MODERNISM AND
TIME MACHINES

Edinburgh Critical Studies in Modernist Culture
Series Editors: Tim Armstrong and Rebecca Beasley

Available

Modernism and Magic: Experiments with Spiritualism, Theosophy and the Occult
Leigh Wilson

Sonic Modernity: Representing Sound in Literature, Culture and the Arts
Sam Halliday

Modernism and the Frankfurt School
Tyrus Miller

Lesbian Modernism: Censorship, Sexuality and Genre Fiction
Elizabeth English

Modern Print Artefacts: Textual Materiality and Literary Value in British Print Culture, 1890–1930s
Patrick Collier

Cheap Modernism: Expanding Markets, Publishers' Series and the Avant-Garde
Lise Jaillant

Portable Modernisms: The Art of Travelling Light
Emily Ridge

Hieroglyphic Modernisms: Writing and New Media in the Twentieth Century
Jesse Schotter

Modernism, Fiction and Mathematics
Nina Engelhardt

Modernist Life Histories: Biological Theory and the Experimental Bildungsroman
Daniel Aureliano Newman

Modernism, Space and the City
Andrew Thacker

Modernism Edited: Marianne Moore and The Dial *Magazine*
Victoria Bazin

Modernism and Time Machines
Charles M. Tung

Forthcoming

Slow Modernism
Laura Salisbury

Primordial Modernism: Animals, Ideas, Transition (1927–1938)
Cathryn Setz

Modernism and the Idea of Everyday Life
Leena Kore-Schröder

www.edinburghuniversitypress.com/series/ecsmc

MODERNISM AND TIME MACHINES

Charles M. Tung

EDINBURGH
University Press

Edinburgh University Press is one of the leading university presses in
the UK. We publish academic books and journals in our selected subject
areas across the humanities and social sciences, combining cutting-edge
scholarship with high editorial and production values to produce academic
works of lasting importance. For more information visit our website:
edinburghuniversitypress.com

Edinburgh University Press Ltd
The Tun – Holyrood Road, 12(2f) Jackson's Entry, Edinburgh EH8 8PJ

First published in hardback by Edinburgh University Press 2019

Typeset in 10/12.5 Adobe Sabon by
IDSUK (DataConnection) Ltd, and
printed and bound by CPI Group (UK) Ltd,
Croydon, CR0 4YY

A CIP record for this book is available from the British Library

ISBN 978 1 4744 3133 0 (hardback)
ISBN 978 1 4744 3134 7 (paperback)
ISBN 978 1 4744 3135 4 (webready PDF)
ISBN 978 1 4744 3136 1 (epub)

CONTENTS

FIGURES

The Plate section can be found between pages 84 and 85.

ACKNOWLEDGEMENTS

It is an ambivalent relief to reflect on the end of a project that should have concluded long ago. I could have then recalled in finer detail all the people, places and cultural things that shaped and inspired it. I do remember first thinking very intensely about finitude and time travel in high school when my father died – the year was 1985, and *Back to the Future* had just been released. Of course, the actual writing of the book took place many years later aboard the very slow time machine, and over that period my understanding of the fantasy of moving in time mutated a great deal. Now that the book is finished, the language for treating the subject's zone of significance has changed too. For instance, the word 'alternative' has come to signify brute ideological denial, bald-faced mendacity and the hateful nationalist right – as in 'alternative facts' and 'alt-right'. The sense of temporal alternatives in this book is beset by these meanings, but I hope it fends them off and continues to signal the tactical search for those threads in a heterogeneous present that connect us to different pasts, timelines and rhythms, as well as their various futures. The lines that are running across our present contain a number of dangers coming down the track(s) at different rates. It feels ridiculous to attempt to be timely about time machines, and yet the reimagination of time and time travel seems more desperate to me now than it did in 1985.

I am thankful to live among good friends and colleagues at Seattle University. My list, in no particular order, includes Kate Koppelman, David Neel, Ken Allan, Naomi Hume, Christina Roberts, Jen Schulz, Molly Clark Hillard,

Allison Henrich, Kristi Lee, Kristen Hultgren, Alli Meyer, Rachel Luft, Jason Wirth, Matt Whitlock, Ali Mian, Maria Bullon Fernandez and so many others. I am grateful to the College of Arts and Sciences and the Provost's Office for summer fellowship support, and to the Popko Lounge in the Lemieux Library for the space to write and chat with many of the folks above. I know I am fortunate to have a less precarious position than many in our profession now and luckier still to work at an institution where the threat of normative time has not overwhelmed the task of thinking against it, and where normative time has not overmanaged the protracted, irregular schedule of intellectual productivity in general. Perhaps it is too self-serving to be glad of a community that lets one be slow, de-synchronise, deviate from the implacable channelling through the standard phases. Nevertheless I am as certain about my gratitude as I am about the pace of my thoughts. Thanks also to those friends and colleagues with whom I've enjoyed sustained and sustaining conversations across multiple conferences and other meet-ups: Benjamin Widiss, Aaron Jaffe, Warren Liu, Gloria Fisk, Joseph Jeon, Jessica Hurley, Leif Sorensen, Judith Roof, Jennifer Fay, Jonathan Eburne, Justus Nieland, Georg Koszulinski and Mark Patterson. They have influenced my thinking in so many ways, but they are not to blame if I have gleaned the most outlandish implications from our exchanges. Finally, I'm grateful to have had great students in whom all the best parts of our discipline live: Olivia Hernandez, Dan Bentson, Erika Bailey, Andrew Battaglia, Ana Lincoln, Rose DeBell, Sheldon Costa, Amanda Uyesugi, Vincent Chien, Grace Goodwin, Natalie Jaech and Alex Hughes.

To be interested in time and its multiplicity is to be drawn out beyond the safety of one's disciplinary niches. I am mindful that hopping around with time machines in the long twentieth century has taken me into zones presided over by authoritative figures with better knowledge of those territories. And at the same time, my narrower focus here, which lands on the relation between canonical modernism and later, more popular cultural objects, has meant that I have not added to the project of expanding the collection of early twentieth-century go-to texts. I hope that the limits and limitations of my scope (and abilities) are not construed as a statement about the value and importance of that project of widening, rescuing and foregrounding. I acknowledge that the choice to concentrate on one set of things is a choice not to pursue other sets, and I have faith that there will be time to balance these choices in other projects.

Different parts of this book have been published in journals: a version of the Introduction appeared in *Configurations* 23.1 (2015); a version of Chapter 4 appeared as 'Baddest Modernism: The Scales and Lines of Inhuman Time', in the *Modernist Inhumanisms* special issue of *Modernism/Modernity* 23.3 (2016); a part of Chapter 1 appeared in *This Year's Work in the Oddball Archive*, ed. Jonathan P. Eburne and Judith Roof (Bloomington: Indiana

University Press, 2015); and a portion of Chapter 2 is about to appear in *ASAP/Journal* 3.3 (2018).

Academic projects are supported by an immense amount of collateral labour and patience. They are propelled by all kinds of conditions of possibility set in motion by generosity, and they often carry with them a trail of sacrifice. I thank all the lucky stars that I get to think and teach for a living, but the most important source of support for the journey of this book has been my family: my mother and brother, the memory of my father, my most patient partner Chau, and our children, Sophie and Ambrose, whose beautiful demands remind me there is nothing like another present. I dedicate this book to them.

SERIES EDITORS' PREFACE

This series of monographs on selected topics in modernism is designed to reflect and extend the range of new work in modernist studies. The studies in the series aim for a breadth of scope and for an expanded sense of the canon of modernism, rather than focusing on individual authors. Literary texts will be considered in terms of contexts including recent cultural histories (modernism and magic; sonic modernity; media studies) and topics of theoretical interest (the everyday; postmodernism; the Frankfurt School); but the series will also reconsider more familiar routes into modernism (modernism and gender; sexuality; politics). The works published will be attentive to the various cultural, intellectual and historical contexts of British, American and European modernisms, and to interdisciplinary possibilities within modernism, including performance and the visual and plastic arts.

Tim Armstrong and Rebecca Beasley

INTRODUCTION: MODERNISM, TIME MACHINES AND THE DEFAMILIARISATION OF TIME

We do not all of us inhabit the same time.

Ezra Pound, 'Dateline'

History is no entity advancing along a single line . . . it is a polyrhythmic and multi-spatial entity.

Ernst Bloch, Heritage of Our Times

Find the strangest thing, and then explore it.
John Wheeler's advice to his students in theoretical physics,
The Life and Science of Richard Feynman

MODERNISM AND TIME MACHINES

Many works of modernist literature and art aspired to the condition of time machines. While an early phase of modernism's history contains the first appearance of such a device in H. G. Wells's *The Time Machine: An Invention* (1895), the aesthetic experiments that we typically associate with the singular noun 'modernism' have not been considered in relation to this foundational science-fiction trope or its numerous offshoots burgeoning through our cultural landscape today. Yet if we reflect on what many of the most famous texts and paintings were doing in form and theme, it is clear that the modernist aesthetic called attention to itself not only as a vehicle for experiencing and moving in time, but also as a technique for rethinking that experience and movement. Moreover, modernist experiments often sought self-consciously to question and reconceptualise time by foregrounding the ways in which their own devices, often in concert with psychological, social and historical mechanisms, structured and produced time. Modernism was itself, in many hitherto-unconsidered senses of the phrase, a time machine.

By reading modernism as a peculiar kind of time machine, this book seeks to expand our sense of both the well-known obsession with time at the beginning of the twentieth century and the popular trope of the time machine. *Modernism and Time Machines* argues that the fascination with time in canonical works of literature and art should be reframed alongside the rise of time-travel narratives and alternate histories, because both modernism and this cardinal trope of science fiction (hereafter SF) have been able to produce a range of effects and insights that go beyond the exhilarations of simply sliding back and forth in history.[1] Together these strands of what was once considered as 'high' art and 'low' popular culture can now be seen to form part of a larger network whose primary function is the defamiliarisation of time itself. Running throughout the twentieth century, this network includes not just literary tropes, formal techniques and SF themes, but also technological, cultural and historical conditions, as well as disciplinary formations such as critical geography and postcolonial historiography. Drawing in part on Deleuze and Guattari's sense of the term, this book describes a larger 'machine' comprising these disparate components, a heterogeneous assemblage whose 'identity' resides in what it does – a configuration of elements, as Levi Bryant defines the machinic, characterised by their outputs and operations.[2] The kind of time machine that I am concerned with in this book – a heterochrony-producing machine, an alternate-history network – is not just the standard aesthetic artefact featured in our critical narratives. That is, this machine is not simply the familiar instrument that symptomatically picks up and sometimes processes the shifting spatio-temporal conditions of modernity. Rather, this oddly articulated time machine is a set of connections that construct and reveal a multiplicity of non-standard times and strange timespaces, and a variety of ways of imagining history otherwise.

In studies of literary modernism that we have now spent two decades recasting, the relations between these elements of the network were construed most often as the familiar oppositions between high art and low pulp, aesthetic self-consciousness and historical determinations, modernism's interiority and modernity's material conditions. In terms of time, for instance, these oppositions formed a picture in which the heightened preoccupation with time that emerged in the late nineteenth and early twentieth century was a poignant turn away from clock time and a shift towards subjectivity and lived experience. In the face of capitalism's standardisation and regulation of time, the acceleration of changes in social life, and the vertiginous elongation of human and planetary history by evolutionary theory and geology, writers and artists were said to have moved inward to explore the workings of memory, the pathos of finitude and the intensities of fugitive moments. As Adam Barrows puts it in *The Cosmic Time of Empire*, 'the dominant critical tendency has been to treat modernist time as a purely philosophical exploration of private consciousness, disjointed from the forms of material and public temporality that standard time attempted to organize'.[3] For Sara Danius in *The Senses of Modernism*, the assumption that modernism responds to 'the growing hegemony of homogeneous time' simply by turning to 'explorations of subjective time' does not allow us to see how literature actually internalised the new technologies of perception in ways that made private experience itself already a composite expression of modern conditions.[4]

Much has been done to complicate these divisions – for the most part by demonstrating the historical nature of what once seemed unhistorical. This has been important work. But if we take seriously the period's interrogations of the form of time and history, then modernism's engagement with history (inclusive of SF) cannot mean simply and solely that the interpenetration of modernism and modernity is reassuringly historical. Like Danius, I think that modernist art and literature did not succumb to the purely 'external' and Luddite dualism pitting aesthetic modernism and its expressions of organicism against technological modernity. However, rather than re-reading subjective 'time-consciousness' for its internalisations of technology, I want to argue, like Barrows, that modernist time machines critique the imperial and commercial 'one, true, "cosmopolitan" time of modernity', but that they do so by revealing or constructing an external multiplicity of material, social and geographical times and histories.[5] Thus, in addition to Barrows's postcolonial treatment of temporal difference, I want to argue for a kind of 'science-fictionalisation' of time and the temporal pluralisation characteristic of recent work in critical geography. The heterochrony machine of which modernism is a part questions and estranges time not only in terms of geographical and political location but also with regard to its rate, scale and number. The modernist time machine complicates the dualism of modernism and modernity not just by treating literature as itself a technology of temporal perception but by revealing the alternative temporality and historicity that make for as many modernisms as there are modernities. Indeed, in this book, 'modernism' functions as shorthand for a pluralisation of time's speed, shape and lines of occurrence. 'Modernism' is the name for its own multiplication of itself and that which underwrites it – a problem that has been taken up in various arenas of inquiry (globalisation studies and postcolonial theory, for instance), and that I address in Chapters 2 and 3.

As a result of the critical tendencies towards anti-technological interiority that Barrows and Danius describe, many of modernism's strangest reconfigurations of time – such as Ezra Pound's claim that 'We do not all of us inhabit the same time' – have come to sound like self-evident descriptions of purely subjective differences.[6] Mark Currie's work in *About Time* has updated our critical appreciation of how our experience of time is organised by the continuous anticipation of narrative and the backward temporality of teleological retrospect, but we have not yet fully grasped how some of modernism's non-narrative, anti-narrative and bad-narrative experiments might have reconfigured the axis of narrativity itself as the non-subjective plurality of physical and material times, rather than the many dimensions of selfhood or experience.[7] *Modernism and Time Machines* takes Pound literally and treats modernism as an exploration of a plurality of different times and kinds of time. While this claim sounds familiar, my argument in this book is that the time-consciousness and perception of temporality that critics treat as the cultural signature of the front end of the century are not just signs of interior resistance to homogeneous, standardised time or idiosyncratic experiences of temporality. They are in many instances registers of non-subjective times as such, and of different ways of construing temporal multiplicity. Modernist literature and art cannot be cordoned off from SF but are instead connected to it. By reading across the ingrained categories that have separated modernism and SF on a variety of grounds (style, genre, narrow periodising factors), this study constructs an expanded field defined by the SF dimensions of the modernist time obsession and the modernist dimensions of SF. Both are distinguished by their radical rethinking of the shapes of time, the consistency of timespace and the nature of history. Closing the distance between these two aesthetic modes requires some comparison of hitherto unnoticed operations and effects of both, but the aim of the project is not a mere catalogue of similar moves in contrasting locations but rather a re-reading of standard takes on modernist temporalities, and vice versa, a revised understanding of the cultural fantasy of time travel.

Thus, Pound's remark that we inhabit different times – the possibility that we might walk halfway down the block and into another epoch, or that we occupy zones constituted by the overlap of varying rates, rhythms and scales – conjures both an SF scenario and a modernist one. Think, for instance, of T. S. Eliot's *The Waste Land*, in which the simultaneous presence of different undead eras constitutes a heterogeneous timescape and redefines 'classicist' modernism as the weird, anachronistic overlap of reference frames. Or the 'Wandering Rocks' episode of James Joyce's *Ulysses*, in which the precise timing and mapping abilities of a chronophotographic method – a series of snapshots tracking movement – call attention to parallax, not only between points of view but between Dublin's various spaces, each elapsing at different rates. Similarly, Virginia Woolf's *Mrs Dalloway* critiques the modern nation as a synchronised, well-proportioned whole by emphasising, in theme and form, a multiplicity of clocks (of which subjectivity is but one), each running differently on a day distended by many forces, not least of which is the daylight saving time that is literally manipulating the clock. Lastly, recall the strange way that William Faulkner's *The Sound and the Fury* maps temporal disjuncture on to US social history by juxtaposing a disenfranchised racial 'timelessness', a lagging Jefferson, Mississippi, and a progressive, industrialised North. Conversely, one might also think of SF's strangely evolved bodies, its visions of alternative histories, and its fascination with slow motion and time lapse as extensions of cubist fragmentation, de-synchronised parallels and temporal disjunction. Modernism's estrangement of time with respect to its rate, scale and number begins to look like the real avant-garde of today's commonplaces in SF and popular culture.[8] In addition to bridging modernist studies and SF scholarship, *Modernism and Time Machines* places twentieth-century time culture and the time-travel trope in direct conversation with critical geography's multiplication of material, social and geographical rhythms, with postcolonial treatments of temporal difference and alternative historical tracks, and with the humanities' so-called speculative turn towards inhuman scales and deep time.

There has not been any substantial treatment of the positive links between the modernist time fixation and either the science-fictional or the alternate-historicist aspects of late twentieth-century culture. Indeed, the prevailing wisdom holds that the earlier interest in time was ultimately a way of ignoring history or maintaining the dominant, progressivist version of it. Thus, modernist time experiments – in the now-too-familiar forms of conservative pastism, ruptural futurism, timeless spatial form and epiphanic or everyday momentousness – have often become negative examples for the other parts of the century, particularly the far end: they appear as forms of escape from the regulatory and standardising forces of modern life into unhistorical zones of temporality and subjectivity, or fortifications of the unilinear time of the dominant capitalist order. As I discuss in Chapter 4, Fredric Jameson has constructed important links between modernism and SF, but they seem to be one-way streets: he sees SF as a radical modernist practice, but does not consider modernism as a kind of SF.[9] Recently, several excellent scholarly works have appeared that call upon postcolonial and materialist positions to problematise the prevailing view of literature's retreat to interior temporalities – by emphasising, for instance, modernism's engagement of global standard time as an imperial instrument (Barrows), its awareness of the technological constitution of aesthetic experience (Danius) and its exploration of uneven development in novels of arrested growth (Jed Esty's *Unseasonable Youth*).[10] However, none connects this critique to SF. *Modernism and Time Machines* builds on this work by linking it to unexpected components of heterochronic culture. Scholars interested in SF and time travel are almost by definition invested in imagining the present and future otherwise, but the intermittent connections drawn by critics between time travel and modernism have focused less on alternative visions of time and history and more on logical paradox, self-reflexivity and playful narrative forms – see, for example, George Slusser and Daniele Chatelain's 'Time Travel and the Modern Geometrical Narrative' (1995) and David Wittenberg's important study, *Time Travel: The Popular Philosophy of Narrative* (2013).[11] Finally, while postcolonial and materialist criticism has done a great deal to theorise historical multiplicity and heterogeneity, the resulting alternative historicism is usually in opposition to both modernism and modernity; and generally critics apply these concepts to broad cultural differences elided by imperialist history and Western historiography, not so much to timespace itself – see Dilip Parameshwar Gaonkar's edited collection *Alternative Modernities* (2001) and Dipesh Chakrabarty's *Provincializing Europe* (2000).[12]

To constellate modernism with the pop-culture trope of the time machine and our contemporary desire to interrogate and revise history is now both untimely and timely. Over the course of the century, the work of producing and tracking the otherness and multiplicity of time has come to seem less and less desirable in direct proportion to the political need for 'simultaneous contradiction' – for concrete opposition and resistance in a straightforward dialectic in an urgently (but falsely) simplified now. Nevertheless, as Ernst Bloch reminded utopian thinkers in the 1930s, 'Not all people exist in the same Now. They do so only externally, through the fact that they may all be seen today. But they are thereby not yet living at the same time with others.'[13] Insofar as modernism can be shown to explore this 'non-synchronous' condition and the strange and uneven coexistence of different times, its 'time cult', as Wyndham Lewis disparaged it, enters not only into a surprising constellation with time-travel and alternate-history narratives, but also with the engaged or potentially engaged interrogations of history in recent academic discourses. Modernism's reworking of the nature of time and modernity itself – as something other than a single line of just-nows strung together, in Walter Benjamin's simile, 'like the beads of a rosary' – connects not only to SF's fantasy of undoing time and the nature of history's line, but also to the impulse of 'historiographic-metafiction' that Linda Hutcheon identified with postmodernism, and to the postcolonial desire, in Dipesh Chakrabarty's words, 'to reconceptualize the present', 'to think [. . .] the "now" that we inhabit as we speak – as irreducibly not-one'.[14] To sketch the outlines of the full heterochrony machine is to begin to see how the political desire to revise history and envision other histories connects to the century-wide imaginative contestation of historical progress and the earlier interest in history's irregular rhythms, its dense divarication of branches, its variety of scales and bundles of non-parallel lines.

The method that *Modernism and Time Machines* employs to explore this not-one-ness in the pace, shape and number of timelines is itself multiple. In attempting to track the components and articulations of a larger, cultural heterochrony machine, this book adopts a 'machinic' posture like that of its subject: it creates assemblages that combine not just objects from different zones of culture, but also different media from different parts of the long twentieth century; and it reads in the unexpected outputs and operations an earnest reconceptualisation of time as not-one. The resulting approach reflects, and reflects on, the subject matter because not only does the heterochrony machine comprise such materials and discourses, but the book's very argument centres on alternative ways of understanding history and conceiving of historicity. My aim is not at all to disclaim the important sequences of previous historical work but to build on them by multiplying the kinds and scales of sequences. At the same time, the book of course narrows its focus to specific targets. Because I am concerned with those aspects of the modernist time obsession that do not focus primarily on psychology, subjectivity and lived experience in its own right, I leave aside the period's interest in the occult version of the fourth dimension, and I avoid paranormal time-slip narratives and dream fiction. Though I find the recovery of lesser-known writers both valuable and necessary, I concentrate here on less-considered connections, unfamiliar combinations that transform how we read the things being combined. By assembling readings of cultural objects' internal mechanisms and themes with larger historical discourses and with contemporary texts and technologies, *Modernism and Time Machines* explores the way modernism, science fiction and features of contemporary experience work together to defamiliarise time and produce new forms of timespace.

The Time(s) Machine

The heightened interest in temporality from the nineteenth century onwards is most often characterised in terms of a rapid and precipitous fall into time, and this interest from the beginning brought with it a new attention to the speeds, shapes and number of times. As I will discuss in the next section, aestheticism and impressionism are incipient moments of an SF reconceptualisation of the nature of times; but here I begin conversely with H. G. Wells's *The Time Machine* as an incipient moment of the modernist time fixation. Modernism is said to have engaged the new pace of railways, automobiles, the telegraph and wireless communication, mass production and urbanisation, by developing an aesthetics of temporal experience that opposed the spatialised time of scientific rationality. Wells's landmark SF text seems to go in the opposite direction: it appears to embrace spatialised time, to explore the progressive or degenerative direction of history, and to reaffirm the model of a single, universal, physical time. In this view, not only does modernism seem unable to handle the heterochronic multiplicity of time except in terms of the subject's lived experience, but Wells's trope of the time machine appears ill-equipped to help defamiliarise time, illuminate other times or produce alternate historicities. However, re-reading Wells's work is crucial to a revised sense of modernism as a major component in a larger heterochrony machine.

To show how Wells's trope is part of the modernist redefinition of timespaces, I want to rehearse briefly what time machines usually signify and accomplish, and how they typically operate within the historicist machine rather than the heterochronic one. The obvious cultural significance of this technology is that its ability to move a traveller backwards or forwards in time, like narrative itself, expresses the fantasy of revising the past and previewing the future. Backward time travel expresses the desire to alter history for a better future, to 'undo' the present, as Catherine Gallagher describes this type of plot, 'by subtracting a crucial past event'; or it aims to highlight in a cautionary way the unintentional revisionary effects on the future of what we do in the past and present.[15] Forward time travel generally foregrounds a vision of historical progress, a culture's extrapolation of its future from its present, or a critique of the present by its imagined consequences. As Jameson's work on utopian SF shows, what many consider the genre's defining feature of 'cognitive estrangement' is in fact an effect of the temporal operation of forward time travel: SF not only works to 'defamiliarize and restructure our experience of our own *present*', but provides a preview or negative outline of the virtually unimaginable corrective sequence that ought to happen in the future, which calls into consciousness and into question the historical sequence that produced the current state of affairs.[16] While there are certainly time-travel narratives that successfully explore different conceptions of time such as the loop or the forking branch, by and large the ordinary time machine transports us in a way that depends upon and reinforces the conception of history as a tight, straight and unilinear sequence, and that reflects and inspires a cultural present's imagination of its own effectuality, responsibility and range of solicitude.[17]

Time travel's affective and epistemological functions – what it allows us to feel and know – are likewise often tied to unilinearity. The thrill of revision, of going back to see, whether in the time machines of museum villages, theme parks or literary texts, is the thrill of witnessing something no longer present, of understanding what is absent. Conversely, the enjoyment of speculative or predictive preview is the pleasure in imagining what the future will be like or in tracking positive or negative outcomes. While in both cases, as Philip Rosen points out, the fantasy provides the sensation of a godlike power to rise above history – of 'a transcendence of [one's own] temporal location and determinations' – time travel also serves, and returns us to, the present, lodged squarely between the past and future. To journey into the past may be to express the 'ambition to have something of the past available to perception in the present [. . .] to freeze time at the service of a beholder or spectator', but it is also, according to Rosen, an expression of historicism and the nineteenth-century heritage project that aligns time's dimensions into a unity, such that the past is always somehow *our* past, the past of our present.[18] Similarly, the journey to the future may be accused of the Olympian overview – a reproach that both

Wells's novel and his ambitious non-fiction *The Outline of History* (as well as its amusingly condensed version *A Short History of the World*) have rightly received – but its excitements and anxieties about what the future holds bring the touristic or imperial flight back down to the more pedestrian understanding of time.[19] The utopian or cautionary imagination of how things could or will be relies on parsimonious consecution *within* the singular causal chain. Whatever will be depends upon what is bequeathed.

Finally, overlapping with these functions, the time machine's movement back and forth tends to have a pedagogical use. Because it presupposes (and produces) the integral role of the past in the constitution of our present and future, the figure can be found in the discourses of many academic fields, not just history, but archaeology, museum studies, genetic anthropology and cognitive psychology.[20] The television show *Doctor Who* was in fact originally an educational programme designed to promote science as well as take viewers back to famous events in history to get a better look.[21] The ordinary time machine is an effective rhetorical and conceptual device that transforms the unfamiliar and hard-to-imagine past or future into a well-furnished site for the present; it immerses our faculties in the exciting range of perceptual and imaginative conditions for understanding something absent. But its epistemological power derives primarily from its unification of time that allows us to track a current state of affairs to its prior cause, and vice versa, a cause to its consequence. Even if the traveller cannot see it, the end of the trip is most often an articulated, genealogical now: the goal of the pedagogical time machine is to be returned to the present or present object, with a happy appreciation of how we arrived here or wherever we are headed.

There is no denying the diagnostic and prognostic powers of the time machine in its dominant form or the contexts that call forth images of these powers from culture. The trope in this form is a part of the historicist machine, doing valuable and compelling work. However, revision, pleasure and pedagogy are not all there is to the time machine and the modernist discourse of which it is a part. Indeed, I want to argue that the most interesting use of the trope is the defamiliarisation of the very model of time that underlies the prevailing understanding of time machines. This temporal estrangement produces the opposite of pedagogy and pleasure: time-travel narratives and twentieth-century time machines – from cubist painting and modernist writing to postmodern alternate history and SF film – often feature the undoing of the lean rectilinearity of historiographic revision and the bewildering of any pleasure we might take in riding the one time that culminates in or follows from us. The defamiliarisation of time seeks in instances of anachronism that which is covered up by the singular noun: differential rates of passage; a variety of scales and shapes of timespace; and a plurality of timelines and histories.

There is, as it were, a heterochrony machine hidden in the idea of the time machine, just as the latter is concealed in the pedestal of Wells's colossal sphinx. Its liberation requires noticing that the very first time machine to appear in literature was not just a vehicle of imperial adventure and prognostication but a potential producer of unfamiliar temporalities in its nascent questions about the interrelated qualities of time's speed, form and number. The SF novelist Harry Turtledove has pointed out that '[w]e're all time travelers, whether we know it or not. We go into the future at a steady rate of one second per second', but Wells's vehicle of time travel helped to make strange the very medium in which we live by featuring a device able to manipulate, outstrip and negate the putatively universal pace of one second per second, the common-sense rate of temporal passage itself.[22] In Wells's novel, the speed of the Traveller's machine, relative to the rate at which the his late nineteenth-century dinner guests' experience is elapsing, varies from 'over a year a minute', to a pace so fast that 'the thousands [of days] hand [on his dial] was sweeping round as fast as the seconds hand of a watch', to the unimaginably 'great strides of a thousand years or more'.[23] The critical and imaginative power of such an ability, as Wells's Traveller points out on the first page of the story, consists in the fact that it can 'controvert [. . .] ideas that are almost universally accepted' (59). Whereas for the Traveller's parlour audience this controversion meant undermining the assumption of the unidirectionality of time and the inescapability of the present, for me the more important challenge posed by the machine's imaginative exploration of the spatial qualities of the 'Fourth Dimension' is its de-synchronisation of our experience from the steady flow of a single, uniform, natural time and the re-synchronisation of it with variable temporal speeds that are explicitly produced. More than a decade before Albert Einstein, Wells's novel shows that a second does not always elapse in a second, as a second (Plate 1).

In addition to its crucial role in modernism's repudiation of one-second-per-second regularity and all that the public clock had come to stand for – capitalist discipline, bourgeois values, modernity itself – Wells's novel is an early example of the modernist push against time's standard scale. The text suggests that the shape and form of time can no longer be thought of as an absolute container or rectilinear line for measuring the duration of things and parsimoniously explaining their emergence. This is why Wells's protagonist constantly revises his 'interpretation' and 'theory' of the history that brought about the future of the Eloi and Morlocks. In the stretching of human history on to multiple scales of deep time (Darwinian and astronomical), time's shape and internal consistency changes in several ways: the stable entities of the nineteenth century, such as a narrativisable history or the category of the human itself, are distended beyond recognition; the significant intervals, phases and period units necessary for defining phenomena, as well as the histories in which they have identities, are possibly of varying length; and the multiplicity of potential genealogies interferes with a singular, scientifically constructed lineage.

Travelling at different speeds in the machine shows a world 'melting and flowing under [his] eyes' (77), and this melting indicates not only the limits of the human sensorium – our physical inability, as the Psychologist says, to perceive 'the spoke of a wheel spinning, or a bullet flying' (67) – but the limits of the Traveller's historiographical scale. Almost 801,000 years into the future, and then 30 million years beyond, the Traveller cannot determine if 'the modification of the human type' (111) and the Eloi's and Morlocks' ways of life are the products of Victorian 'social triumphs' that have eliminated 'the grindstone of pain and necessity' upon which 'we are kept keen' (91–2), or if the 'gradual widening [. . .] between the Capitalist and the Labourer was the key' (109). And between the three-dimensional 'section' of the late nineteenth century from which he comes and the slice of timespace at 802,701, there is a vast four-dimensional corridor filled with many possible strands. Do the Eloi and Morlocks descend from lemurs or apes or any of the other animals the Traveller uses to figure them? While he thinks he has drawn some plausible conclusions, and although the text seems to deliver its social admonitions in a steady voice, the Traveller also admits that he 'had no convenient cicerone in the pattern of the Utopian books' (111).

If, according to Jonathan Bignell, the movements in time-travel texts provide 'fairground thrills', then the different temporal speeds and scales in Wells's novel complicate these pleasures by dissolving time's historiographically manageable shape.[24] The 'hysterical exhilaration'(78) that the Traveller and consumers of imperialist romances feel is generated by what Paul Cantor and Peter Hufnagel identify as a typically Victorian 'journey to the imperial frontier', where European explorers, including modernist protagonists such as Joseph Conrad's Marlow, encounter exotic 'cultures at very different stages of historical development'.[25] But this exhilaration of going-forward-to-go-back on the progressive line of history is countered in Wells by a disorientation that is 'excessively unpleasant' (77), by a 'sickness and confusion' (144). The dissonance seems to exceed any imperialist distaste for the colonised and their often unheard claim to coevalness. The Traveller's confusion is in fact an index of the disintegration of the imperial universal time underwriting the diagnosis and prognosis of both self and other.[26] In its place is the intimation that the shape of time, in addition to irregular tempos, cannot be represented by the straight line uniformly segmented.

The impossibility of thinking time as a rectilinear, unilinear, punctual form whose instants are ever disappearing into an irrevocable past leads to the final aspect of the alternative conception of time in which *The Time Machine* is a crucial early text – its number. While Wells does not explicitly engage the issue of the number of timelines produced by the machine, his novel contains the seed of a whole sub-genre of SF – alternate history – whose proliferation of timelines is a consequence of the agency (and the paradox-avoidance) of time travel. Wells's plot does not extend to the possible consequences of his Traveller's intervention in the Eloi's and Morlocks' history, or the after-effects of his pre-emptively moralising tale about Victorian class divisions, and yet the structure of his novel, as Elana Gomel argues, pits the implication of alternate history against the block universe presupposed by forward time travel. The embedded narrative, told by the unnamed narrator, contains the 'deterministic chronotope of time travel', in which all of past and future time is spatialised and traversable. But the embedded narrative, told by the Traveller himself, employs the 'chronotope of alternative history', in which history is contingent and the future is unknowable.[27] This second understanding of the way time and space are connected reconfigures the progressive/regressive line, at the very least, into a random, open-ended process that the time machine's journey has in fact shaped and altered. Wells left the implications to our imagination, but his novel's utopian investment in evaluating Victorian industrial capitalism suggests very strongly and tantalisingly a timescape in which alternate histories are not only possible but already cutting across the present.[28] While many SF plots allow the alternate timeline to take the place of the former, 'official' timeline, and thus reaffirm the prison house of singular sequence, the point of going back to Wells's first deployment of the time-machine trope is less to suggest that the world's one history could have gone a different way than to prepare for texts that see how history is composed of different ways already going. As Bloch pointed out about the non-synchronous remnants of different parts of the past coexisting simultaneously around one another, 'History is no entity advancing along a single line [. . .] but it is a polyrhythmic and multi-spatial entity.'[29]

TOWARDS A LITTLE ALTERNATIVE HISTORY OF THE MODERNIST TIME CULT

In the decade following the First World War, according to Michael Levenson, 'time became such a dominant concern that it can be taken as a cultural signature'.[30] This obsessive thematisation of time – its movement into the spotlight from the quiet background for plot or the 'invisible medium' of history – had of course begun to surge in the decades before, a current well-documented by Stephen Kern and Tim Armstrong, among others.[31] By the interwar years, this concern seemed to culminate in modernism's distinctive 'Time-consciousness': the lived experience of the 'extra-literary historical realm of novelty [. . .] rapid modernisation in technologies, social relations, religious beliefs, philosophic principles'.[32] Levenson's identification of 'Time-consciousness as an inescapable topos of Modernism' agrees with the majority of critical accounts of early twentieth-century literature and art, including Wyndham Lewis's contemporary, disagreeable antipathy: in the 1920s Lewis had connected the '"time"-notions which have now [. . .] gained an undisputed ascendancy in the intellectual world' to the period's 'time-mind'.[33] In the period after the war, this emphasis on the subjective experience of temporal dynamism and the ubiquitous phenomenologies of flux slowly receded, so that eventually, as Levenson puts it, 'time [. . .] was absorbed back into history'.[34]

If we bear in mind what Wells's text accomplished at the end of the nineteenth century, a constellation of texts begins to appear around it that suggests an alternative reading of the modernist time cult, or at least a way of highlighting an unacknowledged aspect of the time obsession in which poignant interior landscapes are not the ends of the story but the registers and extensions of newly conceived topographies of timespace. In this section, I want to offer a brief re-reading of aestheticism and impressionism, which H. Peter Stowell identifies as the 'incipient moment of literary modernism'.[35] More specifically, these literary and artistic modes have long been treated as the starting point of modernism's 'fall into time': its fall away from timeless values, from the stabilities of the inherited past, and into a medium that makes newness not only possible, but inevitable and inevitably short-lived. As Matei Calinescu argues, modernism signifies 'a major cultural shift from a time-honored aesthetics of permanence, based on a belief in an unchanging transcendent ideal of beauty, to an aesthetics of transitoriness and immanence, whose central values are change and novelty'.[36] The social, intellectual and technological changes underlying this aesthetic shift make the descent into time appear both rapid and deep: the late nineteenth and early twentieth centuries witnessed the rise of technologies of ever-faster production, transport and communication, which contributed to an acceleration of changes in social life, a radical compression and unification of space and a contraction of time in which, as David Harvey says, 'time horizons shorten to the point where the present is all there is'.[37] Moreover, this period had to come to terms with new understandings of the human situation brought about by Charles Darwin's long evolutionary history, Sigmund Freud's psychological depths and Charles Lyell's precipitous bottoming-out of the age of the planet. If modernity, according to Zygmunt Bauman, is 'more than anything else, [the] *history of time*: the time when time has history', that history contains not just a variety of ways of experiencing, marking and telling a faster and longer time, but also a new awareness of a variety of times *per se* generating new experiences, markers and tales.[38] That is, in the prevailing history of modernism's engagement with the pathos and problems of historical being, which repudiates the clock, there is a strand of alternate historicity that proliferates clocks and transforms the 'aesthetics of transitoriness' and the immersion in 'the transient, the fleeting, the contingent', to use Charles Baudelaire's formulation, into an aesthetics of heterochrony.[39]

Both the remorseless rate of change and enormous timescales (in which speed hardly shows up) have bolstered the discourse of the supersession of the past and helped to differentiate modernity from previous regimes of repetition, permanence and timelessness. Two familiar literary expressions of the consequences of temporal speed and depth can be found in Matthew Arnold's vision of a naked historicity exposed by a receding 'Sea of Faith', and in the erosive power of W. B. Yeats's 'time's waters', which hollow out all things, even the love that for Arnold was a poignant last resort.[40] By these lights, the fall into time appears as a postlapsarian 'curse', covering over the radical estrangements of time in breakneck swash, or in the vertiginous elongation of human and planetary history beyond the creationist timeline of six thousand years. This narrative tends to constrain the potential that recent cultural histories have found in the period by writing it into the standard mythology of the new as a function of mere temporal passage. Instead of indexing dynamic, uneven and technologically manipulable times, the elements of the heterochrony machine become ways of accelerating and elongating a single time. Thus, the familiar formulations of the modernist time-story centre on the experience of rupture with the anchoring power of both eternity and tradition; the pathos of the present located in structures of loss, heroic finitude or dilated instantaneity; and the consequent desire for a more primordial, mythic substructure undergirding a temporally fractioned world.

How can we re-read this conjuncture as a point at which a new account might diverge? I would like to return to one of the quintessential formulations of the aesthetics of brevity and temporal passage, Walter Pater's *Studies in the History of the Renaissance*, a text that famously celebrates the fall into time as an 'outbreak of the human spirit' liberated from the eternal truths and immovable solidities of the Middle Ages.[41] Like Wells's description of moving through time, Pater's representation of this freedom relies on the trope of melting: not only the social and moral 'habits' of a 'stereotyped world', but also objects themselves delineated by those habits, dissolve into 'the whirlpool', breaking down into a flood of 'impressions, unstable, flickering, inconsistent'.[42] 'While all melts under our feet' on 'this short day of frost and sun' with no afterlife in reserve, Pater urges us to join this flood of sensuous liberation, availing ourselves of as many 'pulsations' as we can get in our brief interval. In the beautiful final sentences of *The Renaissance*, this aesthetic receptiveness is supposed to yield 'a quickened, multiplied consciousness. [. . .] For art comes to you proposing frankly to give nothing but the highest quality to your moments as they pass, and simply for those moments' sake.'[43] When confronted with the onset of accelerated social change and of commercial regulation of ever smaller durations of life, it is poignant to read Pater's exhortation as the valiant transformation of the linear drama of precisely subdivided temporal passage into powerful instances of existential fulfilment. The aesthetics of transitoriness produces one of modernism's most familiar tropes: the moment. As Matthew Beaumont writes, 'Pater attempted to reclaim, and redeem, the moment. He confronted the sense of instantaneousness characteristic of life in an industrial society through passionate attention to the instant itself.'[44] In the context of a brief, increasingly managed life – '[w]e have an interval, and then our place knows us no more' – one must convert temporal dissolution and evanescence into the conditions for an expansive present.[45]

It is impossible to disagree with this account, to take Pater's famous conclusion as anything other than an epicurean appeal to the impressionist who would pursue 'this quickened sense of life'.[46] However, latent in this story from the beginning is something altogether more strange. In *The Renaissance*, Pater implies that the meditation on the relativity of beauty be extended to the very moments in which perception is situated and determined. That is, the text also hints at the non-concurrence of times 'within time', the dissolution and melting of the everyday conception of time itself. In the 'fruit' of Pater's aesthetic passion is an ontological instability that applies to moments themselves. For instance, in the 'delicious recoil' of 'water in summer heat' – where to divide up the flux of elements and processes according to our needs, past conventions or fixed ideas would be to rest arbitrarily with the mere 'concurrence, renewed from moment to moment, of forces parting sooner or later on their ways' – the spectrum of becoming and 'perpetual motion' extends not only from water to steam, but to 'the elements of which we are composed', and, sooner or later, 'beyond us': 'the action of these forces [. . .] rusts iron and ripens corn'.[47] By paying attention to the differential rates of oxidation, organic maturation and human perception, as well as the molecular recoil of kinetically energised water or the chemical processes of the human body, we get not only a 'quickened, multiplied consciousness', but a quickened consciousness of multiplicity. The relations of this multiplicity allow us to see, for instance, the present not simply as a finely delineated sequence, but as a cross-section of a plurality of times.

To go from the subject's being-*in*-time-as-a-singular-noun to being-among-times requires one to open the momentary ecstasy of the impression to a different sense of time whose multiplication is not simply the result of milking extra pulsations from 'the splendour of our experience and of its awful brevity'.[48] Doing so is a matter not so much of resisting as adding to the prevailing view, since the condition of transitoriness is not eliminated but compounded. Leo Charney summarises the dominant account in a way that recalls Levenson's separation of time from history: 'Pater detached sublime experience from continuity and emphasized that it could reside only inside unique moments of sensual immersion.'[49] But within the 'fruit' of aesthetic passion is also an ontological instability that applies to moments themselves. In the disintegration of the barrier between subject and object, in the erotic confluence that breaks things down and also leads to 'that strange, perpetual, weaving and unweaving of ourselves', the moment gives way to multiplicity and heterogeneity and reveals different strands of elemental processes. Beneath the solid surface of the subject, object *and* the present too, there lurk the 'unstable, flickering, inconsistent' strands of differently paced processes fluctuating through water, iron, corn, the human and time as such. If modernity, as Marx and Engels described it, is a situation in which 'All fixed, fast-frozen relations, with their train of ancient and venerable prejudices and opinions are swept away [. . .] All that is solid melts into air', it is not just because the flow of modernity is uniformly linear and efficiently single-minded in its erosive force, or because history moves on to new stages.[50] It is also because temporal multiplicity exposes that which appears to be unitary or static, even space and time themselves, to be composed of a variety of rates and rhythms, a transverse section of many threads.

Aestheticism's ethos and thematics of transitoriness become matters of method and form very clearly in impressionism. In the visual arts, the repudiation of the timeless and the traditional becomes a literal fracture of the world into short-lived perceptual fragments by a subjectivity whose location in time affords it access to the intensities of the sensuous present. At the level of subject matter, the fall into time entailed a departure from the traditional religious subjects and enduring historical scenes of the Académie des Beaux-Arts' annual salons, and an attempt, by contrast, to render fleeting moments from ordinary lives. But the 'core narrative', as Jonathan Crary calls it, is its formal 'break with several centuries of another model of vision, loosely definable as Renaissance, perspectival, or normative'.[51] The obvious analogue in literature is the break with realism's God's-eye clarity and its well-structured plots by emphasising the limitations of seeing, the fluid and complex play of consciousness and the treatment of life as a contingent flux rather than as 'a series of gig lamps symmetrically arranged'.[52] The rejection of formulaic illusionism – for the innovative impasto of atomised, unblended colour, often *en plein air* for the dramatic shifts of light and atmosphere – seems to rest on the standard narrative of time-consciousness in obvious ways. For impressionist form implied not only that the scene was in time but that the painterly eye and the observer were likewise located squarely in the midst of the same temporal flux. The subject of impressionism was therefore, as Ronald Bernier points out, both the raw materials of perception and experience, and our de-privileged 'variable perception in nature' – that is, the temporally situated process of subjective seeing itself, as opposed to an idealised and static point of view.[53] Likewise, in literature (whose analogous features would be atmospheric and subjective distortion, 'delayed decoding' and situated transmissions of sense), impressionism is said to have played 'a decisive role in [. . .] the long process whereby in every domain of human concerns the priority passed from public systems of belief [. . .] to private views of reality – what the individual sees'.[54]

As in the case of Pater's *Renaissance*, it is not difficult to delight in Monet's compelling dramatisations of 'in-timeness'. For instance, in his series of paintings of Rouen Cathedral, Monet juxtaposes most conspicuously and ironically these temporal themes and forms with an imposing Gothic church, a symbol of spiritual eternity, historical permanence and nationalist pride that dominates the entire canvas. At the top of each of the pictures is what one might be tempted to call the site of the paintings' real subject: a small patch of sky, which seems to be not only a synecdoche for the very cause of the church's shifting appearances, an index of the weather, but also a figure for impressionist technique itself and Monet's serial method. Between 1892 and 1894, Monet made over thirty paintings of the façade of the cathedral by setting up a number of canvases (often ten or more) outdoors. He moved from one to the other as the light continued to change, and then brought them back to his studio for completion. In its composition, this most numerous of Monet's series seems to register temporality as atmospheric fluctuation, the impossibility of a complete capture or record, and as indicated by his return to the studio and his reliance on memory, the limitations of the extemporaneous point of view. While John Klein writes that 'the artist's vision, will, and personal experience generate the variations on the single unifying motif' and therefore, assisted by the fictional unity of 'sequential structure', provides 'the counterbalancing weight' to the incompleteness and ephemerality for which impressionism had so often been criticised, these weights – including the stone face of religious immutability – only seem to accentuate the marks of being in time within each painting and across the series (Plate 2).[55]

But is the painting's meaning centred solely on the fragility and inconstancy of time in modernity relative to an older order, or on the tension between precious moments of individual experience and the larger record of time passing? Or is the Cathedral series, as Rebecca Stern says of the Charing Cross series, 'a new way of telling time'? For Stern, this new way asks us 'to conceive a tale that recorded the machinations of reverie more than the precision of synchronized time that (also) marks modernity'.[56] However, there is another way – beyond the subjective meditation on moments before they advance unremittingly into nothingness – in which Monet is reckoning, recounting or revealing time. Consider that, from Rouen in 1893, as a result of the openness to the temporal variety discovered over the last three years in his serial explorations, Monet remarks in a letter to his wife Alice: 'Everything changes, even stone.'[57] This provocative insight, by intensifying the transitory 'everything' via a figure of solidity, goes beyond the realm of immediate appearances to a range of other processes that are too quickly book-ended by ontological tendencies. Side by side in the Cathedral paintings, then, are the pathos of human being, the temporalities of perceptions and compositional processes, and the changes of stone, whose slow pace make the façade seem immobile and therefore able to take on the additional meanings of the timelessness of religion and the indurate French nationalism propped up by Gothic architecture. Time, in other words, becomes relative times, rates of change in relation to one another. Monet's series foregrounds the aggregation of *different rates of transitoriness*, the bundle of times in which the objects of impressionism are obscured, not just by time's dispersive force or subjectivity's distortions, but by the play of processes and reference frames.

In addition to engaging the remorseless erosive power of the clock, impressionism's melting world, like aestheticism's, is an effect of the emergence of a multiplicity of times, the assemblage of physical rhythms irreducible to the subject. One hundred years after Monet began his Cathedral series, Henri Lefebvre would formulate a 'rhythmanalysis' as the best way to understand this world, in which

> nothing is immobile [. . .] [I]f [the rhythmanalyst] considers a stone, a wall, a trunk, he understands their slowness, their interminable rhythm. This *object* is not inert; time is not set aside for the *subject*. It is only slow in relation to our time, to our body [. . .] An apparently immobile object, the forest, moves in multiple ways: the combined movements of the soil, the earth, the sun. Or the movements of the molecules and atoms that compose it.[58]

The move from timelessness or classical permanence to ephemerality and lived experience need not dead-end in the subject and its lonely surfing of unilinear progression/degeneration. At this early point in the history of the twentieth-century time obsession, what appears to culminate in the quintessentially modernist experience of dissolution can also be read as an emerging recognition of the relations among many times. Time ceases to be an abstract, single, uniform medium or a phenomenological mode of appearances, fracturing instead into the play of relations among a variety of locally inflected sequences and lines of occurrence.

Many Clocks

While the narrative of the fall into time remains compelling, it is not by itself enough to capture the weirdness of radical heterochronic estrangements. Rather than attending to strange, uneven and manipulable times that arise from the period's technologies of rapid production, transport and communication, and from new evolutionary, geological and astronomical understandings of human and planetary history, the prevailing story plugs these familiar factors into the acceleration and elongation of a single time. If we continue to read the phenomenon of speed in terms of an abstract space divided by absolute time (rather than in terms of the relation of peculiar times to the particularities of space), then the time obsession becomes too easily and completely the failed attempt to break with the unitary time that economic modernity both needed and exploited.[59] Modernism was seen to be either thoroughly co-opted by the forces it meant to resist, or it was actually complicit with those forces. In this account, the aesthetics of transitoriness could not outpace the thematics of loss or its underlying sense of time as ever-lengthening distance. It certainly could not outrun capitalism. As Paul de Man puts it in 'Literary History and Literary Modernity', the 'authentic spirit of modernity' witnessed its own efforts at making it new fade from 'an incandescent point in time into a reproducible cliché'.[60] Modernism's 'uniquely shaped flames of the fire' were washed out by the flow of time, and all attempts to be modern foundered on the sudden awareness of, or blindness to, being mired within an unsurpassable time.

However, modernism's reconceptualisation of time, of which Wells must be counted as a crucial part, in fact transformed the singular noun into the relations among variable rates of change and spatio-temporal scales. This more complex picture of the period's time culture is characterised by what Jon May and Nigel Thrift describe as 'a growing awareness of living within a *multiplicity of times*, a number of which might be moving at different speeds and even in different directions', or by what Lefebvre described as heterogeneous rhythms, those relations 'of a time with a space, a localized time, or if one wishes a temporalized place'.[61] As Lefebvre goes on to say, these relative rhythms, which are themselves 'concrete times', 'are not measured as the speed of a moving object on its trajectory is measured, beginning from a well-defined starting point (point zero) with a unit defined once and for all. A rhythm is only slow or fast in relation to other rhythms.'[62] But when we consider the twentieth-century's aesthetic repudiation of 'the one, true time' of the public clock, key examples – Eliot's heterochronic cityscapes, Woolf's multiplicity of imperfectly synchronised clocks, Faulkner's jeweller's shop window filled with unregulated watches, as well as more contemporary interrogations of jumbled geographies and historical unevenness – become absorbed into the historicism machine and the period's anti-rationalist retreat to the subject.

The cultural response to the clock, as Barrows points out, has seemed to depend exclusively on the 'familiar narrative of modernism's affirmation of private, interior time consciousness, which has largely depended on an application of the theories of Henri Bergson'.[63] For Bergson, 'When I follow with my eyes on the dial of a clock the movement of the hand which corresponds to the oscillations of the pendulum, I do not measure duration [. . .] I merely count simultaneities.'[64] These extensive, uniform and de-temporalised simultaneities, which are 'absolutely distinct in the sense that the one has ceased to be when the other takes place', slice and subdivide the heterogeneous temporality of *durée*, 'just as the pendulum of the clock cuts up into distinct fragments and spreads out, so to speak, lengthwise, the dynamic and undivided tension of the spring'. Pure duration is a confluence or interpenetration of interior states into one another, such that their multiplicity cannot be laid out side-by-side in a spatial series. It is rather the continuous, 'heterogeneous duration of the ego, without moments external to one another, without relation to number'.[65]

One cannot ignore the fact that the turn to Bergson's arguments – for dynamic and interpenetrated *durée* against spatialised, uniform and de-temporalised simultaneities – was a real and moving response to the threat of the public clock, its regulated instants and their unyielding pace. As Jacques Le Goff recounts, the mechanical clock, invented in the thirteenth century, began its rise when public and commercial time-reckoning overtook the cyclical schedules of monastic routine and rural life, on its way to becoming 'the measure of all things'.[66] In the nineteenth century, the advance of the clock culminated in the elision of local times in Britain and North America by railway companies (1847 and 1883, respectively), and then on a global scale by the International Prime Meridian Conference (1884), which established a 'universal day' that commenced from a prime meridian – the Royal Observatory at Greenwich – and allowed for the precise parcelling-out of the time zones of the earth in longitudinal segments of fifteen degrees.[67] In Lewis Mumford's well-known account, 'The clock, not the steam engine, is the key-machine of the modern industrial age', since its products – seconds and minutes – move us away from 'eternity [. . .] as the measure and focus of human actions', and towards the single metric necessary for the coordination of nation and empire, as well as for the quantification, regulation and 'work-discipline' of capitalism.[68] So clearly had the clock become the means and 'the symbol of the process of European modernization' that Joseph Conrad built a novel, *The Secret Agent*, around Martial Bourdin's failed anarchist plot in 1894 to blow up the Greenwich observatory, 'the first meridian' and the first tick of the planet-as-clock.[69] The refrain about the impact of the clock on modern life has continued to this day, most recently in John Durham Peters's claim that '[t]he watch is the prime symbol of modernity, a time bomb marking our Faustian mortgage of ourselves to things we did not actively choose but will not give up'.[70]

But the problem that emerged in modernist writing and painting was not only that the modern world had come to rely increasingly on the technological fractioning of time for the purposes of measurement and coordination in ways that had an impact on everything from the structure of human perception to social organisation. It was equally that the clock was part of a larger machine producing the belief that there was only one thing to measure and coordinate. For instance, the coercive power of the public clock in Woolf's *Mrs Dalloway* – its 'shredding and slicing, dividing and subdividing' which 'counselled submission, upheld authority, and pointed out [. . .] a sense of proportion' – derives from its allegiance to the oneness of time.[71] The clock converts the times of bodies, individual wills and local histories, not only in 'the purlieus of London', but 'the heat and sands of India, the mud and swamp of Africa', and elsewhere, into a single universal history.[72] As Barrows explains, the standardisation of time and the fiction of the universal day at the International Prime Meridian Conference in Washington, DC were actually site-specific imperial practices that established England's 'authority to measure, regulate, and delimit the uneven temporalities of global modernity'.[73] The modern clock, when plugged into the larger network that included imperial coordination, progressive history and the work-discipline and timetables of industrial capitalism, forcefully asserts time's independent unity, its absolute rate and its universality. One might say that just when Einstein, Minkowski, aesthetic modernism and time-travel fiction are beginning to reconceptualise the nature of physical and social timespaces, the world witnesses the aggressive institutionalisation of the Newtonian conception of 'Absolute, true and mathematical time', which 'of itself, and from its own nature flows equably without regard to anything external'.[74]

Wells's time machine stands among modernism's earliest challenges to the independence of this empty time measured by the clock. The machine initiated a questioning of the way modernity drained time of spatial specificities and local practices – not simply by travelling inward but by preparing the way, in Einstein's words, for 'as many clocks as we like'.[75] If the expansion of modernity involved, as Anthony Giddens claims, the separation of time and space and the emptying from both of local specificity (such as where the sun appears in the sky at a particular locale), the time machine by contrast required that there be 'no difference between Time and any of the three dimensions of space', as Wells's Traveller says, and it also anticipated that the unevenness of timespace and our various velocities across it allow for clocks to diverge and time to change pace.[76] As W. M. S. Russell points out, Wells's treatment of time as a spatialised fourth dimension anticipates Einstein's rejection of Newtonian time and space in his 1905 theory of special relativity 'by showing that different observers have different timelines', as well as Hermann Minkowski's 1908 reformulation of 'special relativity in terms of a space-time continuum, with time as the fourth dimension'.[77] Moreover, Wells's device does not just rewrite the ontology of things and moments as 'sections [. . .] Three-Dimensional representations of [. . .] Four-Dimensioned being'; it shows us a fourth dimension whose speed and scale vary.[78] Modernism would later connect this variability not only to technology but to the unevenness of literal and figurative topographies to which times are tied, weaving relativity into the smaller reference frames of social space.

By recasting the fall into time as the exploration of temporal multiplicity, we set the stage for a deeper investigation into the relations between the most popular SF figure of the time machine, contemporary historiographic interventions and the wide range of non-narrative temporal orientations in modernism – such as the deep pastism of 'paleomodernism', the epiphanic moment, streams of consciousness, the rapids of the aleatory, or the hyperopic perspectives of far futurism. The time machine comes in many forms – a nickel, ivory and crystal contraption, a blue British police box, a plutonium-powered DeLorean – but some of them, when powered correctly, can function as a controversion technology that overturns our common-sense understanding of time by revealing or producing other times and alternative senses of historical multiplicity. Beyond its typical uses for delight and instruction, the time machine manipulates the putatively universal rate of one second per second, questions the size and evenness of time's periodic units, problematises the timeline's scale, and clarifies and pursues a plurality of histories and epochs that are not integrated, as imperialist historiography conceived it, as phases on a larger progressive line. If temporal plurality can be assembled in what Johannes Fabian describes as 'radical contemporaneity', the time machine reminds us that this 'coevalness' is not a more fundamental here-and-now but a momentary and constructed constellation.[79] As such, this 'present' would evince 'the fragmentary, irreconcilable multidimensionality of the historical', as Srinivas Aravamudan puts it in his examination of the anachronism of 'multiply coexisting temporal orders'.[80] Or it might appear as a strange configuration generated by cross-sectioning many timelines, as a certain strain of SF develops it.

In her diary, Woolf recalls a conversation with Eliot in which she 'taxed him with wilfully concealing his transitions', and it is tempting to think of all modernist techniques as tending towards an undifferentiated Bergsonian process of transition.[81] But one way in which we might bring more clarity to the heterochronic significance of earlier twentieth-century work is to trace its connections to later, more contemporary work about time transit itself, such as Jeremy Shaw's video art series *This Transition Will Never End*. Begun in 2008 with plans for never-ending additions and updates, Shaw's video montages piece together wormhole clips from various time-travel TV shows and films – 'appropriated footage of the un-representable', as Lars Bang Larsen describes it.[82] The project, in Shaw's words, is an 'ongoing archive of appropriated footage taken from a wide variety of movies and television in which a vortex, or any such tunnel-like or spiraling image, is used to represent the slippage of time or a transition from one reality to another'.[83] As Shaw remarks, these vortical representations of dimensional portals figure the history of moving pictures as the history of temporal special effects, while also highlighting the psychedelic fantasy of liberation from everyday constraints and coordinates as 'a ubiquitous representational cliché of the transition into another reality, state, time, etc.' that is paradoxically 'visually un-documentable' (Plate 3).[84]

Shaw's collection of clips offers a critique of the fantasy of hyperspace – what David Wittenberg identifies as the narratologically necessary 'viewpoint-over-histories' brought to light in the latest, crucially visual phase of time-travel fiction. In this phase, paradoxical narrative structures self-reflexively 'expose the postulate of *fabular* apriority', the premise that there must be a 'prior historical or factual story' underpinning a fiction, as well as the way in which that premise serves to hide the fact that 'the real, physical means of prioritizing *fabula*' requires a paratextual act of reading that can visualise and map out fabular sequences, a 'primal scenography of narrative'.[85] However, Shaw's jerky ride of the mash-up of warp-speed scenes does not so much posit the impossibility of accessing hyperspace as suggest that the paratextual, meta-historical impulse to exit a time results in the jump to another reference frame rather than to an absolute timeline. As he says in his interview with Larsen, the fantasy of time travel, like the psychedelic trip, is 'not about "dropping out" to the utopian community or ideals of yesteryear, but it's an acknowledged engagement and dialogue with this proposition of time-slippage'.[86] As Larsen summarises Shaw's wormhole excursions, such time slippage, in contrast to 'phenomenological-type psychedelic works that refer to a supposed fullness "behind" or "before" the representation', suggests a 'different concept of time [. . .] where it isn't that simple to divide things up in pre or post', because the destinations of such transit are different reference frames in which time runs at different speeds and over which no single clock presides.

Wittenberg has argued that 'narrative itself [is] a "time machine"', and that 'literature itself might be viewed as a sub-type of time travel, rather than the other way around'.[87] The reasons are that narrative is 'a mechanism for revising the arrangements of stories and histories', and that literature moves us through times and places in ways more or less attentive to 'the structural time and space of storytelling itself'.[88] The period that this book explores is the period in which literature is arguably most aware of its operations as a machine or set of devices. As Sean Pryor and David Trotter argue in their recent collection on 'modern technographies', literature 'had to get to grips with these new levels of mechanical supremacy, and it did so in part by reconceiving itself as a machine'.[89] Paul Valéry defined a poem as a 'machine producing the poetic state of mind', and William Carlos Williams similarly described poetry as a 'machine made out of words'.[90] Likewise, in critical discourse, one might think of I. A. Richards's riff on Le Corbusier, 'A book is a machine to think with', or Victor Shklovsky's essay 'Art as Device', in which literary technics ironically work to free objects from 'the over-automatization' of perception.[91] If modernist literature specifically aspired to the condition of a machine, it was a distinctly non-narrative one that reworked everything from what Woolf called 'the formal railway line of a sentence' to plot structure itself.[92] It strove to be a very peculiar kind of time machine – not simply a vehicle moving us back and forth in time, or even one with a view of the rails and tracks below, but also one that defamiliarises and reconfigures the very medium that narrative is meant to organise, and that produces a variety of timespaces.

In Chapter 1, I will start with the defamiliarisation and reconfiguration of historicity. Wells's machine produces a vision of what evolutionary biology calls heterochrony, which becomes a figure for the hotchpotch body of history itself. This estranging vision allows for a re-reading of two of the most canonical modernist techniques on record: Pablo Picasso's 'primitivist' warping of painting's timespace and Eliot's fragmentary historical sense. The patchwork historicity that emerges from a return to *Les Demoiselles d'Avignon* and *The Waste Land* connects up with a more explicitly Einsteinian view of history in Murray Leinster's alternate-history story, 'Sidewise in Time', which thematises the convergence of anachronistic presents, irregular trajectories and multiple lines into polytemporal assemblages. Chapter 2 begins by considering the alternate historicity of temporal alongsidedness in the frame of Jameson's and Neil Smith's reading of uneven development. In thinking about the political unconscious of multi-temporality and how the idea of alternatives might be reconsidered, I examine three texts that feature cross-cut parallel timelines: Christopher Nolan's *Interstellar*, Philip K. Dick's *The Man in the High Castle* and Virginia Woolf's *Mrs Dalloway*. By reading these meditations on separate, de-synchronised, but intersecting histories, the chapter constructs a connection between Michel Serres's time-machinic view of crumpled historicity and alternate history's treatment of historical intervention in light of timelines with differing pace, duration and sets of possibility. The new, no longer the result of the radical historical break, must be rethought in relation to the overlap and intersection of tracks that run irregularly through any present.

In Chapter 3, I examine time lag not simply as the difference between two locations on a single timeline, but as the difference between lines themselves with their respective tempos and varying pace. Starting with a reading of 'bullet time' in *The Matrix* as a way of foregrounding relative rates, the chapter moves to Michael Wesely's blurry, record-breaking, pinhole photographs of urban development, before turning to racialised time lag in William Faulkner's *The Sound and the Fury* and the postcolonial exploration of historical difference and behindness in Jessica Hagedorn's *Dream Jungle*. Finally, Chapter 4 examines the twentieth-century aesthetic interest in representing and exploring enormous timescales. Here, too, my focus is not on works that seek out some ultimate, most fundamental time frame, but on texts whose scaling up and zooming out reveals the clash of multiple timescales rather than their dissolution into the very largest. By drawing connections between Wells's time travel, Woolf's far futurism, J. B. S. Haldane's vision of the end of the world in his essay/story 'The Last Judgment' and Olaf Stapledon's unprecedented prolepsis of two billion years in *Last and First Men*, this chapter shows how modernist attempts to picture human life from an estranging distance join with SF's literal movement away from all earthly temporal units. Modernism's technique of expanding perspective connects to and even culminates in SF's extraterrestrial settings and themes by allowing us to view the limits of our time frames in relation to others.

As I hope my account will demonstrate, modernism's literary and painterly experiments, certain time-travel fantasies and some unexpected contemporary cultural objects function as a controversion technology. Towards the end of his career, the Annales School historian Fernand Braudel emphasised that his one 'great problem' – 'the only problem I had to resolve' – had been 'to show that time moves at different speeds'.[93] Well before the Annales approach became synonymous with the imperturbable *longue durée*, Braudel's early breakthroughs in reconceptualising time and history, as Bill Schwarz notes, had

> few conventions in the historiography of the period that could serve as a model. But if the historiography was deficient in this respect there was [. . .] an entire tradition of high modernist literature which devoted its greatest energies to devising narrative forms which could reproduce time moving at different speeds.[94]

Those narrative forms were, of course, famously anti-narrative or non-narrative, and moreover they explored not only timing but also timescales and timelines. If Perry Anderson rightly criticised monolithic modernism as an empty 'portmanteau concept whose only referent is the blank passage of time itself', the irony is that its time fixation produced precisely what Anderson argued that modernism-in-the-singular elides: a 'multiplicity of modernisms'.[95] This multiplicity is not only the embodiment of the 'diversity founded on the far greater plurality and complexity of possible ways of living' – the site-specific 'alternative modernities' that have 'different starting points', as Gaonkar says, and 'lead to different outcomes' – but also the various responses within modernism to the uneven and various times informing their own unevenly distributed and multifarious modernity.[96] The desire to get outside singular, uniform time continues to power the heterochronic machine into the twenty-first century.

NOTES

1. The time machine is a cardinal trope of SF because, as Sean Redmond points out, 'Science fiction is in essence a time travel genre. Events either open in the altered past, the transformed present or the possible future, transporting the reader to another age, place, dimension or world.' Sean Redmond, 'The Origin of the Species: Time Travel and the Primal Scene', in *Liquid Metal: The Science Fiction Film Reader*, ed. Sean Redmond (New York: Wallflower, 2004), 114–15.
2. See Gilles Deleuze and Félix Guattari, *Anti-Oedipus: Capitalism and Schizophrenia* (Minneapolis: University of Minnesota Press, 1983) and *A Thousand Plateaus: Capitalism and Schizophrenia* (Minneapolis: University of Minnesota Press, 1987). For Deleuze and Guattari, a machine is an assemblage of connections among parts that, when plugged into one another, produce new lines of becoming. Levi Bryant's book *Onto-Cartography: An Ontology of Machines and Media* (Edinburgh: Edinburgh University Press, 2014) usefully clarifies how machinic configurations help us to expand definitions of entities based on what they produce and perform. I should mention that my understanding of the way things connect is much less hostile to the discursive.

3. Adam Barrows, *The Cosmic Time of Empire: Modern Britain and World Literature* (Berkeley: University of California Press, 2011), 7.

4. Sara Danius, *The Senses of Modernism: Technology, Perception, and Aesthetics* (Ithaca: Cornell University Press, 2002), 10. Danius argues that 'Conditions of possibility can be traced internally; that is, they are to be understood as a matter of constitution [. . .] Stated differently, technology and modernist aesthetics should be understood as internal to one another' (10–11).

5. Ibid. 4; Barrows, *Cosmic Time of Empire*, 102.

6. Ezra Pound, 'Dateline', in *Literary Essays of Ezra Pound*, ed. T. S. Eliot (London: Faber, 1954), 87.

7. Mark Currie, *About Time: Narrative, Fiction, and the Philosophy of Time* (Edinburgh: Edinburgh University Press, 2007).

8. For general accounts of modernism's 'time-obsession', see Wyndham Lewis, *Time and Western Man* (London: Chatto and Windus, 1927); A. A. Mendilow, *Time and the Novel* (New York: Humanities Press, 1965); and C. A. Patrides, *Aspects of Time* (Manchester: Manchester University Press, 1976).

9. As Phillip Wegner says of Jameson's *Archaeologies of the Future*, one of the study's 'most original contributions is that it enables us to understand science fiction itself as a *modernist* practice'; Phillip Wegner, 'Jameson's Modernisms, or, the Desire Called Utopia', *Diacritics: A Review of Contemporary Criticism* 37.4 (2007): 7, emphasis in original. The connection between modernism and SF is built on Russian formalism's *ostranenie*, which modernist scholarship usually translates as 'defamiliarisation'. Darko Suvin incorporates *ostranenie* into his influential definition of SF as 'the literature of cognitive estrangement': *Metamorphoses of Science Fiction: On the Poetics and History of a Literary Genre* (New Haven, CT: Yale University Press, 1979), 4.

10. See Barrows, *Cosmic Time of Empire*; Danius, *Senses of Modernism*; and Joshua Esty, *Unseasonable Youth: Modernism, Colonialism, and the Fiction of Development* (Oxford: Oxford University Press, 2012).

11. George Slusser and Danièle Chatelain, 'Spacetime Geometries: Time Travel and the Modern Geometrical Narrative', *Science Fiction Studies* 22.2 (1995): 161–86; David Wittenberg, *Time Travel: The Popular Philosophy of Narrative* (New York: Fordham University Press, 2013). Wittenberg does remark that in addition to time travel as a way to 'recover past time', 'one might also argue that certain theoretical problems in literary modernism – for instance, Proustian *rechercher* as an immanent theorisation of the structure and psychology of storytelling, or Joycean and Woolfian experimentation with the spatial and temporal rearrangement of narrative forms – might have encouraged academic literary theorists to notice generic time travel fiction as an opportunity or a challenge' (27).

12. Dilip Parameshwar Gaonkar (ed.), *Alternative Modernities* (Durham, NC: Duke University Press, 2001); and Dipesh Chakrabarty, *Provincializing Europe: Postcolonial Thought and Historical Difference* (Princeton: Princeton University Press, 2000).

13. Ernst Bloch, *Heritage of Our Times*, trans. Neville and Stephen Plaice (Cambridge: Polity, 1991 [1935]), 97.

14. Walter Benjamin, 'Theses on the Philosophy of History', in *Illuminations*, trans. Harry Zohn (New York: Harcourt, 1968), 263; Chakrabarty, *Provincializing Europe*, 249.

15. Catherine Gallagher, 'Undoing', in *Time and the Literary*, ed. Jay Clayton, Marianne Hirsch and Karen Newman (New York: Routledge, 2002), 11.

16. Fredric Jameson, *Archaeologies of the Future: The Desire Called Utopia and Other Science Fictions* (New York: Verso, 2005), 286 (emphasis in original). '[T]he essence of Suvin's theory of cognitive estrangement', as Patrick Parrinder puts it, is 'that by imagining strange worlds we come to see our own conditions of life in a new and potentially revolutionary perspective': 'Introduction', in *Learning from Other Worlds: Estrangement, Cognition, and the Politics of Science Fiction and Utopia*, ed. Patrick Parrinder (Durham, NC: Duke University Press, 2001), 4. See also Robert Scholes and Eric Rabkin, who point out that time machines serve to displace a story's setting into the future, which generates 'the satire of our present world': *Science Fiction: History, Science, Vision* (New York: Oxford University Press, 1977), 176. Jameson's work on SF stresses the temporalisation of cognitive estrangement, showing that defamiliarisation provokes not only a simple comparison or critique of our present, but also a sense of the causal trajectory of current social and material arrangements that could be disrupted by a new and revolutionary vision. As the title of his book *Archaeologies of the Future* suggests, there is, buried in the present, an unimaginable trace of something to come, a utopia ready to be unearthed whose ethical necessity – the feeling that it must follow next – matches with equal force and appeal (but without equal effectiveness) the deep determination of the world as it has come to be.

17. For an account of 'tales of the loop, tales that reaffirm the fixity of events on this continuum', 'stories of alternate timelines and temporal disjunction' and the 'solipsism model', see George Slusser and Robert Heath, 'Arrows and Riddles of Time: Scientific Models of Time Travel', in *Worlds Enough and Time: Explorations of Time in Science Fiction and Fantasy*, ed. Gary Westfahl, George Edgar Slusser and David Leiby (Westport, CT: Greenwood Press, 2002), 11–24. Many of the loop and forking-paths stories do not feature any change in the form of time itself: 'alternate history' usually means just a different and unexpected series of events. After the surge of time-cop stories in the 1950s dedicated to protecting the one true timeline, temporal form does get reconceptualised more and more, and seems to yield, as Brian Stableford argues, the 'multiversal chaos [that] was the inevitable ultimate consequence of the premise [of using a time machine]', perhaps because the alternate-history model often functioned simply as the 'escape route from the logical paradoxes arising from time travel'. But SF's signature method of extrapolation, he writes, 'is most powerful when it conveys a sense of inexorable inevitability'. See Brian Stableford, *Science Fact and Science Fiction: An Encyclopedia* (New York: Routledge, 2006), 534, 533, 175. Also, from the point of view of critical reception, even when the trope seems to be doing something else, such as collapsing history or trapping us in a never-ending present or sending us off on an alternate branch, the time machine tends to become a lesson about the dangers of forsaking that sequence.

18. Philip Rosen, *Change Mummified: Cinema, Historicity, Theory* (Minneapolis: University of Minnesota Press, 2001), 80, 83.

19. H. G. Wells, *The Outline of History: Being a Plain History of Life and Mankind* (London: George Newnes, 1920); H. G. Wells, *A Short History of the World* (London: Cassell, 1922).

20. For instance, in history, see Daniel Rosenberg and Susan Friend Harding (eds), *Histories of the Future* (Durham, NC: Duke University Press, 2005); in archaeology, see Michael Shanks and Christopher Tilley, *Re-Constructing Archaeology: Theory and Practice* (London: Cambridge University Press, 2005); in heritage studies, see Robert Lumley (ed.), *The Museum Time-Machine: Putting Cultures on Display* (London: Routledge, 1988); in genetic anthropology, see Spencer Wells, *Deep Ancestry: Inside the Genographic Project* (Washington, DC: National Geographic, 2006); in cognitive psychology, see Endel Tulving's work on episodic memory in 'Memory and Consciousness', *Canadian Psychology* 26.1 (1985): 1–12, and Thomas Suddendorf and Michael C. Corballis, 'Mental Time Travel and the Evolution of the Human Mind', *Genetic, Social, and General Psychology Monographs* 123.2 (1997): 133–67.

21. Paul Kincaid, 'Time Travel', in *The Greenwood Encyclopedia of Science Fiction and Fantasy: Themes, Works, and Wonders*, ed. Gary Westfahl and Neil Gaiman (Westport, CT: Greenwood Press, 2005), 2: 820.

22. Harry Turtledove, 'Introduction', in *The Best Time Travel Stories of the 20th Century*, ed. Harry Turtledove and Martin Harry Greenberg (New York: Del Rey, 2005), ix. Physicists use this formulation too: 'We are all time travelers. Do nothing, and you will be conveyed inexorably into the future at the stately pace of one second per second.' Paul Davies, *How to Build a Time Machine* (New York: Penguin, 2002), 5.

23. H. G. Wells, *The Time Machine: An Invention*, ed. Nicholas Ruddick (Peterborough, ON: Broadview Press, 2001), 78, 144, 147. Subsequent page references are to this edition and are given in parentheses in the text.

24. Jonathan Bignell, 'Another Time, Another Space: Modernity, Subjectivity, and *The Time Machine*', in *Liquid Metal: The Science Fiction Film Reader*, ed. Sean Redmond (London: Wallflower, 2004), 139.

25. Paul A. Cantor and Peter Hufnagel, 'The Empire of the Future: Imperialism and Modernism in H. G. Wells', *Studies in the Novel* 38.1 (2006): 36, 37.

26. I agree with Cantor and Hufnagel that 'the imperialist expansion of Europe in the nineteenth century opened up the imaginative possibility of time travel', and that the machine itself is constructed out of 'the raw materials of empire [. . .] ivory and crystal' ('Empire of the Future', 37, 54). But the ultimate effect of coming into contact with a primitive past is not only and always a strengthening of the historiographic or evolutionary line stretching from exotic other to civilised self. It very often produced the sense of what Johannes Fabian calls 'coevalness', and, more importantly, a sense of multiple historical tempos whose coevalness is an effect of a specific kind of cross-sectioning.

27. Elana Gomel, 'Shapes of the Past and the Future: Darwin and the Narratology of Time Travel', *Narrative* 17.3 (2009): 334–52. Summarising Stephen Jay Gould's

Wonderful Life, Gomel argues that 'the opposition between Darwin's branching tree and the straight line of progress (or regress) embodies the most fundamental issue regarding the nature of history: the choice between determinism and contingency' (348).

28. There are more than a dozen sequels to *The Time Machine* but, as far as I know, only a few are alternate-history extrapolations in which the next text tries to determine what changes to our history (and that of the Eloi and the Morlocks) Wells's traveller has put in motion. For instance, in Stephen Baxter's *The Time Ships*, the 'official' sequel authorised by the Wells estate, the Traveller discovers that his original voyage and the publication of his story have altered history and produced a new timeline, making it impossible to return to 802,701 to save Weena.

29. Bloch, *Heritage of Our Times*, 62.

30. Michael Levenson, 'The Time-Mind of the Twenties', in *The Cambridge History of Twentieth-Century English Literature*, ed. Laura Marcus and Peter Nicholls (Cambridge: Cambridge University Press, 2004), 197.

31. In addition to Stephen Kern, *The Culture of Time and Space, 1880–1918* (Cambridge, MA: Harvard University Press, 2003) and Tim Armstrong, *Modernism: A Cultural History* (Cambridge: Polity, 2005), see also Peter Galison, *Einstein's Clocks and Poincaré's Maps: Empires of Time* (New York: W. W. Norton, 2003) and Michael O'Malley, *Keeping Watch: A History of American Time* (New York: Viking, 1990).

32. Levenson, 'Time-Mind of the Twenties', 207, 198. The capital 'T' in 'Time-consciousness' indicates not only the grandeur of the topic but also the way in which times have been construed as a proper noun.

33. Ibid. 207; Lewis, *Time and Western Man*, xviii.

34. Levenson, 'Time-Mind of the Twenties', 217.

35. H. Peter Stowell, *Literary Impressionism: James and Chekhov* (Athens: University of Georgia Press, 1979), 9. Stowell names impressionism 'a literary phenomenon of major proportions, as it rendered a furiously changing world, precariously perched for the flight of Modernism into the 20th century' (9).

36. Matei Calinescu, *Five Faces of Modernity: Modernism, Avant-Garde, Decadence, Kitsch, Postmodernism* (Durham, NC: Duke University Press, 1987), 3. There are many variations of this account. In addition to the sources already mentioned in this chapter, see general introductions to modernism such as Christopher Butler's *Early Modernism*; celebratory accounts of the modern such as Marshall Berman's *All That Is Solid Melts Into Air*; and virtually any critical narrative based on Baudelaire.

37. David Harvey, *The Condition of Postmodernity: An Enquiry into the Origins of Cultural Change* (Cambridge: Blackwell, 1990), 240.

38. Zygmunt Bauman, 'Time and Space Reunited', *Time & Society* 9.2–3 (2000): 172, emphasis in original.

39. Charles Baudelaire, 'The Painter of Modern Life', in *Selected Writings on Art and Literature*, trans. P. E. Charvet (Harmondsworth: Penguin, 1992), 403.

40. Matthew Arnold, 'Dover Beach' (1867); Charles Baudelaire, 'The Painter of Modern Life' (1863); W. B. Yeats, 'Adam's Curse' (1903). In 'Dover Beach', religion is

a slackening 'girdle' that can no longer hide or hold together the enticements and horrors of mortality (Matthew Arnold, 'Dover Beach', in *The Poetical Works of Matthew Arnold*, ed. Nathan Haskell Dole [New York: Thomas Crowell, 1897], 213–14); in 'The Painter of Modern Life', Baudelaire opposes the beauty of 'the transitory fleeting element' of modernity with 'the emptiness of an abstract and indefinable beauty, like that of the one and only woman before the Fall' (403); and in 'Adam's Curse', Yeats turns Arnold's 'darkling plain' of the present into an end-of-the-summer dusk in which an unfull moon stands as a symbol of humanity's eviction from the garden of Eden and its temporal punishment, the stripping down of human life to its brief, belaboured finitude (W. B. Yeats, 'Adam's Curse', in *The Collected Works of W.B. Yeats: The Poems*, ed. Richard J. Finneran [New York: Macmillan, 1989], 78–9).

41. Walter Pater, *Studies in the History of the Renaissance*, ed. Matthew Beaumont (Oxford: Oxford University Press, 2010 [1873]), 5.

42. Ibid. 119.

43. Ibid. 120–1.

44. Matthew Beaumont, 'Introduction', in Pater, *Studies in the History of the Renaissance*, xx. For a study on nineteenth-century 'figures of brevity', see Sue Zemka, *Time and the Moment in Victorian Literature and Society* (Cambridge: Cambridge University Press, 2011).

45. Pater, *Studies in the History of the Renaissance*, 120.

46. Ibid. 121.

47. Ibid. 118.

48. Ibid. 120.

49. Leo Charney, 'In a Moment: Film and the Philosophy of Modernity', in *Cinema and the Invention of Modern Life*, ed. Leo Charney and Vanessa R. Schwartz (Berkeley: University of California Press, 1995), 280. In Charney's reading, this detached present becomes cinema's defamiliarising answer to modernity and its empty history: 'This possibility of a sensual present as antidote to the alienation of modernity was the path taken in modernity from Pater's promotion of the sublime moment to Walter Benjamin's notion of shock to Jean Epstein's concept of *photogénie* to Heidegger's own speculation that the "moment of vision" allowed an ecstatic break in the otherwise elusive passage of lost time' (281–2).

50. Karl Marx and Friedrich Engels, *The Communist Manifesto: A Modern Edition* (London: Verso, 1998), 38.

51. Jonathan Crary, *Techniques of the Observer: On Vision and Modernity in the Nineteenth Century* (Cambridge, MA: MIT Press, 1990), 3–4.

52. Virginia Woolf, 'Modern Fiction', in *The Common Reader*, ed. Andrew McNeillie (New York: Harvest, 2002), 150.

53. Ronald R. Bernier, *Monument, Moment, and Memory: Monet's Cathedral in Fin de Siècle France* (Lewisburg, PA: Bucknell University Press, 2007), 13.

54. The description of the shift from the external to the internal, the consensual to the sensory, is E. H. Gombrich's, quoted in Ian Watt, *Conrad in the Nineteenth Century* (Berkeley: University of California Press, 1979), 171.

55. John Klein, 'The Dispersal of the Modernist Series', *Oxford Art Journal* 21.1 (1998): 124. For Klein, the failure of the unity of the series perfectly satisfied the demands of the art market, which wanted to sell individual works that were validated by the coherence of something larger. For the criticism of incompletion, see Louis Leroy's infamous 1874 review of Monet's *Impression: Sunrise*, which gave impressionism its name: 'Wallpaper in its embryonic state is more finished than that seascape.' 'L'exposition des impressionnistes', *Le Charivari*, 25 April 1874, in Linda Nochlin, *Impressionism and Post-Impressionism, 1874–1904: Sources and Documents* (Englewood Cliffs, NJ: Prentice-Hall, 1966), 10–14.

56. Rebecca Stern, 'Time Passes', *Narrative* 17.3 (2009): 236.

57. Daniel Wildenstein, *Claude Monet: Biographie et Catalogue Raisonné*, vol. 3 (Paris: La Bibliothèque des arts, 1974), 1208, quoted in Bernier, *Monument, Moment, and Memory*, 73. Bernier sees the series as multiplicity but ties it to Bergson: 'The philosophy of Henri Bergson, whose central thesis is the primordiality of experiential time – time as flux – provides a practical way of thinking about Monet's achievement. The idea of extended perception I have described in the series of images may be thought of, I want to argue, as like Bergson's extensive consciousness located in time: conscious states understood not [. . .] as a sequence of successive, atomistic, and discrete moments – the time of clocks – but as a multiplicity continually unfolding in "duration"' (57). This reading makes the figure of the Cathedral rhyme with subjectivity as itself an 'enactment of historical continuity' (62), whereas my reading is content to let temporal difference remain un-unified.

58. Henri Lefebvre, *Rhythmanalysis: Space, Time, and Everyday Life* (London: Continuum, 2004), 20–1.

59. According to Jon May and Nigel Thrift, the general account of modern timespace inspired by Marx's insight about the annihilation of space by time focuses on 'a significant acceleration in the pace of life concomitant with a dissolution or collapse of traditional spatial co-ordinates (changes usually expressed via some discourse on *speed* – or space divided by time)'. Jon May and Nigel Thrift, *TimeSpace: Geographies of Temporality* (London: Routledge, 2001), 7.

60. Paul de Man, 'Literary History and Literary Modernity', in *Blindness and Insight: Essays in the Rhetoric of Contemporary Criticism* (Minneapolis: University of Minnesota Press, 1988), 147.

61. May and Thrift, *TimeSpace*, 12; Lefebvre, *Rhythmanalysis*, 89.

62. Lefebvre, *Rhythmanalysis*, 89.

63. Barrows cites Kern's 'Bergsonian reading of modernist time' as 'still the only rigorous attempt to theorize a relationship between standard time and modernist literature' (*Cosmic Time of Empire*, 8). That is, as 'the touchstone for studies of standard time and aesthetics', Kern's book construes modernism as pure resistance to the clock (8–9). My argument is that modernism resists *the* clock by featuring *many* clocks and by acting as a special kind of time-telling device.

64. Henri Bergson, *Time and Free Will: An Essay on the Immediate Data of Consciousness* (London: G. Allen, 1913 [1889]), 108.

65. Ibid. 228, 108.

66. Jacques Le Goff, *Time, Work, and Culture in the Middle Ages*, trans. Arthur Goldhammer (Chicago: University of Chicago Press, 1980), 52; see also 29–42.
67. Ian R. Bartky, *One Time Fits All: The Campaigns for Global Uniformity* (Stanford: Stanford University Press, 2007), 35–47.
68. Lewis Mumford, *Technics and Civilization* (New York: Harcourt, Brace, 1934), 14; E. P. Thompson, 'Time, Work-Discipline, and Industrial Capitalism', *Past and Present* 38 (1967): 56–97.
69. Gerhard Dohrn-van Rossum, *History of the Hour: Clocks and Modern Temporal Orders* (Chicago: University of Chicago Press, 1996), 3; Joseph Conrad, *The Secret Agent* (London: Methuen, 1907), 62.
70. John Durham Peters, *The Marvelous Clouds: Toward a Philosophy of Elemental Media* (Chicago: University of Chicago Press, 2015), 255.
71. Virginia Woolf, *The Mrs. Dalloway Reader* (Orlando: Harcourt, 2003), 286.
72. Ibid. 284.
73. Barrows, *Cosmic Time of Empire*, 19.
74. Isaac Newton, *Mathematical Principles of Natural Philosophy*, trans. Andrew Motte (Berkeley: University of California Press, 1934 [1729]), 6.
75. Albert Einstein and Leopold Infeld, *The Evolution of Physics: The Growth of Ideas from Early Concepts to Relativity and Quanta* (New York: Simon and Schuster, 1938), 181.
76. Wells, *The Time Machine*, 60. In the humanities, perhaps the best-known figuration of time's emptiness – i.e., as an absolute container – is Walter Benjamin's critique of the 'homogenous, empty time' through which humanity is thought to progress ('Theses on the Philosophy of History', 261). However, it is Anthony Giddens who specifies this emptiness as an evacuation of local solar time and 'localised activities', and as time's disembedment from space: 'The invention of the mechanical clock and its diffusion to virtually all members of the population [. . .] were of key significance in the separation of time from space. The clock expressed a uniform dimension of "empty" time, quantified in such a way as to permit the precise designation of "zone" of the day.' Furthermore, 'The separating of time and space and their formation into standardised, "empty" dimensions cut through the connections between social activity and its "embedding" in the particularities of contexts of presence.' See Anthony Giddens, *The Consequences of Modernity* (Stanford: Stanford University Press, 1990), 17, 20.
77. W. M. S. Russell, 'Time before and after *The Time Machine*', in *H.G. Wells's Perennial Time Machine*, ed. George Edgar Slusser, Patrick Parrinder and Danièle Chatelain (Athens: University of Georgia Press, 2001), 50, 54.
78. Wells, *The Time Machine*, 61.
79. Johannes Fabian, *Time and the Other: How Anthropology Makes Its Object* (New York: Columbia University Press, 1983).
80. Srinivas Aravamudan, 'The Return of Anachronism', *MLQ: Modern Language Quarterly* 62.4 (2001): 345–6.
81. Virginia Woolf, *The Diary of Virginia Woolf, Vol. 2: 1920–24*, ed. Anne Olivier Bell (New York: Harcourt Brace Jovanovich, 1978), 67.

82. Lars Bang Larsen, 'PCP: Pop/Conceptual/Psychedelic: Interview with Jeremy Shaw', *C Magazine* 101 (2009): 19.

83. See 'Jeremy Shaw – Degenerative Imaging in the Dark | LambdaLambdaLambda | Artsy', https://www.artsy.net/show/lambdalambdalambda-jeremy-shaw-degenerative-imaging-in-the-dark (last accessed 15 May 2017).

84. Larsen, 'PCP', 20.

85. Wittenberg, *Time Travel*, 145–7.

86. Larsen, 'PCP', 21.

87. Wittenberg, *Time Travel*, 1.

88. Ibid. 1, 46.

89. Sean Pryor and David Trotter, 'Introduction', in *Writing, Medium, Machine: Modern Technographies*, ed. Sean Pryor and David Trotter (London: Open Humanities Press, 2016), 9.

90. Paul Valéry, 'Poetry and Abstract Thought' (1939), in *The Art of Poetry*, ed. Jackson Mathews (Princeton: Princeton University Press, 1989), 79; William Carlos Williams, introduction to *The Wedge* (New York: New Directions, 1969 [1944]), 256.

91. I. A. Richards, *Principles of Literary Criticism* (London: K. Paul, Trench, Trubner, 1924), vii; Viktor Shklovsky, 'Art as Device' (1919), trans. Alexandra Berlina, *Poetics Today* 36.3 (2015): 151–74.

92. Steven Connor, 'How to do Things with Writing Machines', in *Writing, Medium, Machine: Modern Technographies*, ed. Sean Pryor and David Trotter (London: Open Humanities Press, 2016), 19–34; and Virginia Woolf, *A Writer's Diary: Being Extracts from the Diary of Virginia Woolf* (London: Hogarth Press, 1953), 136.

93. See Bill Schwarz, '"Already the Past": Memory and Historical Time', in *Regimes of Memory*, ed. Susannah Radstone and Katharine Hodgkin (London: Routledge, 2003), 135.

94. Ibid. 146. Schwarz claims that Braudel never mentioned modernist experiments because he misunderstood the literary explorations as being 'historically "weightless", capable of understanding subjective time only at the expense of temporalities located socially and externally' (146).

95. Perry Anderson, 'Modernity and Revolution', *New Left Review* 144 (1984): 102. In this critique of Marshall Berman's book *All That Is Solid Melts into Air*, Anderson identifies modernism completely with the aesthetics of transitoriness: 'Modernism as a notion is the emptiest of all cultural categories [. . .] There is no other aesthetic marker so vacant or vitiated. For what was once modern is soon obsolete' (112–13).

96. Ibid. 113; Dilip Parameshwar Gaonkar, 'Introduction', in *Alternative Modernities*, ed. Dilip Parameshwar Gaonkar (Durham, NC: Duke University Press, 2001), 17. Gaonkar's excellent introduction defines modernity as 'an attitude of questioning the present' (13), and then goes on to say that a 'site-based reading [of the global plurality of modernities] decisively discredits [. . .] the inexorable logic that is assigned to each of the two strands [societal and cultural] of modernity. The proposition that societal modernization, once activated, moves inexorably

toward establishing a certain type of mental outlook (scientific rationalism, pragmatic instrumentalism, secularism) and a certain type of institutional order (popular government, bureaucratic administration, market-driven industrial economy) irrespective of the culture and politics of a given place is simply not true. Nor does cultural modernity invariably take the form of an adversary culture that privileges the individual's need for self-expression and self-realization over the claims of community' (16).

I

THE HETEROCHRONIC PAST AND SIDEWISE HISTORICITY: T. S. ELIOT, PABLO PICASSO AND MURRAY LEINSTER

Augmented Temporality

In 2010 'cameraist' Jason Powell received national attention in the USA on a number of news sites and blogs for his 'Looking into the Past' project, which National Public Radio's Robert Krulwich called 'Time Travel on the Cheap'.[1] For this project, Powell searched the online photo archive of the Library of Congress for old black-and-white photographs of landmarks and other still-existing locales in order to take a picture of his hand holding up the photographs against their present-day locations. The vintage photos are perfectly aligned with the backdrop of the present to look like a window into the past. In similar fashion, the 'StreetMuseum' app, launched by the Museum of London in 2010, geotags its archival photographs and paintings of London's 'thousands of years of turbulent history' to their current locations in the city, thereby offering tourists 'a window through time' and embedding portions of the museum *in situ*: users hold their mobile-phone cameras up to a 'present day street scene and see the same London location appear' from the past, either as a simple image or as 'a ghostly overlay on the present day scene'.[2] Speaking of analogous literary devices in SF, the novelist Stephen Baxter describes such 'past viewers' as a 'technology of omniscience' that allows us, as H. G. Wells once put it in his 1921 Neanderthal fantasy 'The Grisly Folk', 'to walk again in vanished scenes, and feel again the sunshine of a million years ago' (Fig. 1.1 and Plate 4).[3]

Figure 1.1 StreetMuseum App: 23 Queen Victoria Street during the Blitz, 11 May 1941, windowed into the present

Against such sunny returns to the past, Baxter provides examples of literary past viewers that present more complicated versions of the past and present. In J. G. Ballard's 'The Sound-Sweep', for instance, the past is not a simple zone worth 'looking into' for clean comparative leaps, but is instead the site of grimy, accumulated residues of minor happenings that must be cleansed and removed from dignified artefacts and present objects. The sweeper can perceive and must 'sonovac' from a thirteenth-century chapel 'all extraneous and discordant noises – coughing, crying, the clatter of coins' that have settled on the 'beautiful sonic matrices rich with seven centuries of Gregorian chant'.[4] Today our augmented presents seem to invite more and more extraneous and discordant noise, with real-time events appearing on television with a ticker-tape of information running along the bottom of the screen, or heads-up displays (HUDs) in cars that float above the bonnet and stitch their operational and navigational data into the environment itself. Examples of 'augmented reality' (AR) are often described in spatial terms: Lev Manovich describes AR as a dataspace, a world 'overlaid with dynamically changing information', a physical space that is electronically enhanced, extended, manipulated and surveilled.[5] However, one might also put more pressure on the temporal dimension of such augmentations and consider the stranger complications of the past and present that such time pollution often achieves. It is not just space but also our sense of time and history that we navigate, congest and perhaps alter by means of these technologies of interface.

Let us consider a sort of temporal AR that has no pretension to omniscience, the all-knowing archivist's impulse to dig up the entirety of the ever-present past underlying the now, nor the desire to build up defensive fortifications of the foreshortened or quietist present. Modernist literary and art history, and certainly SF, contain examples of more powerful and radical versions of 'Looking into the Past' and 'StreetMuseum', kinds of augmented-temporality technology that layer deep time into the present and open windows into multiple pasts in the now – past viewers and time machines that sought to examine the nature and composition of time itself. However, their temporal implications have been interpreted mostly in terms of Bergsonian, ahistorical simultaneity or atavistic recoveries of the deep past, both of which were seen as responses to the unified, punctual time of modernity. As a way of leading into this chapter's primary examples of Pablo Picasso's 'primitivist' views, Murray Leinster's SF and T. S. Eliot's weird historical sense, we might start with a preliminary object of temporal AR that Mark Antliff calls an 'icon of modernism' and Stephen Kern names 'the great symbol of simultaneity': the Eiffel Tower in Robert Delaunay's cubist paintings (1909–14).[6]

Readings of Delaunay's paintings of the Eiffel Tower have tended to emphasise the all-at-once-ness of the non-instantaneous present and its spatially extensive temporal surrounds. Built for the 1889 Exposition Universelle, the tower quickly became a symbol of the modern in terms of its architecture and engineering, and by 1910 it also functioned as part of the clock mechanism helping to manufacture modernity, transmitting the unifying, standardising radio time signal of the local solar time of Paris as France's national time. In 1913 it broadcast the very first time signal (by now Greenwich Mean Time) around the entire globe.[7] Thus, the Eiffel Tower was indeed both the symbol and the instrument of national and international synchronisation, the result of which, as David Harvey argues, was the 'collapse [of] space into the simultaneity of an instant in universal public time'.[8] The effect of simultaneity – that spatially distant observers might know about and experience the same event together at the very moment that it happens – is in fact a symptom of what Harvey described as time-space compression, the shrinking of geographical distance and the flattening of regional time differences by means of capitalist technologies of coordination, communication and transport. By contrast, Delaunay's painting, rendered in a 'primitive', anti-realist style, foregrounds a break from 'the premise that the canvas presents one atemporal moment of vision by a perceiver standing in a fixed position'; in subject matter, the painting would seem to open that present to the analytic run-up and run-off of what Wendy Steiner likened to Gertrude Stein's continuous present, which detaches itself 'from the sense of tradition and temporal continuity of earlier days', that is, from an older 'historiographic ideology' based on progress.[9]

However, that new disruptive continuity and simultaneity tends to be seen in Bergsonian terms as a singular, coherent duration. Patricia Leighten and Mark Antliff discern in this 1911 picture from Delaunay's series, especially in the urban smoke, a symbol of Jules Romains' Unanimism, a figure of intermixture that tinges the multiple aspects of the tower with moody, alogical, empathetic oneness.[10] This interpenetration of cubist facets extends Jean Metzinger's Bergsonian commentary on Delaunay's 'intuition [as] the sudden combustion of thoughts accumulated each day'.[11] The aggregation of Delaunay's own memory, from which he painted the tower, becomes the figure for a larger, social recollection, a gathering of many different views of the tower by many different subjects. Thus, for Antliff, the painting is 'a utopian ode to the possibility of collective consciousness, and with it, collective fraternity'.[12] Delaunay's simultaneity, its multiplicity of views from a series of moments, becomes a social all-at-once-ness, a multiplicity of views from a multiplicity of viewers who are bound to one another through intuition. Leighten and Antliff are convincing in stating that, instead of figuring national unity and progress, Delaunay's paintings make visible all the surrounding differences that are yoked together in a medium that was increasingly homogeneous across space, the medium of happening and rendering that was both public time and the pictorial space of painting (Fig. 1.2).

Blaise Cendrars, in his account of his visit to the tower with Delaunay, claimed that 'Delaunay wanted to show Paris simultaneously, to incorporate the Tower into its surroundings', but what if its surroundings are different times themselves with different pasts?[13] Rather than just the different angles of vision on and from the tower itself, in which 'seen from the first platform, [the tower] spiralled upward; seen from the top, it sank into itself with straddling legs and indrawn neck', the tower's actual milieu is the local and regional times drawn towards the synchronising radio tower, times whose visibility reveals the fault lines in the universal present (whether a punctual moment or a thicker span), the markers of the intersection of many concurrent temporal registers.[14] The strange reality, the total image of the Eiffel Tower is thus not, or not only, defined by subjective difference, or the social construed as many subjective differences; it is also defined by the tempo-geographical variety that cannot be reduced to and by a single uniform time. Here, the simultaneous juxtaposition of multiple instants and points of view does not mean that the multiplicity is ordered up into a shared temporal line; it represents instead the coevalness of times running side-by-side, coeval not in some larger, more fundamental present, but in an expedient timespace of crossings, overlappings and partial encounters. While Harvey reads cubism as 'a movement that tried to represent time through the fragmentation of space [. . .] [which] paralleled the practices

Figure 1.2 Robert Delaunay, *Eiffel Tower*, 1911 (dated 1910 by the artist), oil on canvas, 79½ x 54½ inches (202 x 138.4 cm), Solomon R. Guggenheim Museum, New York. Solomon R. Guggenheim Founding Collection, by gift. 37.463

on Ford's assembly line' (the latter broke up holistic production in order to speed up 'the turnover time of capital'), the aesthetic simultaneity generated by some temporal AR not only displays the Bergsonian aversion to the segmentation and fractioning of time *into a single line*, but also goes one step further in suggesting that temporal heterogeneity is an effect of historical heterogeneity. The mixed and mottled temporality of the subject or the present is the result of the intersection of multiple lines whose pace and starting point are relative not only to longitude on an irregularly spinning globe but to the deformed and deforming localities and their rhythms.[15]

In this chapter, I want to examine two very well-known and canonical cases in art and literature, Picasso's *Les Demoiselles d'Avignon* (1907) and Eliot's *The Waste Land* (1922), along with Murray Leinster's peculiar alternate-history short story, 'Sidewise in Time' (1934). Critics have often complained that the effect of both modernism and AR on our sense of time is negative:

the present is not augmented but diminished and dehistoricised; or the present becomes the triumphant consequence of the march of progressive history. In the case of the former, the past is made present in a spatialised way such that it loses its 'beforeness', its historical depth and determinative force; in the latter, the presence of the past affirms the superiority of the present. By re-reading Wells's representation of the chimerical body by way of the evolutionary-biological concept of heterochrony, this chapter argues for a more complex conception of the past, connecting time machines to modernist AR devices, as well as to later twentieth-century objects examined in this book. Steiner argues that modernist experimentalism 'tells us to think of history in a new way, not as a plotted narrative moving toward a resolution, but as a cubist painting'; the latter 'makes a simultaneity of it [the past]', placing heterogeneous items 'in an aestheticized structure of interrelations'.[16] I would like to read cubism and its simultaneities, along with Eliot's and Leinster's sidewise historical sense, in a more extreme way: the patchwork historicity that results from these aesthetic experiments counters monochronic ways of thinking about history by exploring heterogeneously anachronistic presents, irregular trajectories and multiple lines that converge into polytemporal assemblages. Such temporal augmentations do not just deepen the shallow present but counter the unity and universality of that deep time by a plurality of unexpected pasts with which to align vestiges and fragments in the present.

HETEROCHRONY: HAECKEL, WELLS AND THE POLYTEMPORAL BODY

The refiguration of time as a plurality of times has appeared with increasing frequency in discussions that reconsider both the historical and aesthetic dimensions of modernity. In Dilip Parameshwar Gaonkar's collection *Alternative Modernities*, for example, the pluralisation of modernity marks a rejection of the way modernisation theory's global frame has assumed a single, uniform process modelled on the course of history in western Europe and North America. To claim that different nations and cultures enter the process of modernisation at 'different starting points' and with 'different outcomes' is not simply to assert that diverse contexts are not all equally secular, scientific, bureaucratic and industrialised.[17] It also to imply that the 'course of history' itself – the very temporal infrastructure of modernity, with its 'twin matrix' of 'incessant change and deadening routine' – must be further reconceptualised as site-specific and therefore always multiple.[18] Peter Osborne makes this rethinking of time explicit in his book on contemporary art, *Anywhere or Not at All*:

> the changing temporal quality of the historical present over the last few decades is best expressed through the distinctive conceptual grammar of con-temporaneity, a coming together not simply 'in' time, but *of* times

[. . .] a coming together of *different but equally 'present'* temporalities or 'times', a temporal unity in disjunction, or a *disjunctive unity of present times*.[19]

Osborne briefly uses the term 'heterochronic' to describe an unexpected danger of this 'contemporaneity': that its disruption of modernity's constant transitoriness and perpetual change comes at the cost of the 'conjuncture, or at its most extreme, the stasis of a present moment', that is, the 'annihilation of temporality' characteristic of a culture of the image.[20] One of the most famous uses of the idea of heterochrony has often stood as an example of this danger: in his 1967 lecture 'Of Other Spaces', Michel Foucault used the term to argue that the counter-sites of heterotopia involve not just the reflection and contestation of spatial orders but an 'absolute break with [. . .] traditional time'.[21] His first examples of the way heterotopias are linked to heterochronies are museums and libraries, 'heterotopias in which time never stops building up [. . .] a sort of general archive, the will to enclose in one place all times, all epochs, all forms, all tastes'.[22] While his concept of heterotopia, like heterochrony, is thought to be incomplete or even incoherent, Foucault's idea of the archive has a fairly secure meaning: in *The Archaeology of Knowledge* (1969), the archive is theorised not merely as 'that whole mass of texts' in a repository, but as the 'law of what can be said, the system that governs the appearance of statements as unique events'.[23] However, to emphasise the structure and regulation of the rules of discourse would be to miss the very strange pluralisation that Foucault's less polished thinking might have briefly identified in archives conceived heterochronically.

The heterogeneous pluralisation of times suggested in Foucault's idea of the rupture with 'traditional time' is in fact already present and explicit in the very first context from which the word 'heterochrony' comes: nineteenth-century evolutionary developmental biology. This history of the concept of heterochrony can yield something much more interesting than the simultaneity or stasis of the disjunctive coming-together of times. As the body's hotchpotch of disjunctive timings, heterochrony's biological provenance suggests a multiplicity of ongoing trajectories figured in and as the chimerical body. While the conjuncture of plural times – whether in the form of global history in Gaonkar or the tissue of presentness in Osborne – is always in danger of becoming a de-temporalised convergence in the space of 'the present', what seems 'all here now' is better seen as cuts or fragments of various historical trajectories assembled in relation to each other *as* a 'now'.[24] In 1875, almost a century before Foucault's formulation, and before we had the technology to access the genetic code that informs morphology, the German embryologist and Darwinist Ernst Haeckel coined the term 'heterochrony' (along with 'heterotopy') to describe deviations in the 'traditional time' of the body.[25] In his famous biogenetic law or recapitulation theory, ontogeny always smoothly recapped phylogeny: an organism's development from embryo to adult always replayed every adult stage of its entire species' evolution. In other words, the part not only stood for the whole but archived within it the whole's entire phylogenetic history, one that was always getting longer, growing denser and playing faster. Haeckel imagined, as Stephen Jay Gould points out, 'an even and integrated acceleration of the [series] of entire adult ancestor[s] into earlier and earlier ontogenetic stages of descendants'.[26] However, variations in the onset, offset or pacing of development fragmented both the coherent form of the descendant and the history that it stood for into a de-synchronised set of individual organs, each with its own ontogenetic trajectory. Heterochrony referred to these aberrations in the timing and rate of embryonic development that Haeckel believed prevented the otherwise single-file rehearsal of the past in the morphology of the present. These anomalies notwithstanding, the body was thought to contain regular records of our ancestral past, which Haeckel's well-known and widely disseminated illustration of eight vertebrates at different stages of development made clear (Fig. 1.3).[27]

Although recapitulation theory has been discredited and the embryo illustrations were exaggerated to advance the theory, Haeckel's concept of heterochrony – the deviation from smooth recapitulation – has remained an important idea in

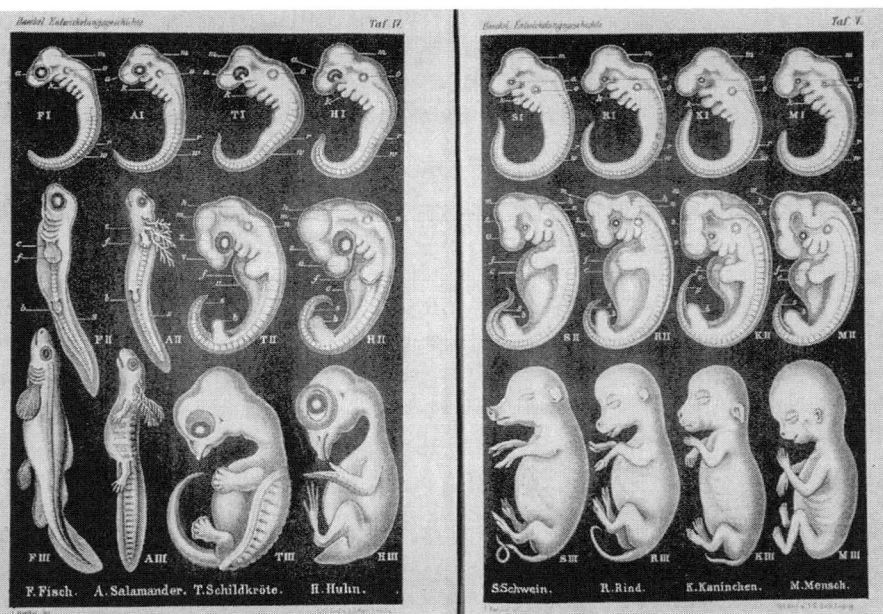

Figure 1.3 J. G. Bach's lithograph of Ernst Haeckel's illustrations emphasising the order of recapitulation, 1874

the life sciences, since it is able to account for variation as such. In fact, as a result of Gould's work, contemporary developmental biology no longer sees heterochrony as an aberration of evolution but as one of its primary mechanisms for generating difference itself. The complete adult image of any previous ancestor never appears in any of the stages of a creature's development, but 'underdeveloped' and 'overdeveloped' traits appear in the hotchpotch of the present. As the palaeobiologist Kenneth McNamara claims, heterochrony is the missing link between the external pressures of natural selection and the internal directives of genetics, and is precisely the way in which evolutionary variation is achieved: 'it explains everything, from the shape of the delphinium flower, to a horse's foot, to the song of a bird'.[28] This mechanism explains how some finches develop slightly bigger bills than others, why dogs resemble juvenilised wolves, and why humans are paedomorphic apes with baby faces but with peramorphic brains that grow for much longer than do the brains of other primates. Heterochrony reveals that our corporeal present is not the culmination of a progressive and uniform linear time; we are rather a 'mosaic of characters, some speeded up, others slowed down, producing one of the more potent cocktails' mixed together over three and a half billion years of life on the planet.[29]

If for Haeckel the body was a figure for linear developmental time, heterochrony's dismemberment of phylogenetic history reconfigured the body as a mosaic of different temporal signifiers, many of which evoke pasts beyond narrowly constructed lineages. Heterochrony turned the body into both the literal repository of and a figure for multiple times and differential rates of change. The body is indeed an archive, but it is a deeply disorderly one. The pasts contained in it are not neatly arranged like library stacks but scattered about in strange arrangements and at different points in their ongoing trajectories. Thus, learning to be modern, as Ezra Pound said of T. S. Eliot's self-modernisation, may have involved 'remember[ing] the date (1914) on the calendar', but it also involved – in so many canonical modernist texts and paintings – the proliferation of clocks and the clash of time-telling devices in disjunctive assemblages.[30] The very concept of generation as a period term was in fact revised in the first third of the twentieth century by sociologists such as Karl Mannheim in order to get beyond the inadequacies of positivist chronologies and successive 'spirits of the age', and to acknowledge 'the mutually fructifying co-existence of multiple times, [. . .] co-existent multiple worlds'.[31] Modernism's time obsession contributed to this revision by pushing the metaphorics of kinship at the heart of generational periodisation to their extreme, calling attention not just to parents and peers but to coeval ancestors from disparate periods, and emphasising not lineage but the biological assemblage of anachronisms.

The heterochrony of modernist figures and techniques is an important aspect of the modernist time fixation that extends far into the twentieth century and to the present. In standard histories of modernism, this multiplication of clocks disappears in the depths of either subjective temporality and its repudiation of precisely fractioned clock time, or the long, subsuming distances of palaeo-modernism's timescales.[32] The nineteenth-century currents that flow into these typical readings of the early twentieth century's time obsession are both materialist and epistemological. First, the technologies of ever-faster production, transport and communication contribute to an acceleration of changes in social life, a radical compression or 'annihilation' of space, and a temporal contraction in which, as David Harvey argues, 'time horizons shorten to the point where the present is all there is'.[33] Secondly, evolutionary theory's long processes, the palaeontological discoveries of Neanderthal and Cro-Magnon skulls and the geological bottoming-out of the age of the planet bring about a fall into deep time.[34] Together, these two currents produce the common account of modernist time-consciousness as the experience of rupture with the anchoring power of eternity and tradition; the awareness of being adrift among 'the transient, the fleeting, the contingent', separated by precipitous and ever-lengthening distances from primordial substructures; and the sense of the present nested squarely in the deep past that constitutes it.[35]

In deep time, the connection between the present and the past was expanded so much that it either snapped, producing only a contrast between overwhelmingly large durations and the increasingly small interval once at its head, or it dilated and thickened to the point that the present became nothing other than the radically deepened past. But the impact of shifting rates of change in relation to deep time did not just result in the cultural ambivalence between an 'aesthetics of transitoriness' and the 'timeless world of myth', as critics have so often said.[36] It also generated the much weirder vision and aesthetics of heterochrony. To rethink this history of modernism by returning to figurations of temporal scale, especially as it was inscribed on the human body and the body of the text, is to see that the crisis of a deepening historicism yielded not just a dwarfing of the frame of human experience or an enlargement of the segment of historical process that we occupy. The discovery of the presence of the deep past also provoked what we might call a compound vestigialisation of the present. Evolutionary biology's conceptualisation of the body became a figure for the temporal hotchpotch of differential rates of change constituting the corporeal present.

This vestigialisation of the present differs from both the phenomenological narrative of multiple temporalities and the usual 'primitivist' framework. The former derives from responses to Henri Bergson's philosophy, which have dominated literary criticism's understanding of the modernist 'time cult' since Wyndham Lewis's reaction to his contemporaries' 'Time-mind' in *Time and Western Man*.[37] Because Bergson's theory of *durée* was, in Adam Barrows's words, 'both backward and inward looking in its orientation', the heterogeneous agglomeration of non-psychological times in modernist cultural production was often melted down into Bergson's conception of time as interior – 'a succession of qualitative changes, which melt into and permeate one another, without precise outlines, without any tendency to externalize themselves in relation to one another, without any affiliation with number [. . .] pure heterogeneity'.[38] But even Bergson's 'intensive' resistance to time as a homogeneous, uniformly divided and singular line has been recast in recent years as support for external and more political conceptions of history – for example, in Elizabeth Grosz's treatment of *durée* as a repository of 'virtualities', a set of 'resources for multiple futures, for open pathways, for indeterminable consequences'.[39]

The heterochrony housed in the material body must also be distinguished from another dominant discourse in modernist studies that swallows up modernism's multiple clocks – primitivism. As I will discuss in the next section, it has been tempting to think of all instances of heterochrony as examples of palaeo-modernism's inscription of myth and the deep past in the present. Disjunctions, mosaics and assemblages are reduced to simple markers of pastness, and therefore become expressions of the period's reactionary pathologisation of the other, its fears of degeneration, and its evasions of the complexities of the historical present. To read heterochrony in this way places it within primitivist discourses that affirm the rectilinear unity of time, with the savage on one end and the civilised on the other, whereas heterochronic bodies suggest a multiplicity of variably deep and heterogeneous timelines, in which the present can be construed not only as points on individual lines containing separate pasts, but as a cross-section of a plurality of those histories. As Dana Seitler's work on atavism shows, the appearance of the archaic past in the present can disrupt 'the modern construction of time as linear and continuous [. . .] undergird[ing] a cause-effect understanding of history', not simply by suggesting a reversible, backward-moving time or a discontinuous eruption of ancestral moments into an 'out-of-order' present. Rather, 'atavism offers up a notion of time as multidirectional and of the body as polytemporal'.[40]

The story of the polytemporal written into modernist heterochrony looks back to a key moment in the exploration of time's disjunctive plurality, H. G. Wells's *The Time Machine* (1895). Roughly contemporary with the high point of Haeckel's career, Wells's text is usually taken to be a query about the progressive or degenerative direction of history, the evolutionary fate of Victorian humanity and its socio-economic structures. However, *The Time Machine* is not just a vehicle of adventure and prognostication; it also works to defamiliarise the very medium in which we live and move by means of a device that challenges time's internal constitution and the putatively universal rate of temporal passage itself. The variable speed of the machine across time reveals the variable rates of time themselves. If the machine's ability to 'controvert one or two ideas that are almost universally accepted' exposes that fact that our experience of the steady flow of a single, uniform, natural time is a fiction built on the 'infirmity of the flesh' and the limitations of human sensory organs, then 'the' history of that flesh is an even greater mystery than the Traveller suspects.[41] His own trip contrasts with the model of time that underlies all his hypotheses about what has happened over the span of 800,807 years (as well as 30 million years).

The Traveller keeps guessing as to how his nineteenth-century present – 'this ripe prime of the human race' – could have culminated in the Eloi and the Morlocks, but he remains unable to generate an adequately complex narrative of change over time, given the dimensions in which and with which he is thinking.[42] His discovery that the paedomorphic Eloi with their 'juvenile' traits are not the evolved masters of, but livestock for, the Morlocks clarifies the power relations of this future present, but it does not solidify in any way his 'developing' explanation that *Homo sapiens* split into two species based on nineteenth-century class divisions.[43] In the largest time frame, those two species seem to become huge crabs and then finally a black, flopping, tentacled creature. But it is clear by this point that connecting 'the Golden Age' to the sunset of humanity, and finally to the red death of the sun, continually falters because the slices of analysis, figured by the discussion of four-dimensioned cuts and the Kodak that the Traveller goes back for, are spaced too far apart. They are, moreover, too uniform. Wells's novel calls its main epistemological trajectory into question by likening the creatures of 802,701 to a number of other animals, such as apes, lemurs and ants, and by peppering itself with chimerical figures such as the sphinx, griffin and faun. The other possible pasts of the Eloi and Morlocks, and the human–animal hybrids, together suggest how any slice reveals an interpenetrated cross-section of heterogeneous strands running through it at different and variable rates.

These visions of the chimerical body can be linked to a range of aesthetic experiments after Wells. Susan Squier points out in 'Embryologies of Modernism' that representations of biological hybridity speak to the modernist interrogation of character, the reconfiguration of 'identity not as stabilized in space and in one time period, but rather as diffused and disseminated across different spaces and times'.[44] For example, Susan Glaspell's 1922 play *The Verge* features a female botanist's vision of social potential in embryological fragmentation and recombination that is simultaneously an expression of modernist aesthetics: 'I want to break it up! [. . .] There would be strange new comings together.'[45] Julian Huxley, grandson of anatomist T. H. Huxley, brother of Aldous and the zoologist who worked with Wells on a textbook, wrote a short story, 'The Tissue-Culture King', whose significance includes the impact of scientific, political and racial forces on the constitution and control of identity. The story centres on 'one of the most celebrated modern embryological techniques' – growing tissue and body parts outside the body.[46] For other writers, the primary goal of this deep reconfiguration of identity was to respond to a temporal-political problem, the brevity of generations: just when people gain enough experience to govern complex civilisations, they get old and die. In his 1921 play *Back to Methuselah: A Metabiological Pentateuch*, George Bernard Shaw imagined that, in the year 31,920 ('As Far As Thought Can Reach'), humans would be able to live indefinitely (until killed by accidents). The diffusion and dissemination of character across spatio-temporal difference that Squier analyses connects to extension and longevity in terms of the recombination of temporally significant parts. Shaw's characters may appear as simple expressions of the desire to escape the temporal limitations of the body: his 'She-Ancient' laments her 800 years of life, one in which she has been 'all sorts of fantastic monsters. I walked upon a dozen legs: I worked with 20 hands and a hundred fingers: I looked to the four quarters of the compass with eight eyes out of four heads.'[47] But these figures that go beyond identities 'stabilized in space and in one time period' also demonstrate and symbolise the relations between the body, aesthetic form and new ways of conceiving the temporalities proper to the uneven and inconsistent topographies of timespaces.

The hybrids and chimeras that haunt Wells's and others' texts, while typically located in the critical discourses of racial pathology and hygiene, also allow us to think the radically heterogeneous forms of the body and history that make both normativity and the identity of pure wholes over time impossible. While on the one hand Wells's protagonist is a fairly typical example of those Victorian adventurers who, in travelling 'to remote corners of empire often had the impression that they were entering the world of the past' and encountering peoples 'at very different stages of historical development', on the other hand the Traveller introduces us to the vertigo and confusion that arise when the very progressive time that underwrites the binary of self and other dissolves underfoot.[48] This ambivalence also characterises 'primitivism' in the visual arts, where imperialism's self-serving and racialising views of history make it nearly impossible to detect a heterochronic exploration of the connections between figures, forms and timespace. It will therefore be instructive to turn to *Les Demoiselles d'Avignon*, the first painting of Picasso's 'African' period and arguably an incipient moment of cubism. No one says strange growths, surreal human–animal hybrids and temporal dismemberment better than him. This painting can be read as part of an alternate-temporality project, as an AR device for looking into the heterochronic nature of time and history.

Pablo Picasso's Cubist AR and Heterochronic History

Usually rendered in terms of sequence, simultaneity and *durée*, cubism's most distinctive characteristics – its subversion of the capture of a scene from a single, static viewpoint – contribute to a larger project and stranger impulse to relativise and multiply. While the relationship between primitivism and cubist experiment is already a part of an art-historical narrative that tracks the development of style from the aesthetic rebellion of the 'wild beasts' to extreme fragmentation and collage, it is worth following the temporal logic linking the interrogation of instantaneity to the idea of the presence of deep pasts. By doing so, one can see how cubism moved beyond impressionism's softer confrontation of the instants necessary for capitalist work-discipline or for a stance against eternity. In contrast to impressionism's desire to complicate the pathos attached to evanescence and to register the different rates of change that cut across the momentary, cubism subverted the mode of representation that had dominated Western painting's techniques and epistemology since the Renaissance by opening up the frozen moment not just to temporal passage or 'the' past, but to a multiplicity of pasts. The painting that many art historians have seen as inaugurating this subversion is Picasso's *Les Demoiselles d'Avignon*.[49]

Formalist accounts of cubism that emphasise its roots in *Les Demoiselles d'Avignon* focus their attention on space in order to explain the radically new pictorial idiom, which was reported to have either 1) problematised illusionistic depth by flattening out space, or 2) extended the primitivist simplification of forms to signify an elemental, pre-civilised contact with reality, a reality that exceeds 'civilised' conventions.[50] In the critical narrative that connected Cézanne, primitivism and the most illegible works of cubism, the brutality of the assault on prevailing modes of realistic representation and world-knowing – that is, on the three-dimensional illusion in which a subject of historic, religious or national importance is rendered (stable) at a single moment in time from a fixed location – came from the savage style for which Cézanne was shorthand. For instance, in 1908 Louis Vauxcelles gave cubism its name by describing Braque's *Houses at l'Estaque* as 'reduc[ing] everything – places and figures and houses – to geometrical patterns, to cubes', and by attributing this reductive energy to both the 'style of Cézanne' and the obsession with the 'art of the Egyptians'.[51] Out of the interest in the primitive and fundamental comes the revolutionary treatment of space. In the following year, 1909, Vauxcelles remarked of Matisse:

> From regression to regression, Matisse goes back to the art of the caverns, to the babble of the infant who with a pointed flint traces the silhouette of a reindeer's head onto the wall [. . .] He schematizes, he synthesizes. And the Kanaka (Polynesian) cubes of M. Braque are the direct result.[52]

Cézanne's solutions to spatial problems line up easily with the rawness of primitivism as an overthrowing of overcooked convention. Both the shallowing of illusionistic depth, which painters achieved by breaking down the shapes of the world into basic forms that cannot be riveted to the grid defined by foreground and background, and the return to old schemes and syntheses, such as those of the painters of reindeer and bison in the Font-de-Gaume cave during the Magdalenian period, add up to the primordial desire to see more, and to embrace those aspects of the world that are uncontainable by academic formulae and Renaissance perspective.[53] Thus, the technical accomplishment of cubism is the breaking open of space for the suprasensible, for the large iceberg of reality of which only the tip is visible in common-sense Euclidean space.[54] This hunger for the suprasensible, for the invisible dimensions of reality, as Linda Dalrymple Henderson has shown, emerges out of a cultural matrix defined by the widespread fascination with the mystical and utopian potential of the geometrical fourth dimension, as well as by the late nineteenth-century discovery of X-rays, radioactivity and the electromagnetic waves used by the wireless telegraph.[55] Henderson argues that it was the enthusiasm surrounding an invisible hyperspace and a distinctly spatial fourth dimension that influenced cubism, and not Einsteinian relativity and a temporal fourth dimension.

It is true that cubism emerged prior to the 1919 popularisation of Einstein's theory, so any argument committed to a directed, unmediated historicist connection would have difficulty creating the chain between the German-born physicist living in Switzerland and painterly experiments in Paris. But the idea of time as the fourth dimension was certainly not unheard of (H. G. Wells's 1895 novel, of course, opens with a meditation on it), and there are other sources for temporal relativity such as anthropology, which I discuss in the Eliot section below. Cubist painters and art critics were clearly trying to formulate, in new painterly styles, the relationship of time to the deformation of the scale and solidity of the world, even though they seemed to limit their attention to the brief duration of the representational present, rather than to fuller and stranger implications of their primordial seeing. In a well-known description by the Puteaux group painter and theorist Jean Metzinger, the cubists had

> uprooted the prejudice that directed the painter to stand motionless, at a determined distance from the object [. . .] They have allowed themselves to move around the object to give a concrete representation of several aspects of it in succession [. . .] The picture used to occupy space, now it reigns in time as well.[56]

The year before, in his 'Note on Painting', he had described this method in reference to Picasso and Braque as a 'free, mobile perspective', which replaces the absolute space determining proportions and relations with a fragmented and faceted multi-dimensional space, swapping the 'dead portion of space' for the dynamism of the 'total image radiat[ing] in time'.[57] Since reconfigurations of space are necessarily reconfigurations of time, one does not have to negate cubism's spatial interventions but only to reincorporate time into the larger 'inflamed aspiration', as Arthur C. Danto put it, 'for alternative realities, new logics, new modes of being' that marks 'at least the first half of our century as a period of the most intense longing for another world since the Middle Ages'.[58]

If the space that the new painting depicted could no longer be seen as Euclidean, how could the time in which the object was situated and constituted still be seen as Newtonian? The short analytic durations sampled in these theoretical formulations appear to be standard clock time, but in what ways are the simultaneous views of a fuller reality no longer the affordances of a time defined as an absolute and neutral container? Time has joined space as one of the very things at issue in modernist painting's exploration of not only its own nature and limits, but the nature and limits of experience and, more importantly, of the histories that are its condition. In most accounts, Bergsonian *durée*, in its explicit opposition to uniform, homogeneous time, has been the accepted companion to non-Euclidean spatial experiments, because it is able to account for the new temporalised ontology that seemed to accompany the new understanding of space as an irregular and dynamic platform or substrate. Henderson argues that cubism's references to time, often expressed as '*la durée*', refer only to Bergson and not to the time of physics: 'Cubism's *durée* was simply the temporal means that enabled the artist to gather and synthesize information about the fourth dimension of space.' Time, she continues, 'plays only a supporting role, allowing the artist or geometer to accomplish the physical or mental movement necessary to form an idea of an object's total dimensionality'.[59] More recently, Henderson has written that 'if there is a sense of time and process' in the fusion of multiple views of something, it is not because cubist painting is 'a record of a figure in motion; instead, time is a means to gather information about higher dimensional space'.[60]

By leaning into the connection between Bergson and the irregularities of physical times in cubism, Leighten and Antliff seem to invert Henderson's formulation: the deformation of space was simply a way of gathering information about a seemingly irrational, non-linear time. Their work has placed Bergson's philosophy squarely at the heart of cubism's temporal project, since the philosopher's ideas motivated and clarified the move against the over-rationalised and regularised space measured by single-point perspective. In such a framework, subjectivity serves as a capacious rubric containing many recognisable modernist tendencies, such as the Nietzschean annihilation of received values and the construction of a mystical authority that filled in the vacuum left by the old order. More importantly, their connection of Bergson and cubism also provides ontological suggestions about the plastic deformations that the substance of the world undergoes in relation to a dynamised and heterogeneous timespace, and about the nature of that timespace in its retention of a deep, interpenetrating past. As Leighten and Antliff show, the cubist fusion of the various aspects of the object into a single image is meant to signify not just the artist's painting-in-time or the indivisible processes of subjectivity expressed in the dynamised surface of the painting, but also non-subjective durations, such as the deep social history valorised in cubist 'classicism', in which the punctual image is replaced by the retention of a long *durée* of the 'race', locality or nation, the social intersubjectivity created by the empathetic intuition of Unanimism, or the *élan vital* running through and constituting the world of seemingly immobile objects.[61]

It is not difficult to reframe in Einsteinian terms the pay-offs of Leighten and Antliff's superb application of Bergsonian philosophy to a non-Euclidean physical world. Antliff writes that the

> distinctions between the *elan* and its material products are lost when the Rhythmists and Cubists intuit the rhythmic properties of 'extensity', the concept of qualitative space the Cubists associated with *passage* [. . .] Indeed, all that distinguishes the melody of matter from that of our own duration is the faster rhythm of the latter in comparison to the former.[62]

The Cézannean-cubist technique of *passage* – the detachment of signifiers of discreteness and solidity from painted objects in order to suggest different sorts of continuity on the canvas and in the world – leads to a comparative sense of the variety of pace. Quoting Bergson's *Matter and Memory*, Antliff points out that 'since all movements possess a rhythm, "it is possible to imagine many different rhythms"'.[63] Henderson has done the definitive research regarding the absence of a direct art-historical influence of Einstein on cubist practice and theory prior to 1919, and I am not trying to insert Einstein as an influence into the early history of cubism. However, it is worth considering the existence of a strand of ideas and agendas in cubist work for which Einstein came to stand so easily as a signifier.[64] The interrogation of Euclidean space was *also* a questioning of Newtonian time, of a single container housing apparently solid and locatable objects that might otherwise be seen precisely as 'figures in motion'. The smaller-scale model in cubism for thinking an assemblage of many Einsteinian reference frames – not merely many tempos within a singular time, but many different times as such – was the heterochronic body, especially in Picasso. Picasso's heterochrony has important historiographic implications.

Picasso's *Les Demoiselles* connects the exploration of the punctual instant to the exploration of a plurality of histories. It is an experiment in placing completely different histories side-by-side, an examination of the way the fragmentation of the present is a symptom of the fissures of an uneven temporal landscape. Most contemporary readings of this painting emphasise the historical pathologisation of the other, fears of racial and sexual degeneration, and the evolutionary justifications for the colonisation of Africa; moreover, they warn us off mid-century interpretations that redeployed the framework in which non-Western subjects and artefacts were uprooted from their contexts and relocated to the back of a typological scheme, the front of which was modernity and civilisation. Both threatening and celebratory encounters with the primitive have always seemed to involve, as Mark Antliff and Patricia Leighten point out, a movement 'into an "infantile" past, as if travelling through time rather than space'.[65] There are two big dangers in modifying the simple, primitivist time-travel scenario. The first is that, in fracturing history itself, we might also suffer the loss of determinate causality, which critics have seen in formalism's retreat from history, postmodernism's play and time travel's fantasies of temporal (and therefore contextual) transcendence. But I want to underscore that the problem is not sequence itself, but the fact that there is more than one. Taking our inspiration from Ernst Bloch, we might say that the political problem is knowing which history or set of histories is the right one for addressing the present that we are addressing. In any case, I am not interested in either condemning the painting or exempting it from the play of forces and discourses that it obviously both negotiated and participated in. The second danger is that we risk returning to and redeploying the racist romanticisations of African, 'Oceanic' and other non-Western art. As with Eliot's use of anthropology, to take seriously the idea that non-Western art does indeed signify the deep past is to buy all-too-credulously into the ideological construct of colonial domination and capitalist exploitation. But, as I will show, the painting forcefully critiques the progressive history used to justify empire, and therefore forces us to rethink tempo-racial exoticisation as just a marginal social location or anterior historical position (Plate 5).

It is important to contextualise the painting, but we should note that the canvas provides no simple dramatisation of backwards time travel. While the painting tempts us with the vision of unilinear human development and cultural hierarchy, its shifts across the canvas from left to right resist any reading centred on the trip from the now of the French brothel, to the Spanish prehistory of the Iberian figures, to the deep African roots of 'time immemorial'. As even William Rubin notes, 'none of the African pieces Picasso saw in his first few years of fascination with "art nègre" were more than just decades old', and yet the trajectory of Picasso's interests from Iberian sculpture to African and Oceanic work was seen as 'a journey back in time, to the beginnings of art'.[66] That is, all signifiers of Africanness were drawn from contemporary art, whereas the Iberian elements – the bulging, lozenge-shaped eyes, huge scroll-like ears and wedge noses – were inspired by stone reliefs dating from the fifth to third centuries BCE.[67] The present of the French bordello is neither the end of the evolutionary line, nor the archive that contains all pasts. Likewise, the African past is not the ultimate deep frame containing Spanish and French history, if we can even use these adjectives of continent, race and nationality without scare quotes. This deceptive disruption of ordering (from earliest to latest) unsettles any interpretation of the painting as a smooth, precipitous descent to the origins of humanity and culture, or as a simple simultaneity in which that single origin is ever-present in modern life.

Instead, as Christopher Green's work on *Les Demoiselles* shows, the painting 'dramatises difference through confrontation', both stylistic and cultural, of European and African, and calls attention to a 'non-European present', a now that belongs to others from another place with another set of cultural and individual determinations and destinies, which nevertheless has become entangled in a most appalling way with a now that seeks to appropriate it to its own sense of historical unfolding. The canvas thus stages parallel timelines running concurrently through the scene in the bordello, as well as through the Iberian moment from 2300 to 2600 years ago and perhaps the longer duration connecting the latter to the former.[68] For Green, the discontinuity is epitomised in the stark juxtaposition of two cultures – archaic European and African – a juxtaposition that cannot be construed as a temporal sequence or an equation, because to move across the canvas is to experience the clash that produces the very 'horror' at the heart of the painting's understanding of the violent intersection of these histories. Rather than assimilating the non-European to the European in a stylistic fusion as Matisse's *Bonheur de vivre* does (a dissimulation of conflict and domination), and rather than collapsing the particularity of many cultures into a single signifier of the primitive or exotic (there is more than one), *Les Demoiselles* stages a jarring concurrence of histories, one running through an archaic Iberian moment, represented by the two central figures, and one running through a primitivised but coeval Africa, represented by the two right-hand figures. Reading Africa as a figure of the latest rather than the earliest time calls attention to the ways in which the history of Europe is implicated in the way that Africa appears in the now. The forcible intersection of these two coeval histories (along with the third of the brothel in Avignon) has provided the material for important historical interpretations and critiques of the painting – from Leighten's highlighting of the contradictions between the painting's anti-colonialist critique of the subordination of Africa and the colonial discourse that was fed by even the most avant-garde representations of Africa; to Green's emphasis on the unrepressed and unresolved ambivalence staged in the painting; and to David Lomas's reading in which Picasso's 'historicization' of Western ideals of beauty was in fact a symptomatic superposition of racist attitudes about 'primal' African sexuality on to the European prostitute as a social and physical degenerate.[69]

Additionally, in this augmented reality of the brothel, in the alternate temporalisation of its present, the painting highlights discontinuity not only across the canvas in the shift from Iberian to African figures, but also *within* the figures themselves. For instance, each figure is not a pure representative of a particular people and a historical stage but a hybrid. Masks or mask-like faces rest atop bodies that do not match up. Limbs appear inconsistent with bodies (as in the figure on the far left of the canvas). Rubin, who ultimately sees a clear shift from archaic to 'tribal' art in the painting, has nevertheless identified in the figures on the right-hand side the mixtures of 'African' sculptural shapes and the 'Oceanic' palette of orange, blue, yellow and white.[70] It becomes very difficult to align a figure with a single specific culture and history, since, as Rubin points out, Picasso worked according to his conceptions of tribal art rather than literally copying it.[71] More importantly, the 'proto-cubist' faceting appears not as the result of movement of the figures or the painter, but as a set of shifts, collisions and overlappings of completely different scenarios. It is not just that 'there are no discernible light sources for the various hatchings and shadings', but that there is a variety of inconsistent sources throughout the painting.[72] The bordello curtain, peeled back like a corner of paper, reveals a frontalised backdrop crinkled like yet more paper or fabric, which seems to enfold or unfold depressions in space and strange shadows around nearly all of the figures' heads, hips and arms. While the asymmetries in the faces and bodies are obviously subversions of conventions and ideals of beauty, they are also the consequence of these distortions in space and history.

In addition to avoiding the redeployment of the myth that a coeval Africa is the childhood of Europe (and yet also, in representing the time before history, a symbol of transcultural timelessness), *Les Demoiselles* asks us to consider, perhaps in spite of itself, that places have histories of their own, and furthermore, that national histories are but one kind of history. The painting's use of atavism in theme and technique not only disrupts any fantasy of internal homogeneity of time and history. It also foregrounds a multiplicity of times and histories rather than a single sweeping chronology showing transhistorical themes – the purity of raw perception, a mystical and monistic natural fecundity, the foundations of social order, desire and death, savage modernity, and so on. What is notable about Picasso's painting is not that these themes are absent, but that they are not distributed across the canvas as a singular coherent narrative. Each figure we encounter is an obvious hybrid resisting typological and individual consistency. The bodies are discontinuous amalgams, and the timespace of the canvas itself is deeply irregular – and all aspects of physical discontinuity in style and subject matter express the heterochronic event-space of history itself.

Murray Leinster's Sidewise Historicity and T. S. Eliot's Strange Historical Sense

Les Demoiselles' reference to deep time did not only challenge shorter-term histories, punctual temporalities and religious narratives as ways of making sense of the present. Its staging of the confrontation of *different* deep times called attention to the alternate historicity of the present, the actual, coeval histories of others that are alive in 'the present'. Leighten argues that Picasso's understanding of history is not the racist evolutionary-progressive model: while he makes use of the anthropological construction of the primitive, he does so precisely at the moment (1905–06) when colonial abuses in Africa were being spotlighted by socialist and anarchist protest, and he demonstrates an awareness of the problematic nature of the discourse of blackness generated by ethnological racism.[73] I will not attempt to do the same for Eliot, but will rather only try to distinguish his early thinking about time as it connects to a much more heterochronic historical sense than Eliot studies is accustomed to thinking about. To do this, I will turn first to Murray Leinster's later fantasy of moving sideways across time, before coming back to the ways in which Eliot picks up on the late nineteenth-century idea of heterochrony and its early twentieth-century application to historiography.

Murray Leinster's short story 'Sidewise in Time' (1934), after which the Sidewise Award for Alternate History is named, focuses not on a single forking of human history but rather on the patchwork of many unfamiliar times and historical outcomes.[74] Leinster's vision of 'the present' is not of a singular, self-consistent temporal location linked to the past and future; rather, it highlights strange intrusions into the smooth regularity of historical timespace from different pasts/histories and, by implication, various futures. That is, in moving sideways, the text reveals a North American present defined by an east coast ruled by a Confederacy that won the Civil War, pre-industrial Chinese colonial settlements around the Potomac, a post-Cambrian jungle in Tennessee and a Russian Alaska and California. The main character, maths teacher James Minott, takes his students to investigate these intrusions into history by other histories, which begin with a series of phenomena such as the discovery that 'the speed of light was not an absolute', an extreme solar flare, and the transformation of a giraffe into 'two slightly pulsating fleshy masses' that become two separate half-sized giraffes (69–70). Shortly after these occurrences, Roman soldiers appear in a suburb of Joplin, Missouri (75), and a 'jungle such as paleobotanists have described as existing in the Carboniferous period' appears in Bryan, Ohio (78), out of which a dinosaur emerges. These intrusions soon add to a growing number of temporal synecdoches in which Romans, Vikings, Chinese, Native Americans and Russians govern what appears to Minott's crew as alternate histories. Moving sideways across this riven topography symbolises the transverse cut one must make in order to construct a shared present; moreover, it shows us, as Minott explains, that the conception of time as a singular 'path instead of a direction' with 'one present and one future' (98) blinds us to the reality that 'there are an indefinite number of possible futures' and, as his student Blake infers, 'any number of pasts besides those written down in our histories. And – it would follow that there are any number of what you might call "presents"' (99, 100).

Although the narrative positions Minott and Blake as contrasts, both Minott's plan to find a profitable present and history that he can dominate and Blake's plan to return the universe to 'normal' provide similar political and affective pay-offs. The story is filled with racist anxiety about rice fields in the US occupied by the 'slant-eyed, terror-stricken face' (88) and things in the tall grass near Fredericksburg, VA 'that looked human, but weren't' (90). Blake's redefinition of historicity generates the plot quest of seeking to avoid 'a path of time in which America has never been discovered by white men' (101), and of a fearful sidestepping around any history that would begin to evaluate its relation to a 'scalping party of Indians from an uncivilized America' (139). Leinster's time-travel fantasy about moving sideways across times rather than backwards and forwards in a singular time ends up, as John Cheng writes, 'reinforc[ing] its linearity mathematically and historically'; indeed '[m]ost interwar time-travel stories', as he points out, 'returned their travelers from their adventures to an unchanged present', and maintained the sense of historical agency that evaporates when the alternate-history genre gets too preoccupied with the cumulative swirl of plural contingencies in the past.[75] For Cheng, the invocation of Einstein in many of these stories serves these typical time-travel premises while disabling the 'historical agency [. . .] at the core of his association with time travel'.[76] Even though Einsteinian spacetime in general relativity departed from rectilinear temporality in favour of tempo-topological complexity, science fiction largely 'adhered to a Euclidean sensibility', because its ambition was simply to move back and forth in time at will.[77]

While Leinster's characters experience these temporal anomalies as catastrophic fragmentation, the story's reconceptualisation of historicity reconfigures the relation between, and the constitution of, the present and the past. In crossing the fault lines of different time zones and histories, the characters encounter a 'scrambling of space and time' (106); but in moving transversely through timespace, the story reveals that the bumpy plane of the present comprises a variety of intersecting and parallel trajectories. As Minott explains it, the sideways movement across this patchwork reveals that fault lines are in fact the borders of 'units from one time-path', and these time-paths are, in perhaps an unintentionally fitting pun, 'elevators with many stories' (107). Significant portions of the earth's surface experience a shift into 'some other time-path than its own', and as a result, 'the dialectics of philosophy have received a serious jolt' (138). The sidewise historicity that deformed the object-world and canvas-space of cubism connects to this interwar fantasy of complex historical temporalities, which in turn plugs into later SF explorations, such as Octavia Butler's *Kindred*, in which the uneven historical terrain of the present is defined by a courthouse, a library, an old church, a Burger King, a Holiday Inn and a wall with the protagonist's arm fused in it, each place bearing witness to the different rates of institutional change and oppression in which African American life is lodged, as well as to the intense tactical nightmare of bending the arc of history in more hopeful directions.

It might appear outlandish to suggest that Eliot's historical sense is likewise plugged into modernism's heterochronic historicity, that the body of Eliotic tradition is, like the temporal tissue of his poem *The Waste Land*, a hotchpotch drawing its units in a sidewise movement across time-paths of varying length and pace. But I want to argue that the poem stands as an assemblage of coeval ancestors from disparate periods and, moreover, operates in clear ways as a heterochronic StreetMuseum or AR, an unreal real-time HUD that not only windows the deep past into the present but reconfigures time and history as such. The earliest negative review of Eliot's pre-*Waste Land* work explicitly maligned that windowing and reconfiguration as cubist: in 1916 Arthur Waugh saw the young poet as part of a 'literary rebellion' defined by 'the unmetrical, incoherent banalities of these literary "Cubists"'.[78] The connection between *The Waste Land* and cubism has been made with modest frequency, and focuses on the stylistic similarities and parallels.[79] However, what remains to be done is to connect the more radical understanding of cubist temporal experiments to Eliot's disruption of unilinear and rectilinear time.

In his 1919 article 'Ben Jonson', Eliot mentions 'systems of non-Euclidean geometry' and connects the mathematics of curved spaces to 'a new point of view from which to inspect [the world]'.[80] But we also know that seeing the world anew for Eliot meant seeing it in relation to a past no longer conventionally defined as simply before, but as persistent and co-present. The understanding of time in *The Waste Land* and in Eliot's critical writing of this period is marked by contradictory characterisations that seem to define modernism as a whole: neo and palaeo; avant-garde and reactionary; innovative and traditional. The poem enjoys a long-standing reputation for revering a homogeneous past and, in its reach beyond a merely literary history, for displaying what Marc Manganaro calls 'the most famous use of anthropology in modernist literature'.[81] On the other hand, the work continues to be seen in light of its technical innovations and its interest in the problem of the new, which were the results of Eliot's 'formative and sustained exposure to, and involvement with, the ferment of the European artistic avant-garde'.[82] These contradictions have tended to cancel each other out in the larger reactionary resolution that was his life, a movement of closure that seems to confirm that his engagement with the new served only his retreat into the old.

However, Eliot's construction of tradition prior to his religious conversion can be a good deal stranger than we have allowed it to be. I acknowledge the impact of Eliot's conservative politics and Anglo-Catholicism on his poetry without placing the challenge of Eliot's early thinking – to the punctuality of the disconnected modern moment, the self-undermining drive towards novelty, and the monistic unity of Bergsonian duration – in a neutralising narrative that terminates in the belief that 'history is a pattern / Of timeless moments' ('Little Gidding', V).[83] That is, Eliot's use of the past contains the potential for opening up the present to a multiplicity of intersecting times or planes of happening. However, in the many studies of the 'historical sense' at the heart of his concept of tradition (the 'perception, not only of the pastness of the past, but of its presence'), Eliot's conception of time has been understood in terms of unilinearity or timelessness, or a combination of both, 'a single eternal order'.[84] Prior to the 1980s, when Tatsushi Narita, Robert Crawford and Marc Manganaro began filling out the picture of the anthropological, 'primitivist' Eliot, the *locus classicus* for understanding his conception of the past was his 1919 essay, 'Tradition and the Individual Talent', in which Eliot defined the historical sense as an awareness that 'the whole of the literature of Europe from Homer and within it the whole of the literature of his own country has a simultaneous existence and composes a simultaneous order'.[85] Understandably, for decades critics have read this simultaneity of the past and present as static and atemporal. M. A. R. Habib says that 'in Eliot's view of tradition, the notion of time [. . .] is a static one whereby present and past are united in an eternal stasis' and 'is anything but historical, depending as it does on a repression of time'.[86] Over seventy years ago, in the mid-1940s, Joseph Frank aligned Eliot's fusions with the atemporality of the Poundian image, 'the intellectual and emotional complex in an instant of time', which he held up as the modernist model *par excellence*.[87] According to Frank, just as Eliot's 'instantaneous presentation' of 'disparate ideas and emotions' serves to 'undermine the inherent consecutiveness of language', so does the 'juxtaposition of past and present' generate a non-sequential 'timeless unity', a spatialised contemporaneity in which 'history becomes ahistorical'.[88]

In accounts of cubism as in Eliot studies, the clear antidote to this ideal, ahistorical, unilinear order has been Bergsonism, whose exclusive hold on the heterochronic in these realms has been powered by our own unihistoricist commitments. The insights have been useful, of course, and anchored in sets of facts: David Tomlinson has argued that *The Waste Land* is a Bergsonian-cubist poem, and we know that Eliot heard Bergson lecture in Paris in 1911, the year when cubism's notoriety was boosted by the exhibition at the *Salon des Indépendants* in which Delaunay, Metzinger, Albert Gleizes and Fernand Léger had a whole room. Bergson had become well known by 1911, the year *Creative Evolution* was translated into English, when vitalist, processual ideas such as 'there are no things, only actions' were useful in combating the overly mechanistic and deadening aspects of scientific and everyday ontologies.[89] And Eliot confirmed, in retrospect, that 'the spiderlike figure of Bergson' hung over 'the new ways of painting' and was a subject that 'was apt to become involved with discussion of Matisse and Picasso'.[90] In 1921 Eliot began work on *The Waste Land* in the immediate aftermath of Picasso's exhibition at the Leicester

Galleries in London, which Eliot indicates that he saw in the March 1921 'London Letter' in *The Dial*.[91] Thus, when we hear in Eliot's 1919 lecture to the Arts League of London, 'Modern Tendencies in Poetry', a companion piece to 'Tradition', that the continuity of the creative present 'keeps the past alive' (in contrast with, say, the 'mummified stuff from a museum' cited in his 1923 *Ulysses* essay), we can easily pair the statement with Bergson's definition of duration as 'the continuous life of a memory which prolongs the past into the present' that then ceaselessly changes by containing 'the heavier and still heavier load we drag behind us as we grow older. Without this survival of the past into the present, there would be no duration, but only instantaneity.'[92] Likewise, when thinking about *The Waste Land*'s 'mythical method', the 'juxtaposition of disparate historical images' that 'transforms the past into the present of the indicative; and in doing so [turns] history into myth', we can easily turn to the Bergsonian cubism that Tomlinson reads as a model of 'techniques for presenting disparate material simultaneously: technical solutions to Eliot's problem of representing the penetration of ancient memory into the present'.[93]

I do not wish to negate any of these insights but would only like to make space for a string of ideas running through these radical aesthetic experiments and science-fictional fantasies of the twentieth century. The strain of relativity that came through cubism and Picasso, which emerges in an expansion of temporal range by various time machines and conceptual devices, suggests the penetration of the present by any number of possible lines, and not just a monolithic ancient memory. Indeed, Eliot's discussion of Joyce's 'mythical method' in 'Ulysses, Order, and Myth', which in Frank's estimation 'sees the actions and events of a particular time only as the bodying forth of eternal prototypes', references Einstein in assessing how modernism was trying to make sense of 'the immense panorama of futility and anarchy which is contemporary history': Joyce's method 'has the importance of a scientific discovery [. . .] In manipulating a continuous parallel between contemporaneity and antiquity, Mr. Joyce is pursuing a method which others must pursue after him. They will not be imitators, any more than the scientist who uses the discoveries of an Einstein.'[94] If Einstein functions as a general cultural signifier for the absence of any absolute time frame or historiographic container in which to determine true simultaneities, then Joyce's mythical parallelism is not the construction of a unified order anchored by Homer. The solar eclipse in 1919 that validated and made famous Einstein's general theory of relativity, which predicted that the gravity of massive objects warps spacetime and would make light appear to bend, is the analogue for what an ancient Greek parallel or, more dramatically, what 'the rock drawing of the Magdalenian draughtsmen' can do: both can demonstrate a warping of the field of the historical sense and a transformation of tradition into a number of different reference frames.[95] While there is certainly a sense that Eliot's definition of tradition invokes a Bergsonian, extra-historical presence of dead ancestors – it is characterised as non-progressive ('art never improves'), accumulative (it 'abandons nothing *en route*') and deep (it does not 'superannuate' the prehistoric art of the Dordogne caves) – it was also meant, as Caroline Patey argues, to open 'a crack in the wall of historical time, cutting deep, as it were, into the homogeneous fabric of [Eliot's] essay'.[96]

The strange presence of the rock drawings was intended to destabilise the placid order of the Western canon by means of the shocking insertion of the 'primitive'. However, this shock is produced not simply by the rush of a temporal bottoming-out, a conceptual intervention in which the floor of both the present and the canonical past drops out from under us, but also by the ability of the juxtaposition or simultaneity to deliver a 'criticism of the evolutionary or sequential approach to the "primitive"' as well as 'the identity/simultaneity of the "savage" and the "civilized"'.[97] Eliot's critique of the discourse of primitivism is precisely what should allow us to free his 'historical sense' from history as a singular path, but the reading of simultaneity as 'identity' – the idea that the past is always simultaneous with the present because it *is* the present – impedes our ability to see Eliot's fascination, especially in *The Waste Land*, with strange non-identities of contemporaneity. Indeed, the widespread critical use of Eliot's review of *Ulysses* to illuminate his concept of the historical sense and his poem attests to the tendency to neutralise Eliot's understanding of the fabric of time by reducing it to myth (such that myth reinforces racist progressive history). As Tim Armstrong has pointed out, 'the gesture toward "mythical time" can more readily be seen as exposing a lack of coherence rather than suggesting the integration that Eliot proposed in "Ulysses, Order and Myth"' – a movement 'through a collection of time worlds'.[98] In arguing against an Eliot of integration and the idea of simultaneity as identity, I would emphasise precisely that lack of coherence, Eliot's investment in relativity, and that strand of his thinking that reconceptualises the present. In this reconceptualisation, the present is not the linear sum of prior moments but a tissue of diverse timelines that are still unfolding, timelines whose intersection with our own perceptual duration generates manifestations of other pasts rather than merely the otherness of the past.

If we can think about *The Waste Land*'s deployment of myth as an activation, at least partly, of temporal relativity and jarring discontinuity, rather than of cultural comprehensiveness and the historiographic lump or bolus that Eliot came to associate with Bergsonian *durée*, then the figure of Tiresias, 'the most important personage in the poem, uniting all the rest' who, according to Eliot's note, melt and merge into her/him/them, will have to make space for other key signifiers of the poem's larger ambitions. Terry Eagleton has described Eliot's use of anthropology as comprising 'totalizing mythological forms' that shore up his 'authoritarian cultural ideology'; indeed, 'the historical secret of that most recurrent of modernist formulas, the shocking conjunction of the very old and the very new, the archaic and the avant garde' is the covert desire to 'regress to the pre-industrial, a closed, cyclical, naturalised sphere of relentless fatality where historicity is suspended'.[99] However, as Christopher Herbert has argued in 'Frazer, Einstein, and Free Play', Frazerian anthropology and Einsteinian physics are 'two cognate branches of a single revolutionary modernist discourse': the 'chief principle of navigation' in Frazer's method was, as in Einstein's universe, 'that time [. . .] is not uniform and absolute but radically differential'.[100] Frazer's time travel, like Eliot's extreme juxtaposition, is powered by a relativising impulse rather than a totalising one, a conceptual fantasy that opens one to different coordinate systems and a 'thought-world where fixed hierarchies of time and place are abruptly dissolved'.[101] The use of myths from Frazer's *The Golden Bough*, Jessie Weston's *From Ritual to Romance* and other sources to create parallels with early twentieth-century London and other places is not simply to construct, as Cleanth Brooks's once influential account cast it, 'surface parallelisms which in reality make ironical contrasts' between the past and present.[102] Rather, the stranger version of Eliot's notion of the presence of the past, his reconfiguration of simultaneity and his deep time that amalgamates but does not improve should be seen as an outgrowth of his critique of anthropological universalism, and his poem's exploration of the relativity of depths, scales and rhythms.

Eliot's interest in anthropological constructions of the primitive began quite early and grew into a well-defined critique of the unilinear evolutionary framework, before it became an aspect of his authoritarian cultural ideology. Drawing on Tatsushi Narita's work on Eliot's first encounter as a 15-year-old boy with 'primitive' peoples at the 1904 St Louis World's Fair (the Louisiana Purchase Exhibition), Ronald Bush shows that the young Eliot's fascination with one of the fair's main attractions exposed him to the temporal racism that informed the 'Congress of Races', which, as a heuristic device for understanding the spatial exposition of the world, distributed its peoples along a historical axis from 'the primitive' to 'the modern'. More often than not, deep time has unified the diversity of times by collapsing the divarication of branches (let alone the disconnected branches) back into the length from trunk to root, a single human history. Along this length, many human cultures were claimed to 'have been left behind in the race of progress', as Lewis Henry Morgan wrote in his 1877 book, entitled *Ancient Society; or, Researches in the Lines of Human Progress from Savagery through Barbarism to Civilization*. 'The history of the human race is one in source, one in experience, and in progress', he argued; '[s]ince mankind were one in origin, their career has been essentially one, running in different but uniform channels upon all continents'.[103] While Bush sees Frazer in line with the comparativist 'armchair' ethnology of figures such as Morgan and E. B. Tylor, he points out that Eliot formed a critical position in relation to the defining feature of evolutionary comparativism – its universality uniting all into a single developmental trajectory.[104] As early as his 1913 Harvard paper on 'The Interpretation of Primitive Ritual' for Josiah Royce's seminar on comparative methodology, Eliot had understood Lucien Levy-Bruhl's critique of armchair anthropology, agreed with it, and moreover had criticised Levy-Bruhl's critique for drawing a hierarchical 'distinction between primitive and civilized mental processes altogether too clearly'.[105]

Eliot's position on the lack of distance between primitive and civilised would seem to suggest the identity of the two, in which both the civilised (poet) and savage alike share a pre-logical, non-dissociated sensibility.[106] There is no doubt that Eliot was partly enthralled with the idea of a relation between modern urban civilisation and non-Western cultures; as Chinua Achebe points out in reference to Joseph Conrad's fascination with Africa, it is an identity that brings a self-congratulatory modernity 'low' by the racist construction of kinship between 'civilisation' and the ugly, the savage and the horrific.[107] In Johannes Fabian's analysis of the temporal assumptions underlying ethnographic representation and its legitimation as a science, the allochronism that posited 'others' as located in the past, positive or negative, 'promoted a scheme in terms of which not only past cultures, but all living societies were irrevocably placed on a temporal slope, a stream of Time – some upstream, others downstream', that is, located differently within a single, unified time.[108] Eliot's use of primitivism in *The Waste Land*, of course, participates in the representation of non-European cultures in terms of regressive inferiority or the rejuvenating exoticisation of that backwardness, both of which rely on distancing the 'other' along a single line of evolution, with European 'civilisation' at the arrowhead present. However, as Bush points out, Eliot's critique of Levy-Bruhl was meant to suggest a relativity that he found in Emile Durkheim's *The Elementary Forms of the Religious Life* (1915) – a relativity based in socio-cultural locality and the social production of 'mentalities'. 'When Eliot spoke of "Magdalenian draughtsmen" in 1919', writes Bush, 'his ethnographic coordinate was not Morgan but Durkheim, who had dramatically turned away from evolutionism toward the skeptical relativism that would more and more constitute the twentieth-century study of anthropology.'[109] As Eliot remarked of the overdetermining plurality of timelines in his 1918 review of James Rendel Harris's comparative study of the evolution of gods from plants across many cultures:

> If Dr. Harris is ever found to be wrong, it will be because he clings tenaciously to a single (vegetable) line of descent. This line is certainly traceable, but it seems possible that a developed god may have an extremely complex parentage, not to be reduced to a single root.[110]

The otherness of multiple lines of descent can, of course, be as racist as the back-of-the-line allochronism informing the larger part of the primitivist project, a way of excluding the knowledge of complex parentage by way of a polygenic relocation of differences to their own zones of history. However, heterochrony insists on both internal heterogeneity and historiographic multiplicity, the consequence of honouring what Mark Rifkin calls 'temporal sovereignty' in the context of Indigenous peoples' histories.[111] If *The Waste Land* can be said to be heterochronic, at least in part, it is because the poem's view of the past is not a simple windowing into modernity's single line of descent, but rather a walk through London with a strange AR app or glasses, a traversal across 'time worlds'. Just as Picasso's *Les Demoiselles* quotes deep time as a way of staging the confrontation of different pasts running through the present, so too does *The Waste Land* present cracks in the wall of historical time that disrupt and contradict what Patricia Rae argues is its 'comparativist museum display'.[112] Whereas art historians have interpreted the governing trope of a bordello in Picasso's painting as positioning the spectator within a critique of sexualising and gendered coordinates that inform totalising desires, literary scholars have likewise read the floor plan of Eliot's poem as a museum in which artefacts have been salvaged, decontextualised and placed into 'the neatly organized glass cases of the ethnological museum'.[113] However, it is also the case that both painting and poem place audiences within a sidewise historiographic itinerary that fractures the very idea of 'history as such' and disrupts our sense of the fundamental unity of time in which there is one past that leads on to one present and one future (whether that unity derives from anthropological narratives of the species, literary history or other modes of unifying and universalising history).

If the journey through *The Waste Land* is meant to demonstrate Eliot's understanding of (the state of) tradition, in what ways would we revise the definition of his historical sense to account for the poem's suggestions of biological heterochrony, and more clearly and assertively, its examples of patchwork historicity and its performance of polytemporal assemblage? In the universe of *The Waste Land*, we come across bats with baby faces, automatic human engines and a chimerical logic informing the fitness of certain transformations. With regard to the latter, think of the stag that must justly receive the suffering inflicted by violent male desire for which it is the figure, or the singing or chattering bird whose transformation or expression of suffering is placed in some kind of physical equation with human responses to injury and trauma. But more convincing than these are the poem's numerous anachronistic juxtapositions that become science–fictional as their overloaded metaphoricity tips the Bergsonian identity of A and B, past and present, into a Leinsterian vision of history: Stetson in the Punic War and First World War; Jesus of Nazareth appearing in the Antarctic as well as on the road to Emmaus, where hooded hordes of Russian revolutionaries are all Tiresiases falling into the 'cracked earth' of geopolitical and historiographic division; and at the end, 'when Thunder asks what sound like really important questions', as Manganaro comically puts it, 'when you have no idea how you got to India', the Fisher King sitting on the bank of the Ganges.[114] While Eliot's poem is almost always construed as an example of (the aspiration to) the totality of Western culture, one could easily argue that the text is working towards the opposite: in Manganaro's reading, the connections of 'identities of people with places get profoundly and powerfully confounded'.[115]

The poem's performance of 'amalgamating disparate experience' has always emphasised Eliot's explicit description of the poet's mental work in 'The Metaphysical Poets' of 'always forming new wholes'.[116] In *The Waste Land*, the figure of this process of combination is Tiresias, whom the footnotes name as 'the most important personage in the poem, uniting all the rest'. Easily paired with the method of 'continuous parallel' are the Bergsonian merging and melting of all the different characters from different eras into the blind prophet from Thebes, who in his lives as both a woman and man has 'Perceived the scene' of sexual assault and indifference just as he foresuffered it and foretells the rest (ll. 215–48). In this reading of Eliot's historical sense, as the music from the typist's gramophone mixes with Ariel's song along the Strand, a busker's mandoline on Lower Thames Street and Wagner's Rhine maidens singing in the Thames, Tiresias gathers all the women and men from the present and the past into themself, an image of the constitutive retentions in 'Tradition', of the vigorous inscription of ancestors' immortality in the innovative poet's bones, and of the identification of what has passed with 'that which we know'.[117] Like the Sibyl of Cumae with whom the poem opens, also a tragic prophet, Tiresias 'functions as Eliot's "higher" viewpoint which will include and transmute the figures in *The Waste Land*', as Jewel Spears Brooker and Joseph Bentley argue, 'unifying incompatible worlds'.[118] The epigraph in which the Sibyl is cited in a Roman text by a character who quotes the seer in Greek ultimately becomes a symbol for so many readers not of the disjunctive intersection of the Greek colony of Cumae with later Roman power and wealth, but rather of a 'synthetic perspective', 'a sort of fourth dimension, from which viewers can look at the contemporary world from a sufficient distance to make that world appear to have an order'.[119]

However, in addition to the integrative and synthetic, *The Waste Land*'s amalgamations also seem to aspire to heterochronic collocation – a 'heap of broken images' (l. 22) that does not melt into a larger whole but instead mashes together units from different time-paths, and evokes a number of branches growing 'Out of this stony rubbish' (l. 20). This is why, for Manganaro, Tiresias is less a figure for totalisation than the 'ethnographer-gatherer and curator' formed by 'Boasian relativist anthropology', and the poem itself is a particular kind of museum, a 'literalized Boasian storehouse' in which 'artifacts are inserted as witness to *specific* epochs, cultures, or subcultures: the words of Shakespeare, Kyd, and Queen Elizabeth evoke Renaissance

England; pub conversation evokes British working-class life; citations of and commentary on the Upanishads evoke "traditional" Indian religion and culture'.[120] The unreconciled ambivalence in Franz Boas's thought between 'culture as an "accidental accretion of individual elements"' and culture as an integrated totality shows up in the poem's tension between the metonymic impulse, which configures individual fragments as synecdochic parts of a geographically bounded cultural trajectory, and the more Bergsonian metaphorical process of 'like producing like': 'ancient Tereus' is likened to 'the young man carbuncular', the goddess Diana is layered on to or 'stacked up against Mrs. Porter, the First Punic War up against the First World War'.[121] If Manganaro is interested in collocation as a kind of ethnographic whole, his attention to the heterogeneous stuff of any total, synchronic cross-section of culture reminds us that the bits and pieces – the content of primitive ceremonies, myths, legends, biblical allusions, children's songs, folklore, ragtime, newspapers, opera, pub gossip – belong to whole, diachronic time-paths that are not represented but evoked, 'elevators with many stories'.

Were one pressed to come up with an alternative emblem for the poem's deformation of historicity, a decent candidate might be the changing windows that give upon different scenes from different histories – the various 'other withered stumps of time' in 'A Game of Chess' that lean out from the pictures or tapestries on the walls, crowding in on the present, infiltrating it and changing its meaning with pasts and possibilities that Madame Sosostris, even with her mixed pack of cards, cannot fully read. The formal and semantic spaces of the poem are warped by the rich profusion of histories that do not layer into each other without remainder, or become versions of the same eternally repeating phenomena. Thus, Michael Whitworth reads *The Waste Land*'s jumble of forms and tropes as manifestations of 'distortion, crumpling, puckering, and warping' in the 'homaloidal', Euclidean space of literal communication.[122] The vestiges of literary forms and modes are strewn across the body of the text: remnants of sonnets mixing into popular music, traces of the lyric combining with the dramatic, biblical verse commingling with nursery rhymes. The mishmash in 'The Fire Sermon' of Andrew Marvell's 'To His Coy Mistress', John Day's *The Parliament of Bees*, the Actaeon and Diana myth, and a popular or bawdy ballad – when the speaker 'from time to time' hears 'The sound of horns and motors, which shall bring / Sweeney to Mrs. Porter in the spring' (ll. 196–8) – brings together the following semantic threads: the urges and urgency of acting in the moment in relation to much more capacious time frames; a chronicle of bee-like human activity, 'the doings, the births, the wars, the wooings' in *The Parliament of Bees*; an older tale of bestial transgression and its fitting punishment; and a brothel scenario, possibly from the First World War.[123] Whitworth reads this technique as superimposition, in which, for example, the intersecting layers allow the word 'horn' to refer 'both to hunting horns and car horns, and by extension, to a feudal world and the modern urban world'.[124]

Eliot's superimposition is an imperfect and incongruent tiling that Whitworth sees best described in the (non-Euclidean) geometrical vocabulary that twentieth-century critical discourses used to understand (Einsteinian) experiments in both literature and the visual arts. For example, in Brooks's visualisation of figurative language, 'metaphors do not lie in the same plane or fit neatly edge to edge. There is a continual tilting of the planes; necessary overlappings, discrepancies, contradictions.' Likewise, in Jacob Korg's discussion of *The Waste Land*'s 'modern art techniques', the poem's collage is the equivalent of cubism's multi-aspectual space of 'overlapping planes'.[125] If this is so, the deformation of aesthetic space and the imbrication of reference frames do not just shatter the illusionism that renders objects and moments whole against a homogeneous backdrop only to merge them again in a synthetic topographical-tempographical constitution of objecthood and time. Rather, the heap of planes is a historiographic intervention, a collocation with heterochronic implications. In the present of Sweeney's and Mrs Porter's encounter, a host of trajectories shoot through, some connecting with one another or with other strands in the poem, some remaining completely parallel: the play of seventeenth-century timescales with sexual pursuit in England; the question of animal self-government and the administration of justice, which windows into the scenic immediacy of an ancient Roman treatment of pursuit and punishment by one's own desires or the predatory desires of others; the violent and mechanising forces of the First World War; and the exploitative systems of sex work.

The multiple and irregular dimensionality of *The Waste Land* accounts for why the poem has appealed to writers and thinkers interested in significantly more complex conceptions of history than the dominant historical sense. Neil ten Kortenaar has pointed out that Kamau Brathwaite drew on Eliot's poem for his trilogy *The Arrivants*, because what he and other West Indian poets 'heard in the classic modernist was the Euro-American's own creolization' and 'the <<riddims>> of St. Louis', to quote Brathwaite's 'History of the Voice'.[126] Likewise, Eliot's work appealed to Ralph Ellison, because its 'range of allusion was as mixed and varied as that of Louis Armstrong'; Eliot represented to these writers 'not the White [Atlantic] but the Greater, always already creolized Atlantic'.[127] Similarly, Mara de Gennaro argues that Eliot's comparativism has appealed to postcolonial thinkers and writers, because it can serve to undermine canonical authority and provoke the imagining of which voices are excluded. Even though they appear 'too discrepant politically to be responsibly considered together', de Gennaro believes that returning to Eliot's *The Waste Land* after reading Aimé Césaire's *Cahier d'un retour au pays natal* (*Notebook of a Return to the Native Land*, 1939) reveals that both share an interest in and method for engaging 'cultural plurality and an attendant psychic confusion' that cannot be dispelled by any 'straightforwardly ethnocentric clarity'.[128]

That method is a disjunctive 'comparative poetics' that is cast here in linguistic terms but is easily convertible into temporal ones. De Gennaro hears in Eliot and Césaire an untimely and disruptive shifting that is 'neither obscuring through translation nor thematically resolving the mutual foreignness of the languages and discourses they interweave'.[129] Her reading of Tiresias tacks away from the prevailing understanding of them as the personification of comprehensive fragmentation, towards a diasporic and postcolonial understanding in which they figure as disjunctive amalgamation. As she argues,

> The seemingly stable and unified 'I' that conceals within itself an indefinite number of disparate voices makes this [Tiresias's] passage, and *The Waste Land* more broadly, a poetic world not of mergings whose stability and universal import we can believe in, but of intersecting perspectives whose appearance of congruency and transferability can mask considerable instability and difference.[130]

This instability and difference of perspectives, voices and discourses is, of course, also the literal instability and difference of worlds and histories. Postcolonial historicity, which I discuss more fully in Chapter 4, acknowledges discursive multiplicity and hybridity as a matter that is simultaneously literal, physical and material, especially with regard to archipelagic, anachronic and allochronic constellations of components. Discourse is at once expressive of and coterminous with the fact that 'for Caribbean history, time becomes responsive to the archipelagic irregularity of space', as Bill Ashcroft puts it, and that this geographic specificity determines the idiosyncrasy and plurality of histories and reference frames.[131]

Whereas Leinster's historical topography seems to emphasise the pasts that might have been, in contrast to Eliot's variety of pasts that were and are, both gesture towards the availability of different historical lines running through the heterochronic detritus in the present. What Armstrong says of *The Waste Land*'s thematics and drama of form could apply equally to Leinster's science-fiction plotting of the present. That is, in the process of trying to 'disinfect waste coded as "feminine"', the text simultaneously foregrounds its own constitution out of the waste products of the past, the excessive 'piling of allusions and eclectic cultural borrowings' without 'any redeeming vision of social order, or [. . .] internal aesthetic of efficiency'.[132] Of modernist fantasies of aesthetic negations, themselves shot through with contradiction, Armstrong remarks that often 'the waste materials of capitalist civilization are investigated for the traces of hidden histories, startling juxtapositions, or alternative temporalities which might rupture the seamless totality and apparently inevitable flow which is capitalism'.[133] If there is no redeeming order or internal mechanism for efficient integration, and no single-minded negation of capitalism, it is because the body of the text and the body of history incorporate heterogeneous units that are themselves not integral to the synchronic cut of a present but part of different trajectories. The questing speaker of Eliot's poem might move in the final section from Jerusalem, around the Mediterranean, and from north Africa across central Europe to Vienna, and then London, just as Leinster's story moves around the US and follows Professor Minott and his students around Virginia, and Picasso's visitor to the time bordello appears to move from Spain to France and Africa. But each location, site and decontextualised fragment is a synecdoche for distinct diachronic strands. As Seitler says of the disruptive appearance of 'morphological retrogressions' on the atavistic body, the sporadic interruption of an unexpected past 'does not confer on the present a reassuring sense of a collective relation to tradition but disruptively impinges on the celebrated understanding of modernity as a wholly modern, progressing and progressive, period of time'.[134]

Seitler reads the medical photograph as 'a temporal practice' that delineates the difference between past and present, a way of quarantining one from the other, even while photographs are always potentially 'atavistic, composite spaces of perpetual return, sites of recurrence whereby the present is always also, instantly, an indication of the past'.[135] This chapter has focused on modes of seeing that reveal how persistence is not a matter simply of continuing extension but also of coeval lines. From the modernist technique of juxtaposing fragments, to the science-fictional plot of a sidewise journey across times, to the augmentative multiplication of windows in the digital age, the presence of the anachronistic item is not simply an invitation to see the past in the present, but to see many pasts jostling in a coordinated set of possible presents that we call 'the present'. As we will see in the next chapter, if the past cannot be taken to be a single, enormous comet's tail stretching always behind us, then the present's irregularities, shapes and multiplicity likewise appear as alternate-historical striations generating strange de-synchronised potential.

NOTES

1. Robert Krulwich, 'Time Travel On The Cheap', *The Picture Show: Photo Stories on NPR*, https://www.npr.org/sections/pictureshow/2010/01/looking_backwards.html (last accessed 22 December 2017). To view more of Powell's photos, see 'Looking Into the Past', http://jasonepowell.com/albums/looking-into-the-past/ (last accessed 22 December 2017).
2. Museum of London's website: https://www.museumoflondon.org.uk/Resources/app/Dickens_webpage/home.html (last accessed 30 October 2018); interview with Vicky Lee, Marketing Manager for Museum of London, 1 June 2010, http://electronicmuseum.org.uk/2010/06/01/streetmuseum-qa-with-vicky-lee-museum-of-london (last accessed 11 October 2018).

3. Stephen Baxter, 'The Technology of Omniscience: Past Viewers in Science Fiction', *Foundation: The International Review of Science Fiction* 29.80 (2000): 97. H. G. Wells's story, 'The Grisly Folk and Their War with Men', was published in *Storyteller Magazine*, April 1921, quoted in Baxter, 'Technology of Omniscience', 106.
4. J. G. Ballard, 'The Sound-Sweep', *Science Fantasy* 13.39 (1960), quoted in Baxter, 'Technology of Omniscience', 98.
5. Lev Manovich, 'The Poetics of Augmented Space', *Visual Communication* 5.2 (2006): 220.
6. Mark Antliff, *Inventing Bergson: Cultural Politics and the Parisian Avant-Garde* (Princeton: Princeton University Press, 1993), 61; Kern, *Culture of Time and Space*, 81.
7. Kern, *Culture of Time and Space*, 81, 14. See also Bartky, *One Time Fits All*, 127–8: 'Paris time' is the 'mean solar time along the meridian of the Paris Observatory'.
8. Harvey, *Condition of Postmodernity*, 266.
9. Wendy Steiner, *The Colors of Rhetoric: Problems in the Relation Between Modern Literature and Painting* (Chicago: University of Chicago Press, 1982), 180, 187–8.
10. Mark Antliff and Patricia Leighten, *Cubism and Culture* (New York: Thames & Hudson, 2001), 93–7.
11. Jean Metzinger, 'Notes sur la peinture', *Pan* (October–November 1910), 49–52. This translation, by Jane Marie Todd, comes from Mark Antliff and Patricia Leighten (eds), *A Cubism Reader: Documents and Criticism, 1906–1914* (Chicago: University of Chicago Press, 2008), 77. In *Inventing Bergson*, Antliff uses a different translation: 'Intuitive, Delaunay has defined intuition as the brusque deflagration of all the reasonings accumulated each day' (61).
12. Antliff, *Inventing Bergson*, 61.
13. Blaise Cendrars recalling Delaunay's project in 1931, quoted in Antliff and Leighten, *Cubism and Culture*, 96.
14. Ibid.
15. Harvey, *Condition of Postmodernity*, 267, 266. Antliff writes that if 'Cubist fragmentation of space is related by Harvey to the accelerated time imposed by capitalist rationalization', we must remember that this was 'the very "public time" that the Bergsonian Cubists, Fauvists, and Futurists so vehemently rejected' (*Inventing Bergson*, 177). However, this rejection also opened up a historiographic possibility that cannot be adequately conceptualised in terms of Bergson's philosophy.
16. Steiner, *Colors of Rhetoric*, 191.
17. Gaonkar, 'Introduction', 17.
18. Ibid. 3.
19. Peter Osborne, *Anywhere or Not at All: Philosophy of Contemporary Art* (London: Verso, 2013), 17; emphasis in original.
20. Ibid. 24. In his discussion of the problematic nature of contemporaneity, Osborne says that the 'co-presentness of a multiplicity of times associates the contemporary [. . .] with the theological culture of the image', and he cites Michael Fried's famous line 'presentness is grace' (24). The presentness in the representational form of the image is an 'annihilation of temporality' (24).
21. Michel Foucault, 'Of Other Spaces', *Diacritics* 16.1 (1986): 26.

22. Ibid. Foucault's next example is the opposite and related 'to time in its most fleeting, transitory, precarious aspect': fairs that 'teem once or twice a year with stands, displays, heteroclite objects, wrestlers, snakewomen, fortune-tellers' (26).

23. Michel Foucault, *The Archaeology of Knowledge*, trans. A. M. Sheridan Smith (New York: Pantheon Books, 1972), 126, 129. 'Heterotopia' appears in the preface of *Les mots et les choses: une archéologie des sciences humaines* (Paris: Gallimard, 1966), a year before the lecture 'Of Other Spaces', which was never published in Foucault's lifetime. The 1967 lecture was published in 1984, several months after Foucault's death; the English translation was published in 1986. Edward Soja calls Foucault's account of heterotopia 'frustratingly incomplete, inconsistent, incoherent': *Thirdspace: Journeys to Los Angeles and Other Real-and-Imagined Places* (Cambridge: Blackwell, 1996), 162. For a good summary of similar complaints as well as a clear articulation of the usefulness of the concept, see Peter Johnson, 'Unravelling Foucault's "Different Spaces"', *History of the Human Sciences* 19.4 (2006): 75–90.

24. Gaonkar pushes against the de-temporalised space of world history by foregrounding the 'critical band of variations consisting of site-specific "creative adaptations" on the axis of convergence (or societal modernization)'. Convergence is the 'acultural theory' of the unilinear and 'inexorable march of modernity [that] will end up making all cultures look alike', regardless of culturally specific conditions and interactions ('Introduction', 18, 17).

25. The term first appears in 'Die Gastrula und die Eifurchung der Thiere', *Jenaische Zeitschrift fur Naturwissenschaft* 9 (1875): 402–508. For its first appearance in English, see Ernst Haeckel, *The Evolution of Man: A Popular Exposition of the Principal Points of Human Ontogeny and Phylogeny* (New York: D. Appleton, 1879).

26. Stephen Jay Gould, 'The Uses of Heterochrony', in *Heterochrony in Evolution: A Multidisciplinary Approach*, ed. Michael L. McKinney (New York: Plenum Press, 1988), 2.

27. Plates IV–V in Ernst Haeckel, *Anthropogenie: oder, Entwickelungsgeschichte des Menschen* (Leipzig: Engelmann, 1874). J. G. Bach's lithograph of Haeckel's illustrations shows a fish, salamander, turtle, chick, pig, cow, rabbit and human, and affirms 'the more or less complete agreement, as regards the most important relations of form, between the embryo of man and the embryo of other vertebrates,' which is 'more complete, the earlier the periods of development', and 'retained for longer, the more closely the corresponding mature animals are related in descent'. Nick Hopwood, 'Pictures of Evolution and Charges of Fraud: Ernst Haeckel's Embryological Illustrations', *Isis* 97.2 (2006): 292.

28. Ken McNamara, *Shapes of Time: The Evolution of Growth and Development* (Baltimore: Johns Hopkins University Press, 1997), 46.

29. Ibid. 282.

30. Ezra Pound to Harriet Monroe, London, 30 September 1914, in *The Letters of Ezra Pound, 1907–1941*, ed. D. D. Paige (New York: Harcourt Brace, 1950), 80.

31. David Kettler and Colin Loader, 'Temporizing with Time Wars: Karl Mannheim and Problems of Historical Time', *Time & Society* 13.2–3 (2004): 157. Mannheim

complicated the biological fact of common chronological location by breaking the interval of generation into other necessary and sociologically relevant elements, such as different participations in different shared fates and perceptions of history ('actual generations'), and different responses within a cohort to these shared experiences (which he called 'generational units'). See Karl Mannheim, 'The Problem of Generations', in *From Karl Mannheim*, ed. Kurt Wolff (New Brunswick, NJ: Transaction Publishers, 1993), 351–98.

32. The term 'paleo-modernism', paired with 'neo-modernism', comes from Frank Kermode, 'The Modern', in *Modern Essays* (London: Collins, 1971), 39–70.

33. Harvey, *Condition of Postmodernity*, 240.

34. For example, Charles Darwin's publication of the *Origin of Species* in 1859 and James Hutton's *Theory of the Earth* in 1795.

35. Baudelaire, 'The Painter of Modern Life', 403. The standard sites that express these currents include the pace of urbanisation, mass production, railways, automobiles, the telegraph and the vertiginous elongation of human and planetary history.

36. Calinescu, *Five Faces of Modernity*, 3; Joseph Frank, 'Spatial Form in Modern Literature', in *The Widening Gyre: Crisis and Mastery in Modern Literature* (New Brunswick, NJ: Rutgers University Press, 1963), 60.

37. See Lewis, *Time and Western Man*.

38. Barrows, *Cosmic Time of Empire*, 11; Bergson, *Time and Free Will*, 104.

39. Elizabeth Grosz, *The Nick of Time: Politics, Evolution, and the Untimely* (Durham, NC: Duke University Press, 2004), 253. The vitalist echo in Gaonkar's pluralisation of modernity as 'variations consisting of site-specific "creative adaptations"' ('Introduction', 18), and the combination of Darwin and Bergson in Grosz's work resonate in exciting ways with the non-subjective character of heterochrony. The Deleuzean distinction between the virtual and actual is in some ways less radical than the actual multiplicity of histories running through heterochronic bodies, but the critical potential – of opening up a 'nick' in time to refuse the inevitability of the present and to sponsor multiple futures – is similar.

40. Dana Seitler, *Atavistic Tendencies: The Culture of Science in American Modernity* (Minneapolis: University of Minnesota Press, 2008), 172, 7. In this study, the idea of heterochrony is implicit in Seitler's references to polytemporality, which can be defined, by way of her examples of atavisms, as the existence of different moments from the past in the present, different 'times' bubbling up into what is otherwise 'continuous forward movement' (7). It would hardly be a giant leap to see some of those coeval moments not as coming from 'the' past, but as synecdochic vestiges of different pasts as such, pasts that are still ongoing.

41. Ibid. 59, 60.

42. Ibid. 120.

43. For more on neoteny and paedomorphic characteristics, see Kirby Farrell, 'Wells and Neoteny', in *H.G. Wells's Perennial Time Machine*, ed. George Edgar Slusser, Patrick Parrinder and Danièle Chatelain (Athens: University of Georgia Press), 65–75. As far as I know, Farrell is the only critic ever to have written on some aspect of biological heterochrony in Wells.

44. Susan Merrill Squier, 'Embryologies of Modernism', *Modernism/Modernity* 3.3 (1996): 147.
45. Quoted in Squier, 'Embryologies of Modernism', 147.
46. Ibid.
47. Bernard Shaw, *Back to Methuselah: A Metabiological Pentateuch* (London: Penguin Books, 1990), 296.
48. Cantor and Hufnagel, 'Empire of the Future', 36, 37.
49. Cubism is hailed as 'the single most important development in the history of twentieth-century art' in Neil Cox's *Cubism* (London: Phaidon, 2000). This description seems to appear in some form in nearly every critical treatment. In *The Age of the Avant-Garde, 1956–1972* (New York: Farrar, Straus and Giroux, 1973), for instance, Hilton Kramer says that Matisse 'turned his attention for the first time to a confrontation of the single most important development that had occurred in painting [. . .] the creation of Cubism' (181).
50. This tradition of *Demoiselle* criticism begins with Daniel-Henry Kahnweiler's *Der Weg zum Kubismus* (Munich: Delphin, 1920), and carries on through Alfred Barr's *Picasso: Forty Years of His Art* (New York: MOMA, 1939), John Golding's *Cubism: A History and an Analysis, 1907–1914* (London, 1959) and Cox's *Cubism*. All see Picasso's work as the beginning of cubism's revolutionary break with the norms of the past by means of its self-reflexive examination of aesthetic procedures, with differing opinions on whether *Demoiselles* itself counts as a cubist painting proper. For a historically situated account of cubism's genesis and significance, see the excellent and pointedly titled *Cubism and Culture* by Antliff and Leighten.
51. Louis Vauxcelles, 'Exposition Braque. Chez Kahnweiler, 28 rue Vignon', *Gil Blas*, 14 November 1908, in Antliff and Leighten (eds), *A Cubism Reader*, 48.
52. C. Estienne, 'Des Tendances de la peinture moderne: Entretien avec M. L. Vauxcelles', *Les Nouvelles* (20 July 1909), 4, quoted in Antliff and Leighten, *Cubism and Culture*, 53.
53. These 16,000-year-old paintings were discovered by Denis Peyrony in 1901 and toured by T. S. Eliot in 1919. On the excessive nature of reality, see Albert Gleizes and Jean Metzinger: 'Reality is more profound than academic recipes, and more complex as well', *Du 'Cubisme'* in Antliff and Leighten (eds), *Cubism Reader*, 419.
54. Euclid's three-dimensional geometry was correlated with 'the quantitative measurement governing perspective' in painting (Antliff and Leighten, *Cubism and Culture*, 68), and informed the values favouring such practices as the clear delineation of forms, the distinction between foreground and background, and the assumption of a smooth, consistent space that does not violate commonsense postulates or axioms, such as the non-convergence of two parallel lines (or inversely, in its original formulation, the convergence of two non-parallel lines). The influence of mathematicians such as Poincaré and Riemann on cubism, thinkers who questioned Euclid's parallel postulate by considering curved space, multi-dimensional spaces and irregularity, ought to show that cubism was less about flatness than the multiplicity of forms existing beyond the limitations

of the Renaissance medium. Once painters break with Euclidean regularity, they begin to come to terms with the fact that figures and objects and reality itself do not just change shape and properties when they shift position; they change temporalities.

55. See Linda Dalrymple Henderson, *The Fourth Dimension and Non-Euclidean Geometry in Modern Art* (Princeton: Princeton University Press, 1983), ch. 1; Linda Dalrymple Henderson, 'X Rays and the Quest for Invisible Reality in the Art of Kupka, Duchamp and the Cubists', *Art Journal* 47.4 (1988): 323–40; Linda Dalrymple Henderson, 'Editor's Introduction', *Science in Context* 17.4 (2004): 445–58.

56. Jean Metzinger, 'Cubisme et tradition', *Paris-Journal*, 18 August 1911, 5, in Antliff and Leighten (eds), *Cubism Reader*, 123.

57. Metzinger, 'Note sur la peinture', in Ibid. 76.

58. Arthur C. Danto and Linda Dalrymple Henderson, *The Fourth Dimension and Non-Euclidean Geometry in Modern Art, The Print Collector's Newsletter* 16 (May–June 1985), 64.

59. Henderson, *Fourth Dimension*, 91.

60. Linda Dalrymple Henderson, 'Four-Dimensional Space or Space-Time? The Emergence of the Cubism-Relativity Myth in New York in the 1940s', in *The Visual Mind II*, ed. Michele Emmer (Cambridge, MA: MIT Press, 2005), 355–6.

61. See especially Chapter 2, 'Philosophies of Space and Time', in Antliff and Leighten, *Cubism and Culture*, in which they show how Bergson's anti-rationalist *durée* combined with Henri Poincaré's relativistic conventionalism to generate the Puteaux cubists' sense of the 'rhythmic' nature of space, their mixing and melting of disparate temporal and spatial views on the plane of the canvas, and the alogical feeling or intuition evoked by the deformed ontology of unstable, unhomogeneous entities.

62. Antliff, *Inventing Bergson*, 100–1.

63. Ibid. 101. Antliff translates Gleizes and Metzinger's claim that the only difference between cubists and impressionists is a 'difference of intensity' to mean that impressionism is relegated to a 'slower rhythmic realm', based on the fact that 'in Bergson's cosmology, matter itself possesses a latent consciousness, taking its place as the slowest rhythm on the scale of being whose degrees of rhythmic tension are a function of the degree of freedom inherent in their activity' (101).

64. In 'Four-Dimensional Space or Space-Time', Henderson argues that the Einstein–cubism connection was promulgated widely and wrongly for the first time in Sigfried Giedion's *Space, Time and Architecture* (1941) and in Paul Laporte's art criticism at the end of the 1940s.

65. Antliff and Leighten, *Cubism and Culture*, 28. As they put it succinctly, 'African, Oceanic and even Middle Eastern and North African cultures have been said to mirror the "childhood" of Western civilization [. . .] As such the term "primitive" is part of a larger discourse concerning the role of temporal constructs in power relations between cultures, propped up by racial theories of inferiority' (28).

66. William Rubin, 'Picasso', in *'Primitivism' in 20th-Century Art: Affinity of the Tribal and the Modern*, ed. William Rubin, vol. I (New York: Museum of Modern Art, 1984), 243, 242.

67. Rubin nevertheless maintains that 'tribal works were associated by Picasso's generation with the earliest phases of civilization, in accordance with a highly simplistic model of world history', Ibid. 243.

68. Christopher Green, '"Naked Problems"? "Sub-African Caricatures"? *Les Demoiselles d'Avignon*, Africa, and Cubism', in *Picasso's Les Demoiselles d'Avignon*, ed. Christopher Green (Cambridge: Cambridge University Press, 2001), 130; Christopher Green, 'An Introduction to *Les Demoiselles d'Avignon*', in Green (ed.), *Picasso's Les Demoiselles d'Avignon*, 2.

69. See David Lomas, 'In Another Frame: *Les Demoiselles d'Avignon* and Physical Anthropology', in Green (ed.), *Picasso's Les Demoiselles d'Avignon*, 104–27. See also Sander Gilman, *Difference and Pathology: Stereotypes of Sexuality, Race, and Madness* (Ithaca: Cornell University Press, 1985).

70. See Rubin, 'Picasso', 256–8. Here 'Oceania' means Vanuatu, then the New Hebrides. The colours come from Aoba and Malakula works that Picasso would have seen during his visit to the Trocadéro.

71. Ibid. 260–1.

72. Arthur I. Miller, *Einstein, Picasso: Space, Time, and the Beauty That Causes Havoc* (New York: Basic Books, 2001), 123.

73. See Patricia Leighten, 'Colonialism, l'art Negre, and *Les Demoiselles d'Avignon*', in Green (ed.), *Picasso's Les Demoiselles d'Avignon*, 77–103.

74. Murray Leinster, 'Sidewise in Time', *Astounding Stories* 13.4 (1934): 10–47; reprinted in *The Time Travelers: A Science Fiction Quartet*, ed. Robert Silverberg and Martin Harry Greenberg (New York: D.I. Fine, 1985), 67–142. Subsequent page references are to the reprint edition and are given in parentheses in the text. The Sidewise Award was established in 1995 by critics Steven H. Silver and Evelyn Leeper and NASA scientist Robert B. Schmunk.

75. John Cheng, *Astounding Wonder: Imagining Science and Science Fiction in Interwar America* (Philadelphia: University of Pennsylvania Press, 2012), 201.

76. Ibid. 188.

77. Ibid. 190.

78. Arthur Waugh, 'The New Poetry', in *T. S. Eliot: The Critical Heritage*, ed. Michael Grant, vol. 1 (London: Routledge & Kegan Paul, 1982), 69. Waugh's review of Ezra Pound's *Catholic Anthology*, which had published 'The Love Song of J. Alfred Prufrock' and several other early poems, attacked all of 'the New Poetry' in the collection, but singled out passages from Orrick Johns, Pound and Eliot. Waugh connected these poets with cubism because of Dorothy Shakespear's Vorticist design on the cover of the volume. Her 'geometrical device, suggest[s] that the material within holds the same relation to the art of poetry as the work of the Cubist school holds to the art of painting and design' (68).

79. For the critical treatments of *The Waste Land* and cubism, see Jacob Korg, 'Modern Art Techniques in *The Waste Land*', *Journal of Aesthetics and Art Criticism* 18.4 (1960): 456–63; David Tomlinson, 'T. S. Eliot and the Cubists', *Twentieth-Century Literature* 26.1 (1980): 64–81; Jewel Spears Brooker and Joseph Bentley, *Reading The Waste Land: Modernism and the Limits of Interpretation* (Amherst, MA: University of Massachusetts Press, 1992), ch. 1, 'A Wilderness of Mirrors: Perspectives on

the Twentieth Century'. In the latter, in ways similar to Henderson's treatment of the fourth dimension, Brooker and Bentley read Eliot's cubism as an idealist response to the collapse of subject–object dualism, which seeks a multidimensional transcendence allowing one to see the wholeness of life that is invisible in a three-dimensional representational and epistemological frame.

80. T. S. Eliot, *The Sacred Wood: Essays on Poetry and Criticism* (London: Methuen, 1920), quoted in Brooker and Bentley, *Reading The Waste Land*, 28.

81. Marc Manganaro, 'Mind, Myth, and Culture: Eliot and Anthropology', in *A Companion to T. S. Eliot*, ed. David E. Chinitz (Chichester: Wiley-Blackwell, 2009), 79.

82. Giovanni Cianci, 'Reading T. S. Eliot Visually: Tradition in the Context of Modernist Art', in *T. S. Eliot and the Concept of Tradition*, ed. Giovanni Cianci and Jason Harding (Cambridge: Cambridge University Press, 2007), 120.

83. T. S. Eliot, *Collected Poems, 1909–1962* (New York: Harcourt, Brace, 1963), 208. In his 'A Draft of a Paper on Bergson' (Houghton Library, Harvard University Collection, MS, 1910–11), Eliot wrote that Bergson's philosophy tended towards a monism in which ultimately there 'will only be a single eternal present. Timelessness of another sort.' For an excellent synopsis of this paper, see Paul Douglass, *Bergson, Eliot, and American Literature* (Lexington: University Press of Kentucky, 1986), 59–61.

84. T. S. Eliot, 'Tradition and the Individual Talent', in *The Sacred Wood: Essays on Poetry and Criticism* (London: Methuen, 1920), 49. 'A single eternal order' is what Ronald Bush identifies as the critical consensus in 'The Presence of the Past: Ethnographic Thinking/Literary Politics', in *Prehistories of the Future: The Primitivist Project and the Culture of Modernism*, ed. Elazar Barkan and Ronald Bush (Stanford: Stanford University Press, 1995), 24.

85. Eliot, 'Tradition and the Individual Talent', 49. Bush's excellent essay examines a number of Tatsushi Narita's articles, including 'Eliot and the World's Fair of St. Louis – His "Stockholder's Coupon Ticket"', *Studies in Social Sciences and Humanities* 26 (March 1982): 1–24; Robert Crawford, *The Savage and the City in the Work of T.S. Eliot* (Oxford: Clarendon Press, 1987); and Marc Manganaro, '"Beating a Drum in a Jungle": T. S. Eliot on the Artist as "Primitive"', *Modern Language Quarterly* 47.4 (1986): 393–421.

86. M. A. R. Habib, *The Early T. S. Eliot and Western Philosophy* (Cambridge: Cambridge University Press, 2008), 200, 166.

87. Ezra Pound, *Literary Essays of Ezra Pound*, ed. T. S. Eliot (London: Faber, 1954), 4.

88. Frank, 'Spatial Form in Modern Literature', 9–10, 59. Frank published 'Spatial Form' serially in *The Sewanee Review* 53.2 (1945), 53.3 (1945) and 53.4 (1945), and later collected these articles in *The Widening Gyre*. All citations are from the book. The cast of scholars who think Eliot's investigation of temporality led only to the ironic, and ultimately religious, repudiation of time is too long to list. It would include Lyndall Gordon's biographical work in *Eliot's Early Years* (Oxford: Oxford University Press, 1977), which casts the early work as already on the way to his religious poetry. Much of the debate in recent decades about Eliot's anti-semitism tends to link very tightly his thinking on time, his religious views and his prejudice. For the discussion entitled 'Eliot and Anti-Semitism: The Ongoing Debate' (I and II), see *Modernism/Modernity* 10.1 (2003): 1–70.

89. Henri Bergson, *Creative Evolution*, trans. Arthur Mitchell (New York: Henry Holt, 1911), 248.

90. T. S. Eliot, 'Books of the Quarter', *The Criterion* 13.52 (1934): 451–2.

91. Tomlinson, 'T. S. Eliot and the Cubists', 66.

92. T. S. Eliot, 'Ulysses, Order, and Myth', in *Selected Prose of T. S. Eliot*, ed. Frank Kermode (New York: Harcourt Brace Jovanovich, 1975), 177; Henri Bergson, *An Introduction to Metaphysics*, trans. T. E. Hulme (London: G. P. Putnam's Sons, 1912), 44.

93. Joseph Frank, 'Spatial Form: An Answer to Critics', *Critical Inquiry* 4.2 (1977): 237–8; Tomlinson, 'T. S. Eliot and the Cubists', 78.

94. Frank, 'Spatial Form in Modern Literature', 60; Eliot, 'Ulysses, Order, and Myth', 177.

95. Eliot, 'Tradition and the Individual Talent', 51.

96. Ibid.; Caroline Patey, 'Whose Tradition? T. S. Eliot and the Text of Anthropology', in *T. S. Eliot and the Concept of Tradition*, ed. Giovanni Cianci and Jason Harding (Cambridge: Cambridge University Press, 2007), 161. Michael Hollington argues that Eliot probably visited one of the Dordogne sites (La Madeleine or Les Eyzies) rather than Niaux, a correction to Hugh Kenner's account, in 'Some Art-Historical Contexts for "Tradition and the Individual Talent"', in Cianci and Harding (eds), *T. S. Eliot and the Concept of Tradition*, 140.

97. Patey, 'Whose Tradition?', 164.

98. Tim Armstrong, 'Modernist Temporality: The Science and Philosophy and Aesthetics of Temporality from 1880', in *The Cambridge History of Modernism*, ed. Vincent B. Sherry (Cambridge: Cambridge University Press, 2016), 41.

99. Terry Eagleton, *Criticism and Ideology: A Study in Marxist Literary Theory* (London: Verso, 1976), 148; 'Modernism, Myth, and Monopoly Capitalism', in *The Eagleton Reader*, ed. Stephen Regan (Oxford: Blackwell, 1998), 281. He goes on to say that 'Modernism as a movement [. . .] sought like Joyce or Eliot to isolate the deep structures of all such parochial [non-international] experience, to sweep them up in the great global mythological cycles [. . .] it couldn't avoid miming the habits of international capitalism itself, which is quite as blindly indifferent to particular times and places as *The Waste Land* or the *Cantos*' ('Modernism, Myth, and Monopoly Capitalism', 283).

100. Christopher Herbert, 'Frazer, Einstein, and Free Play', in *Prehistories of the Future: The Primitivist Project and the Culture of Modernism*, ed. Elazar Barkan and Ronald Bush (Stanford: Stanford University Press, 1995), 135, 155; see also Christopher Herbert, *Victorian Relativity: Radical Thought and Scientific Discovery* (Chicago: University of Chicago Press, 2001), ch. 5, 'Frazer and Einstein'.

101. Herbert, 'Frazer, Einstein, and Free Play', 155.

102. Cleanth Brooks, *Modern Poetry and the Tradition* (Chapel Hill: University of North Carolina Press, 1939), 167.

103. Lewis Henry Morgan, *Ancient Society; or, Researches in the Lines of Human Progress from Savagery, through Barbarism to Civilization* (New York: Henry Holt, 1877), vi–vii.

104. On evolutionary comparativism, see Patricia Rae, 'Anthropology', in *A Companion to Modernist Literature and Culture*, ed. David Bradshaw and Kevin J. H. Dettmar (Oxford: Blackwell, 2008), 92–102.

105. Manuscript p. 5, John Hayward Bequest of T. S. Eliot papers in King's College Library, Cambridge; quoted in Bush, 'Presence of the Past', 36.

106. On the connection of this identity of past and present to Eliot's idea of the dissociation of sensibility, see Patey, 'Whose Tradition?' and Manganaro, '"Beating a Drum in a Jungle"', 398–9.

107. Chinua Achebe, 'An Image of Africa', *Massachusetts Review: A Quarterly of Literature, the Arts and Public Affairs* 18.4 (1977): 782–94.

108. Fabian, *Time and the Other*, 17.

109. Bush, 'Presence of the Past', 41.

110. Review of Rendel Harris, *The Ascent of Olympus*, *Monist* (Oct. 1918), 640; quoted in Crawford, *The Savage and the City*, 70.

111. See Mark Rifkin, *Beyond Settler Time: Temporal Sovereignty and Indigenous Self-Determination* (Durham, NC: Duke University Press, 2017), which I discuss in the next chapter in relation to nonsynchronous histories.

112. Rae, 'Anthropology', 100. Mark Manganaro writes that *The Waste Land* performs 'the function of an "ethnographic museum"' and is most often read 'in terms of the fate of cultural artifacts that are borrowed, torn, stolen from their "original" or at least prior contexts'. Marc Manganaro, *Culture, 1922: The Emergence of a Concept* (Princeton: Princeton University Press, 2009), 43, 41.

113. Leo Steinberg, 'The Philosophical Brothel', *October* 44 (1988): 7–74; Susan Hegeman, *Patterns for America: Modernism and the Concept of Culture* (Princeton: Princeton University Press, 1999), 33.

114. Manganaro, *Culture, 1922*, 54.

115. Ibid. 53.

116. T. S. Eliot, 'The Metaphysical Poets', in *The Annotated Waste Land with Eliot's Contemporary Prose*, ed. Lawrence Rainey (New Haven, CT: Yale University Press, 2005), 198.

117. Eliot, 'Tradition and the Individual Talent', 52.

118. Brooker and Bentley, *Reading The Waste Land*, 54, 46. Eliot's dissertation on F. H. Bradley analysed this higher viewpoint as relational experience.

119. Ibid. 52.

120. Manganaro, *Culture, 1922*, 45, 41.

121. Ibid. 50.

122. Michael H. Whitworth, *Einstein's Wake: Relativity, Metaphor, and Modernist Literature* (Oxford: Oxford University Press, 2001), 220.

123. See T. S. Eliot, *The Annotated Waste Land with Eliot's Contemporary Prose*, ed. Lawrence Rainey (New Haven, CT: Yale University Press, 2005), 103.

124. Whitworth, *Einstein's Wake*, 221.

125. Cleanth Brooks, *The Well-Wrought Urn* (London: Dennis Dobson, 1968 [1947]), 6, quoted in Whitworth, *Einstein's Wake*, 225; Korg, 'Modern Art Techniques in *The Waste Land*', 457.

126. Neil ten Kortenaar, 'Where the Atlantic Meets the Caribbean: Kamau Brathwaite's "The Arrivants" and T. S. Eliot's "The Waste Land"', *Research in African Literatures* 27.4 (1996): 18. Kortenaar cites Edward Kamau Brathwaite, 'History of the Voice, 1979/1981', in *Roots* (Ann Arbor: University of Michigan Press, 1993), 286 n. 34.

127. Ralph Ellison, 'Hidden Name and Complex Fate', in *The Collected Essays of Ralph Ellison: Revised and Updated*, ed. John F. Callahan (New York: Modern Library, 2011), 203. Ellison writes, '*The Waste Land* seized my mind [. . .] Somehow its rhythms were often closer to jazz than were those of the Negro poets [. . .] there were its discontinuities, its changes of pace and its hidden system of organization which escaped me.' Kortenaar, 'Where the Atlantic Meets the Caribbean', 18.

128. Mara de Gennaro, 'A Return to *The Waste Land* after Césaire's *Cahier*', *Comparative Literature Studies* 52.3 (2015): 484, 483.

129. Ibid. 483.

130. Ibid. 501–2.

131. Bill Ashcroft, 'Archipelago of Dreams: Utopianism in Caribbean Literature', *Textual Practice* 30.1 (2016): 99. This is, of course, a controversial position, given the vexed history of modernism's relationship to Africa and fantasies of Africa, and the ways in which it has involved different kinds of evasions to reframe modernity in terms of global capitalism. For a recent summary of these tensions that result in the insistence on what Fredric Jameson argues is a 'singular modernity', see Mark DiGiacomo, 'The Assertion of Coevalness: African Literature and Modernist Studies', *Modernism/Modernity* 24.2 (2017): 245–51.

132. Tim Armstrong, *Modernism, Technology, and the Body: A Cultural Study* (Cambridge University Press, 1998), 70.

133. Armstrong, *Modernism: A Cultural History*, 5.

134. Seitler, *Atavistic Tendencies*, 67.

135. Ibid. 77.

2

ALTERNATE HISTORY AND THE PRESENCE OF OTHER PRESENTS: VIRGINIA WOOLF, PHILIP K. DICK AND CHRISTOPHER NOLAN

The strange historicity of plural times has already been well theorised as a symptomatic cultural logic of the long twentieth-century present. In this theorisation, the experience of multi-temporality arises from the political unconscious that Fredric Jameson identified as 'incomplete modernization', in which people 'still live in two distinct worlds simultaneously'.[1] Jameson describes this aspect of modern life in his conclusion to *Postmodernism* in more or less science-fictional terms: the temporal thematics of modernism is the logic of this transitional economic period and should be seen as 'uniquely corresponding to an uneven moment of social development, or to what Ernst Bloch called "the simultaneity of the nonsimultaneous" [. . .] the coexistence of realities from radically different moments of history – handicrafts alongside the great cartels, peasant fields with the Krupp factories or the Ford plant in the distance'.[2] In contrast, by the 1990s Jameson's postmodern present had at last become 'more modern than modernism itself': 'we are no longer encumbered with the embarrassment of non-simultaneities and non-synchronicities. Everything has reached the same hour on the great clock of development or rationalisation (at least from the perspective of the "West").'[3] In 'full postmodernity' there is no more unevenness or strange temporal juxtaposition, because the total domination of capital has made everything fully contemporaneous.

The disappearance of alternatives and the end of temporality are direct consequences of this complete-modernisation-as-postmodernity thesis from the point of view and material position of the West. Stuck in an eternal present, the rising frequency of apocalyptic fiction in the twentieth century signals a frustrating retreat to the sublime distractions of world catastrophe, rather than a genuine grappling with the state of emergency and the resiliently opportunistic implosion that is the current, dominant economic system. Among the terabytes of thinking about the state of things in the twenty-first century is the bit of critical folk wisdom, often attributed to Slavoj Žižek, which traces back to Jameson: 'Someone once said that it is easier to imagine the end of the world than to imagine the end of capitalism.'[4] The refusal to succumb to this failure of imagination, for Jameson, means getting *post-contemporary* – breaking with and getting beyond modernisation and its destruction of historicity in order to grasp the process historically. Lamenting the return of attention to the modern in a *Singular Modernity*, Jameson, perhaps a bit self-servingly, insists that 'no "theory" of modernity makes sense today unless it comes to terms with the hypothesis of a postmodern break'.[5]

Imagining alternatives might require getting past the onrush of quickly evaporating nows, but it does not require breaking with the multi-temporal. Indeed, as Neil Smith argues in *Uneven Development*, the weird and even science-fictional *temporal alongsidedness* that Jameson describes is not the effect of incomplete modernisation, but in fact one of the necessary outputs and aims of the capitalist operating system. In the 2007 'Afterword to the Third Edition' of *Uneven Development*, Smith recaps his argument that, in contrast to Marx's insight about the synchronising 'annihilation of space by time' of a global market, capitalism requires and produces unequal terrain and differential temporalities at every scale – globe, nation, region, city, neighbourhood. In between remarks on Margaret Thatcher's dictum that 'there is no alternative' and Donna Haraway's comment in the 1990s that 'I have lost the ability to think of what a world beyond capitalism would look like', Smith warns 'left apocalypticism' to keep its focus on the source of multi-scalar disaster and the production of spatial scale itself.[6] In his 'Afterword to the Second Edition', Smith discusses John Berger's line that 'Prophecy now involves a geographical rather than historical projection' by connecting it with Jameson's spatial analyses and with Foucault's pronouncement that 'We are in the epoch of simultaneity [. . .] the epoch of juxtaposition [. . .] of the side-by-side.'[7] Against both Fukuyama's thesis that the 'universalization of Western liberal democracy' meant that struggles 'would be localized and peripheral' at the end of history, and Jameson's portside of this argument, in which the global capitalist present is the end of temporality and the waning of historicity, Smith warns against an 'arrogant ethnocentrism' that would justify 'depriving history' to those who are in different ways 'struggling for the chance to have the merest say over their own historical destiny'.[8]

Smith's argument spells out the primary political unconscious of multi-temporality, and we could easily think of the increasing interest in other moments and temporalities around the globe as itself symptomatic of the way capital accumulation requires 'social and spatial differentiation', as well as different times.[9] But perhaps the failure of imagination is less the inability to imagine capitalism and modernity ending *once and for all*, than the vision of history as a singular time whose present can be ended absolutely by means of a radical break. In conjunction with the postcolonial alternative modernities thesis, which I will discuss in Chapter 4, we might put more pressure on the historiographic idea, inseparable from the geographic one, that there really are a number of different times, and thereby revise our sense of what the alternatives are. One could do this without denying the impact of the economic underwriting of the historical, but one would have to consider the ways in which current modes of always historicising are themselves not neutral and sometimes, even in the argument for alternative modernities, not capable of acknowledging what Mark Rifkin calls 'temporal sovereignty'. In *Beyond Settler Time*, for instance, Rifkin argues against the idea of simply constructing a more 'inclusive version of "history" or the "present"', because Indigenous peoples seek both to critique 'notions, narratives, and experiences of temporality that de facto normalise non-native presence, influence, and occupation', and to insist on multiple frames of reference – temporal sovereignty rather than temporal recognition within present coevalness, based on 'landedness, governance, and everyday socialities'.[10] In opposition to modernity and history as 'a singular temporal formation that itself marks the sole possibility for moving toward the future', Rifkin's discussion of Indigenous peoples' futures allows us to consider the political unconscious of the notion of the political unconscious, and his interest in adapting Einstein's work on temporal reference frames forces us to shift the way we think about the new and the alternative, not as the product of an explosive event *within* history, but as the result of assessing differently paced, non-synchronous, but often intersecting lines, of attempting to bend them, reorder them or shift tracks.[11]

This chapter addresses the aesthetic exploration of historical alternatives by thinking about strange conceptions of historicity and the fantasy of alternate histories in three different texts: Virginia Woolf's *Mrs Dalloway* (1925), Philip K. Dick's *The Man in the High Castle* (1962) and Christopher Nolan's *Interstellar* (2014). Each of these texts not only thematises the condition of temporal alongsidedness but also formally structures itself by means of cross-cut parallel plotlines and side-by-side timelines that de-synchronise from one another. I will begin with the most recent cultural object, Nolan's film, which uses parallel editing, normally deployed to construct simultaneity, to represent the de-synchronisation among reference frames. I will then travel back to Woolf's modernist text as an early model of this very specific sort of alternate history, a text that is likewise a kind of post-apocalyptic meditation on a variety of rhythms in a present interpenetrated by what might have been and what comes next. I will end by reading Dick's text, which like Woolf's novel features two main characters who never meet and live in timelines with differing pace, duration and sets of possibility. While *The Man in the High Castle* fits squarely into the alternate-history genre, it is not interested simply in a mutation of a past sequence that produces a forking historical path with an altered present and future, but in the reconfiguration of alternativity, historicity and the present in the context of diverging concurrent trajectories.

CROSS-CUT NON-SYNCHRONOUS TIMES IN *INTERSTELLAR*

Christopher Nolan's 2014 film *Interstellar* might contain the longest cross-cutting in cinema history – from around the 1:18 mark to nearly the end of this 2-hour 49-minute film.[12] This technique of parallel editing, in which a film cuts back and forth between two alternating sets of action in separate locations and weaves them together, usually functions to establish the simultaneity of the actions. Immersing us in the flow of diegetic time, the parallel edit reconfigures the relations between shots from a cumulative sequence of *and-then*s to its opposite: a simultaneity or *meanwhile* that is now energised by suspense and the desire to overcome the distances traversed by the cross-cutting.[13] However, in *Interstellar*, as in Nolan's previous film *Inception* (2010), parallel editing establishes two reference frames running at distinctly different rates. Whereas parallel actions normally reinforce the unity and uniformity of both diegetic time and the time of the world in which it is situated, cross-cutting in this most scientifically realist film seems to structure a non-synchronous diegesis for a distinctly heterochronic universe.[14]

The film's formal interest in de-synchronisation becomes its primary plot difficulty, as a world searching for a viable future encounters solutions and additional challenges from different times. In the film, the protagonist Joseph Cooper (Matthew McConaughey) is asked to pilot a mission to find a habitable planet either for the mass exodus of humans from a mid-apocalypse Earth doomed by blighted crops and suffocating dust, or for a clutch of 5,000 human embryos to reboot humanity elsewhere. Aware of the effects of special and general relativity, Cooper tells his daughter Murphy (Mackenzie Foy) that he will return and gives her one of two watches perfectly synced. 'By the time I get back', he says, 'we might even be the same age.' After passing through a wormhole that has appeared near Saturn, Cooper and the crew arrive in the vicinity of the black hole Gargantua and undergo extreme time dilation on an orbiting planet where, as Kip Thorne pencilled out, 'time flows sixty-thousand times more slowly than on Earth'.[15] When the crew is delayed on the planet by enormous waves caused by extreme tidal forces, they know that the several hours spent retrieving information on the planet's viability and the astronaut

Miller's fate has cost them twenty-three earth years. From this point forward in the film, the parallel editing cuts between Murphy's timeline on earth and her father's increasingly de-synchronised timeline – not between distant places within a singular timespace, but between different planets and systems, completely different reference frames. In a moving scene, when Cooper returns to the spacecraft *Endurance* from Miller's planet, the ship has collected twenty-three years' worth of video messages, which we watch with him elliptically from the beginning as a kind of time lapse: his son has had a baby and eventually gives up on ever hearing back from Cooper; his father-in-law has died; and his daughter Murphy, now a scientist in her mid-30s (Jessica Chastain), has finally sent her first message to Cooper on her birthday, when she has turned the same age as her father (Plate 6).

The film's drift towards the value of synchronisation is, of course, more accessible than, and certainly competes with, its fascination with non-simultaneity. The video screen on the *Endurance* that provides us with a window on to the life elapsing more quickly on earth evokes Edwin Porter's bubble insert in the opening shot of his 1903 *The Life of an American Fireman*, a construction of simultaneity in a film once considered to contain the earliest example of cross-cutting.[16] Alluding to the history of interweaving parallel strands of action together in narrative cinema, this image of communication technology drops into the diegesis as both the material support and the figure for the instantaneity of affective connection. This immediate affective link then gets folded into the film's larger power-of-love theme, in which Dr Amelia Brand (Anne Hathaway) describes love as the inexplicable medium that 'transcends dimensions of time and space' and 'as an artifact of a higher dimension that we can't consciously perceive'. For Vivian Sobchack, the connection and unification constructed by the technique and indeed the medium itself contributes to the film's success: citing Nolan's full awareness that 'cinema is, itself, a time machine', she argues that *Interstellar*'s multiple dimensions of the narrative, structure and 'immersive mise en scène' find resolution 'by unifying – their different immensities and seemingly incompatible values' (Fig. 2.1).[17]

Time machines, in both form and theme, in medium and diegesis, do frequently produce resolution and synchrony. In *Interstellar*, the fifth-dimensional 'bulk' imagines history as a completed and manipulable film reel as well as a total library, a space in which Cooper realises that it is he and future humans who will have (and have already) mastered time and are sending messages back to the past in order to save humanity (the 'ghost' in the bookshelf). This fantasy of the bulk courts the convergence and closure typical of parallel edits. The film's 'narratively mind-bending and visually stunning' climax in this space depends on a time-travel plot device whose bootstrap loop hooks on to the logic of the just-in-the-nick-of-time rescue or reunion set up by cross-cutting.[18] As Raymond Bellour has demonstrated, such unifying closure often involves

Figure 2.1 Edwin Porter's bubble insert in *The Life of an American Fireman* (Edison Manufacturing Company, 1903) and Christopher Nolan's video screen in *Interstellar* (Legendary Pictures, 2014)

the alternation of male and female who come together in the proper, heteronormative present of the narrative.[19] According to Doane, the parallel edit that ends in heterosexual reunion is a common narrative answer to the medium's problem of 'a cinema that affirms time as continuity', a time machine that keeps on cranking forward.[20] *Interstellar* features a double reunion: that of

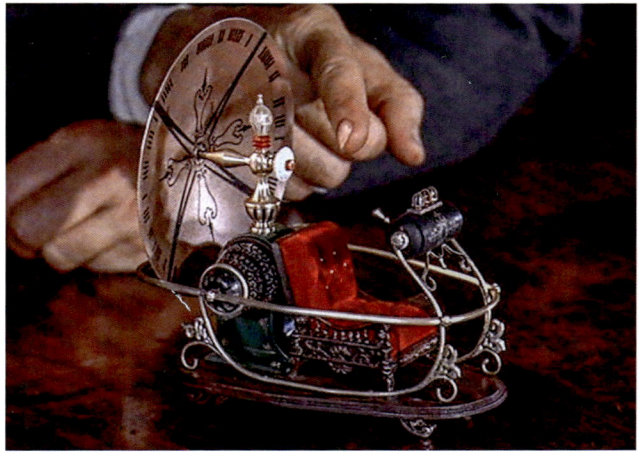

Plate 1 The model of the time machine in George Pal's *The Time Machine* (Metro-Goldwyn-Mayer, 1960)

Plate 2 Claude Monet, *Rouen Cathedral, West Facade, Sunlight*, 1894, oil on canvas. Courtesy of the National Gallery of Art, Washington, DC

Plate 3 Jeremy Shaw, *This Transition Will Never End* (2008), stills from single-channel video. Courtesy of Jeremy Shaw and KÖNIG GALERIE, Berlin

Plate 4 Jason Powell, *Looking Into the Past: Leader Theater, 9th St., Washington, DC* (2010), original photograph *The Wolverine* (1922)

Plate 5 Pablo Picasso, *Les Demoiselles d'Avignon*, 1907, oil on canvas.
Museum of Modern Art, New York, © 2018 Estate of Pablo Picasso /
Artists Rights Society (ARS), New York

Plate 6 Christopher Nolan's *Interstellar* (Legendary Pictures, 2014),
'Time will run differently for us?'

Plate 7 Amazon Prime's *The Man in the High Castle* (Amazon Studios, 2015)

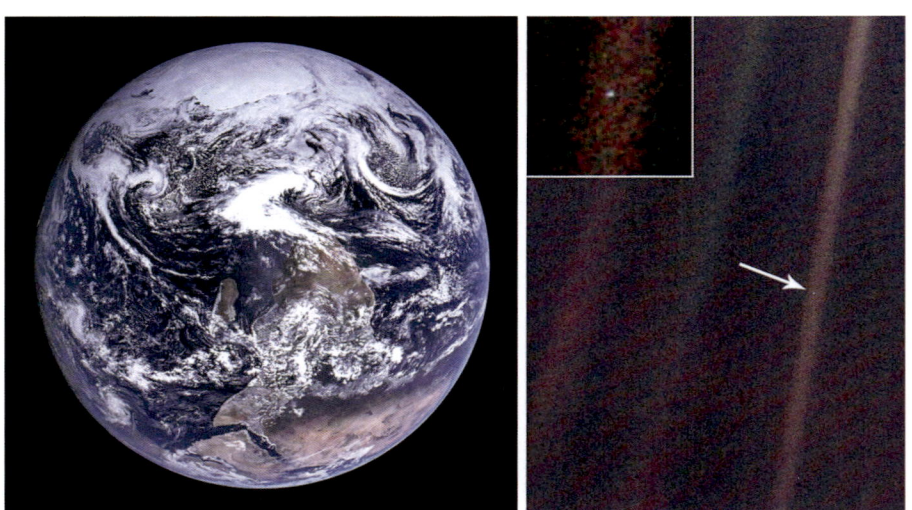

Plate 8 'The Blue Marble', taken by *Apollo 17* crew, 1972, and 'Pale Blue Dot', taken by *Voyager 1*, 1990. Courtesy of NASA

father Cooper and daughter Murphy (after a separation of nearly eighty earth years), and the suggested reconnection of Cooper and Dr Amelia Brand as the new Adam and Eve of Edmund's planet. These images of time as continuity not only affirm the escapist fantasy expressed by Professor Brand (Michael Caine) at the secret NASA facility: 'We're not meant to save the world; we're meant to leave it.' They also join with the images of cornfields and baseball to suggest the temporal resolution into the ultimate unilinear historicity of apocalyptic form itself.

While the dominant impulse of the alternate-history genre (and certainly space-exploration SF) may often be the desire to evacuate the present, the dream of a mass exodus from history, we might consider the tension in the film between cross-cutting's function of immersion and the peculiar combination of out-of-syncness and egressive desires, between the thematics of reunification and the plotlines' coeval non-simultaneity. For both the movie's characters and its viewers, the stage of action is a Jamesonian scenario in which global capitalism has both ended history and sparked an exigent fantasy of living elsewhen. Even if we do not read the figures of the bulk and the wormhole and the desire for an exit as an escapist dream of history-transcending extra-dimensionality, but only as the assertion of another, different time, is it not the case, as Peter Osborne points out, that the Blochian 'historically differential temporal multiplicity of non-sametimeness' is already the default state of capitalism today?[21] Jamesonian critics such as Phillip Wegener see the 'resurgence of interest in the science fiction subgenre of alternate history' as a way of reimagining 'the present as history', a rethinking of the present that is neither the 'stereotypically modernist totalitarian closure of rigid historical determinism' nor 'the postmodern free play of radical contingency', but a hopeful and political specification of the possibilities that follow from a determinate past.[22] Michael Löwy's gloss on Walter Benjamin becomes a mission statement on the value of alternate history:

> Against the history written by the victors, the celebration of the *fait accompli*, the historical one-way street and the 'inevitability' of the victory of those who triumphed, we must come back to this essential proposition: each present opens up onto a multiplicity of possible futures. In every historical conjuncture, there were alternatives.[23]

However, when the genre construes history as multiple – that is, not only possible futures but also actual presents and pasts – historicity often appears less promising. Criticising such plurality, Osborne asks: '*From within which time(s) does the political agent/subject of politics act?*'[24]

For all its failings to picture the differing arrival times of disaster, *Interstellar* remains an interesting heterochronic exploration that aligns with a current running through modernist and alternate-history attempts to think about alternatives in new ways, and to process formal and thematic interests through cross-cut de-synchronisation. This alignment allows us to consider the ways that multiple histories – including the different temporal scales of other collective histories, such as global warming or the Anthropocene – put pressure on the functions of aesthetic mediation. Like the video screen on the *Endurance* or the other figures of the time machine, including the bulk, such mediation is less about instant connection and love than about the ability to diagnose those forces that synchronise differential timeliness facilely or violently, or that arrange the multiplicity of histories in 'reciprocal indifference'.[25] As a relativistic mediator, time-machinic aesthetics mark the gap between timelines and spark the desire for the outside of any singular timespace.

Sobchak writes that Nolan's treatment of the bulk reveals a simple truth that is decidedly not aporetic: 'it is certainly possible to alter whatever present we happen to presently occupy'.[26] This broadly construed and instantly comforting takeaway could perhaps be reformulated to account for the importance of de-synchronisation to the idea of historical alternativity: any present that we presently occupy belongs to a line or sequence of events that is one in a bundle of many, but it also belongs to a construction of evenness (likewise called the 'present') that is a transverse cut across those simultaneous but non-synchronous timelines characterised by differential rates of change. In this context in which histories are not superseded but carry on in varying durations, directions and pace, what does the concept of alteration mean?

Interstellar belongs to a class of alternate history that thematises the process of altering history in relation to the problem of varying rhythms and various timelines (social, political, environmental and astrophysical). Its narrative of exiting one historical track – so as to be able to view it and send messages (via a library) back to specific moments – entails a more critical insight that heterochronic time machines can work to de-sync us from our present pace and the timelines/deadlines it has created, not simply by transporting us to a timeless, dehistoricised omniscience, but rather by moving us disjunctively across warped timespaces. In that engaged de-synchronisation in which tracking different timelines becomes possible (always from another reference frame), possibility and contingency thus become a matter not of finding the right moment for right action in a singular chain of events, but of larger kinds of intra- and multilinear assessments and timings.

Einsteinian Historicity in Mrs Dalloway

Mrs Dalloway is a novel defined by the running of different clocks simultaneously, which makes for a stranger construction of the present than we typically ascribe to Woolf. In most accounts, these ubiquitous public time signals are part of the novel's cross-cutting technique, which allows the reader to establish the logistical and thematic connections between disparate events at various moments of the day. Readers intermittently hear Big Ben striking the hour throughout a novel originally organised into twelve sections.[27] Even its chime on the half-hour serves to mark the coincidence of a number of happenings: at 11:30 a.m. Elizabeth Dalloway appears for the first time, interrupting Peter Walsh's question 'Are you happy, Clarissa?'; and Peter leaves Clarissa's house with 'the sound of all the clocks striking' (236), with St Margaret's clock also punctuating Peter's thoughts of Clarissa's past rejection of him, of his presence in London after so many years, and of, 'as if there rolled down to him, vigorous, unending, his future' (238). In this example, after stalking a young woman across Piccadilly, Peter unknowingly crosses paths with Septimus and Rezia in Regent's Park, where both parties are killing time before appointments (with divorce lawyers and Dr Bradshaw, respectively). Later, when Septimus and Rezia leave their meeting with Dr Bradshaw in London's medical district, 'the clocks of Harley Street' echo Bradshaw's bio-regulatory emphasis on 'proportion' and 'counselled submission, upheld authority, and pointed out in chorus the supreme advantages of a sense of proportion, until the mound of time was so far diminished that a commercial clock, suspended above a shop in Oxford St, announced [. . .] that it was half-past one' (286). And when Clarissa is thinking about the 'degradingly poor' Doris Kilman, whom the Dalloways have hired as a history tutor for Elizabeth, and contemplating the problem of different spaces – 'here was one room; there another' (309) – she hears 'the other clock, the clock which always struck two minutes after Big Ben [. . .] coming in on the wake of Big Ben, with its lap full of trifles' (309–10) (Fig. 2.2).

In the critical history of *Mrs Dalloway*, mapping the novel has been not only a matter of tracing the characters' spatial movements and figuring out, by means of the many clocks, which events are taking place simultaneously; it has been a thematic exploration, as well, of whether the accent falls on the violence of mass coordination and unification, or on the beauty of bringing things together. In the former, the multiple clocks form a chorus singing of a disciplinary 'proportion' that abets the forces of nationalist and imperialist 'conversion'; in the case of the latter, synchronisation is a post-war difficulty that can be resolved in the pathos of calling moments together into an interpenetrated present, a rich and mottled now that contains not only the past but different points of view. Thus, in discerning the significance of the novel's flipping between various plotlines and itineraries, critics have often seen its primary contrast as one between masculine and feminine time – metaphors for modes of organisation, from perception to social life. For Makiko Minow-Pinkney, Big Ben stands for the law of the Father, which 'dissects the continuum of life and imposes a structure'.[28] As the characters move through the city, for example,

Figure 2.2 Cover of *Mrs Dalloway* (Paris: Le livre de poche, 1982),
illustrated by Jacques Rozier and Monique Gaudriault

the clock's striking resonates with the motor car's 'violent explosion', the back-firing heard simultaneously as 'a pistol shot' and 'the voice of authority' (205). The throbbing motor car, whose pulse is felt throughout the entire social body, terrifies Septimus but enthralls the crowd, which believes it carries 'the endur-ing symbol of the state' (207), unifying everything from shoppers who think 'of the dead; of the flag; of Empire' and drinkers fighting in a back-street pub, to 'girls buying white underlinen [. . .] for their weddings' (209). The novel explicitly thematises time as a technology of coordination and convergence by connecting it to William Bradshaw, 'the priest of science', who defines madness as 'not having a sense of proportion' (279, 281). In preaching 'divine proportion' – the ability to size the parts of mental and political life properly – Dr Bradshaw 'made England prosper, secluded her lunatics, forbade childbirth, penalised despair, made it impossible for the unfit to propagate their views' (283). This gendered, eugenic list of biopolitical domestic accomplishments is linked to 'conversion', the imperial project of imposing proportion 'in the heat and sands of India, the mud and swamp of Africa', but also in the 'purlieus of London', the wilderness at the edge of the royal forest that involved heavy policing (284).

By contrast, but likewise an example of synchronisation, Clarissa's party is for many critics the emblem and the result of Woolf's technique – her 'discovery', when the text was still called 'The Hours', of how she 'dig[s] beautiful caves behind [her] characters [. . .] The idea is that the caves shall connect, & each comes to daylight at the present moment' (95). Instead of violence and coercion, but still premised on individual parts tending towards dissolution, the party signifies 'the traditionally feminine project', as Elizabeth Abel writes, 'of constructing social harmony through affiliation rather than conflict'.[29] Not only does the party stand for the technical achievement of rendering, in David Daiches's early assessment, 'the flux of experience' and creating 'all transitions from one part to another in such a way that the unity of the work is emphasized', but also the novel's vision of social harmony relies on the repetition of elements, memories and persons from the past, 'the raising of the dead', as J. Hillis Miller puts it, all of which are reassembled in 'the present as a completed whole, or [as] it moves toward such completion'.[30] *Mrs Dalloway*'s various itineraries end up at Clarissa's victorious party, tunnelling their way through the duration of the novel's subterranean layers into the present.

On this view, that particular present, in which heterogeneous moments from the past merge and interpenetrate, is deeply Bergsonian. In his account of how 'some people count the successive strokes of a distant bell', Bergson determines that there are 'two kinds of multiplicity', one that is made up of homogeneous, spatially extended and mutually impenetrable units, 'to which the conception of number is immediately applicable'; and the other defined by intensive states of consciousness that 'permeate' – a term as Woolfian as it is Bergsonian.[31] Hearing the bell and telling the time is less a matter of counting the strikes than it is an act of 'gathering, so to speak, the qualitative impression produced by the whole series'.[32] If one desires to speak of simultaneity in Bergson at all, one would not be referring to the process of reconciling places with certain times but rather, as Michael Whitworth remarks, rethinking contemporaneity in terms of 'smearing and blurring': 'viewed as durée, every moment of time is simultaneous with every other', because none is fully discrete and 'every moment of durée overlaps every other'.[33] The difference between Bergsonian and Einsteinian simultaneity turns on time's relationship to space, its spatialisation. With respect to Woolf's novel in particular, Whitworth stresses the Einsteinian character of modernist heterochrony over Bergsonian durational heterogeneity: 'The simultaneity of *Mrs. Dalloway* and other works of high modernism is heterochronic: it brings together two or more diverse times as if they were simultaneous.'[34]

Without denying the novel's deep investment in refusing to say of itself (and of its characters and indeed moments themselves) 'I am this, I am that' (200), one would also have to note the general consensus on 'the extreme particularity of time and place in *Mrs. Dalloway*', which presents to readers, as Andelys Wood observes, an invitation to track 'the characters in a network of spatial and temporal relationships as they walk through London', and offers the opportunity to chart critics' attempts to make sense of these itineraries in relation to the theme of synchronisation itself.[35] Wood observes a number of cross-cut juxtapositions: at noon, when 'Twelve o'clock struck as Clarissa Dalloway laid her green dress on her bed, and the Warren Smiths walked down Harley Street'; at 3:30 p.m., Elizabeth Dalloway's 'boarding the bus back toward Westminster [which] is intercut with Septimus's perceptions of his Tottenham Court Road sitting room'; and at 6:00 p.m., the ambulance carrying Septimus's body, which Peter hears as he thinks about the civilised 'efficiency, the organisation, the communal spirit of London' (331).[36] Interwoven with these observations about the novel's timing is Wood's attention to characters and critics along a number of highly significant routes: Clarissa's circuitous path to Mulberry's flower shop (with a return home by 11:00 a.m., the first clear time in the book), which is directly across from Septimus and Rezia's starting point on their way to the doctor's appointment; Peter's two-and-a-half-mile walk at 11:30 a.m. from his surprise visit at Clarissa's to Regent's Park, where he awakens from a nap at 11:45; Richard Dalloway's return home by 3:00 p.m. along Dean's Yard, after his late lunch meeting with Lady Bruton and Hugh Whitbread. While the coincidences encourage attention to precise timing and the significance of coming together, the characters' movements seem to demonstrate 'discrepancies, even impossibilities', since 'nearly all the walks that clearly structure the novel must take considerably longer than the time so precisely allotted to them'.[37] For Wood, these discrepancies are deliberate: Woolf was 'herself an experienced London walker', and her novel consciously defies regulation by clocks and resists rational proportion, emphasising instead 'the web of relationships', 'the ability of characters to experience "time in the mind", in defiance of the clock', and the excavations of a past covered over by post-war rebuilding or hidden beyond perspectival limits.[38]

Whereas for Wood, Woolf's precise use of clocks is precisely to push away from them and their role in threading disparate scenes together, for Ronald Walker clock time and its quantitative determinations allow the reader to develop an awareness of, to feel metronomically, the different tempos of being in time that exceed the clock. Walker measures the 'narrative rhythm' in *Mrs Dalloway* by developing a 'time-space index' that compares the intervals of the novel's present in 1923 to the frequency of external analepses, flashbacks to events prior to the present day, which retard or accelerate the narrative tempo.[39] His detailed analysis establishes that Woolf has squeezed seventeen hours into the twelve unnumbered sections, whose lengths vary from 2.9 pages to 86.8 pages, with each page, for reference's sake, averaging around 3.5 minutes.[40] One useful takeaway of Walker's work is that the present in Woolf is never what one thinks it is, fluctuating in duration between spans that provide a sense of speed and fluidity, and dense units that dilate the now and shoehorn lengthy thoughts and disruptive, extra-diegetic memories into it. Ultimately the novel's rhythms find their balance in Clarissa's ability 'to be; to exist; to sum it all up in the moment as she passed' (352); the clock's multiplicity and discrepancies are resolved in her gift for complex, cumulative there-being which represents a present whose structure resembles and culminates in the openness of the ending itself. Both plot and technique render fully 'that constant flux which is time present, and which [. . .] is also a continuum comprised of past, present, and future'.[41] For Walker, the specific composition of this flux and 'the felt dynamics' of the combinations of 'rhythmical deviations' provide the experiential meaning of Woolf's art.[42]

One can understand without much effort critics' desire not to leave the novel mired in its discrepancies and to convert the text's multiplicity into a unified whole. Clearly, in this novel and across her oeuvre, Woolf demonstrates an immersive interest in a variety of kinds of time coming together: moments of being; crystallised, diamond moments; waves; standardised proportion; gendered time; subjectless history and inhuman time, among others. What is undeniably appealing about Clarissa's character and the novel itself is their full submersion in the flux of the moment and the persistence of memory that is one of modernism's signature preoccupations. The first pages of the novel exemplify this 'in-ness' in time and provide an answer to the key question of 'why one loves it so, how one sees it so':

> In people's eyes, in the swing, tramp, and trudge; in the bellow and the uproar; the carriages, motor cars, omnibuses, vans, sandwich men shuffling and swinging; brass bands; barrel organs; in the triumph and the jingle and the strange high singing of some aeroplane overhead was what she loved; life; London; this moment of June. (4)

The repeated preposition emphasises the setting as not just the spatial situatedness in the heart of empire, the seat of government and 'the midst of ordinary things' (309). 'In' also signifies temporal immersion, *in medium temporum*: mid-year (June), mid-month ('the middle of June', 196) and mid-week

(Wednesday, 207). After hearing 'the hour, irrevocable' from Big Ben followed by the sensation of dissolution, Clarissa performs the heroic recuperation of meaningful duration heightened by her situation in a singular current that flows towards death.

However, in recounting the variety of tempos within the time presided over by Big Ben, the novel also asks us to recast temporal multiplicity: it is not 'musical', like the clock's warning (196), but cacophonous. Following the passage above, which one critic has said 'may be one of the noisiest in all of Woolf's work', the novel discerns in a Wednesday morning a number of differing tempos:

> And everywhere [. . .] there was a beating, a stirring of galloping ponies, tapping of cricket bats [. . .] the grey-blue morning air, which [. . .] would unwind them, and set down on their lawns and pitches the bouncing ponies whose forefeet just struck the ground and up they sprang, the whirling young men, and laughing girls [. . .] who, even now, after dancing all night, were taking their absurd wooly dogs for a run; and even now, at this hour, discreet old dowagers were shooting out in their motor cars [. . .] (197)[43]

These rhythms that are ticking in their various ways in what Clarissa feels is 'this, here, now in front of her' (200) are experienced from a privileged point of view as flowing into the 'waves of that divine vitality' that emanate from the expanding circles of the tolling clock and through the network of daily activities (199). Certainly, they may be understood as unified by the Englishness of a certain class. However, the novel presents us not only with other perspectives in which this noise is experienced quite differently, but also with a demonstration that the din is equally a number of rhythms that coexist but do not merge.

If Clarissa does not make anything of the differences between these tempos and temporalities that seem to her to merge into one another in some larger ecstasy of connection, the novel fairly quickly begins to foreground disjunctive rhythms and, ultimately, different timelines. These timelines are co-present but de-synchronised from each other, and never come together in any substantive way, except for brief moments of intersection that can only be seen from the critical position of yet another reference frame. The novel's various clocks gesture towards the reality not only of the sensuous texture of a multiplicity *in* time, but also of the stark divisions, durations and rates among a plurality of times. The critical history of *Mrs Dalloway* has emphasised the time of the mind or Bergsonian *durée*, even when thinking through clock time and its discrepancies. What would the text yield if we bracketed the novel's unarguable interest in subjectivity and memory in order to pursue Woolf's more adventurous exploration? Instead of the psychological and canonically modernist drama of temporal immersion, the emphasis would fall on a less familiar (but equally modernist) idea – that of the unsynthesisable side-by-side-ness of plural times, and of the alternate-historical impulse to exit a timeline and imagine a different history. Woolf, of course, worried that the 'reviewers will say that it is disjointed because of the mad scenes not connecting with the Dalloway scenes', but it has been perhaps too much of a capitulation to this worry and to the anticipated consternation of reviewers that we have overemphasised the connection of the novel's various tunnels in daylight at the present moment.[44] Like *Interstellar*'s cross-cutting between plotlines that are related but de-synchronised, *Mrs Dalloway*'s method asks us to consider the way in which narrative and history itself can be structured heterochronically. Neither the novel's form and style, nor its themes, are primarily about coordination and synchronisation – quite the opposite. What is interesting and powerful about the text is the fact that the side-by-side, 'the sane & the insane', remain so unreconciled and unsynthesised.[45]

The inspiration for a resistance to a unitary clock time is not Bergson but Einstein: rather than a repudiation of clock time, the novel features a multiplication of clock times. In the novel's explicit mention of Einstein – in which 'Mr. Bentley, vigorously rolling his strip of turf at Greenwich', sees the skywriting aeroplane speeding away as a symbol of 'man's soul; of his determination [. . .] to get outside his body, beyond his house, by means of thought, Einstein, speculation, mathematics, the Mendelian theory' (218) – Whitworth sees a contrast 'between the earth-bound Bentley and the soaring Einstein' that valorises science and 'alludes to Einstein's role in changing ideas of space and time'.[46] The contrast between, on the one hand, the mundane and pedestrian at Greenwich, locus of the prime meridian and the standardisation of time, and on the other, the flights of thought, carriers of the payloads of relativity, activates for Whitworth a consideration of what he calls, in a well-crafted oxymoron, 'Einsteinian simultaneity'.[47] We might think of Whitworth's heterochronic reading of 'simultaneity as literary form' as a timely update of 'spatial form', Joseph Frank's term for the way in which the modernist text 'eliminates any feeling of sequence by the very act of juxtaposition'.[48] Long considered a centrepiece of modernist aesthetics, simultaneity is invariably construed as a convergence in a moment, 'an aesthetic ordering based on synchronicity, the logic of metaphor' in which, as Eugene Lunn writes, '[t]hings do not so much fall apart as fall together, reminding us of the derivation of the ubiquitous "symbol" from the Greek *symballein*, "to throw together"'.[49] However, here, in the case of Einsteinian simultaneity, Whitworth shows how the technique of juxtaposition, which Frank cast as a spatialisation of past and present 'locked in a timeless unity', is not a freezing or elimination of time, but rather a gathering of anachronistic elements, arriving like rays of light from different times and reference frames in the cosmos at a particular now.[50]

But let us push Einstein's thought experiments in simultaneity even further – not only to the insights that the now is not what it seems, since historicity comprises a multitude of clocks, but also towards an implication of alternate history that, in probing the limits of one's time, one can jump tracks or alter a track by means of other tracks. The central problem of relativity was for Einstein the problem of simultaneity: as he wrote, 'all our judgments in which time plays a role are always judgments of simultaneous events'.[51] That is, to determine the time of some event requires one to reconcile it with the simultaneous display of a nearby clock. But timing is much more complicated when dealing with more than one place and with faraway events, because different frames of reference produce irreconcilable descriptions of the same phenomena. In Einstein's thought experiment from his famous 1905 paper on special relativity, two bolts of lightning strike the front (A) and back (B) of a moving train at the exact moment that the precise centre of the train passes an observer on the platform. Since the lightning strikes are equidistant from the observer, the light from both the front and the back of the train reaches the observer at the same instant, and the observer judges that they occur simultaneously. However, for an observer located exactly at the centre of the train, which is moving forward at high speed, the light from location A will reach her first since the distance is decreasing between her and location A, the site of the lightning strike at the front of the train. For the observer on the train, lightning strikes A and B are not simultaneous. Moreover, from either onboard or platform position, there is no way to tell if the train or the train station, as non-accelerating inertial contexts, is at rest or in motion, since the laws of physics obtain in exactly the same way in both. There can be no absolute simultaneity in Einstein's thought because 'no special frame of reference exists from which the motions of all others can be judged'.[52] According to Peter Galison, Einstein's thought experiment centres around the question of '[h]ow [. . .] we synchronize our distant clocks' in the absence of a master clock. This problem must take into account distances and the speed of the synchronising signal, a difficulty rooted not in the ethereal realm of pure thought but in the material networks of telegraph wire, train tracks, standardised time and a Swiss patent office in which, as Adam Frank puts it, the young Einstein's 'day job was to evaluate designs for electromechanical time coordination devices'.[53]

In addition to the counter-intuitive fact that the now is not what it seems, Einstein's work opened the way for rethinking the nature of time as such, and for considering the possibility of forward time travel (the ability to outstrip the constraints of one particular history), which forms the premise of *Interstellar* as well as countless other science fiction texts. Einstein's heterochronic and multi-temporal present destabilises what we take for granted – an absolute plane of happening in which one sequence is true, and against which all individual events can be ordered. Whatever simultaneity can be generated must be acknowledged as a convention, Galison explains, as 'nothing more than the coordination of clocks by a crossed exchange of electromagnetic signals, taking into account the transit time of the signal'.[54] Moreover, if the speed of light, regardless of reference frame, never changes and is a universal constant, which Einstein postulated in his theory of special relativity, then distance and duration must become flexible and elastic. Because velocity comprises measurements for length and duration, '[t]here is no one length for an object', as physicist Adam Frank puts it, and there is no one time between events: '[i]nstead of a single overarching Newtonian cosmic time, there was now a relativistic patchwork of times, each measured by observers moving relative to one another'.[55] Thus, Einstein's daydream, when he was 16, of what he would see if he were to ride a light beam later generated the terms for the stranger realities of the twin problem, in which one twin, who flies away from earth at very high speeds, returns to find that he is now much younger than his sibling because his time ran slower than the earthbound twin's clocks. In Woolf's novel, Mr Bentley's view of the aeroplane evokes both a 'simultaneity' of timelines themselves, the plural reference frames in which clocks are ticking at different rates, and the alternate-historical longing of the characters 'to get outside [their] body, beyond [their] house', the desire, in measuring one frame against another, to exit one's own.

Beyond Mr Bentley and the aeroplane's evocation of Einsteinian special relativity, *Mrs Dalloway*, like *Interstellar*, is actually structured by means of parallel timelines that de-synchronise from one another. The critic who comes closest to capturing the science-fictional quality of Woolf's interest in relative times and multiple clocks is Paul Tolliver Brown. In 'The Spatiotemporal Topography of Virginia Woolf's *Mrs. Dalloway*', Brown argues that the discrepantly timed walks in the novel 'draw attention to the fact that her characters inhabit a relative setting' and are 'walking through the city [. . .] at a slightly faster pace than their presumably stationary environs'.[56] For example, Clarissa's shopping trip to Bond Street would have required a taxi in order to return by 11:00; Peter's unlikely two-and-a-half-mile trip to his nap in Regent's Park takes place in less than fifteen minutes; and Richard's impossible return from Lady Bruton's lunch by 3:00 would compress a number of time-consuming activities into a matter of minutes. Rather than treat these anomalies as a vague resistance to clock time, Brown reads the fast-motion walks as evidence that 'Woolf's Londoners are no longer in sync with a single perspective of time and space, because they no longer inhabit a mechanistic London' but a relativistic one; indeed, critics who fixate on the unrealistic timing of the characters' paths 'affiliate themselves with Big Ben and base their calculations on a single, accelerated system moving at a much different speed than the characters themselves'.[57] In light of the overarching theme of a changed world after the war, Brown argues that the characters' fast-motion times suggest that those who 'remain mostly stuck in the Victorian past' would experience 'a greater amount of time to stroll the streets [. . .] than Big Ben would seem to denote to readers'.[58] In his reading of the aeroplane scene, the various perspectives are in fact 'a conglomerate of different referential frames', and Mr Bentley at Greenwich, thinking about Einstein, evokes a contrast between the two-dimensional grid of GMT and the geodesic arcs and curved, non-Euclidean spaces of Riemannian geometry. Thus in the relativistic landscape of the novel, the difference between Big Ben and St Margaret's chime, which comes two minutes after, signifies 'the idea that there are multiple present moments, thus introducing the concept of relative simultaneity'.[59]

These are important insights that begin to emphasise the temporal discrepancies in a new way. Rather than celebrating convergences or revelling in the tensions among parts, Brown's framework of a relativistic London suggests different times rather than different moments or subjective inflections. With respect to the novel's temporal disjunctions, the furthest that critics have gone with *Mrs Dalloway* has been to highlight the 'depiction of synchronously lived moments of multiple characters [. . .] a clear deployment of cubist strategy', as Jennie-Rebecca Falcetta has argued.[60] For Falcetta, the text's temporal discrepancies demonstrate that 'Woolf collapses time', the outcome of rendering experience 'as plural realities of the same geographical space, moment in time, event, or phenomenon, thus asserting the presence of dynamic, simultaneous perspectives'.[61] This account draws on Wendy Steiner's reading of cubist simultaneity, which teaches us 'to think of history in a new way, not as a plotted narrative moving toward a resolution, but as a cubist painting whose elements maintain their heterogeneity – objects, people; things, signs [. . .] the contemporaneous, the anachronous – in an aestheticized structure of interrelations'.[62] Such readings of the novel's cross-cutting treat Einstein's influence as a current that feeds into the well-established Woolfian metaphorics of plural subjectivities: in *Orlando*, for instance, in which literary form and biographical time-keeping must grapple with 'sixty or seventy different times which beat simultaneously in every normal human system so that when eleven strikes, all the rest chime in unison', Julia Briggs cites the presence of Einstein's special relativity in the way that 'Woolf links her multiple internal clocks with the multiple selves that inhabit us'.[63] The cubist rendition of 'multiple subjective Londons' echoes the temporal plurality within the self that multiplies the selves, 'of which', as *Orlando* puts it, 'there may be more than two thousand'.[64]

However, the strangeness of the Einsteinian twinning of selves depends crucially on the simultaneity, the contrastive parallel co-presence, of multiple non-subjective times themselves. There can be no doubt that Woolf was deeply interested in subjective temporalities. As Leena Kore Schroder points out, Woolf's 'Evening Over Sussex: Reflections in a Motor Car' recounts the way in which motoring in a Singer in 1927 generated for the autobiographical subject 'a polyphony of selves that range as fluidly over the Sussex landscape as they do through time, spanning its reference from the arrival of William the Conqueror [. . .] through the present moment, to what Sussex will be "in five hundred years to come"'.[65] However, the Woolfian time machine – whether automobile or aeroplane, or the walks and 'tunnels' that constitute *Mrs Dalloway* as a demonstration of 'postmodern geography' – not only produces a topography in which subjects' imagined spaces fold into real, physical, collective ones,[66] it also constructs space 'as the dimension of multiple trajectories, a simultaneity of stories-so-far', to use Doreen Massey's formulation, 'a dimension of a multiplicity of durations'.[67] Just as moving across time opens up the dynamic heterogeneity of spaces, moving across spaces produces the temporal multiplicity both within history and *of* timelines.

As in *Interstellar*, the two main plotlines in Woolf's *Mrs Dalloway* diverge from one another so as to produce a most striking vision of the heterochronic present and to imply a deeply moving desire for alternative historical possibilities. Even without modifying our understanding of Woolf's work, her treatment of historical periods is already rich and provocative: think, for instance, of the way she figures the drawing room in 'A Sketch of the Past', a memory of her father in which 'two different ages confronted each other [. . .] at Hyde Park Gate. The Victorian Age and the Edwardian Age. We were not his children; we were his grandchildren. [. . .] We were living say in 1910; they were living in 1860.'[68] Many of the readings of *Mrs Dalloway* emphasise precisely this confrontation of a post-war present and the remnants of an earlier social order. But as we read what we take to be a poignant figurative treatment – of a sympathetic 52-year-old ruling-class character, nostalgic for a time 'before the War, [when] you could buy almost perfect gloves' (202), as she and her family face a new era defined by the rise of the Labour party – we are tempted to remain on the historiographic tracks whereby the past necessarily falls away as modernity arrives (which intensifies the pathos). In this way, we underestimate the victorious staying power of certain historical trajectories and the differences among them.

Once Septimus and Rezia's path divaricates from Clarissa's on Bond Street, the two plotlines begin to differ widely. Building on Brown's argument that the characters are moving at different speeds in relation to Big Ben as the novel's way of conjuring differential frames of reference, my claim simply adds that the different fates of these characters (and the different questions about the uncertainty of their fates) signify an alternative historicity. This historicity is striated by sequences of varying lengths and rates of change, and marked by a longing for the new that draws less on the radical historical break as such and more on shifting tracks in a region of overlap and intersection. Plainly stated, in this modest adjustment to our reading of *Mrs Dalloway*, the novel's backdrop of extreme synchronisation foregrounds the contrasts between characters whose individual paths signify larger currents running transversely, and mostly in parallel, through the present: primarily, between a historical track that is dilated and distended in all sorts of ways (memory, Daylight Saving Time) and a plotline that is foreshortened and foreclosed (war trauma, suicide), but also in relation to other trajectories (for instance, the colonial administration of India, the struggles of the 'New Woman'). Ultimately, the novel calls attention to narration itself – both as tracking and as flipping from one path to another. Narration's parallel edits do not synchronise the events taking place in London, but locate the intersections (violent, sympathetic) of timelines. Narration here is not a mode of connection, but a way of performing a desire for an outside, an exit, another time altogether.

The central contrast in Woolf's critique of 'the social system' is, in her words, between 'the sane & the insane side by side' – between Clarissa Dalloway, middle-aged protagonist preparing for a party, and Septimus Warren Smith, shell-shocked war veteran who commits suicide – but their parallel paths are distinctly uneven, and they are clearly not living in the same historical now, let alone a larger psychological space.[69] For these characters, whom Elizabeth Lamont describes as both 'psychic doubles' and 'geopolitical doubles', the 'present', misrecognised as a neutral container in a singular historical current, appears and is experienced differently by these Einsteinian parallels (if not quite twins): to Clarissa, the 'War was over [. . .] thank Heaven – over' (196–7), and her trajectory through the plane of the present allows her to relish the vital flow of the June day; but for Septimus, the war continues, stuck on repeat, so that the world of everyday London constantly 'wavered and quivered and threatened to burst into flames' (15).[70] The most striking feature is the shape and differential rhythm of this parallel. Although she is a middle-aged character with a heart condition, Clarissa's plotline spans the length of the novel, is marked by her enjoyment (like Peter's) of the lengthened daylight and prolonged evening of 'Mr. Willet's summer time' (340), and signifies in broad thematic terms longevity and continuity. Septimus, by contrast, occupies a truncated line: one of 'many millions of young men' swallowed up by London, he disappears in the ninth section of Mrs Dalloway, and signifies a futureless world powered by a different temporality. This temporality, as all Bergsonian readings of the novel have rightly pointed out, is structured by explosive and disconnected nows, a present that is thoroughly disarticulated by all the unified clocks – Big Ben but especially the biopolitical 'clocks of Harley Street' that are '[s]hredding and slicing, dividing and subdividing' the day, his life, and the possible courses of life for his entire class (286). If Septimus can be said to 'return' in the final pages of the novel in Clarissa's thoughts, it is only to underscore that the larger historical lines they inhabit remain largely distinct, but have crossed at key junctures to show how the theft and violence of time in one world enables the rich enlargement, dilation and flow of it in another. Clarissa, fearfully hearing the clock's 'striking the hour, one, two, three', feels 'glad that he had done it' (363); her temporal privilege allows her to see Septimus's escape from the disciplinary powers 'forcing your soul' as an obligation to return to her synchronising pleasures, to 'feel the beauty [. . .] feel the fun' (363).

There is no doubt that the larger historical forces for which their individual lives stand have crossed one another in causal ways, and yet the novel foregrounds that the two characters never meet, and that the rhythm and end of their Wednesday differ dramatically. In Woolf's short story 'Mrs. Dalloway in Bond St', Clarissa contemplates the relationship between her present (construed as the national present) and the war, while 'the [shop-girl] moved like a snail': in the glove shop just before the car's backfiring, Clarissa thinks that 'Thousands of young men had died that things might go on' (23). It is, of course, precisely this self-serving ruling-class view that is responsible for the ascendancy of one history over another, of a sequence that subsumes and converts all others to its cadence. This view of going on by putting all things into proportion (including the harm to others caused by proportion) is what underwrites Clarissa's belief that after '1918 to 1923' people's appearances, behaviour, their writing and life arcs (courtship, marriage) are remarkably different (258); and it affords Richard and his circle, all of whom succumbed to and 'liked continuity', 'the sense of handing on the traditions of the past' (300), and the illusion they relish that they are progressive reformers, as Alex Zwerdling argues, despite their 'British Empire, tariff-reform, governing-class spirit'.[71] Indeed, 'the separate worlds she created in *Mrs. Dalloway*', as Zwerdling remarks, are where we find Woolf's 'most searching account of the class isolation of her society'.[72] As outlandish as it might seem, the discrepant pace between those worlds – with one coming to a premature end and the other valiantly pressing on in what her class presumes to be the universal, historical present – encourages us to take Zwerdling's insight literally. The separate worlds that Septimus and Clarissa and her friends inhabit are isolated timelines cannot be made to accord with one another, even though there are points where they touch, points of violent intersection, moments of dominating synchrony – as when Peter, hearing the ambulance carrying Septimus's body (impaled on the rusty spikes of Mrs Filmer's area railings, the harshest image of unitary clock time), reckons smugly that this is 'civilisation', 'the efficiency, the organisation, the communal spirit of London' (331).

By postulating the 'sovereignty' of different histories without denying their causal co-implication – the temporal disparities and varying futures between, say, the lineage containing 'courtiers once in the time of the Georges' (197) and the line shortened and accelerated by the persistence of the other's violence – it is easier to feel the strange pathos of the as yet unrealised paths that the novel dreams about. One has to do with the war itself. While for most characters the war is over and its destruction is sublated in proportional continuity, the novel suggests an alternate history that is not in all cases a desperate fantasy, a history still waiting to achieve critical mass. It does so by way of a different doubling: Clarissa and Doris Kilman. Clarissa hates every way in which Doris differs from her: the latter has 'a really historical mind'; is close to her daughter; is religious; is insensitive to the class manners and dress code from which she is excluded; is poor. And yet Clarissa also realises that 'with another throw of the dice [. . .] she would have loved Miss Kilman! But not in this world. No' (203). The biggest difference is, of course, that Doris's 'family was of German origin; spelt the name Kiehlman in the eighteenth century' (306), an issue that gets her sacked from her job as a history teacher during the war. As Christine Froula argues, this comparison allows the novel to evoke 'a defeated and still belligerent postwar Germany' and an England 'heedless of the political consequences of the international class oppression instituted at Versailles', where the treaty that ended the war also demanded harsh reparations from Germany in excess of 100 billion marks.[73] Resigning in protest as British Treasury officer, John Maynard Keynes, Woolf's friend, wrote in *The Economic Consequences of the Peace* (1919) that these punitive reparations would doom 'European civilization struggling forwards to a new order' by 'reducing Germany to servitude for a generation' and 'depriving a whole nation of happiness'.[74] Considering Keynes's prospective anxieties about the treaty's disastrous outcome (yet another war) from a retrospective position, the historian and biographer Robert Skidelsky writes, 'Had Keynes's 1919 programme been carried out, it is unlikely that Hitler would have become German Chancellor.'[75]

The question of the direction of Doris's path is not just about whether the First World War will carry on by other means, and run in tandem with the tenaciously persistent governing class, but also one about where the history of self-supporting middle-class women will go in economic, social and sexual terms. The novel is not too optimistic about the economic outlook, at least in relation to this individual character or Septimus. When Doris, who 'had always earned her living' (307), goes with Elizabeth to the Army and Navy Stores, she is shown to be 'lost' and 'hemmed in' by commodities that stand for a set of lives or little sequences that are not and perhaps will never be within reach: administrative assignment or holiday in the colonies ('trunks specially prepared for taking to India'), childbirth and marriage ('accouchement sets and baby linen') and Bloomsbury life in general ('hams, drugs, flowers, stationery') (314). Rhyming in appearance and staying power with Septimus in his 'shabby overcoat', Doris – in a well-worn mackintosh, 'degradingly poor', probably 'hungry' (305, 311) – tells Elizabeth that '[l]aw, medicine, politics, all professions are open to women of your generation' (312). It is in this hope, fortified by her love for Elizabeth, that the novel gestures at a ready, concurrent line of history, with its own sequences of key events, recuperative and proleptic narrativisations, and branches of possibility.

The feeling that life, with another throw of the dice, could have been otherwise, and that an alternative coeval historical line could yet become more visible and secure (via narratives, events, institutions and material conditions) is perhaps most perceptible in Clarissa's flashbacks to her youth at Bourton, when her life was at a crucial juncture. Having made a calculated decision to become 'Mrs. Richard Dalloway' (202) after rejecting Peter Walsh's proposal of marriage, Clarissa remembers – with joy but also within a more diffuse mood of regret – 'this falling in love with women' (222), 'the most exquisite moment of her whole life' (225), the kiss with Sally Seton. For Kate Haffey, the kiss and the diamond moment of its memory serve two functions: Clarissa's 'yielding to the charm of a woman' (221) signals the novel's interest in queer temporality, those disruptions of heteronormative development 'from childhood through adolescence to marriage and reproduction'; and the memory of it in Clarissa's present demonstrates the power of the 'queer moment' to undo the linear dividing and subdividing into normative and chronological stages of life, thus emphasising the novel's Bergsonian form, marked by 'the very presence of [the] past' and 'the simultaneous presence of multiple identities'.[76] For Haffey, 'This is not a text about moving from the past into the future, but rather one about the preservation of the past', a moving attempt to hold on to that which 'crashes through all the barriers meant to keep the past and the present separate'.[77] However, Haffey concludes her argument suggestively in the other temporal direction: in 'presumptive heterosexuality, [the] future is often pre-imagined', ending in marriage and reproduction; but 'within queer temporality', the moment of the kiss 'is the opening to a future that is not yet decided'.[78]

The future is not yet decided simply because the structure of time, on the most familiar model, is open-ended (one of literary studies' most hopeful adjectives for several decades), but also because different timelines have different possibilities latent within them, and the cross-sectioned plane we call 'the' future contains its own unpredictable constellation of differently weighted, concurrent paths of potentiality. Thus, as Susan Squier points out, Clarissa's paths through Westminster and Bond Street, 'haunts of male political and female social power', are placed in contrast with her daughter Elizabeth's bus ride 'up the Strand, a newly booming center of male and female commercial and professional life', which suggests 'the changing status of women in postwar England'.[79] The shift here from mother to daughter is not simply about alternativity-as-the-next, but about the future as possibility arising from out-of-sync trajectories. Elizabeth is 18, the same age as Clarissa at Bourton: whereas her mother was, in Jane Marcus's words, 'the lesbian who marries for safety and appearances [. . .] and chooses celibacy within marriage, no sex rather than the kind she wants', Elizabeth thinks of new possibilities – a doctor, a farmer, an MP (287–8). These are options that require, in some instances, a confrontation between queer histories of gender and sexuality, and the different itineraries of her mother and Septimus.[80] Tamar Katz has argued that, although 'urban time creates pauses of anticipation' in *Mrs Dalloway*, she is struck by 'how little this text imagines the future; how little it cares for the future tense': in her view, it is only Elizabeth's bus ride to the Strand that 'promises a different future for women and a different engagement with London'.[81] The novel does not sketch out a future, but I would argue that the text seems to care deeply about rethinking the future tense. The future could be something other than the undecidable but monolithic zone floating down into the domain of the present and replacing it. If the queering of futurity in resistance to the normative ordering of life in modern chrono-biopolitics is implied in the novel's thematic parallel of Clarissa/Sally and Elizabeth/Doris, then the novel's probing of alternative futures recasts potentiality as a question of the relation between diverse currents that combine in certain ways (causally, fatally, reparatively) at certain points, and remain merely parallel at others.[82]

It is difficult to shift the emphasis from the novel's clear thematic and formal interest in moments (the text's seventy references to moments, its synchronisation of scenes) and the counter-insistence by critics that such moments are resisted or redeemed by Bergsonian durational flows.[83] But it is the timeline or reference frame that allows us to best understand the novel's method of flipping frames or switching tracks, a technique that performs a desire for an exit to a different time. Paul Saint-Amour has argued that, if we link 'the omniscient narrator [. . .] to a specific figure or conceit within the diegesis', then *Mrs Dalloway*'s aeroplane, whose distanced perspective allows for the novel's mappings and timings, might be seen to reconfigure the 'gaze of total war' from its mission of reconnaissance to the pacifist work of tracing 'the spider's thread of attachment' (297), 'the fragility of interdependence, the susceptibility of the whole social matrix to trauma'.[84] To temporalise the plurality of these threads is simultaneously to assert that the other clocks, like the other lighthouse in Woolf's next novel, are 'true too'; to highlight not only immersion in time but also the exclusion from some other times and the dream of escape from one's framing sequences. It is also to rethink the new in terms not of the continual explosive appearance of the future into the present, displacing it into the past, but a matter of already existing sequences coming near or crossing paths.[85] Sara Ahmed's *The Promise of Happiness* takes Clarissa's 'hints of a life she might have lived' as the novel's way of foregrounding how becoming 'proximate' to others' unhappiness might help us acknowledge our connections and generate solidarity in the recognition of our distance from the illusion of happy objects. *Mrs Dalloway*'s less touching but perhaps more moving approach is its cross-cut comparisons of how some arcs end, how others continue, and how newer tracks struggle to begin.

ALTERNATE PRESENTS IN *THE MAN IN THE HIGH CASTLE*

At the end of 2015 a number of news articles reported that Amazon Studios' adaptation of Philip K. Dick's *The Man in the High Castle*, which had debuted in November, had become Amazon Prime's most-streamed original series, following the success of its pilot episode, released earlier in January, which had been its most-streamed pilot.[86] The show's advertising posters redesigned the US flag to feature a Nazi eagle, and plastered it, along with the Imperial Japanese rising sun, in the New York City subway, though the Metropolitan Transportation Authority was forced to remove the posters after public outcry. By the time the second season was released at the end of 2016, the conclusion of the US presidential election marked the start of a resurgence of white supremacist politics and a rise in hate crimes across the country. Dick's 1962 novel, as the inspiration for a popular instance of 'what almost was' fiction, had come to seem like a Tlönian realisation of an improbable, 'populist', counterfactual path. The Amazon show's increased attention to the Japanese protagonist, Nobusuke Tagomi, and his flip into an alternate universe that resembles ours seemed to dramatically ironise a situational irony: we are aware of what Tagomi does not know, namely, that the show's alternate-alternate reality was once our world or approximated it, but against all expectations, the fiction in which he normally resides is now our universe (Plate 7).

Scholars have dated the appeal of the genre of alternate history to very recent decades. Matthew Schneider-Mayerson claims that 'true alternate history' – which Karen Hellekson defined as fiction dedicated to a plausible rather than fantastical present that emerges as a consequence of a 'nexus event' – was not even 'fully recognized as a genre until science-fiction reviewers Steven H. Silver and Evelyn Leeper and NASA scientist Robert B. Schmunk established the Sidewise Awards for Alternate History in 1995'.[87] 'True alternate history' emerged at that moment out of a militaristic, anti-welfare-state, anti-1960s libertarianism typified by Newt Gingrich, who is himself the co-author of an alternate-history fiction, *1945*.[88] Phillip Wegner locates the 'resurgence of interest in the science fiction subgenre of the alternate history' after the turn of the millennium. As he argues in his book on the long 1990s, the reason for the revival of interest in the 'what if' of counterfactual narratives is that the period 'between two deaths' – defined on the one hand by the fall of the Berlin Wall and the end of the Cold War, and on the other by 9/11 and the beginning of the War on Terror – sparked a widespread reimagination of 'the present as history', a reaction to the end-of-history thesis that neoliberal accounts first heralded.[89] This rethinking of the present has been neither the 'stereotypically modernist totalitarian closure of rigid historical determinism' nor 'the postmodern free play of radical contingency', but a hopeful and political specification of the possibilities that follow from a determinate past.[90] The genre of alternate history is a device for finding the alternatives in every historical conjuncture.

Leaving aside the question of the popularity of the genre, we can travel back earlier than the 1990s to see how a peculiar kind of 'what if' fantasy follows from modernist time machines. The period between the two world wars was in general a time of peak alternativity and a crucible for *what-if*s, whether this upsurge in imagining history otherwise be related to the second-modernist scopings ('airmindedness') that I discuss in Chapter 5, the actuarial-futurist impulse of New Deal/Welfare State modernisms in the US, or the fear of 'fascist dictatorships, and the increasing likelihood of another total war', to quote Thomas Davis.[91] For example, in 1931 the journalist J. C. Squire edited a collection of essays by well-known academic and political figures called *If It Had Happened Otherwise*, a collection that Stephen Badsey says is arguably the most 'significant work of counterfactual history to appear in the interwar years', the 'first counterfactual best-seller'.[92] This volume features Winston Churchill's contribution, 'If Lee Had Not Won the Battle of Gettysburg', an alternate-alternate history, in which the historiographic imagination is positioned in an alternate world from the outset, a world in which the Confederate States has won the Civil War, and imagining history differently from there. Such thought experiments, or thought gags, often feature the impulse of self-interested utopian fantasy aimed at fortifying the present. As Badsey points out, the interwar years in Britain featured lots of counterfactual historicising as part of a general thrust at improving military operations – 'what if we could have done it better?' Or they feature a parodic impulse aimed not so much at cutting off a key event at the pass (in Churchill's essay, this event is the First World War), but rather at preventing the serious exploration of 'if' in the first place (e.g., the satirical 'what if Grant had been drinking at Appomattox?'). Indeed, it was towards the end of the 1930s that the idea of a historical divergence point received its casting as the 'Jonbar point' or 'hinge': in John Williamson's novel *The Legion of Time* (1938), a young boy, John Barr, will alter the history of the world if he picks up a magnet rather than a pebble, the former leading to John's scientific career, which enables a technological utopia named Jonbar, the latter to a 'shiftless migratory' life in which his atomic inventions are discovered by those who dominate the planet.

While this period seems to produce a crescendo of hypotheticals, I want to focus on a peculiar characterisation of contingency and possibility – not so much as a pivot point of divergence, but as a function of the heterochronic clash of times. That is, how do we think the emergence of the future not in the fantasy of a completely different world but in treatments of overlapping ones, universes that intrude into others such that the present appears shot through with anachronism? This way of thinking about the new – not as the result of a radical break but as the rearrangement of concurrent tracks – begins in Wells's time-travel fantasy, and more explicitly appears in the alternate-history form of his later 'cross-time' narrative *Men Like Gods* (1923), in which the protagonist flips into an alternate universe where a young Churchill, played by the character Rupert Catskill, attempts to conquer this utopia. Heterochronic historicity finds more figural solidity in Murray Leinster's 'Sidewise in Time' (1934), which I discussed in Chapter 2. Focused not on a single forking of human history but rather on the patchwork of many unfamiliar times and historical outcomes, Leinster's vision of 'the present' highlights strange intrusions into the smooth regularity of historical timespace from different histories. Similarly, L. Sprague de Camp's 'The Wheels of If' (1940) features a protagonist distributed across various versions of US history, trying to make peace between indigenous peoples and the dominant culture of Viking-ruled America.

Like Woolf's modernist text, Dick's *The Man in the High Castle* is a novel structured by parallel plotlines in which two main characters never meet. In the world of the novel, the Allies have lost the Second World War, and the USA has been divided into the 'Pacific States of America' (PSA) governed by Imperial Japan, the 'United States' ruled by Nazi Germany, and a buffer zone of 'Rocky Mountain States' (RMS). In this universe, the path of Nobusuke Tagomi, a bureaucrat in the San Francisco Trade Mission whose role is ancillary to but crucially entangled in the dramatic action of the novel, does not cross the path of Juliana Frink, a likewise 'minor' main character whose meeting with Hawthorne Abendsen, the author of an alternate history within the novel, ends the book. Like Woolf in *Mrs Dalloway*, Dick similarly uses focalisation shifts and coincidence as a way of synchronising disparate events in a post-war world. Dick's 'multifocal narrative' creates a 'narrative polyphony' in which each of the text's perspectives and segments are harmonised by an 'introductory sentence or subordinate clause which sets up the time and place'.[93] The formal fact that nearly all of the novel's chapters and sections begin with the specifics of setting seems to resonate nicely with thematic focus on the location of agency and historical change, the coordinates at which history can become otherwise. Together, form and theme create the 'suggestion inherent to the novel', writes Kathleen Singles, 'that one, specific point in [the novel's alternate] history is contingent – in this case, Zangara's shot on FDR in 1933, a single bullet in a single instant. But everything that follows is governed by the principle of necessity.'[94]

To think through the possibilities and direction of history, the characters make frequent use of the *I Ching* ('Book of Changes'), a text dating back to the Zhou dynasty (1100–400 BCE) that divines the right course of action to take based on randomly constructed hexagrams.[95] This plot device is also the central plotting device: both the intra-diegetic author Hawthorne Abendsen and Philip K. Dick himself use the *I Ching* to construct their fictions. As the latter reported in an interview, the divination tool 'governed the direction of the book': 'I threw the coins and wrote the hexagram lines they [the characters] got [. . .] If it had said [to the character Juliana] not to tell him [Abendsen of the assassination plot], I would have had her not go there.'[96] While Abendsen is reluctant to reveal his 'technical secrets' – whether 'it's genuine underneath [. . .] or done with wires and staves and foam-rubber padding' – his wife Caroline reveals that 'One by one Hawth made the choices [. . .] By means of the lines. Historic period. Subject. Characters. Plot. It took years. Hawth even asked the oracle what sort of success it would be.'[97] The combination of contingency, choice and oracular knowledge in Dick's self-reflexive fiction seems to emphasise an attentiveness to *what is possible when*, based on both synchronic networks of connection and diachronic chains. Frank Frink, the Jewish American master forger whose counterfeiting and concealment from the Nazis are at the centre of the novel's focus on the production of historicity, understands his use of the *I Ching* as a discernment of 'the tenor of the Moment' (21), a consultation of hexagrams that are

> Random, and yet rooted in the moment [. . .] in which his life was bound up with all other lives and particles in the universe [. . .] all connected in this moment of casting the yarrow stalks to select the exact wisdom appropriate in a book begun in the thirtieth century B.C. (19)

In this first appearance of the *I Ching*, Frink's exaggerated sense of its age aligns nicely with the novel's emphasis on the illegibility of the present as a simultaneity of distant events whose effects might be causally entangled, because media such as the ancient text both signify this enigmatic simultaneity and allow the text to construct it via cross-cutting. Indeed, the text shifts to Tagomi for the first time by means of the book, which Tagomi turns out to be using at the same time that Frink is wondering 'who else in the vast complicated city of San Francisco was at this same moment consulting the oracle' (21). Later, when Frink is again using the *I Ching* and ruminating on what small events might set the Third World War in motion, he articulates the thematic significance and narrative purpose of the divination device: 'It's the fault of those physicists and that synchronicity theory, every particle being connected with every other; you can't fart without changing the balance in the universe' (55). Like the telephone that Gunning argues drops into the diegesis in order to justify cinematic constructions of simultaneous actions, the *I Ching* is a medium that functions to bring characters into the same moment in a text that is raising the question about the nature of moments and of history itself.

Indeed, in *The Man in the High Castle*, Dick connects what the oracle does and means to media as such. Like the *I Ching*, various media conduits allow us to date the novel's multiple strands of action to a particular time. The momentous synchronising event in the novel is the death of Chancellor Martin Bormann and the transfer of power to Herr J. Goebbels, a figure who signifies for the reader the fascist command of mass media. The radio delivers the

Denver announcer's 'news of Chancellor Bormann's death' to Juliana in Canon City, Colorado (86). Simultaneously, in the next section, Nobusuke hears his assistant Mr Ramsey over his intercom's tiny speaker: 'Sir, news has just come from the press service below. The Reichs Chancellor is dead' (92). Juliana, after seeing an article in *Life* magazine entitled 'Television in Europe: Glimpse of Tomorrow', thinks of the rise of TV as a spreading German phenomenon and imagines 'what it's like to sit at home in your living room and see the whole world on a little grey glass tube' (77–8). Media link the characters chronologically and represent the achievement of synchronicity as an effect of Nazi and imperial control that delivers a specific future as much as a unified present, both historicist linearity and global synchrony.

This emphasis on the network of connected particles in and *as* the now gives rise to the fascination around causality that is thematised by the novel, and leads characters to wonder which element they should press on in 'the balance in the universe'. According to Rudolf Wegener, the German intelligence officer disguised as Mr Baynes who has travelled to the Pacific States of America to prevent a nuclear attack on the Japanese, the Nazis' 'sense of space and time' – which looks past the particles of 'the here, the now, into the vast black deep beyond', so as to be 'the agents, not the victims, of history' (45) – should be contrasted with the tactical and ethical imperative to 'be small' (46). Likewise, when Frank Frink thinks 'I'm too small' in relation to the course of history, he wonders, 'Can *anyone* alter it? [. . .] All of us combined [. . .] or one great figure [. . .] or someone strategically placed, who happens to be in the right spot. Chance. Accident. And our lives, our world, hanging on it' (55). Tagomi, who does happen to be in the right place to kill the assassins sent to murder Wegener and General Tedeki, believes that his terrible historical agency (the taking of human lives to defend those who would disrupt the Nazi plan of attack) can be neutralised by a retreat into 'living day to day': 'I will go and find the small. Live unseen at any rate' (213). Paul Mountfort points out that the novel pits the synchronic view of time and history against linear causality, building a contrast between '[d]iachronic causality, the single string of causes, the billiard ball theory of change', on the one hand, and an 'immense synchronic interrelationship, as a web of overdetermination', on the other.[98] In Hilary Dannenberg's study *Coincidence and Counterfactuality*, this opposition is the difference between '*mono-* versus *multicausality*', between a simple chain in which 'one antecedent leads to an outcome' and a much more opaque set of 'chaotic causal networks' in which 'perceivable causal-progenerative paths dissolve and are replaced by the interference of complex networks of causal interaction, which are inscrutable to the human mind'.[99]

It is true that the novel courts this tension between the large-scale vision of history embodied by the Nazis' technological progress and domination, and the small-scale interactions of everyday life whose synchronic butterfly effects are the illegible origins of major diachronic shifts in world history. Robert Childan, the antiques dealer who despises his rich Japanese clients' 'mania for the trivial' and for cultural artefacts such as legal documents, Mickey Mouse watches or 'authentic American folk jazz' (110), admires the German 'dream' articulated as a clear techno-historical sequence: 'It's the dream that stirs one. Space flights first to the moon, then to Mars' (30). For Childan, Nazi progress on the unilinear historical track is also the primitivist premise realised as a military outcome: 'the Slavs had been rolled back two thousand years' worth, to their heartland in Asia [. . .] Back to riding yaks and hunting with bow and arrow [. . .] All a thing of the past' (29). By contrast, characters such as Wegener wonder whether a missed appointment at a rendezvous point 'may start a chain reaction' (163). In this opposition, the large marches forward with violent inexorability, whereas the small, by accident, might alter a world, like Frink's little piece of jewellery or artwork. And the drama built around the authenticity or fakeness of objects and identities draws its energy from the characters' confusion, both comic and dangerous, about the provenance of things and of change.

However, the novel's interest in alternate historicity is not just about finding the right, authentic, original moment to alter history's path, but also about learning to think about history differently. This altered conception of history in *The Man in the High Castle*, as in *Interstellar* and *Mrs Dalloway*, is produced by the de-synchronisation built into its structure. As in Woolf's text, critics have discovered temporal discrepancies in Dick's novel that are seen to resonate with the 'fraudulent sense of time' embodied by the counterfeit antiques that Childan is unknowingly selling.[100] But the most important discrepancy for my purposes is not simply about inauthenticity but about timelines. While Dick's text appears to use parallel edits to bring together a number of simultaneous distant actions, in fact cross-cutting reveals two major plotlines that fall out of sync, such that the scene that ends the novel is actually chronologically prior to the climactic shoot-out in Tagomi's office by around two weeks. I will return to this divergence of plotlines in the text and the significance of their non-synchronicity in relation to counterfactual possibilities, but there is more to say about the novel's conception of history and the historicity of objects in its lead-up to the structural manifestation of this thematic interest in (the historical position of) being outside the stream of history.

One can approach Dick's redefinition of historicity by juxtaposing a passage in his novel on the state of history with one from the philosopher Michel Serres. In one of his conversations with Bruno Latour – the one in which he provides his famous figure of time as a crumpled handkerchief where two distant points can become 'suddenly close, even superimposed', and 'two points that were close can become very distant' – Serres provides an example of the heterochronic nature of history that is very similar to Bloch's diagnosis of the 'non-simultaneity' that gave a foothold to fascism in the 1930s: 'everyone is amazed that after 1935 the Nazis, in the most scientifically and culturally advanced country, adopted the most archaic behavior. But we are always simultaneously making gestures that are archaic, modern, and futuristic.' As he explains, 'every historical era is likewise multitemporal, simultaneously drawing from the obsolete, the contemporary, and the futuristic. An object, a circumstance, is thus polychronic, multitemporal, and reveals a time that is gathered together, with multiple pleats.'[101] Similarly, in reflecting on what for both character and reader is an unexpected turn in history, Frink thinks about the horror of the Nazi liquidation of Africa, '[t]hat huge empty ruin':

> Wiped out to make a land of – what? [. . .] Maybe even the master architects in Berlin did not know. Bunch of automatons, building and toiling away [. . .] Ogres out of a paleontology exhibit, at their task of making a cup from an enemy's skull, then the whole family industriously scooping out the contents [. . .] Then useful utensils of men's leg bones [. . .] The first technicians! Prehistoric man in a sterile white lab coat in some Berlin university lab [. . .] A new use for the big toe; see, one can adapt the joint for a quick-acting cigarette lighter mechanism. (17)

In both instances, neither history itself nor the objects that seem to lie inertly 'in' it are identifiable as pure markers of a single moment or stage in history. Frink's example of the lighter resembles Serres's analysis of a 'late-model car', whose contemporaneity is an aura or smokescreen hiding its construction as 'a disparate aggregate of scientific and technical solutions dating from different periods': 'this part was invented at the turn of the century, another, ten years ago, and Carnot's cycle is almost two hundred years old [. . .] [T]he wheel dates back to neolithic times.'[102]

As the novel's attention moves from the figure of the lighter to the art object, its emphasis shifts from fake historicity to alternate historicity, and as a result, the primary critical task flips from seeing through falsehoods to authentic historical conditions, to discerning the outsides of timelines amid a cluster of many times. However, the figure of the lighter, as a multi-temporal technological advance whose folds include the bones of the enemy, at first snaps into alignment with the novel's presentation of the 'whole damn historicity business' (65), introduced by Wyndam-Matson, the owner of the factory that supplies 'forgeries of pre-war American artifacts' to the antiques market (51). Wyndam-Matson explains to his evening visitor Rita that no object actually 'has history in it', that it is impossible to distinguish a cheap Zippo lighter from one that was in Franklin D. Roosevelt's pocket when he was assassinated (66). The aura of history, as he says, is 'in the mind', not the object; historicity, as his business bears out, is produced by 'some sort of document. A paper of authenticity' (66). The mention of FDR locates the significance of the lighter close to the nexus point of this alternate history's generic 'great-manism', since it is his assassination in the world of *The Man in the High Castle* that leads to the Allies' defeat in the Second World War. In *The Grasshopper Lies Heavy*, the alternate history within the novel, FDR is likewise linked to historical divergence, in this case, as Rita reports, to a second-order hypothetical in which 'Germany and Japan would have lost the war' (69).

Like the forged but fully functional Colt .44 with which Tagomi defends the lives of Wegener and Tedeki (possibly preventing the Nazis' nuclear Operation Dandelion), the Zippo lighter sparks a multifaceted anxiety that historicity is a fabrication, but also that historicity is the implacable subtext underwriting the value of a world, its contents and whatever slim possibilities for different worlds exist within it. Frink's Civil War knock-offs and Wyndam-Matson's specimens of falsified time-space coordinates provoke historiographic demystifications akin, as Childan puts it, 'to primal childhood awakening; facts of life' (141), while simultaneously operating to uphold and potentially alter the novel's alternate-historical timeline. These utopian functions would seem to suggest that objects with a hidden, manufactured history or no historicity, like the key 'small' characters and people in the Rocky Mountain States whom Joe Cinadella describes as '[o]ut of the stream of events, left over from the past' (89), trump artefacts and identities validated by official history, no less manufactured. But it is not so much the demystification or evacuation of historicity that produces alternate-historical possibilities and heterochronic conceptions of time, but the reconfiguration of it in the novel's treatment of art objects that are themselves thereby redefined.

Frink's career change from forging old artefacts to creating contemporary art objects might not at first glance suggest Serres's non-synchronous assemblages but rather a kind of pure presentness emptied of the past and its various contests and contrivances of legitimation. Paul Kasoura, the wealthy young Japanese collector with a critical historical sense, finds Frink's silver 'little blob' lacking in historic value, but later attributes this vacuum of historicity to the object's enrapturing 'wu', the Chinese concept of thingness in which, as one critic defines it, 'things work out their destinies in accord with their intrinsic principles'.[103] Kasoura describes the artefactuality of Frink's jewellery to Childan by way of a contrast with pastness:

> I recall a shrine in Hiroshima wherein a shinbone of some medieval saint could be examined. However, this is an artifact and that was a relic. This is alive in the now, whereas that merely *remained* [. . .] I have come to identify the value which this has in opposition to historicity. I am deeply moved, as you may see. (171)

And Frink's pin, which Tagomi purchases from Childan after returning the now eventful Colt .44, seems to be the gateway to historical alternativity: having killed two German agents in his office, Tagomi tries to calm himself by meditating and sensuously experiencing the 'small silver triangle', which opens up a completely foreign universe in which everything is reversed or upside-down. In this alternate universe, Tagomi's familiar Chinese pedecabs are replaced by cars big and 'unfamiliar in shape' (223), Americans of European descent do not yield to Japanese people in cafés, and a 'hideous misshapen thing on the skyline' is revealed to be the Embarcadero Freeway (a structure that existed in Dick's San Francisco, twenty-seven years before the Loma Prieta earthquake). 'Where am I?' asks Tagomi. 'Out of my world, my space and time [. . .] I broke from my moorings and hence stand on nothing' (224).

While Dick is clearly asking us to imagine this alternate-alternate world as our own (and as the seemingly opposite universe of the diegesis), he has already constructed a major obstacle to a simple dialectical flip. Not only does *The Grasshopper Lies Heavy* not quite match our own history's set of events, but *The Man in the High Castle*'s treatment of alternate-historical things offers us a conception of the new, quite different from that of novel's characters, that resonates with its de-synchronising form. With respect to the historical coordinates of the book's objects, we might think of Dick's challenge in terms of a question that the anthropologist Christopher Pinney poses in 'Things Happen: Or, From Which Moment Does That Object Come?': 'what if, instead of assuming that objects and culture are sutured together in national time-space, we start looking for all those objects and images whose evidence appears to be "deceptive" and whose time does not appear to be "our" time?'[104] Pinney wants material culture studies 'to envisage images and objects as densely compressed performances unfolding in unpredictable ways', rather than reading them as presences on a timeline, and he wants us to consider that these performances may not be fully contemporary with other cultural phenomena that appear in the same epoch.[105] His epigraph quotes Siegfried Kracauer's *History: The Last Things before the Last*: 'The overstuffed interiors of the second half of the nineteenth century belonged to the same epoch as the thoughts born in them and yet were not their contemporaries.'[106] But the key point is not just that the contingent appearance of non-contemporaneous phenomena occupy the same moment, which the historiographic pressure to represent '*the* social' and '*the* times' oversimplifies or erases, but that history itself comprises 'a series of cataracts, each pursuing their own uncontemporaneousness in incoherent trajectories'.[107] The cross-sectioning necessary to give us a picture of cultural context at a moment of the calendar necessarily reduces the irregular striations or cataracts to homogeneous instants placed on an even, smooth transverse plane, and the sequence of transverse cuts of the socially contemporaneous becomes history in the singular, rather than the thick bundle of uneven and internally different strands.

Thus, the more interesting opposing term to the 'whole damn historicity business' is not the orientalist purity of an empty presentness that leads to a radical break, but rather the non-synchronous currents running through a cross-sectioned now that can no longer be seen as singular, or whose is singularity is merely provisional, a relation constructed between two or more frames of reference. Frink's pins are 'tiny imperishable seeds [. . .] the contracted germ of the future' (217), not because as Kasoura concludes 'an entire new world is pointed to, by this' (171), but because they provoke Tagomi's insight into the nature of historicity, which Juliana also experiences. Both characters are thus able to travel to the edges of their reference frames and to a new sense of potentiality born of differential timelines that are already in process. If, as Dannenberg says, the immersiveness created by coincidence plots serves narrativity and produces the quality of how tellable a story is, then both of Dick's characters, by contrast, push themselves and readers outwards, modifying the dream of the outsides of various historical and political rhythms typical of this genre, its out-of-time-ness, and turning it into a query about the constitution and duration of different collective timelines. Dick's self-referential ending about the conditions of narrativity of *The Grasshopper Lies Heavy* places the narrativity of *The Man in the High Castle* not only on non-converging life plots that Dannenberg sees as characteristic of counterfactual and postmodern multiple-world fictions, but on divergent reference frames or timelines whose differential temporal consistency determines the shape of those worlds and fictions. In this situation, the possibility of an alternative or the new is a matter of relations between times – intersection, slowing, accelerating or bending certain arcs towards other outcomes.[108] Tagomi's flip into an alternate history, mentioned above, is the one that spectacularly confirms the genre's premise that history can fork otherwise. But it is Juliana's parallel plotline, in comparison, that yields the most important insight into an alternative conception of the present as multiple de-synchronised lines.

From the beginning, the text certainly encourages us to synchronise Juliana's buffer-zone timeline in the RMS and the PSA sequence of events, with which it is formally intertwined. Her journey parallels Tagomi's: in John Rieder's summary, 'both Tagomi and Juliana find their everyday existence disrupted by the entrance into it of disguised Germans, and the result, for each of them is the eruption of a moment of extraordinary violence'.[109] In chapter 12, Tagomi shoots the men whom Herr Reiss sends to assassinate Wegner and Tedeki; in chapter 13, Juliana kills 'Joe Cinnadella' when she discovers he is an SD agent sent to murder Abendsen. Like Tagomi, Juliana has a strange historiographic-metafictional moment, but one that is more critically heterochronic. Before arriving in Cheyenne, Wyoming, she reads a passage from *The Grasshopper Lies Heavy* in which Abendsen envisions a USA where 'the colour problem had by 1950 been solved. Whites and Negroes lived and worked and ate shoulder by shoulder, even in the deep South; World War Two had ended discrimination' (156) – we begin to see that the significance of Abendsen's utopian yearning is not a matter of an unrealistic radical break. Tagomi flips not into a perfect world but into one of *our* racist post-war diners. Alternate historicity is rather a matter of beholding different trajectories in objects and worlds, and of navigating and engaging non-contemporaneous currents with various futures that have never disappeared. In the 'high castle', which turns out to be a 'single-storey stucco house' (240), after learning that *The Grasshopper Lies Heavy* was constructed by the *I Ching*, Juliana says to a comically fatalistic Abendsen, 'you showed that there's a way out' (244). But instead of a postmodern ending with a character exiting the constraints of her own fiction, the novel concludes with Juliana 'retracing her steps back down the flagstone path [. . .] onto the black sidewalk' (248) and 'searching up and down the streets for a cab or a car' (249), a scene that is totally out of sync with the previous crescendo of world-historical intrigue.

This de-synchronisation is not merely at the level of content: Juliana's serendipitous intervention in the plot to kill 'the man in the high castle', and her meeting with Hawthorne Abendsen that concludes the novel, actually take place well *before* Tagomi's climactic pre-emptive killing of the *Sicherheitsdienst* assassins and his momentary glimpse into another world. Her out-of-sync plotline is described explicitly (by Joe) as outside the stream of history – in the buffer zone, the Rocky Mountain States. In chapter 9, the careful cross-cutting that has established simultaneity between distant actions opens up a two-week gap between Tagomi's, Frink's and Childan's events in the PSA, and Juliana's plotline in the RMS, which appears to run without interruption for four consecutive days. Campbell describes this parallel, initially all synchronised to Chancellor Bormann's death, as a set of 'atemporally juxtaposed narrative lines': Frink appears 'after two weeks of nearly constant work' (129), Childan has been inspecting his compromised merchandise for a 'couple of weeks' (140), and Tagomi and Baynes have had a strangely longer 'terrible two weeks' (147) of seventeen daily calls to the Trade Mission in anticipation of the meeting with General Tedeki disguised as Mr Yatabe. Meanwhile, Juliana goes fairly directly, without ellipsis, from Canon City to Denver, and finally to Abendsen's house in Cheyenne, Wyoming.[110] Conspicuously lacking the two-week gap, Juliana's compressed plotline arrives at the metafictional moment in which we watch her discover the edge of a fiction as the limitation of one strand of history – its specific shape, pace and duration – in relation to other strands. The significance for the reader is related to Paul Kasoura's identification earlier in the novel of a 'form of fiction possible within the genre of science fiction', namely the 'alternate present' (109). In this fiction, our conception of 'the' present is altered by a strange sense of alternativity.

Campbell's takeaway from the novel's exploration of 'Dickian time' appears uncontroversial: Dick's 'alternate view of time' foregrounds the idea that 'both linear and synchronistic times exist and are accepted within the narrative' – both the billiard-ball and butterfly-effect versions of temporal sequence.[111] Paul Saint-Amour's more provocative interpretation is that, while counterfactual fiction appears to be premised on the idea that 'history proceeds via moments of extreme, often traumatic discontinuity', texts such as *The Man in the High Castle* express a longing for the more butterflyish continuity of the welfare state by 'replac[ing] it, or threaten[ing] to replace it, with a fascist warfare state'.[112] Such novels, by subtracting FDR and New Deal programmes, counterpose 'the fascist state's predestinarian historiography [that] cannot admit of alternate outcomes' to a more desirable, contingency-sensitive counterfactualism. Saint-Amour's reading of Tagomi's trip to a world marked by 'an altered civil infrastructure' and the absence of certain public works is that it attempts to spark a longing 'to remediate historical wrongs and thus to bend one timeline in the direction of another', yet also blocks it by making racial segregation 'an unavoidable part of the longed-for homeworld'.[113]

To Campbell's and Saint-Amour's accounts I would add that the option the novel offers is not just an either/or between the counterfactual contingency of a world otherwise and the actual world as it could not have otherwise become. This is the primary opposition that Russell West-Pavlov writes is at stake in postmodern and postcolonial critiques of 'the temporal logic underlying modern historiography', and which is called into question by 'alternative or virtual or "counterfactual" histories'.[114] However, Dick's novel poses the otherwiseness of history as a matter of the forms, shapes and constitution of history that in some instances are marked by the problem of contingency/necessity, but just as often are defined by plural strands of history and their degrees of intersection/overlap, our desire for reparative bending, or the fact of indifferent paralleling. If the effect of the racist diner's familiarity is that the novel invites us to return affectively to this homeworld, it is also true that we recognise the diner scenario because it has not disappeared. It continues and has been awaiting a new emphasis and visibility in a sequence marked by the return of Nazis to the public sphere. As the process of cross-cutting and its effect of simultaneity give way to the effect of their heterochronic relations and the divergence, convergence and paralleling of lines, counterfactual possibilities must be reconfigured for an alternate temporal operating system. They are not simply the next moment as it breaks with the previous one, but the qualities of the next heterogeneous plane cutting across a number of chains or sequences.

Jane Bennett and William Connolly illuminate Serres's model of heterochronic assemblage by underlining its 'logic of could happen'. While Serres's conception of a polychronic, multi-temporal history has provoked objections that, in Latour's succinct paraphrasing, 'your history is not historicist' and 'one has the impression that you have a time machine', Bennett and Connolly point to an earlier formulation by Serres that figures how historical causation is not undone by complicating the rigid onto-temporal negations of the advancing clock: 'A seed-corn dies, and it dies. The seed-corn dies, and it sprouts. It sprouts and it is meager [. . .] It sprouts and it multiplies, exponentially, it overruns the place.'[115] In his conversation with Latour, Serres points out the not-historicist, alternate-historicist simultaneity of the non-simultaneous in which it appears that time is the friend of all manner of excluded middles, often making 'co-possible two contradictory things'.[116] He makes this point via a grimly comic anecdote of accidental relativity: 'some brothers, in their seventies, were grouped around their father for a funeral vigil, weeping for a dead man aged thirty or less', for the slow movements of a glacier had revealed their father, who had disappeared a half-century earlier in the mountains, 'perfectly conserved, youthful, from the depths of the cold. His children, having grown old, prepare to bury a body that is still young.'[117] Art and philosophy, he goes on to suggest, are likewise time machines, not just because they have the ability to conserve, but because they produce and reveal anachronisms. While I have avoided the vocabulary of flux in order to navigate around things flowing together in modernist-Bergsonian discourse and the erosion of collective temporal sovereignties, Serres's use of hydrodynamic concepts – surges, fluctuations, bifurcations, rhythms, turbulence and temporary stabilisations – is part of a time-machinic mode that allows us to draw new insights from twentieth-century streams of time, narration and consciousness.[118] As Serres says to Latour, 'time doesn't flow; it percolates [. . .] [I]t passes and doesn't pass [. . .] [I]n a filter one flux passes through, while another does not.'[119] From the chaos of these contingencies and irregularities of ubiquitous noise, possibilities and alternatives emerge and do not emerge in strains that connect, mix, de-synchronise and never touch.

NOTES

1. Fredric Jameson, *A Singular Modernity: Essay on the Ontology of the Present* (London: Verso, 2002), 141, 142.
2. Fredric Jameson, *Postmodernism, Or, The Cultural Logic of Late Capitalism* (Durham, NC: Duke University Press, 1991), 307. It is worth pointing out that these coexistent realities are not just objects or sites but also disjunctively constellated affects, as Jameson goes on to analyse Kafka's 'Trial' in terms of the simultaneous 'pleasurability' and 'nightmares' (308–9).
3. Ibid. 310.
4. The idea appears first in Fredric Jameson, *The Seeds of Time* (New York: Columbia University Press, 1994), xii, and then in 'Future City', *New Left Review* 21 (May/June 2003), 76. For a quick history of this idea, see Matthew Beaumont, 'Imagining the End Times: Ideology, the Contemporary Disaster Movie, Contagion', in *Žižek and Media Studies*, ed. Matthew Flisfeder and Louis-Paul Willis (Basingstoke:

Palgrave Macmillan, 2014), 79–89. The 'someone' who Jameson doesn't remember is H. Bruce Franklin, who claimed that J. G. Ballard 'magnificently projects the doomed social structure in which he exists' – but, Franklin continues, 'What could Ballard create if he were able to envision the end of capitalism as not the end, but the beginning, of a human world?' H. Bruce Franklin, 'What Are We to Make of J.G. Ballard's Apocalypse?', in *Voices for the Future: Essays on Major Science Fiction Writers*, ed. Thomas D. Clareson (Bowling Green, OH: Popular Press, 1979), 105.

5. Jameson, *Singular Modernity*, 94. A Duke University Press editor explained in a voicemail to Scott McLemee that 'post-contemporary' means to 'place the present within a historical narrative, while recognizing that the contemporary is always already disappearing'. Scott McLemee in 'Jameson and Son', *Lingua Franca* 5.5 (1995): 11.

6. Neil Smith, *Uneven Development: Nature, Capital, and the Production of Space*, 3rd edn (Athens: University of Georgia Press, 2008), 241, 266.

7. Ibid. 223.

8. Ibid. 233.

9. Ibid. 254.

10. Rifkin, *Beyond Settler Time*, viii, 9, x.

11. Ibid. 15.

12. Christopher Nolan, *Interstellar*, DVD (Warner Home Video, 2014).

13. See Mary Ann Doane, *The Emergence of Cinematic Time: Modernity, Contingency, the Archive* (Cambridge, MA: Harvard University Press, 2002), ch. 6, 'Zeno's Paradox: The Emergence of Cinematic Time', 172–205.

14. Nolan invited CalTech theoretical physicist Kip Thorne to serve as an executive producer in order to ensure accurate visualisations of the astrophysical and science fictional. See Thorne's tie-in book *The Science of Interstellar* (New York: W. W. Norton, 2014).

15. Ibid. 163.

16. The first film to feature this effect was in fact Porter's 1903 *The Great Train Robbery*. For an account of how Porter's *Fireman* does not deserve this distinction, see Charles Musser, *Before the Nickelodeon: Edwin S. Porter and the Edison Manufacturing Company* (Berkeley: University of California Press, 1991), 'A Close Look at *Life of an American Fireman*', 212–34.

17. Vivian Sobchack, 'Time Passages', *Film Comment* 50.6 (2014): 22.

18. Ibid. 24.

19. See Raymond Bellour, 'To Alternate/To Narrate', in *Early Cinema: Space, Frame, Narrative*, ed. Thomas Elsaesser and Adam Barker (London: British Film Institute, 1990), 360–74, as well as Mary Ann Doane's brief discussion of this alternation in *Emergence of Cinematic Time*, 196.

20. Doane, *Emergence of Cinematic Time*, 196.

21. Peter Osborne, 'Out of Sync: Tomba's Marx and the Problem of a Multi-Layered Temporal Dialectic', *Historical Materialism* 23.4 (2015): 45.

22. Phillip E. Wegner, 'Learning to Live in History: Alternate Historicities and the 1990s in *The Years of Rice and Salt*', in *Kim Stanley Robinson Maps the Unimaginable:*

Critical Essays, ed. William J. Burling (Jefferson, NC: McFarland, 2009), 98; Phillip E. Wegner, *Life between Two Deaths, 1989–2001: U. S. Culture in the Long Nineties* (Durham, NC: Duke University Press, 2009), 101.

23. Michael Löwy, *Fire Alarm: Reading Walter Benjamin on the Concept of History*, trans. Chris Turner (London: Verso, 2005), 115, quoted in Wegner, *Life between Two Deaths*, 100.

24. Osborne, 'Out of Sync', 46; original emphasis. The object of Osborne's critique is Massimiliano Tomba's book *Marx's Temporalities* (Chicago: Haymarket Books, 2013) and the earlier model of temporal plurality in Ernst Bloch's multiversum, both of which seem to create, in Osborne's words, 'an aporia of the temporal position of the political agent' (21).

25. Tomba, *Marx's Temporalities*, xiv.

26. Sobchack, 'Time Passages', 24.

27. For the restoration of the original section breaks and other elements in the British editions of the novel, see the new Cambridge critical edition, Virginia Woolf, *Mrs Dalloway*, ed. Anne E. Fernald (Cambridge: Cambridge University Press, 2014). While I like the way that the number of original sections evokes more strongly the earlier project title 'The Hours' (but without directly corresponding to the diegetic hours), my reading is not dependent on it or on any of the variants. So for my purposes here, I have used the Harcourt edition with the supplementary apparatus: Virginia Woolf, *The Mrs. Dalloway Reader* (Orlando: Harcourt, 2003). Subsequent page references are given in parentheses in the text.

28. Makiko Minow-Pinkney, *Virginia Woolf and the Problem of the Subject* (New Brunswick, NJ: Rutgers University Press, 1987), 82.

29. Elizabeth Abel, 'Narrative Structure(s) and Female Development: The Case of *Mrs. Dalloway*', in *Virginia Woolf*, ed. Rachel Bowlby (London: Routledge, 2013 [1992]), 80.

30. David Daiches, *Virginia Woolf* (Norfolk, CT: New Directions, 1942), 53, 62; J. Hillis Miller, 'Repetition as the Raising of the Dead', in *Fiction and Repetition: Seven English Novels* (Cambridge, MA: Harvard University Press, 1982), 177.

31. Bergson, *Time and Free Will*, 86–7.

32. Ibid. 86.

33. Whitworth, *Einstein's Wake*, 191.

34. Ibid. 185–6.

35. Andelys Wood, 'Walking the Web in the Lost London of *Mrs. Dalloway*', *Mosaic: An Interdisciplinary Critical Journal* 36.2 (2003): 19.

36. Ibid. 23.

37. Ibid. 19.

38. Ibid. 19, 25, 28.

39. Ronald G. Walker, 'Leaden Circles Dissolving in Air: Narrative Rhythm and Meaning in *Mrs. Dalloway*', *Essays in Literature* 13.1 (1986): 60.

40. Ibid. 62–3.

41. Ibid. 78.

42. Ibid.

43. Victoria Rosner, '"Life Struck Straight through the Streets": *Mrs. Dalloway* as City Novel', in *Approaches to Teaching Woolf's Mrs. Dalloway*, ed. Eileen Barrett and Ruth O. Saxton (New York: Modern Language Association of America, 2009), 39.

44. Woolf, *Diary, Vol. 2*, 323.

45. Ibid. 207.

46. Whitworth, *Einstein's Wake*, 186.

47. Ibid. 187.

48. Ibid.; Frank, 'Spatial Form in Modern Literature', 59, 10.

49. Eugene Lunn, *Marxism and Modernism: An Historical Study of Lukács, Brecht, Benjamin, and Adorno* (Berkeley: University of California Press, 1984), 35.

50. Whitworth, *Einstein's Wake*, 189; Frank, 'Spatial Form in Modern Literature', 59.

51. Arthur I. Miller, *Albert Einstein's Special Theory of Relativity: Emergence (1905) and Early Interpretation (1905–1911)* (New York: Springer, 1997), 371.

52. Adam Frank, *About Time: Cosmology and Culture at the Twilight of the Big Bang* (New York: Simon and Schuster, 2011), 134.

53. Galison, *Einstein's Clocks and Poincaré's Maps*, 19; Frank, *About Time*, 125.

54. Galison, *Einstein's Clocks and Poincaré's Maps*, 306.

55. Frank, *About Time*, 134.

56. Paul Tolliver Brown, 'The Spatiotemporal Topography of Virginia Woolf's *Mrs. Dalloway*: Capturing Britain's Transition to a Relative Modernity', *Journal of Modern Literature* 38.4 (2015): 25. In his essay 'Clarissa's Invisible Taxi', John Sutherland writes, 'How did Clarissa get back from upper Bond Street so quickly? [. . .] The solution [. . .] is blindingly obvious. She took a taxi [. . .] For "upper-middle-class ladies" in 1923 to take a mile's walk to the florist's to save a servant's legs was unusual to the point of eccentricity.' John Sutherland, *Can Jane Eyre Be Happy? More Puzzles in Classic Fiction* (London: Icon, 2017 [1997]), 222–3. Andelys Wood says, 'Peter, a man of fifty-something, has covered more than two miles in less than fifteen minutes: no wonder he needs a nap.' She says of Richard's under-examined walk, 'No matter how "eager" Richard is to go "straight" to his wife, he doesn't have time to buy flowers and still arrive in Dean's Yard as Big Ben begins to strike 3:00' ('Walking the Web', 21, 24–5).

57. Brown, 'Spatiotemporal Topography', 25.

58. Ibid.

59. Ibid. 27, 32.

60. Jennie-Rebecca Falcetta, 'Geometries of Space and Time: The Cubist London of *Mrs. Dalloway*', *Woolf Studies Annual* 13 (2007): 125.

61. Ibid. 114.

62. Steiner, *Colors of Rhetoric*, 191; quoted in Falcetta, 'Geometries of Space and Time', 127.

63. Virginia Woolf, *Orlando: A Biography (Annotated)*, ed. Maria DiBattista (Orlando: Harvest, 2006), 223; Julia Briggs, *Reading Virginia Woolf* (Edinburgh: Edinburgh University Press, 2006), 134.

64. Falcetta, 'Geometries of Space and Time', 115; Woolf, *Orlando*, 230.

65. Leena Kore Schroder, '"Reflections in a Motor Car": Virginia Woolf's Phenomenological Relations of Time and Space', in *Locating Woolf: The Politics of Space and*

Place, ed. Anna Snaith and Michael Whitworth (New York: Palgrave Macmillan, 2007), 138.

66. See the introduction to Anna Snaith and Michael Whitworth (eds), *Locating Woolf: The Politics of Space and Place* (New York: Palgrave Macmillan, 2007).

67. Doreen Massey, *For Space* (London: Sage, 2005), 24.

68. Virginia Woolf, *Moments of Being*, ed. Jean Schulkind (New York: Harcourt, 1985), 147.

69. Woolf, *Diary, Vol. 2*, 248, 207.

70. Elizabeth Clea Lamont, 'Moving Tropes: New Modernist Travels with Virginia Woolf', *Alif: Journal of Comparative Poetics* 21 (2001): 173. As Paul Saint-Amour writes, 'Much work on the novel during the last two decades has focused on a stereopair different from "the sane & the insane": that of the civilian and the soldier'; Paul K. Saint-Amour, 'Air War Prophecy and Interwar Modernism', *Comparative Literature Studies* 42.2 (2005): 130–61. Saint-Amour's article gives an excellent account of recent scholarship on the stereopair.

71. Alex Zwerdling, *Virginia Woolf and the Real World* (Berkeley: University of California Press, 1986), 129.

72. Ibid. 119.

73. Christine Froula, 'Mrs. Dalloway's Postwar Elegy: Women, War, and the Art of Mourning', *Modernism/Modernity* 9.1 (2002): 139.

74. John Maynard Keynes, *The Economic Consequences of the Peace* (London: Macmillan, 1920), 225, quoted in Froula, 'Mrs. Dalloway's Postwar Elegy', 140.

75. Robert Skidelsky, *John Maynard Keynes: Hopes Betrayed, 1883–1920* (London: Macmillan, 1983), 399. See Froula's discussion, 'Mrs. Dalloway's Postwar Elegy', 139–44.

76. Kate Haffey, 'Exquisite Moments and the Temporality of the Kiss in *Mrs. Dalloway* and *The Hours*', *Narrative* 18.2 (2010): 138, 144, 145.

77. Ibid. 149.

78. Ibid. 159.

79. Susan Merrill Squier, *Virginia Woolf and London: The Sexual Politics of the City* (Chapel Hill: University of North Carolina Press, 1985), 102.

80. Jane Marcus, *Virginia Woolf and the Languages of Patriarchy* (Bloomington: Indiana University Press, 1987), 118.

81. Tamar Katz, 'Pausing, Waiting, Repeating: Urban Temporality in *Mrs. Dalloway* and *The Years*', in *Woolf and the City*, ed. Elizabeth F. Evans and Sarah E. Cornish (Clemson, SC: Clemson University Digital Press, 2010), 3, 7, 8.

82. 'There are alternative futures', Banfield writes, 'contained in the combination of fact and viewpoint making up its accumulation of retrospect.' In her reading, Elizabeth is the 'bearer of future possibility'. Ann Banfield, *The Phantom Table: Woolf, Fry, Russell, and Epistemology of Modernism* (Cambridge: Cambridge University Press, 2000), 895.

83. See David Dowling, *Mrs. Dalloway: Mapping Streams of Consciousness* (Boston, MA: Twayne Publishers, 1991), 128.

84. Saint-Amour, 'Air War Prophecy', 117 nn. 36, 119.

85. Virginia Woolf, *To the Lighthouse* (New York: Harvest Books, 1981 [1927]), 186.

86. See Natalie Jarvey, '"The Man in the High Castle" Is Amazon's Most-Watched Original', *The Hollywood Reporter*, 21 December 2015, http://www.holly-woodreporter.com/live-feed/man-high-castle-is-amazons-850422 (last accessed 11 October 2018); and Elizabeth Wagmeister, '"The Man in the High Castle" Becomes Amazon's Most-Streamed Original Series', *Variety* (blog), 21 December 2015, http://variety.com/2015/tv/news/the-man-in-the-high-castle-amazon-ratings-viewership-1201665925/ (last accessed 11 October 2018).

87. Matthew Schneider-Mayerson, 'What Almost Was: The Politics of the Contemporary Alternate History Novel', *American Studies* 50.3 (2009): 64–5.

88. See Karen Hellekson, *The Alternate History: Refiguring Historical Time* (Kent, OH: Kent State University Press, 2001).

89. Wegner, *Life between Two Deaths*, 175.

90. Wegner, 'Learning to Live in History', 98.

91. Saint-Amour, 'Air War Prophecy'; Michael Szalay, *New Deal Modernism: American Literature and the Invention of the Welfare State* (Durham, NC: Duke University Press, 2000); Thomas S. Davis, 'Late Modernism: British Literature at Midcentury', *Literature Compass* 9.4 (2012): 328.

92. Stephen Badsey, '"If It Had Happened Otherwise": First World War Exceptionalism in Counterfactual History', in *British Popular Culture and the First World War*, ed. Jessica Meyer (Boston, MA: Brill, 2008), 360.

93. Darko Suvin, 'P.K. Dick's Opus: Artifice as Refuge and World View (Introductory Reflections)', *Science Fiction Studies* 2.1 (1975): 9, 10.

94. Kathleen Singles, *Alternate History: Playing with Contingency and Necessity* (Berlin: Walter de Gruyter, 2013), 155.

95. Paul Mountfort, 'The *I Ching* and Philip K. Dick's *The Man in the High Castle*', *Science Fiction Studies* 43.2 (2016): 287. Mountfort treats the *I Ching* as the novel's 'central plot device' and provides a good synopsis of the critical history of the *I Ching* in relation to Dick's novel.

96. Arthur Byron Cover, 'Vertex Interview with Philip K. Dick', *Vertex* 1.6 (1974), http://www.philipkdickfans.com/literary-criticism/frank-views-archive/vertex-interview-with-philip-k-dick/ (last accessed 11 October 2018).

97. Philip K. Dick, *The Man in the High Castle* (New York: Penguin Books, 2001 [1962]), 243, 245. Subsequent page references are to this edition and are given in parentheses in the text.

98. Mountfort, 'The *I Ching* and Philip K. Dick's *The Man in the High Castle*', 301. Mountfort is quoting Jameson's discussion of the locus classicus of butterfly effectuality, Ray Bradbury's 'A Sound of Thunder' (Jameson, *Archaeologies of the Future*, 89).

99. Hilary P. Dannenberg, *Coincidence and Counterfactuality: Plotting Time and Space in Narrative Fiction* (Lincoln: University of Nebraska Press, 2008), 114–15.

100. Laura E. Campbell, 'Dickian Time in *The Man in the High Castle*', *Extrapolation: A Journal of Science Fiction and Fantasy* 33.3 (1992): 193. For example, as Campbell points out, Childan has an appointment with Tagomi at 2:00 p.m., which he afterwards complains lasted for 'almost four hours in all' (50). However, *after* the store has reopened (in the evening), a disguised Frink enters his shop to

tell him that some of his antiques are fake. Childan sends his merchandise to a lab at Berkeley for testing, which impossibly calls him back at 3:00 p.m.

101. Michel Serres and Bruno Latour, *Conversations on Science, Culture, and Time*, trans. Roxanne Lapidus (Ann Arbor: University of Michigan Press, 1998), 60.
102. Ibid. 45.
103. Patricia Warrick, 'The Encounter of Taoism and Fascism in Philip K. Dick's "The Man in the High Castle"', *Science Fiction Studies* 7.2 (1980): 50, quoted in Hellekson, *Alternate History*, 70. Jianjiong Zhu contends that the novel calls not on the Taoist understanding of *wu* but on the Zen Buddhist conception in which the 'suchness of things' is an emptiness in the viewer beyond intellection. Jianjiong Zhu, 'Reality, Fiction, and Wu in *The Man in the High Castle*', in *State of the Fantastic: Studies in the Theory and Practice of Fantastic Literature and Film*, ed. Nicholas Ruddick (Westport, CT: Greenwood, 1992), 108.
104. Christopher Pinney, 'Things Happen: Or, From Which Moment Does That Object Come?', in *Materiality*, ed. Daniel Miller (Durham, NC: Duke University Press, 2005), 262–3.
105. Ibid. 269.
106. Siegfried Kracauer, *History: The Last Thing before the Last* (Princeton: Markus Wiener Publishers, 1969), 147, quoted in Pinney, 'Things Happen', 256.
107. Pinney, 'Things Happen', 264
108. See Dannenberg, *Coincidence and Counterfactuality*, 5–6.
109. John Rieder, 'The Metafictive World of *The Man in the High Castle*: Hermeneutics, Ethics, and Political Ideology', *Science Fiction Studies* 15.2 (1988): 220.
110. See Campbell, 'Dickian Time in *The Man in the High Castle*', 194, especially her helpful 'Event Chart' (199–200).
111. Ibid. 192.
112. Paul K. Saint-Amour, 'Counterfactual States of America: On Parallel Worlds and Longing for the Law', *Post-45* (blog), 20 September 2011, http://post45.research. yale.edu/2011/09/counterfactual-states-of-america-on-parallel-worlds-and-long-ing-for-the-law/ (last accessed 11 October 2018).
113. Ibid.
114. Russell West-Pavlov, *Temporalities* (London: Routledge, 2013), 74–5.
115. Serres and Latour, *Conversations on Science*, 54, 44; Michel Serres, *Genesis* (Ann Arbor: University of Michigan Press, 1995), 69, quoted in Jane Bennett and William Connolly, 'The Crumpled Handkerchief', in *Time and History in Deleuze and Serres*, ed. Bernd Herzogenrath (New York: Continuum, 2012), 157.
116. Serres and Latour, *Conversations on Science*, 49.
117. Ibid. 61.
118. See Bennett's and Connolly's reading of Serres's *Genesis* in 'The Crumpled Handkerchief', 157–8.
119. Serres and Latour, *Conversations on Science*, 58.

3

TIME LAGS AND DIFFERENTIAL PACE: BULLET TIME, WILLIAM FAULKNER AND JESSICA HAGEDORN

In Lana and Lilly Wachowski's film *The Matrix*, the protagonist Neo (Keanu Reeves) kicks off the movie's climactic sequence by setting out to rescue Morpheus (Laurence Fishburne), the man who helped Neo unplug from a simulated 1990s world that sentient machines use to pacify human brains while their bodies are farmed for bio-electric power. The year of this dystopian setting is unclear: the Resistance believes the year to be 2199, but we learn in later films that there have been multiple iterations of the Matrix, recent versions of which actually include a rebellious Zion (the refuge of unplugged humans) as a kind of pressure-release, a way of protecting the machines' power grid. Moments after Neo's famous bullet-dodging scene against faster-than-real agents, we begin to encounter deviations from actions represented at a uniform speed, whether fast, slow, or 1x: the 'Rescue of Morpheus' sequence involves speed-ramping and a variety of slow-motion speeds between and within shots. Stranger than the simple speed-up or slow-down of action, as Lisa Purse points out, characters and objects begin to move in different frames of reference within the same shot.[1] As the helicopter that Trinity (Carrie-Anne Moss) is piloting begins to crash in slow motion over him, Neo looks up in what appears to be real time and utters her name, while Tank (Marcus Chong) presumably hears 'Trinity' in a squeaky, high-frequency pitch, as he listens to the rescue operation from the ship *Nebuchadnezzar*. When the helicopter crashes, it sends ripples through the glass-and-steel grid of the office building, figuring curved, uneven and malleable timespaces. Neo looks down on the explosion in a time rendered identical to that of the audience, while the flames, debris and smoke billow out at a slower speed.

This temporal assemblage was not what the film became known for, if it was noticed at all. Rather, the buzz about the film centred on its seeming opposite: what Bob Rehak calls the 'frozen-time aesthetic' of 'bullet time', exemplified by the scene in which Neo, having grown more confident in his powers as 'the One', is able to perceive and move so quickly that he can evade the agents' bullets, while the audience is granted a similar ability to freeze the projectiles visually in mid-air and rotate around them.[2] Instead of showcasing temporal multiplicity, bullet time seemed to consolidate thereness and presence, drawing on the technique's lineage in 360-degree product viewing on online shopping websites, in the spectacularising of products in Matthew Rolston's mid-1990s' television advertisements for Gap Khakis and, more famously, Michel Gondry's commercials for Smirnoff and Polaroid. The commercial use of what was then called 'the Gondry effect' displayed the 'mastery of the frozen moment', in order to simulate the simple presence of the commodity, so that buyers could pause to rotate and re-examine the item before purchasing it, or verify its non-illusory substance like a magician waving a cane above and below an exhibit (Fig. 3.1).[3]

The technological history and critical readings of bullet time in *The Matrix* support the view that the representational technique is best understood as a 'romanticization of the pause', an 'uncanny ride from an illusion of movement to one of sculptural freeze'.[4] Certainly, the film's unveiling of the effect in the first moments of the movie, when police barge into a hotel room and shout 'Freeze!' at Trinity, suggests at the outset that both the wonder at spectacles and the analysis of actions derive from the ability to immobilise or decelerate the fleeting moment so that it remains in clear and present view. From Eadweard Muybridge's use of multiple cameras to capture a single moment from different positions in 1887, or Harold Edgerton's stroboscopic capture of high-speed events such as bullets puncturing playing cards in 1964, to Tim Macmillan's work with arrays of pinhole cameras in the early 1980s, eventually marketed as 'Timeslice' technology: the history of bullet time seems to announce its ambition to freeze time. Recent critical accounts of bullet time are similarly focused on temporal arrest: many film scholars in Wanda Strauven's 2006 collection of essays, *Cinema of Attractions Reloaded*, upload Gunning's argument about the spectacular, anti-narrative nature of early cinema – the emphasis on 'theatrical display [. . .] over narrative absorption' and 'delight [. . .] from the unpredictability of the instant' – into the new operating system of digital special effects. The accent thus falls on the intensification of 'thereness' in the new ability to freeze and encircle.[5]

However, the spectacle of bullet time and its mid-air immobilisations of a seemingly weightless world can also be seen as dilations and contractions of

Figure 3.1 Matthew Rolston's GAP khakis commercial (1998)
and Activeden's 360° product viewer

events relative to speed and scale. If 'the obfuscation of an object can be the requisite result of gaining greater access to its material components', as Bill Brown has pointed out with reference to MRIs, then in the case of bullet time, the clarifying deceleration and lightening of the object might be considered the product of access to the variable material temporalities that together constitute a present.[6] Like its older relative cubism, which rendered its objects across multiple timespace dimensions, bullet time shows presence to be an assemblage of differing times rather than a single instant solidified by differing angles. If special effects participate in an 'aesthetics of astonishment' that ruptures the linear drive of narrative, this particular attraction calls attention to the different drives, rates and timelines that narrative must always straddle and often repress. The freezing or slowing is an effect of the construction of a single, virtual motion-picture camera moving at impossibly fast speeds. John Gaeta, the visual effects supervisor for the movie, used 122 computer-triggered still cameras surrounding the actor, combined with two 1000-fps motion-capture cameras, topped off with CGI frame interpolations.[7] The super-realist excess of frames, together with compositing software (Kodak's Cineon), transforms the problem of realism's continuity of motion into a question about the variable speeds of viewing, as well as the variable rates of change among elements within shots. In bullet time, as the object's or actor's movement continues along its trajectory in 'real time', we begin to orbit in fast motion. While seeming to freeze and float, bodies are still on their way down but appear suspended relative to the acceleration of the viewer.

The different speeds and shifting pulls would seem, more than anything else, to signal the technological fantasy of transcending and manipulating time and history from without. As Purse argues, the 'film's ability to manipulate the spatial and temporal dynamics of its visual narration mirrors Neo's own developing ability to manipulate the spatial and temporal dynamics of the Matrix program'.[8] However, in addition to this fantasy of transcendence, bullet time can also suggest a variety of timelines that elapse in varying ways. Just as the unity of the virtual camera is the effect of the multiplicity of camera positions and digital frames, so too is the unity of time an amalgam of multiple histories. Gaeta claims that virtual cinematography creates a better immersion in a world's events and objects and in 'the truthfulness of the space around them', but bullet time also seems to boot us out of that seamless space by means of disjunctive discrepancies.[9] Action cinema generally 'strives to offer a theme park of attractions: music, color, story, performance, design, and the sense of improbably fast motion [. . .] to seduce the audience into surrendering to the ride', and no one would deny that this is true of the attractions in *The Matrix*.[10] But bullet time also serves immersion's opposite – an array of temporal exits that piggy-back on the film's theme of transcending simulation for a fundamental reality, but whose destination is equally an awareness of a criss-crossing of times and narratives. That is, the discrepancies between rhythms and rates of change can, of course, be contained by the dream of the One who jumps levels and departs from the clocks and physics of the Matrix, but the figure of the digitally constructed attraction in the film's formal and thematic constitution produces more than SF's usual kinetic and kaleidoscopic sublime. If the 'cinema inherits the kaleidoscopic possibilities of amusement park rides', the emergent, egressive power to see in science-fiction films often manages to tie itself to something other than a transcendent utopian location, as Scott Bukatman points out, 'less a place, a fixed site, than a trajectory' – indeed, 'a field of possible, and multiple, trajectories'.[11]

This chapter examines how H. G. Wells's time machine initiates a focus on revealing, producing and moving across multiple trajectories. I look first at Michael Wesely's record-breaking pinhole photographs from *Open Shutter* (2004) and the way in which his long exposures use the effect of blur to connect relative rates of movement to larger histories as such. I then travel back to William Faulkner's *The Sound and the Fury* (1929) in order to show how the novel is crucially concerned with racialised time lag not simply between two points on a single historical line, but between different histories that move at different rates and go their own ways. Here, the temporal aspect of double consciousness – of always living in someone else's time and yet also located in a distinctive history marked by laggy access – leads to a consideration of postcolonial treatments of time lag and the way in which historical behindness opens on to the tangle of histories that appears synecdochically in the plane of the present as heterogeneity. I turn finally to Jessica Hagedorn's *Dream Jungle* (2003), which stages the collision, overlap and differences between the story of Magellan's 'discovery' of the Philippines, the 1970s hoax of the uncontacted

'Stone Age' Tasaday people, the filming of contemporary US history in *Apocalypse Now* in Mindanao, and the long-running Moro insurgency. Each of these texts contains a bullet-time scene in which the dilation of the encounter of disjunctive rhythms reveals a heterochronic assemblage of time-paths and historical frames.

WELLSIAN BULLET TIME MELTING AND FLOWING AND MICHAEL WESELY'S PINHOLE BLURS

The view from the Time Traveller's vehicle in H. G. Wells's *The Time Machine* produces a thrilling cinematic effect in its movement through the increasingly rapid 'palpitations of night and day'.[12] As the Traveller accelerates from one second per second to 'over a year a minute' and soon 'great strides of a thousand years or more', he describes 'trees growing and changing like puffs of vapour, now brown, now green; they grew, spread, shivered, and passed away. I saw huge buildings rise up faint and fair, and pass like dreams. The whole surface of the earth seemed changed – melting and flowing' (76). The 'slowest snail that ever crawled', he says, 'dashed by too fast for me' (77). Early cinema was interested in Wells's view without fully grasping its heterochronic potential. The filmmaker Robert Paul was so taken in 1895 by the protagonist's ride to 802,701 that he applied that year for a patent to construct a time-machine simulator out of film, panoramas and dioramas.[13] Naturally, George Pal's film adaptation of Wells's novel in 1960 shows how easily the time machine's view can be equated or reduced to the production of the cinematic illusion itself: the palpitations of night and day become the flicker of the medium, and the swift elapsing of time is rendered as the time lapse of flowers blooming and dying, fruit ripening and rotting, and most self-reflexively, the sun moving repeatedly across the chronophotographic cells of the Traveller's solarium window (Fig. 3.2).

However, Wells's text is clear that visibility is a matter of rates in relation to one another, particularly the relative slowness of sense and representation. In his response to the Traveller's demonstration of the smaller model of the time machine at the first dinner party, which grew 'indistinct' like a ghost before vanishing, the Psychologist explains: 'We cannot see it, nor can we appreciate this machine, any more than we can the spoke of a wheel spinning, or a bullet flying through the air' (67). In Wells's *National Observer* text (published serially from March to June 1894), the Traveller remarks that '[a]s soon as the pace became considerable, the apparent velocity of people became so excessively great that I could no more see them than a man can see a cannon-ball flying through the air'.[14] Wells's bullet time emphasises the 'relativity of the in/visible', to use Keith Williams's formulation, not only in terms of the limitations of our perceptual organs, but also with respect to the temporal pace underlying perception itself. Wells's Psychologist ties this relativity to the movements of the time machine itself: 'If it is travelling through time fifty times or a hundred times faster than

Figure 3.2 The solarium windows, the flowers and snail from George Pal's *The Time Machine* (Metro-Goldwyn-Mayer, 1960)

we are, if it gets through a minute while we get through a second, the impression it creates will of course be only one-fiftieth or one-hundredth of what it would make if it were not travelling in time' (67). In surfing through a range of temporal rates, the machine adds to the aim of transport a more important function, namely to reveal or construct the relativity of times that enables the fantasy of surfing to begin with. 'Endemic to both high and low modernism', time travel both generates relativity and, as Williams puts it, 'seems to derive from [. . .] Wellsian relativisation (accelerated, dilated, reversed, subjectivised) towards the turn of the century'.[15]

If this relativisation includes the relation to subjectivity, it is not reducible to it. Rather, it locates the self as one reference frame among others, each of which may require a separate clock. The text's understanding of perception as a function of timing mechanisms and shutter speed, as well as of the movements of object and subject, suggests an important connection between the philosophical and psychological thinking of the period and its developing technologies of representation and projection. In his *Principles of Psychology*, William James describes a scenario similar to what the (cinematic, organic, figurative) time machine makes possible:

> Suppose we were able, within the length of a second, to note 10,000 events distinctly, instead of barely 10 [. . .] The motions of organic beings would be so slow to our senses as to be inferred, not seen [. . .] But now reverse the hypothesis and suppose a being to get only 1000th part of the sensations that we get in a given time, and consequently to live 1000 times as long. Winters and summers will be to him like quarters of an hour [. . .] [T]he motions of animals will be as invisible as are to us the movements of bullets and cannon-balls; the sun will scour the sky like a meteor, leaving a fiery trail behind him.[16]

To shoot forwards and backwards like a bullet at certain speeds (distance/time) produces perceptual shifts that become ontological ones, but to shoot forwards and backwards through time itself is to encounter the differential speeds of time, to begin to journey across distinct timespaces in which reference frames lag behind or surge apace in relation to one another.

If one effect of looking across time frames is the experience of disjuncture, the other major result is blur, the dominant way in which contemporary cinema represents wormhole travel, and a defining feature of modernity that figures how a once 'fixed, fast-frozen' world begins to 'melt into air'.[17] From Marx and Engels to Wolfgang Schivelbusch, this trope of dissolution oversees the transformation of time itself from a stable landscape of eternal repetitions to a panoramic rush in which 'velocity blurs all foreground objects'.[18] Whether the driving force of this transformation is 'the constant revolutionizing of production' or the experience of train travel, this new constant movement becomes both the medium and the object. However, as Wells's text suggests, the prevailing way of thinking about this blur – the subject moves or the camera gets bumped – should be qualified to emphasise the rate of movement of the object relative to the rate of movement of the viewing apparatus. To consider the distortions in view caused by a fast object relative to a slow eye opens up that relation/relativity to any number of different ratios, as well as to the larger implication that Martin Jay draws from his study of blur: that 'there is no master temporality subsuming all the others'.[19] The ratio not only determines what appears solid and what appears undefined and ghostly, but also points to 'plural chronologies', as Jay points out: 'understood temporally', blur 'make[s] us aware of what Ernst Bloch famously called [. . .] "non-synchronicity", in which the residues of a not fully dead past and the potential of a not yet realised future coexist uneasily with the time of the transient present'.[20] More importantly, beyond the non-sequential coevalness of past, present and future, this non-synchronicity defines a kind of decortication of different times from time-in-the-singular: 'differential times underpin the experience of blur'.[21]

Instead of the exploration of blurred boundaries between past, present and future, or the proliferation of differential times, the history of time lapse and the motion picture is a chronicle of the eradication of blur. In the technical development from the capture of motion to the rendering of it by means of motion, chronophotography marks the moment in the 1870s not when interpenetrated *durée* and plural chronologies become the focus of representation, but when photographic emulsions become sensitive enough for the short exposures necessary to represent clearly the phases of a moving object. Questions about an accelerated world – such as Leland Stanford's about whether all four hooves of a racehorse lose contact with the ground – became answerable by high-speed, short-exposure photographs (by Eadweard Muybridge in 1877), which seemed to yield a clarity born of stillness.[22] But since that clarity could only be achieved by a change in the relationship between the viewing technology and the world, the attraction of photography's 'arrest of motion' should be recast as the effect of the acceleration of the *viewing apparatus* relative to the fast-moving object or process.

Cinema requires an equivalence of speeds in order to generate the materials for the smooth simulation of motion. Figuratively speaking, if blinking were the act that completed a phase of the viewing process (both the fixing of the image and the generation of enough material to constitute movement), then the eye must blink with a speed and at a rate that is commensurate with the pace of the object. While a founding aspiration of film was to a frame rate of short exposures that would produce a one-to-one representation of reality, the technology's emergence from chronophotography's ability to capture more frames for a represented duration (whether by increasing the frame rate of the camera or the number of cameras) means that cinematic realism was born in the possibilities of slow-motion clarity. Time lapse, as a thinning of frame density rather than an increase, is the opposite and initially promises to complicate permanence by making visible the movements of (and within) solidities or slow processes. Its purpose is to compress and accelerate a duration by spacing out the capture of the phases of the moving object. By slowing down the blinks or spacing out the intervals between which frames are exposed, time appears to speed up, which yields a clearer picture of processes normally prevented by life rhythms and deficiencies in patience. What is hidden in stasis or slowness must be sped up to be seen, such as the germination and growth of a bean in the botanist Wilhelm Pfeffer's 1898 time lapse, gradual shifts in landscapes, the decay of a corpse, or the comedy of time lapse itself in a witty five-minute version of Godfrey Reggio's 1982 film *Koyaanisqatsi*.

However, if the thing we want to see is the relation between times itself, perhaps the clearest sense of heterochronic lags and differential pace comes from the point of view of the slowest snail, rather than the perspective of the bullet and the high-speed camera – or at least an alternation, implied or explicit, between speeds. The German photographer Michael Wesely, who holds the record for the longest photographic exposures in history, some over three years in length, goes beyond the seductions of sheer transience in blur to the tracking of the relationships between rhythms, timelines and scales.[23] To create the city shots in *Open Shutter*, Wesely built special pinhole boxes mounted on steel tripods that were fixed in concrete, which use an incredibly sensitive emulsion that could not be calculated in advance. He could not predict but was curious about the impact of the variability of the exposure length on what comes into view in the shots. These longest of blinks, with a frame rate of one, thus make strange the regularity and uniformity of the motion of the object or world as the basis for marking time in the singular. The content of the photos – the multiplicity of rates and rhythms that come to constitute what a city is – pushes against the idea of a tick as that which contains evenly recurrent moments and contributes to a homogeneous periodicity (Fig. 3.3).

Wesely's experiments in temporal blur and exposure not only critique photography's putative mission to capture, freeze and preserve the singularity of what Cartier Bresson called 'the decisive moment', they also register a dissatisfaction with the concept of the present as a continuous site of solidity, in which the sensuous availability and aesthetic thereness of the world are scaled to a single narrative clock of the human. In 1988, when given an assignment in portraiture, Wesely claimed that because he was unable to 'collect the best moments or find them in my contact sheets', it would be better to 'collect millions of moments in one picture'.[24] Like his long-exposure shots, all of his early portraits feature the exposure time in the title, because, as he says in an interview, 'Time itself is the subject, manifesting itself in many details.'[25] However, by the mid-1990s, Wesley had begun to shift from the mere accumulation of moments sequentially collecting along a single timeline within the photo to the tracking of different sequences collecting in separate lines. Realising that his exposures of three-to-four months were a 'not really significant time frame', he decided to go for a much longer duration, a year. By enlarging the time frame to a year, and later three years, the photographic capture of human scales defined by the revolution of the earth around the sun yields a number of other periodicities

Figure 3.3 Michael Wesely, *9.8.2001 – 7.6.2004 MOMA, New York* in *Open Shutter* (2004), and *8 Min. Emilio Vedova* in *Portraits* (2013)

and scales: not simply the construction of buildings layer-by-layer, but also solar repetition scoring streaks across the image as a moving object from our vantage point; glints of cumulative presences, but also haphazard bright spots that may have simply caught the sun at just the right spot in the duration; ghostly traces of recurrent events; and the low-intensity marks or virtual disappearance of the everyday movements of humans. While the framework of these photos points to 'an architectural view' – because the relative stasis of buildings creates clear and stable images – 'the details', says Wesely, 'are the essential things'.[26] These details, marked by the full gamut of illegibility that Wesely identifies with time and timings, undo the value of the moment, year or any other privileged unit as the foundation for a picture in general and for a picture of time as a unitary medium in particular. As he says of the sun's path in his photographs, '*the lines in the sky put our existence, us, our planet into context with [. . .] the Universe, which coexists on an entirely different time scale*'.[27]

Beyond the most obvious contrast between human and planetary scales, Wesely's photos open themselves to everything in between. The photograph becomes the space of intersecting timelines and timescales. Many of his exposures in *Open Shutter* appear as simple records of construction and renovation

– such as the 1997 pinholes of Potsdamer Platz in Berlin, at the time the largest construction site in Europe, as well as the images commissioned by the Museum of Modern Art in New York, which tracked the museum's renovation and expansion in the early 2000s. However, Wesely's blurs pick up a whole host of other concurrent processes: for instance, the ironic juxtaposition of the speed of the administration and scheduling of urban construction with the more visible regularity of social routines and the traffic of everyday activities repeatedly flowing through the channels formed by the city. The New York pinholes were open from 2000 to 2003, during which time the Twin Towers fell, no doubt altering the light like the weather; the Potsdamer Platz images track the development of a site that was destroyed in the Second World War and physically divided between East and West during the Cold War. Together, these photos in *Open Shutter* thus take as their subject the bookends of a period that, in Phillip Wegner's account, generated neoliberal narratives of the end of history while also sparking utopian dreams of possibility in the wake of the Cold War. But Wesely's images present the underlying, ghostly obscurities of the one-take picture of historical progress. They inhabit those spaces where history had for a time purportedly come to an end or elapsed with a vengeance – and in doing so, they raise the question, not so much what comes next, as what is being erected on daily, monthly and yearly rhythms at various scales? What is possible among the trajectories made visible by the accumulation of transverse layers of periodicities, whose varying pace appears in varying intensity and clarity?

Wesely's temporal blurs and variable flows, though they perhaps resemble palimpsestic, Bergsonian responses to complaints about modernist fragmentation or transitoriness, or more elaborate Barthesian records of mortality, can in fact be, like bullet time in film, a way of tracking different processes and timelines that underlie, constitute and ultimately undermine a present that can no longer be regarded as in sync with itself. In 1929 John Crowe Ransom conceptualised blur as 'a modernistic effect quite like flux in the temporal arts': blur is simply the interpenetration of objects, as flux is the interpenetration of moments. He recuperated blur's aesthetic fuzziness by claiming it to be a more complex exploration of 'the particularity which real things possess' and the 'infinities of quality with which [abstract scientific constants] are invested in reality'.[28] The profusion of detail complicates the rendering of a clear picture. But there are other reasons why an object or a now might not be crisply and uniformly rendered. Instead of an object or a present losing its distinctness via mergers with what is contiguous (other objects, or past and future), we might consider a time-machinic effect in which objects and presents exist in, and are viewed from, a variety of timelines and reference frames. While it is tempting to collapse all variations in pace and rates of change to one fundamental time and ultimate scale, the time machine takes us to spaces governed by separate clocks and helps to make clear the stakes of chronological and historical disjunction.

If we return to certain modernist explorations of time lag and historical de-synchronisation, the stakes of the relations between different clocks become palpable, arresting and spectacular in social and political terms.

Clock Time, Racial Timelines and Faulkner's Differential Rates

The Sound and the Fury is a modernist text overrun by clocks, which most readers prefer to hear as a unified chorus about time as an implacable metaphysical force. In Faulkner's novel, there is most famously the Compson family watch, which, despite his attempts to break it, continues to tick in Quentin's pocket all day on 2 June. On the wall of the Compsons' kitchen is a broken, one-handed cabinet clock that is three hours behind, which Dilsey knows how to read correctly. The novel is strewn with components of earlier time-telling devices such as shadows and water, and elements of modern time regulation, such as the telegraph. There are pulsing veins, skeletons and gendered and raced bodies on which time is being inscribed as a furiously jumbled tale. The novel ends with an image of a backward clock, as Benjy and Luster circle anti-clockwise in a dilapidated surrey around the statue of a Confederate soldier in Jefferson. However, the image that we encounter in the second section of Faulkner's book – an image that is both quintessentially modernist and strangely science-fictional – fractures this unity: Quentin sees in a jeweller's window a display of 'a dozen watches' with 'a dozen different hours', each with an 'assertive and contradictory assurance'.[29] Walking around Cambridge on the day of his suicide, he makes an effort to avoid knowing what time it is, but is everywhere prevented from forgetting the hour. Realising that there are clocks 'high up in the sun', embedded in his body and 'ticking away in my pocket', he decides perversely to enter the jeweller's shop, in which the sound of his pocket watch that he isolates in his head is transformed into a cacophony 'of ticking, like crickets in September grass' (53). Quentin asks 'if any of those watches in the window are right?' (53); the jeweller tells him that 'they haven't been regulated and set yet' (54).

The interpretation that established clock time as the unified refrain of Faulkner's work (and the basis of his 'metaphysics') was Jean-Paul Sartre's 1939 essay, 'On *The Sound and the Fury*: Time in the Work of Faulkner', still seen by some to be 'the best essay on Faulknerian time'.[30] In Sartre's reading, clocks create and represent a catastrophic present, 'which creeps up on us and disappears': all passing moments are consigned to an all-consuming past, and the future is something that simply 'does not exist' until it flickers into/as the diminished present.[31] Famously, he figures the novel's theme and technique in his image of 'a man sitting in an open car and looking backwards. At every moment, formless shadows, flickerings, faint tremblings and patches of light rise up on either side of him, and only afterwards, when he has a little perspective, do they become trees and men and cars.'[32] Whereas Sartrean temporality is, as Justin Skirry points out, 'a subjective process whereby the For-itself projects itself towards a possible future self', Faulknerian time is the external medium of loss, which can only be experienced as extreme blur and whose clocks evoke only the pathos of sheer passage.[33] In Skirry's gloss, 'Sartre criticizes Faulkner for maintaining a chronological metaphysics of time under which consciousness is determined by the sum of its misfortunes, leaving his characters without their future possibilities.'[34] In Sartre's reading, the characters' passivity, confusion and futurelessness motivate the novel's desperation for an 'access to a time without clocks', and justify the urgent if impossible necessity that '[f]or Faulkner, time must be forgotten'.[35]

Mid-century American criticism after Sartre generally agreed with his characterisation of the Compsons but sought to separate their temporal pathologies from Faulkner's own metaphysics of time. That is, clock time was the condition and springboard for what critics have long seen as the two main possibilities for interpreting Faulkner's response to modernity: either he valorises subjective experience, informed by Bergson's antipathy for clocks; or he hopes for transcendence, in death or church.[36] However much (or little) these two interpretive paths have differed, they share a desire to defend Faulkner by showing the ways in which his novel seeks to oppose and exceed the depredations of the clock. For instance, in his influential reading 'Concepts of Time in *The Sound and the Fury*' (1954), Perrin Lowrey was one of the first to delineate different conceptions of time in the novel – a separate one for all three sections devoted to Benjy, Quentin and Jason, which were etiological critiques of the 'clocks and watches and references to time [that] provide a ticking refrain to the central action', and one for the final chapter featuring Dilsey, who by contrast 'is aware of time [. . .] in what might be called the "correct way". She is neither obsessed with time [. . .] nor is she insensible of it [. . .] Through her eyes the reader sees the Compson family in the proper historical perspective, which a correct time-sense gives.'[37] Dilsey's 'correct' lived experience of time as continuity serves as a healthy repudiation of the Compsons' catastrophic time, because it enables her to see through the deceptive appearance of clocks and read them properly. When the broken kitchen clock 'struck five times', Dilsey knows precisely what time it is: '"Eight oclock", Dilsey said' (171). The *durée* that Lowrey valorises secures its status as temporal paradoxically by transcending the clocks that 'slay time [. . .] clicked off by little wheels' (54).

Likewise, Dilsey serves as the novel's mechanism for 'the reader to achieve a final perspective on the lives of the Compsons' and to understand Faulkner's true metaphysics, according to Olga Vickery's '*The Sound and the Fury*: A Study in Perspective', also published in 1954.[38] This metaphysics centres on 'that vital impulse behind all things', as she suggests in a later essay, and opposes the clocks that obscure temporality by representing its moments as 'isolated and discontinuous' and without a future.[39] Caddy is for Vickery the embodiment of these clocks, the focus of the Compsons' fiction of order, purity and stability, as well as 'the instrument of its destruction'.[40] She is 'almost a symbol of the blind forces of nature' that will undo all such fictions.[41] Ultimately, it is Dilsey's association with a more capacious naturalism of redemptive cyclicality – described as a 'continuous process' in which past and present 'are both contained in and their contours subtly altered by an eternal growing present' – that 'throw[s] the final illumination not only on Caddy and the whole sequence of events that started with her affair but also on what each of the Compsons believed her to be'.[42]

Given the sympathies of American literary criticism from the 1950s onwards, it is not surprising to find Cleanth Brooks cresting this trend of distinguishing Faulkner's understanding of time from the Compsons' doom, and his attempts to steer it away from Bergsonian vitalism, whose influence he claimed was 'generally overestimated and [. . .] occasionally pushed to absurd lengths'.[43] For Brooks, it is true that the temporality of the 'stream of living consciousness [. . .] has little to do with the time that is measured off by the ticking of the chronometer', and that, as Sartre claimed, the Compson brothers are futureless and therefore 'not free'.[44] Following Lowrey, he sees Benjy as 'locked almost completely into a timeless present'; Quentin's obsession with the past is indeed 'a repudiation of the future' that 'finds symbolic expression in his twisting the hands from his watch'; and Jason is 'always racing the clock and [. . .] usually late'.[45] However, the solution to 'the saddest word of all' in the larger chorus of clocks is not a fluid, interpenetrated and 'intensive' temporality but the paradoxically timeless time of the eternal, mythic and universal.[46] Again, the figure who emerges as the symbol of 'a proper notion of time' is Dilsey, for whom 'neither the past nor the future is oppressive, because to her they are all aspects of eternity'.[47] Because her balanced understanding comes from her belief 'in an order that is grounded in eternity', 'past, present, and future gathered together in a total pattern', Dilsey is able to endure the 'disintegration of modern man' in which individuals are 'lost in private worlds'.[48] By contrast, as a representative of 'familial and cultural unity', and with a 'view of the world and mankind [that] is thoroughly Christian', Dilsey receives and projects the novel's Easter Sunday vision of transcending profane time – 'a vision of eternity which gives meaning to time and will wipe away all tears in a final vindication of goodness and in a full consideration of those who mourn'.[49]

If we are to revise our consideration of Faulkner's treatment of time, we will have to avoid trying to decide which character embodies the most salutary orientation towards it and instead turn to the more contemporary interest in history, but with a major difference. Rather than simply bringing US social and economic history to the fore, we must listen to the 'assertive and contradictory' differences within the din of de-synchronised ticking that Faulkner's text explores.

While some of these variations might be differences between individuals, the novel maps subjective and mythic temporalities on to the unharmonisable clocks of social and economic histories. There is no orchestration into a concerted music of time or eternity, but only the plural juxtapositions of discordant ticks and the timelines they represent. What has appeared to both sympathetic and unsympathetic audiences alike as an eternal present (with an anachronistic past still in it), or an obsession with unstoppable and unsurpassable passage, or a desire to escape to a timeless order, can be read together as parts of a larger heterochronic landscape, a disjunctive present, with other presents and different historical lines running through it. This reading does not entail the erasure of the other temporal orientations that critics have seen in the novel, but only the recognition that the novel's interest in temporal difference is literal, and that the text meditates on what temporal passage in one particular frame of reference looks like from another frame. As in the works of other modernists seen to push against 'the one true time' of modernity, Faulkner's clocks can be treated as explorations of the lag between differently paced histories rather than as affirmation of idiosyncratic time-consciousness, or as evidence for the primitivist thesis on the lag of 'underdevelopment' within a single, absolute reference frame.

As my brief run through Faulknerian time studies makes clear, the novel certainly encourages readers to relish the singular timeline as a site of loss, where 'tomorrow, and tomorrow, and tomorrow' creep into the present and immediately become past. We are invited to valorise the novel's mythologising of this loss in the unmistakably Christian terms of desire's tragic fall into the endless undressings of signifiers from signifieds. However, we should also pay close attention to the pathos of the novel's comparisons of different rates of change with each other. The most striking example of this comparison, in a novel that arguably is constituted entirely by such comparisons, comes almost directly after Quentin leaves the jeweller's shop filled with the contradictory, unsynchronised clocks: having purchased the flat-irons for his suicide, Quentin boards a streetcar in which the only available seat is next to a well-dressed African American man wearing 'a derby and shined shoes' (55). Sitting shoulder-to-shoulder with this man in the tram sparks Quentin's insightful but also deeply limited awareness that his own racialising identification of this man with the epithet 'nigger' – and indeed race as such – is nothing more than an 'obverse reflection' of the dominant culture at any given moment (55). His discomfort with the man's co-presence provokes a memory of his train trip back to Mississippi earlier in the year, in which, having crossed over into the south in Virginia, he realises that he 'had missed Roskus and Dilsey' (55).

As the text makes clear, what Quentin remembers missing, while riding on the tram in Boston, is a specific kind of spatial and temporal relationship that he has with African Americans in the South. He recalls waking up on the southbound train to the absence of movement. Raising the window blind, he discovers a 'car [. . .] blocking a road crossing', and as a result, 'a nigger on a mule in the middle of the stiff ruts, waiting for the train to move' (55). The image of the African American man and his mule – 'with that quality [. . .] of shabby and timeless patience, of static serenity: that blending of childlike and ready incompetence and paradoxical reliability' (56) – is the familiar, racist projection of obverse behindness and timelessness with which Quentin also connects Dilsey and Roskus. As John Rieder says of SF's emergence from and indebtedness to colonialist constructions of anachronism, such a juxtaposition bears 'the mark of anthropological difference', an anachronism featuring 'an incongruous co-habitation of the same moment by people and artifacts from different times'.[50] But the plural here refers to positions on a universal line of history: in this colonial ideologeme, those who literally occupy the now are affirmed and fortified by the position of those who are considered 'to exist in the past – in fact, to be our own past'.[51] Relative to constructions of whiteness in the South, the man on the mule serves to remind Quentin that 'You are home again' (55). As the temporal opposite of Northern modernity, Southern blackness has always been the primitivist anterior to the singular present for the Compsons; in the North, however, things that were arranged in a before/after relationship are now coeval but moving along paths at different rates. Indeed, Quentin's memory of the South and its frozen binaries of race, gender, region and class have all been illusions: as if captured in bullet time, the stasis of the train, the man and the mule, as well as the juxtaposition of Quentin and the well-dressed man on the streetcar, gives way to various trajectories and intersecting speeds.

The novel juxtaposes Quentin and the well-dressed man on the tram to suggest not so much that they share the same, singular present – as if the man on the mule had joined the Great Migration and arrived in Boston as an instantaneously post-racial equal. Rather the streetcar/train scene suggests that African Americans, the Compsons and white Northerners (with whom Quentin is obviously not fully simultaneous) are all on different trajectories moving at different rates that, of course, have intersected in crucially causal ways but also peel off into different paths and futures. To make the case that Faulkner's novel is doing more with lag than showcasing the primitivist idea that black is behind white on the unified line of history, I want to dig more deeply into the meaning of the constellation of images that we encounter from the novel's second section onwards: clocks, technologies of transport and work, the telegraph and racial timelines. Quentin, his brothers and even Dilsey may want to escape, stop, conquer or transcend clock time (the bad premise of their 'reducto absurdum', to use Mr Compson's malapropism), but the novel registers something odd in time lag that will be accentuated in Jason's comic belatedness and blindness to uneven economic timescapes, and the novel's presentation of the provincialisation and racialisation of times.

Jewellers, Observatories, Telegraphs and
Historiographic Bullet Time

Boston jewellers' clocks, trains, the telegraph: this specific constellation of images that we encounter in the novel's second section occurring in 1910 – itself an analeptic break from the chronologically disordered plot taking place in 1928 – illuminates the very production of modern clock time and the history of attempts, motivations and consequences of eliminating time differences and lag. In the late nineteenth century, so connected were the clock, train and telegraph that if you were to come upon a wire and pull it, as Peter Galison argues, you would very quickly discover an 'opalescent' mesh connecting a number of entities, including academic fields (e.g., physics and engineering), government institutions (e.g., geodetic surveys and international committees on measures and conventions), train tracks and the technology of ever more precise clocks.[52] This meshwork comprised the infrastructure for organising and coordinating faster and more efficient movement, communications and production. Modern time in its most familiar form – synchronised, precise and increasingly brief – emerged from this set of connections and seemed to become load-bearing itself. As Adrian Mackenzie points out, 'clocktime may well be the most ubiquitous of modern technical infrastructures', since 'clocks are deeply embedded in diverse scientific, cultural, institutional, economic, and military realities'.[53] In Sue Zemka's account, the moment is the 'central artistic conceit of industrial culture', because its simultaneity with other distant nows was both the instrument and byproduct of modern infrastructure (railways, telecommunications, the factory system), and because so many late nineteenth- and early twentieth-century writers attempted to reappropriate the moment as a perceptual and aesthetic vertex/vortex that might free us from this regulatory matrix.[54]

If, as Mackenzie argues, 'infrastructural technologies are constantly "conjuring nature" into a particular representational framework', then it is clear from both the novel and US history that these particular technologies are part of a larger machine producing isochronic and isotopic unity.[55] As it turns out, Boston and Harvard were important components in this machine, geared to impose an absolute spatio-temporal uniformity on local irregularities of both the natural and social world, and to minimise or eliminate lags between longitudinally diverse timescapes within unified zones. In my brief retelling of this story about technologies of time, what appear as aspects of *The Sound and the Fury*'s passive setting – Boston and Harvard – will emerge in the foreground as significant actors in the drama of both symptomatic and strategic de-synchronisation. Quentin's drama of temporal pathology depends on the way Harvard connects to the history and instruments of time's standardisation and unification.

Prior to the end of the nineteenth century, the norm across the US (indeed across the world) was 'a profusion of competing local times [. . .] variously determined and variously maintained', as Carlene Stephens has pointed out.[56] In the US, prior to standardisation, '[m]ost often a local jeweller, who might also have been an amateur astronomer, kept the community time standard'.[57] Unhappy with this state of affairs, the astronomer and head of the time service at the Harvard College Observatory, Leonard Waldo, complained that 'people have been dictated to by their jewelers' who 'insist on a time which shall appeal to the local time of their customers'.[58] In the years leading up to the US and Canadian railways' resetting and regulating of their clocks in 1883, Waldo had become a nationally recognised voice for the scientific management of standard time and was in the process of forming his own Standard Time Company in order to compete with the Western Union Telegraph Company in the sale of time signals authenticated by astronomy. Western Union had cultivated a relationship with the US Naval Observatory since 1865, the end of the Civil War, by trading its telegraph services in exchange for free time signals, and as a result it eventually enjoyed a 'virtual monopoly on the commercial signalling of time', selling the precise synchronisation of 'house, office, or manufactory' to Washington, DC time for a subscription fee of $75–375 per year.[59] While his business venture did not succeed, Waldo contributed to the eventual drift away from Washington time to Greenwich time by stoking up what Galison calls the 'cultivated precision mania of the Harvard Observatory [that] had come to resonate not only among astronomers but also among high-end watchmakers and their gentlemanly New England customers. The culture of precision ticked sooner and louder in Boston.'[60]

In cultural terms, to be 'on time' – on exactly the right time – was to be worldly and virtuous. The Massachusetts senator Edward Everett, a high-profile public figure, had pointed out in an 1856 dedication speech at the Dudley Observatory that localised clocks are of limited value compared to the 'celestial mechanics' tracked by astronomy, because the former 'keep home time alone, like the good traveller who leaves his heart behind him'.[61] But for Waldo, to be not-all-there and stuck in one's insular 'home time' was not just an inconvenience but a social ill. In his article 'The Distribution of Time' (1880), Waldo argues that the 'character of a people in the scale of civilization is the promptness with which they transact their business'.[62] Because the US had no unified standard to establish even regional time, that business was marked by the chaos of 'factory operatives [who] begin work on railroad time and stop on local time', the inter-city 'jostle and inconvenience' of 'stock-exchanges, business offices and the banks [that] close with a difference of ten minutes' and 'the thousand engagements broken by the discrepancies of time'.[63] But more perilous than these headaches, idiosyncratic local times provided by jewellers were bad for 'the masses', who could only be improved, he thought, by cultivating in them 'a certain precision in doing the daily work of life which conduces, perhaps, to a sounder morality'.[64]

It was precisely on this association of punctuality with moral constitution that the International Time Recording Company, which would go on to become IBM, marketed its timeclock, a device whose prototype was invented in 1888 by William Bundy, a jeweller in New York, to record and tabulate employees' hours. The ITRC's 1914 catalogue advertises its timeclock as a machine that 'induces punctuality by impressing the value of time on each individual' and furthermore would also 'weed out [. . .] undesirables' – 'men irregular in appearance, who come late and go out at odd times'.[65] This sentiment, which served as a marketing tool for Waldo, piggy-backed on updated narratives of idleness. In an example provided by Michael O'Malley, a fifth-grade lesson in 1881, printed in *McGuffey's Readers*, could blame a train collision, a business failure and the death of an innocent man on lateness: 'The best laid plans, the most important affairs, the fortunes of individuals, honor, happiness, life itself are daily sacrificed because somebody is "behind time".'[66] As Robert Levine points out, in Horatio Alger stories the acquisition of a good suit and a pocket watch, both of which Faulkner poignantly ironises in Quentin on his last day, are 'the two most crucial events marking the hero's graduation to the middle class'.[67] To succeed in life – economically, morally, psychologically – was to be in precise sync.

The lagless exactitude in science and culture that Waldo was trying to market widely was the product of machinic connections, originating in Cambridge, between clocks, observatory functions, telegraph wires and trains. The inventor of the first electrically distributed public time service was in fact the first director of the Harvard Observatory (1839–59), William Bond, the son of a prominent Boston clockmaker. Bond's work helped to establish the first regional time standard or 'zone' (New England), which anticipated and set the stage for the 1884 International Meridian Conference and its decision to use the Greenwich Observatory as the prime starting point for demarcating the isochronic segments of the universal day.[68] Bond was not just an astronomer but someone with connections to commercial shipping and government mapping: he owned a firm that supplied, rated and repaired marine chronometers for businesses at the Boston port and the Navy. Because of these connections, the US Coast Survey enlisted Bond and the astronomers at the Harvard Observatory to assist with longitudinal measurements in 1848. During this collaboration, Bond worked out a way to determine longitude more accurately and to minimise the errors of the 'personal equation' – the lag in different people's response times while timing astronomical events and transits – by using an 'automatic circuit interrupter in place of human nerves and muscles as the connecting link between the astronomical clock and the electric wire' of the telegraph.[69] That is, instead of calculating longitude by observing the moment a star crossed a reticle in a telescope and noting that moment on a discrepant clock, and then using the difference between that time and a distant observatory's time in order to figure out how far away it is (given that one hour is 15 degrees if a full 360-degree rotation of the globe takes 24 hours), Bond used a break-circuit device attached to an astronomically set clock to broadcast its ticks through the telegraph, and he devised a receiving machine, a drum chronograph, that would mark on paper rotating on a drum both the beats of the clock and the observer's telegraph signal at the instant of the star's transit.[70] As Galison summarises Bond's innovative combination of telegraphy, clocks and astronomy, 'Why not make the escapement of a clock act like a telegraph key so the ticks would be heard anywhere and everywhere' and 'let the clock-driven signal mark on a smoothly turning cylinder located far from the clock?'[71] This process, known as the 'American method' by British astronomers, was awarded a medal at the 1851 Crystal Palace Exhibition in London, and adopted by the Astronomer Royal at Greenwich. It made 'Cambridge [Massachusetts], not Washington [. . .] the reference point on the North American continent for US and Canadian government surveys'; and Cambridge was synced to Greenwich.[72]

Harvard's innovations in precision would contribute to both national and international temporal unification. Shortly after his work with the Coast Survey, Bond converted the American method used in specialised geodetic and astronomical applications into a public service delivering *gratis* true local time throughout New England. As Carlene Stephens writes, Harvard's distribution of the time signal was the 'world's first public time service based on clock signals *telegraphed* from the observatory'.[73] The method for ascertaining the truest local time possible, its lag-free distribution and its cost became good justifications for adopting it as a standard elsewhere. In 1849 the New England Association of Railway Superintendents voted to adopt a regional time standard based on 'the true time at Boston as given by William Bond & Son', and required that 'all station clocks, conductors' watches, and all time tables and trains should be regulated accordingly'.[74] Because Bond had measured his meridional lines west from the maritime reference point of Greenwich rather than east of Washington, DC, the first formal US regional time zone in New England was established in relation to this longitude, anticipating not only the railways' national agreement on a uniform time standard and multiple zones in 1883 (which Ian Bartky observes was Greenwich's 'first international use as a *land* time standard' in the world), but also the International Meridian Conference's adoption of Greenwich as the reference point for the universal day in 1884.[75]

If Boston/Harvard is a key site in the developing circuits of isochronic and synchronic machinery, Faulkner's use of this setting offers a direct critique of the metaphysics and the politics supported by the history of time standardisation, its connection to the regulations for safer train travel, and the dependence of both on communication infrastructure. That is, to bring together discordant clocks, the figure of the trains whose coordination necessitated standardisation and the telegraph wires required to eliminate lag between longitudinally diverse timescapes within unified zones is to create an active backdrop against which de-synchronisation and lag appear in sharp relief. Faulkner's exploration/depictions of the regional and racial variations in historical pace, material access to goods and communicative immediacy pushes against the metaphysics and politics of synchronisation and, moreover, reveals the phenomenon of lag to be more than simple delay or behindness, the subsequence of arrivals in the taken-for-granted present. Rather, in recognising that what appears as the present and time-in-the-singular is in fact composed of a variety of different paces that themselves do not sync up even while they might intersect and cross paths, Faulkner's text makes clear the cost of the single temporal line and the elimination of the local difference that unitary history has often construed as the permanent past.

Let us return to the scene immediately following Quentin's experience of the jeweller's unsynchronised clocks, the scene in which he sits next to a well-dressed African American man on the Boston streetcar and remembers the man on the mule he saw on his Christmas holiday train trip from Harvard back to the South. We can begin by noting how this scene seems to form a complex meditation on where different populations are located in what Waldo called 'the scale of civilization' – a set of unilinear temporal relationships registered in both social and technological terms. In the South, African Americans lag behind the Compsons, which Faulkner allows us to measure in Quentin's brief exchange as the distance from the train window to the mule. As Quentin also recalls on this day in 1910, his family proudly sports 'the first auto in town' – a gift from Herbert Head to Caddy (59) – at a moment in their family history when they are hoping to keep pace and face by attaching themselves to the son of a Northern banking family, and by sending their eldest child to Harvard. From Quentin's position – in the regional frame of reference, but also figuratively on a train that runs on uniform standard time, however imperfectly (and here temporarily delayed) – the man on the mule appears outside of time: 'motionless and unimpatient' (56). The train is, as Cynthia Dobbs notes, an 'emblem of modern change', whereas the man on the mule is described desperately by Quentin in naturalistic terms as 'carved out of the hill itself' (55), a reassuringly primitivist sign of 'home' for him.[76] As George Ellenberg notes, the mule, so ubiquitous in the South that by the mid-1920s it comprised 'nearly three-fourths of work animals in the Lower South' and numbered 4.5 million, stands clearly as one of the repressed elements of Southern history, helping to constitute it but excluded from it.[77] In the set of racist associations around 'beasts of burden', mules were metonyms for black bodies themselves, a technology of labour associated so strongly with the history of slavery and the failed promises of the Federal government's redistribution of '40 acres and a mule' that, as Ellenberg argues, only a mass migration from the land could counter 'the power of the mule/African American nexus' that had generated 'powerful justification for keeping blacks in the fields'.[78]

While African American characters in the novel are marked by the absence of progress in the South, stuck in kitchens and fields and built into hills, in the North they appear – to Quentin and to many readers – to share in the same, singular present on the streetcar. It appears as if the Great Migration from the land has enabled the man on the mule to catch up with white modernity, sharing space and history with Northern streetcar riders. In 1910 that process had only just begun, but by the late 1920s, the time of the Compsons' jumbled present and the publication of the novel, the first wave of migration had already seen an enormous number of African Americans moving out of the South. As Cheryl Lester argues, Faulkner's streetcar/train scene in particular registers an obvious anxiety about the beginnings of the Great Migration, in which 2.5 million African Americans abandoned the rural South for northern industrial cities from 1915 to 1930.[79] As she notes, Faulkner travelled out of the South for the first time by train in 1918, during 'the first peak of black migration', and therefore 'joined the stream of northbound migration'.[80] If technologies of transport are a general symbol for modernity, their specific valences in this context touch on some of the raced consequences of this trip: the streetcar serves as the site of uncomfortable racial proximity – 'a long-standing *topos* in the literature of migration' – while the train quite literally conveys (the defection and disaffection of) black labour.[81] In Lester's important reading, even the novel's longing for Caddy, 'thematized as the primary cause of change', is a displaced desire for disappearing black bodies, especially the body of the ageing mammy Dilsey, a 'ruin or landmark' signifying the profound shift in the South 'from an agrarian to an industrial economy and from a rural to an urban society'.[82] From the Compsons' perspective, counted in this 'loss' would be the diminishing opportunities for the rituals of 'racial etiquette' used to confirm the status of white superiority and wealth. In Quentin's memory this etiquette appears as the benevolence-generating game of 'Christmas Gift' that he plays with the man on the mule, to whom he flings a quarter from the train window. Thus, if African Americans appear in the North on the same vehicles as Quentin, the novel would seem to suggest that it is because they are leaving behind their position of always being behind, and because the fortunes of the Compsons are going in reverse.

While the two men seem to be passing each other from opposite directions while sitting in the Boston streetcar in a singular timeline that renders them coeval, we might consider the ways in which the larger scene is a kind of bullet-time exposition of various rates of change crossing paths but also going their own ways. The man from Quentin's memories – the man 'in the middle of the stiff ruts' who 'didn't have a saddle' and whose 'feet dangled almost to the ground' – seems to have arrived figuratively and miraculously in the North in a derby hat and shined shoes (55), but the significance of his arrival is not that African American history is now united with and included in 'official national history' and Northern white modernity. It is rather that his presence serves to accentuate how different the regional and racial timelines are, and how lag is not just about the difference in position within a single line, but also the difference between lines themselves. That is, the presence of the man with shined shoes in the seat next to Quentin allows the text to position Quentin and the South, as well as blackness, in relation to industrial modernity – all three of which have differing trajectories. While both the man on the mule and the man on the streetcar are presented alongside Quentin, these scenes allow us to think about the various vectors and paces that problematise any singular rectilinear account of history.

Faulkner makes these relative positionings and intractable arcs explicit in many ways. At the level of the narratorial present itself, where the reader seems to 'hear' the novel directly, the shifting narrative locus warps and destabilises our access to the text, not only because the story is told out of order from unusual points of view, but also because in this book reception lags behind voice in exaggerated ways – a kind of modernist Doppler effect. Consider the moment when Quentin encounters the three boys fishing near the Larz Anderson bridge who point him to a Unitarian church clock. Quentin has asked if there are any factories around that might tell him if it is one o'clock. They hear the Southern accent as a mark of blackness: '"He talks like they do in minstrel shows" [. . .] "Aint you afraid he'll hit you? [. . .] You said he talks like a colored man"' (76). This moment of the text's self-awareness serves to provincialise and racialise the entirety of the text, particularly the fourth section of the novel, which is rendered in the third person. Readers become conscious that hearing the novel in 'standard' non-accented English is a sign of inhabiting a specific time frame and cultural space. In the three first-person sections, whose linguistic register does not appear to be explicitly regionalised and raced in the specific ways that African American speech is represented, the text's self-conscious thematising of the inflections and accents of consciousness highlights the laggy distortions that the novel's critical history has left largely undetected, and points to the novel's ambitious refusal to identify the South (or the North) with the normalised and normalising present.

Country Suckers Time vs. Colored People's Time

Likewise, Jason's use of Western Union's service to play the cotton futures market emphasises in a comic way Southern lag and its difference from the Northern/national itinerary. Part of the hilarious drama of Jason's section is the enormous amount of money he is losing, the full extent of which he is unaware of, because Western Union provides him with market reports that are too late to act on.[83] At 5:10 p.m. he receives a telegram from New York advising him to sell his futures contracts because the 'market will be unstable, with a general downward tendency' (153). When Jason sarcastically proposes to send a telegram that says 'Buy [. . .] Occasional flurries for purpose of hooking a few more country suckers who haven't got in to the telegraph office yet' (153), the telegraph operator confirms the difference between Country Suckers Time and the New York Stock Exchange: 'He looked at the message, then he looked at the clock. "Market closed an hour ago"' (153). It is already 6:10 in the Eastern Time Zone. The late delivery of news and the time differences between EST and CST come to stand not only for Jason's personal failure to be at the right place at the right time (a large part of the reason why the Western Union agent is unable to deliver the telegrams to him on time), but also for the economic and racialised historical differences that the novel expresses in temporal terms.

The latter is the most dramatic way in which the novel demonstrates that the problem of the twentieth century, to modify W. E. B. Du Bois's famous assertion, is the relationship of timelines to the colour line. The Compsons and others can perceive Southerners as lagging behind the nation and the North in ways that they believe liken them to African Americans, because, as Michael Hanchard puts it, 'unequal relationships between dominant and subordinate groups produce unequal temporal access to institutions, goods, services, resources, power, and knowledge'.[84] Although they are passing each other in Faulkner's train/mule scene, one cannot equate a laggy *no-longer* position of a white Southerner in the North with a laggy *not-yet* position of an African American in the South (the Compsons' pathetic delusion). Moreover, the novel does more than construct a single line or queue of temporal access and location. To better understand this accomplishment, we should shift from the temporalised pathos of the Compsons to that of the Gibsons, the novel's African American characters, and put more pressure on the novel's portrayal of behindness within US history.

On the one hand, the novel explores what Hanchard calls 'racial time', 'a more total imposition of dominant temporality than an abstract, acultural labor time (since slaves would have had to change their position within the mode of production by transforming themselves racially)'.[85] It is possible to measure the degree of the imposition of hegemonic isochrony, as well as the proximity to centres of material power, by timing the wait that a subordinate group has 'for goods and services that are delivered first to members of the dominant group', and by noting instances of 'time appropriation' when symptomatic lags (or historical erasures) are tactically deployed to effect 'positive change in their overall position and location in society'.[86] 'Modernity in black' means abiding and enduring, but it also means explicitly acknowledging and strategically mobilising one's difference from modernity in general, which according to Frank Kirkland 'fosters the belief that a future-oriented present, severed from any sense of an historical past, can yield culturally distinctive and progressive innovations'.[87] By contrast, African Americans' relationship to modernity 'promotes the conviction that a future-oriented present can be the fortunate occasion in which culturally distinctive innovations are historically redemptive of a sense of past' – a specific past that cannot and should not be relinquished because its erasure, and with it the obliteration of any possible future, was precisely what slavery accomplished.[88] This framework of waiting, time appropriation and redemption provides a more powerful way to reflect on Dilsey's association with eternity.

Racial time begins less as a critical concept that enabled socio-political mapping than as a racist reading of African Americans' relationship to the clock, whose pendulum, as Marx pointed out more generally, marked out 'the subordination of man to the machine', but also 'as accurate a measure of the relative activity of two workers as it is the speed of two locomotives'.[89] If the clock reduced the human being in general to the quanta of labour time, then what has come to be known as 'Colored People's Time' (CPT) began as a belief in the slave worker's unfitness for modern quantification and efficient activity. As Mark M. Smith argues, the fact that Southern planters attempted to cultivate the same clock discipline associated with Northern factories has been insufficiently acknowledged for two reasons. First, the entire antebellum South, including its slaves, was understood as 'bound to the rhythms of nature', and was therefore associated with premodern, task-oriented temporality.[90] And secondly, African Americans were seen not only as 'adopting presentist and naturally defined notions of time', but also as incapable of clock discipline, a perception with a long, racist history.[91] For instance, the explorer Mungo Park remarked of Africans in 1799: 'Loss of time is an object of no great importance in the eyes of the Negro. If he has anything of consequence to perform, it is a matter of indifference to him whether he does it to-day or to-morrow, or a month or two hence.'[92] Smith also cites the principal of the Laing Normal and Industrial School for Freedpeople, Abby D. Monro, a white Northerner: 'we live in a country where no note is taken of time [. . .] "Shortly" and "directly", common expressions, may mean an hour, a day, or a week hence [. . .] It seems to be one and the same to these people.'[93] As Jason Compson puts it so crassly while Earl is closing up the hardware store, 'the only place for them is in the field, where they'd have to work from sunup to sundown. They can't stand prosperity or an easy job' (156).

On the other hand, while the novel represents the difficulty of this temporal-material queue, it also suggests a heterochronic configuration of history. Dilsey knows exactly how much the dress that her daughter Frony is wearing to Sunday services costs: 'You got six weeks' work right dar on yo back' (180). To wait on the Compsons is to wait longer – for an impatient Mrs Caroline Compson and her family. The racist attribution of African Americans' incapacity to internalise good time habits and respect for the clock served as justification for what Smith calls 'time obedience', 'enforced or imposed by time-conscious planter-managers through the threat or use of violence'.[94] While resistance to obedience was a matter of racial essence in the eyes of many white Southerners, it became simultaneously a tactic for contesting and opposing the oppressive machinery of both nature's racialised 'scale of civilization', to return to Waldo's formulation, and the technologically coordinated 'promptness with which they [had to] transact their business'.[95] CPT was thus both a temporal position to which African Americans and others were and are consigned, as well as a temporal tactic that people of colour recognised they could sometimes use. Since they occupied a position of behindness that often fell off the outer edge of history into timelessness, slaves and freedpeople often found that by means of lateness or slowness they could resist 'planter-defined time during and after slavery'.[96]

However, Faulkner's Gibsons stand less for resistance than for a need to acknowledge a history defined by different coordinates and rhythms. John Streamas points out that CPT is in fact 'the time-dimension of [. . .] double consciousness'.[97] We might define CPT, then, in a modification of Du Bois's formulation, as the sense of always living in and according to someone else's time, a feeling of this two-ness, of being in a timeline in which one's soul is measured by the tape of a world that looks on in amused contempt and pity, as well as of being in a distinct history marked by exclusions from and laggy access to history in the main, but operating in a different way. For Streamas, the former time – of a racialising capitalist modernity – is punctual and never-ending, whereas 'CPT envisions endings [. . .] as the very point of resistance'.[98] In his argument, to humanise time by means of narrative closure secures and redeems a lost past (to see the ending enables one to see the beginning, the first by means of the last), and pushes back against the steady ticking of the empty present. What Smith defines as 'the preferred means of protest' of freedpeople – their 'careful withdrawal and rationing of their labor power (what the planters described as lethargy)' – opens up the possibility of a subversive appropriation of conventional narrative form, a form that carves a definitive shape out of homogeneous time.[99] For our purposes, we should note that Faulkner's novel does not foreground narrative closure as the completion of a singular arc. *The Sound and the Fury* ends not simply with Benjy travelling anti-clockwise around a Confederate monument. Luster, Dilsey's grandson, is there too. Although Luster is at work driving Benjy in the horse-drawn carriage, and is abused by his employer Jason for going in the wrong direction around the statue, the novel leaves us with Luster holding the reins. While Faulkner in his Appendix to *The Sound and the Fury* may have wanted merely for the Gibsons to have 'endured' (215), his novel indicates an awareness that they will go their own way, with a past yet to recover and redeem, and an array of futures to claim.

Hanchard asks if the presence of what Paul Gilroy calls the 'counterculture of modernity' perhaps 'hint[s] at one of several divergent paths of modernity'.[100] The significance of *The Sound and the Fury* is not only in its spotlighting of lag but also in its interest in heterochrony. Whereas historicism is defined by Benjamin as the force that relegates alternatives to the zones of the irrational/backward while also producing such zones, the task for heterochronic historicism is, to use David Lloyd's words, to retrieve 'the different rhythms of historically marginalised cultures and the alternative conceptions of cultural and social relations that account for their virtual occlusion from written history'.[101] The other temporalities and the imagination of 'alternative ways of being' are the means, as he says, for 'a different future'.[102] If this is so – if different cultures and social formations have different pasts and dispositions towards the past, different presents, and the possibility of different futures – then it is worth thinking of *The Sound and the Fury* as tracking the lag and differences between wholly different timelines and historical trajectories, even if they necessarily or accidentally cross paths or run intermittently in parallel.

POSTCOLONIAL HISTORIES AND HETEROCHRONIC LAG IN JESSICA HAGEDORN

That black and white, and North and South, are not synced up is uncontroversial, but Faulkner's exploration of lag is more interesting than a representation of x-behind-y-behind-z. His style and subject matter have been recognised as working archipelagically, as Hugues Azerad says, 'to undo the vision of reality and truth as singular, introducing the multiple, the uncertain, and the relative', and as helping to initiate the transnational turn, according to Saldivar and Goldberg, by locating the US South within the 'processes of modernization and [. . .] dependency' defining the wider Global South.[103] It is thus useful to consider the construction of heterochronic lag, in Faulkner's text and elsewhere, in relation to postcolonial historicism and global historiography. Time lag, in Homi Bhabha's well-known formulations, is both the assigned condition of postcolonial belatedness and behindness, as well as the opportune instability and gap in identities of all kinds (linguistic, epistemological, psychic, political) that threaten and contest colonial power. The presence of lag – of distances in signification, for example – raises 'the question of cultural difference and incommensurability', as Bhabha says, 'not the consensual, ethnocentric notion of the pluralistic existence of cultural diversity'.[104] Indeed, the disruptiveness of lag, its presence as the 'incommensurability where differences cannot be sublated or totalized', resists the oneness and wholeness of history as such: postcolonial time lag opposes 'the ideological discourses of modernity that attempt to give a hegemonic "normality" to the uneven development and the differential, often disadvantaged, histories of nations, races, communities, peoples'.[105]

In this framework, lag is not simply the delayed arrival on the one, true timeline; it is the contestation of the shape and constitution of that timeline itself. There is no way to take this idea other than literally. In Bhabha's thought, the single line of history is itself one of the 'technologies of colonial and imperial governance', and thus the critique of lag as a condition is not merely aimed at restoring those who have been cast as primitive and archaic to the present as coeval beings.[106] The critique of the positioning of the margins must be paired with the power of lag to reconfigure the nature of history and coevalness as such. If 'the most fundamental source of colonial power is the very idea of historical temporality, or history itself', as Satoshi Mizutani puts it, then history must be dismantled as the illusion of a homogeneous national present within (or as) a unified global history.[107] This imperative continues to raise the perplexing question, in Bhabha's words, of how we can conceive 'a social imaginary based on the articulation of differential, even disjunctive, moments of history and culture'.[108] The whole is necessarily a fiction, and one might say that this fiction should be rewritten along the lines of a science fiction, a fiction in which the absolute, singular time of reality is 'provincialised' as an illusory narrative with specific spatio-temporal coordinates, and in which the construction of a larger whole foregrounds the stitching together and coeval articulations of various fragmentary historical narratives and lines running at various rates.

As critics have pointed out, the dangers of this temporal heterogeneity thesis are several. To insist on a discontinuous history – one that is not part of a single continuum – participates in the primitivist relegation of difference to faraway timespaces and, as Johannes Fabian argues, denies to different histories their coevalness with Western/European history. Keya Ganguly points out that 'Fabian's harshest criticism is reserved for relativistic cultural perspectives that, under the cover of valorising the distinctiveness of the other, end up unable to reckon with the sameness of the "one history that leads from the slingshot to the megabomb"'.[109] Like the timeline drawn out by Stanley Kubrick's famous match cut in *2001: A Space Odyssey* of the prehistoric bone spinning in the air and the futuristic space station rotating in space, Fabian's 'one history' would be the only, solitary terrain of struggle, despite the provincialisation of it at the core of many of its critiques. Thus, Ganguly worries that Bhabha's idea of lag 'reproduces an old-fashioned nativism about the so-called alterity of postcolonial cultural practices', and reminds us that to hypostatise 'the "otherness" of time itself' is to ignore one of Jameson's key points, which is that 'capitalist modernity serves as the de facto referent for any understanding of postcolonial culture'.[110]

There are other justifiable anxieties about historical multiplicity and 'temporal sovereignty'.[111] Simon Gikandi argues that postcolonial temporality 'cannot – does not – reject the temporality of modernity because modern time is a significant part of its prehistory. Indeed the postcolonial condition is embedded, through colonialism and nationalism, in the politics of modernity.'[112] For Gikandi, the post- is a truly temporal prefix, but one that solidifies the connection with modernity rather than severing it. Because the opposition of Western progressive reason to anachronistic and regressive lag reinforces the narrative of modern hegemony, formulations of globalisation have tried to construe the present as multiple, different and simultaneously modern. These accounts would disrupt modernity in the realm of culture and the imaginary, when in the material, political realm, the very 'category of time [its totalising and unitary character] is itself indistinguishable from the hegemony of European modernity', and the transnational pluralisation of times and modernities remains rooted in a singular overarching history.[113] Moreover, the fragmentation of history is not so much a mode of resistance as it is a condition, a symptom of modernity and of the rise of global capitalism.

The question of the number of modernities, and hence of histories, has been a pressing issue for some time in a field premised on the relationship of culture to the referent of the 'modern'. As his title *A Singular Modernity* suggests, Jameson argues that the plurality in the lived experience of modernisation and its superstructural expressions are the result of the transitional phases of one, underlying, capitalist world system. As Neil Lazarus puts it, Jameson's formulation 'stands as a compelling repudiation of the various recent attempts to pluralize the concept of modernity through the evocation of "alternative", "competing", or "retroactive" modernity/modernities', because it refuses the 'diffusionist model' of modernity in which the qualities of the modern radiated outwards from Europe to non-European peripheries, a movement that is 'historicism' itself.[114] In diffusionist historicism, the propagation of an original European modernity delivers late instructions to different places through distorting conduits on how to be modern. But Lazarus's re-reading of Jameson shows that multiple expressions of modernity across the globe should not be construed as alternatives to an original Western modernity so much as the simultaneous consequences of and responses to

> production for exchange rather than use; monetization; private ownership; the development of specifically capitalist markets (involving 'free wage labor', the buying and selling of labor power) and of ancillary systems and institutions designed to enable and facilitate the consolidation, extension, and reproduction of [. . .] capitalist class relations.[115]

In Jessica Hagedorn's novel *Dream Jungle* (2003), the lag experienced by the characters who live in the Philippines, at a distance from but within the orbit of various neocolonial centres, reveals a need to acknowledge a causal intersection between modern European history, US history and the history of the peoples of the archipelago. However, Hagedorn's lag shows us that we can do so without having to insist that those histories are one, that their rhythms and significant units of measurement and memorialisation are identical, or that the construction or recognition of an alternative historical track is an evasion of the impact of Western capitalism. Indeed, while a good portion of the pathos of the novel is inextricable from the violence necessary to keep the histories of the US and the Philippines interpenetrated or at least aligned, the force of Hagedorn's exploration derives from the question not simply about where her characters come from, but where they are headed, the pathos of possibilities.

In her previous novel *Dogeaters* (1990), the world of the Philippines is defined not only by the colonisation of its imagination by American mass media, by the spectacular matrix that Guy Debord figured as a nightmare guardian of a society's sleep, but also by the spectacles' laggy arrival times and the chronological disorder built into characters' understandings of their world and identities, and into the disordered narrative form itself.[116] The first characters we meet in *Dogeaters* are in fact the movie stars Jane Wyman, Rock Hudson, Agnes Moorehead and Gloria Talbott, recalled in the novel's metafictive 'technicolor' style by one of the primary narrators, Rio Gonzaga, as the interior lining of her 1956 Manila universe. The expensive, air-conditioned space of the Avenue Theater advertises itself as 'Manila's "Foremost! First-Run! English Movies Only!" theater' – for those Filipinos who desire and can afford to keep abreast of imported cultural currents.[117] However, at the end of the novel, when one of the characters steps out of the narrative frame to correct Rio's account (and destabilise the entire fiction based loosely on the Marcos-era Philippines), we learn that 1956 may have been 1959, and 'We got movies late in those days, don't you remember? They advertised them as "first-run", but it wasn't like it is now [. . .] the movies were as much as two or three years behind the times.'[118]

This laggy relationship is treated implicitly in her later book *Dream Jungle*, where Hagedorn is interested in framing out-of-placeness and anachronistic unbelonging in the postcolonial present within a deeper timeline. The novel is structured by several different plots that seem to work together in sync. The first is Antonio Pigafetta's sixteenth-century account of Magellan's 1521 'discovery' of and death in the islands that the Spanish later named for Prince Philip. This historical sequence of events is paralleled by the 1970s narrative of Zamora López de Lagazpi who 'discovers' the lost 'Stone Age tribe' of the Taobo. Zamora's name suggests that he is the descendant of the Spanish conquistador Miguel López de Lagazpi, who established the first colony in the Philippines in 1565 – a lineage that, as Zamora knows, powerful people such as the president (Marcos) desire for themselves. Zamora's family history is a legacy that the wealthy mestizo also actively extends. His story of encounter with the Taobo and their usefulness to the president on the eve of martial law is based on Manuel Elizalde's 1971 discovery of the uncontacted people, the Tasaday, who made international headlines in the 1970s and were accused of being a hoax in the late 1980s, after

Marcos was deposed.[119] This plotline is juxtaposed with the story of *Napalm Sunset*, a fictionalised but unambiguous account of Francis Ford Coppola's filming of his Vietnam War picture *Apocalypse Now* in the Philippines. The novel produces this juxtaposition of Zamora–Taobo and *Napalm Sunset* by following its primary focus, the trajectory of a young girl, Rizalina Cayabyab, who comes to work with her mother at Zamora's compound in the Hollywood Hills neighbourhood of Manila from a Muslim region of Mindanao, the fictional Sultan Ramayyah. Rizalina runs away from the Legazpi mansion at 12 and reappears soon after as Jinx, a sex worker at the club Love Connection, where she meets an actor in *Napalm Sunset*, Vincent Moody, whom she accompanies back to the movie set in her home town near Lake Ramayyah.

The belatedness of the Philippines, where things keep coming late and remain out of place, is inscribed on the landscape itself, a landscape that critics have seen as the postmodern ground and emblem of Hagedorn's style of pastiche. When Vincent Moody lands in Manila from Los Angeles, he is astonished when driven

> past swamplands and crumbling colonial ruins, past jazzy discotheques, grand hotels, and haunted cathedrals [. . .] squatters' shacks on vacant lots, past brand-new skyscrapers make of smoky glass and steel. Billboards advertised kung-fu movies, Camay soap, and Kikkoman soy sauce [. . .] *Aji-No-Moto*, *Magnolia*, *Cortal*, *Rufina Patis*, *Eye-Mo*. Red-and-white Coca-Cola signs shimmered in the sunlight.[120]

This backdrop, like Jameson's description of peasant fields, Krupp factories and Ford plants, evokes not the postmodern waning of historicity but rather, it would seem, the transitional unevenness of capitalism across colonised spaces. Such a scenario seems to be a case, calibrated for the Filipino situation, of what Perry Anderson describes as 'the complex and differential temporality in which episodes or eras were discontinuous from each other, and heterogeneous within themselves'.[121] In this way, disjunctive constellations such as Lazarus's 'St. Petersburg in the 1870s, say, Dublin in 1904, Cairo in the 1950s, a village on a bend in the Nile in the Sudan in the 1960s' should not be considered as examples of alternative modernities, but of 'coeval [. . .] modernities or, better yet, peripheral modernities [. . .] in which all societies shared a common reference provided by global capital and its requirements'.[122]

However right, obvious and unavoidable it is to note the text's exploration of the peripheral status of the Philippines' present and, as Shyh-jen Fuh describes it, 'the historical sedimentation of its colonial legacies', the novel also raises the question of other and alternative historical tracks and possible futures, which exist in the world of *Dream Jungle* as both conditions and desires.[123] For Hagedorn, in *Dogeaters* as in *Dream Jungle*, alternativity is figured as insurgency and the revolutionary enclave, which hover in the background; but the fact that there is more than one temporal reference frame to consider is why the later novel is more diffident about revolution. As its title suggests, *Dream Jungle* appears to be focused on the various ways in which the archipelago has served as a fantasy space for colonial, postcolonial and neocolonial projects in the one history that leads from the conquistadors' jungle to the Americans' blockbuster. The singleness of that history is in tension with the polyvalent, contradictory potential of the jungle: the jungle is simultaneously the historical location of the descendants of 'exceedingly backward' peoples (named 'negritos' by the Spanish and pictured as 'physical and mental weaklings', as a 1903 *National Geographic* article describes them), the site of the impossible project of postcolonial nationalism, and the object of material and cultural exploitation by globalised multinational capitalism (Fig. 3.4).[124]

If there is something like a bullet-time scene in Hagedorn's novel, it is Rizalina's glimpse of Bodabil, the Taobo boy whom Zamora has brought back from 'the Stone Age' of the mountainous jungle region around Lake

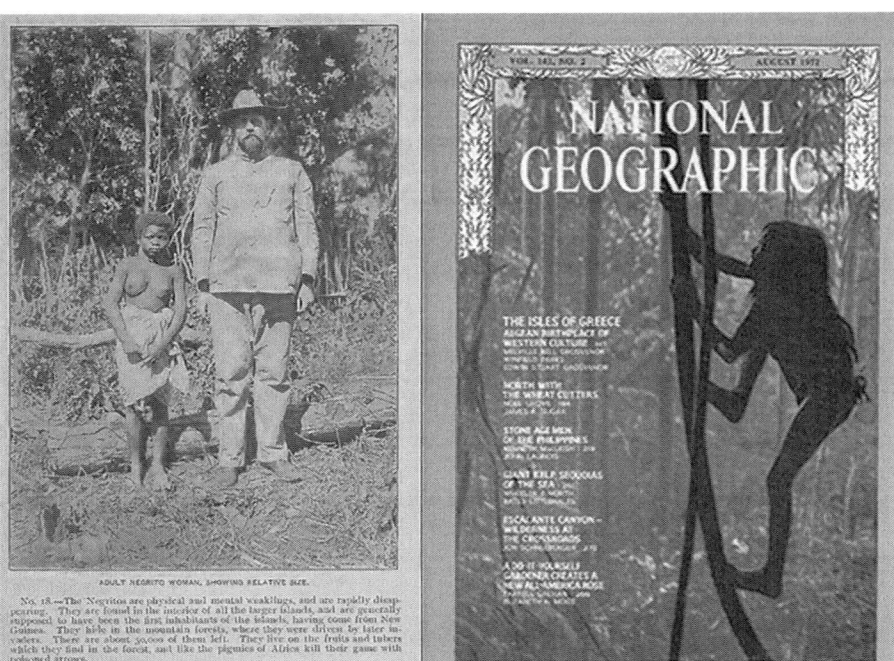

Figure 3.4 *National Geographic* photograph of negritos as 'physical and mental weaklings' (1903), and *National Geographic* cover on the Tasaday people (August 1972)

Ramayyah to the 1970s in Manila. The same age as Bodabil, Rizalina sees 'a skinny boy with long hair hanging loosely down his back [. . .] who crouched, enchanted, in front of the flickering TV screen' (34). However, this image is immediately placed under suspicion, as the focus of Hagedorn's juxtaposition seems to veer away from the constellation of Rizalina's trajectory from servitude to sex work, an emblem of indigeneity, and the technology of mass-mediated history in thrall to US culture. Instead it seems to tend towards the postmodern thematics that Hagedorn is known for: the production of the fiction of authenticity by the all-encompassing media mechanisms that yoke the fiction of the pure past to the global fantasy of a shared, singular future in which everyone has a place. In 'The Tasadays: The Stone Age Cavemen of Mindanao', the 1971 *National Geographic* article on which this plotline is based, Kenneth MacLeish ('Ken Forbes' in the novel) writes that as he and Elizalde ('Zamora') approached the Tasaday caves, led by their guide Balayem ('Duan'), Elizalde 'whispered "That must be it!" We moved closer [. . .] We stepped into the Stone Age [. . .] [W]e two, visitors where none had visited before, sat in silence, dazed as travelers in a time machine might be dazed upon arriving at their most distant destination.'[125]

Having flown to the Mindanao rainforests in helicopters, MacLeish recounts that Elizalde's party, 'skyborne creatures of man's most advanced and tormented society, and they, perhaps the last of the world's innocents, watched each other across the full span of cultural evolution'.[126] As a possible hoax, the fantasy of the Tasaday's/Taobo's timeline is not that it has been hitherto separate, just now crossing paths with modern history in the Philippines; rather, the uncontacted tribe belongs to the history of the 'most advanced' and may itself be a spectacle serving that history. The fact that Elizalde discovers the 'primitive' aboriginal people and together with Marcos provides a media diversion on the night before the president declares martial law (in response, as the novel suggests, to the communist guerilla insurgency and the beginning of the Moro Rebellion) indicates that Zamora's anthropological discovery is not only a repetition of 'the first moment of colonial encounter', but also a spectacle that abets the US-backed regime.[127]

In this reading, the parallel would be about recurrence rather than the coevalness of histories. As Shu-ching Chen argues, Zamora's return to the jungle is an attempt to recover the origin of the nation, and simply 'replicates the territorial imagination and spatial logic of imperialism'.[128] In relation to the city, the jungle of lost tribes is, as it was for the Spanish, feminised and backward or static. It is an example of the contradictions surrounding what Anne McClintock calls 'anachronistic space': 'Since indigenous peoples are not supposed to be there – for the lands are "empty" – they are symbolically displaced onto [. . .] *anachronistic space*', where they 'exist in a permanently anterior time [. . .] as anachronistic humans, atavistic, irrational, bereft of human agency'; by contrast, 'white male patrimony is violently assured as the sexual and military insemination of an interior void', of the 'virgin space'.[129] In *Dream Jungle*, the jungle is doubly displaced: if the Taobo and Bodabil are, like Elizalde's Tasaday, a nationalist fabrication with a colonialist pedigree for neocolonialist purposes, then the image of the crouching indigenous boy in front of the TV simply fortifies a theme that Hagedorn's work is known for – the simulation of origins, the fakeness of personal and national identity – and feeds into the novel's later exploration of the mass-mediated present in *Napalm Sunset/Apocalypse Now*. And the story of the making of the film turns out to be the story of the erasure of the historical particularity of the Philippines' colonial situation: the film can only critique US imperialism in Vietnam by 'render[ing] the archipelago invisible' and 'figuring it as a geographical substitute for Vietnam/Cambodia'.[130] Filipino actors are made to play Vietnamese soldiers; 'loincloth-wearing Filipino extras [are] playing mountain tribesmen' (245); and the two Southeast Asian jungles are interchangeable, because white American audiences will not notice or care.

However, the text seems intent on making the erasure of distinctions and contrasts conspicuous, and on pointing out the inadequacy of a single overarching historiographic umbrella, whether that be the power of imperial ethnology or Marxist critiques of global capitalism, however useful and even necessary the latter might be in explaining the present. One of the ways in which the novel raises the question of heterochronic lag between distinctive histories is by exploring 'the Philippines as an extension and manifestation of the US South', as Vernadette Vicuña Gonzalez writes, and by clarifying the 'racial logics' that organised the labour system as well as the socio-cultural domain in both the American South's and the Global South's 'coeval histories and colonial economies'.[131] In Gonzalez's argument, *Dream Jungle* links the 'ethnographic fantasy of the native in the former American colony to a cinematic war drama based on Conrad's *Heart of Darkness*', and thereby foregrounds the racialisation of Filipinx people as negritos, 'little brown brothers' and sexually exotic sisters, immediately following the Spanish-American War in 1898, in relation to both the subjugation of African Americans in the American South and US imperialism in Vietnam.[132] As Gonzalez reads Jessie Tarbox Beals's photographs of the 1904 World's Fair in St Louis, which featured the grotesque 'living exhibition' of 1,100 'savage' Filipinos, 'the colonization of the Philippines and the American project of "uplift"' were constructed 'as parallel to the reconstruction of the American South': 'Fairgoers superimposed the familiar racializations of the South onto the new brown savages of the US empire.'[133] Thus, the novel focuses on *Napalm Sunset* as an extension of 'the visual technologies [. . .] instrumental in rationalizing and producing an iconography of savagery, a narrative of civilizing, and evidence of the successful disciplining of the native body'.[134] Hagedorn's representation of the film highlights a director, Tony Pierce, who quotes Conrad's paradigmatic text about colonial time travel – 'we were trav-elling in the night of the first ages' (247); it foregrounds the erasure of the Filipino and Vietnamese contexts under the historically persistent sign of the primitive; and it brings into view the global economic imperatives of cheap labour that underwrites these erasures.

The long simultaneity of imperial and global-capitalist primitivism is nev-ertheless complicated by the presence of elements that resist or escape the syn-chronising mechanisms of Pierce's production and its requirements of colonial mimicry (whether the peoples of the Philippines find themselves mimicking Europeans, European Americans, African Americans or Viet Cong). As in the discussion above of CPT as 'the time-dimension of double consciousness', a laggy two-ness gives way to a heterochronic multiplicity, and the jungle emerges, beyond the twin aspects of nationalist origin and colonial backdrop, as the actual location of insurgency and resistance. There are a number of examples of a monolithic illusion giving way to plural rates of change and trajectories of history. The 'Indians' that Pierce's son sees near Lake Ramayyah are, as Janet Pierce corrects him, 'not *Indian*, Jesse. They're *Himal*' (218). The novel makes a point of describing the face of the actor Billy Hernandez, who has 'played every imaginable ethnic type in movies, on television, and onstage' in the US (194): Billy's face is described in the text as Taino, referring to the indigenous peoples of the Caribbean islands also colonised by the Spanish, whose histories have not disappeared but abide. Likewise, whether or not the Taobo are 'authentic' or paid actors, what they signify is one history among a cluster of histories in the Philippines that cannot be used to ground nationalist historiographic unity and that in fact problematise such unity. As Janet Pierce writes in her diary about shooting their film about the Vietnam War, 'We're in the middle of a real war', 'the civil war in Mindanao' (276), a conflict that continues to this day. Accord-ing to Amy Kaplan, Pierce's/Coppola's reliance on Marcos's support and the 'rented military equipment from the US built army of the Philippines' are the novel's way of figuring 'the horrors of American imperialism in Vietnam', which offers an obvious irony: 'the breakdown between fiction and history in these glaring parallels between the present in the Philippines and the [immediate] past of Vietnam do not make Eleanor or Francis Coppola reflect on their participa-tion as filmmakers in the dynamics of empire'.[135] However, the scene in ques-tion also represents and exemplifies, stands for and as, the continued unfolding of another history: in *Apocalypse Now* as in *Napalm Sunset*, the attack scene using Filipino military aircraft playing American helicopters shows the choppers 'suddenly turn out of line as they are radioed by their commanders to fight a political insurrection in the immediate vicinity'.[136]

The significance of the flight path is that, while the frames defined by Spanish imperialism, US colonisation and neocolonisation, and postcolonial nation-building overlap in significant ways, they also contain non-identical paths forward. At the level of the individual, Hagedorn is less sanguine in *Dream Jungle* than in *Dogeaters*. Rizalina escapes the Philippines but ends up, ambiguously, in Moody's old place in Santa Monica. Like Elizabeth Dalloway, she receives a sketch of possible futures when she is younger: '"Your future is" – my mother paused, thinking hard – "filled with hope. You could become a nurse, Lina. Or a bank teller [. . .] Or maybe a teacher like that woman you admire so much"' (14). But Rizalina believes that the Bic pen and pink notebook on which she uses a portion of her first month's salary (73) will record a 'future of shit', since her family history is one of 'Washerwomen, *yayas*, cooks, housecleaners, gardeners who [. . .] hardly ever saw their own families' (15). Zamora's voice ends the novel: the final chapter, narrated in 2000 from a marble mantelpiece in New York where his daughter keeps the urn of his ashes, recounts an unhappy life plagued by 'my diabolical virus, my cancers, my non-immune system' (321). It may seem as if the novel's sole purpose is to draw a single line from the account of one coloniser in 1521 to another voice from the dead in 2000, with the main characters' lives being pulled directly into the new imperial centre of the US. However, the novel also alerts us early on, through the photojournalist Ken Forbes's retrospection, to a variety of futures that point to other histories, collective sequences that may share certain key events with, but remain de-synchronised from, history in the main. In the text, ostensibly offstage, the Moro National Liberation Front guerillas shoot down Zamora's helicopter pilot Buzz Ramos, and the Himal elders and guides ''Aket and Duan survived well into their nineties' (87). If the jungle, as Chen argues, 'is inscribed by the uncanniness of two temporalities: the fascination with the ahistorical timeless imaginary of the nation, and the imperialist symbolic order that gives rise to the homogenous linear national pedagogy', it also contains and stands for the incommensurable histories that began before Magellan and continue on, slowly, and without Americans.[137]

What seems offstage and out-of-sync is actually running side by side with a host of other sequences, rhythms and sets of possibilities. In part two of *Dogeaters*, 'The Song of Bullets', the world that is governed by lies, 'tsismis' (gossip) and mass media is disrupted by another timeline, joined late by the main character Joey after Senator Avila (Aquino) is assassinated. This timeline, defined by Joey's re-education in the jungle by the insurgents, ends in the future tense, when Daisy 'teaches him how to use a gun'.[138] Warren Liu says of the techno-Orientalism in SF that what many texts find most concerning 'is not the threatening savage eternally lurking at the periphery of the civilized, but the threat of an inappropriate disordering of the synchronization among past, present, and future'.[139] This disordering, as Liu argues, 'skews the future': 'the queer future, it turns out, is that which potentially counterfeits the "natural" inevitability of the present, thereby exposing it as the future's *asynchronous past*'.[140] If one of the 'pitfalls of the term "post-colonialism"', in Anne McClintock's formulation, has been that 'the theory promises a decentering of history in hybridity, syncretism, multi-dimensional time, and so forth, [while] the *singularity* of the term effects a re-centering of global history around the single rubric of European time', then we might add the following to Liu's excellent account: the past no longer lines up with the present, and the future no longer aligns with the present from which it presumably flows, because the singularity of the term 'time' yields to other histories coursing through any particular slice of contemporaneous non-sametimely happenings.[141]

NOTES

1. Lisa Purse, 'The New Spatial Dynamics of the Bullet-Time Effect', in *Spectacle of the Real: From Hollywood to Reality TV and Beyond*, ed. Geoff King (Bristol: Intellect, 2005), 151–60.
2. Bob Rehak, 'The Migration of Forms: Bullet Time as Microgenre', *Film Criticism* 32.1 (2007): 35.
3. Richard Linnett, 'The Gondry Effect', *Shoot* 39.19 (1998): 25, quoted in Eivind Røsaak, 'Figures of Sensation: Between Still and Moving Images', in *The Cinema of Attractions Reloaded*, ed. Wanda Strauven (Amsterdam: Amsterdam University Press, 2006), 334 n. 9.
4. Rehak, 'Migration of Forms', 26; Røsaak, 'Figures of Sensation', 323.
5. See Tom Gunning, 'Attractions: How They Came into the World', in Strauven (ed.), *The Cinema of Attractions Reloaded*, 31–40; Tom Gunning, '"Primitive" Cinema: A Frame-Up? Or, The Trick's on Us', in *Early Cinema: Space-Frame-Narrative*, ed. Thomas Elsaesser and Adam Barker (London: British Film Institute, 1990), 95–103; and Tom Gunning, '"Now You See It, Now You Don't": The Temporality of the Cinema of Attractions', *Velvet Light Trap: A Critical Journal of Film & Television* 32 (autumn 1993): 3–12.
6. Bill Brown, 'Materiality', in *Critical Terms for Media Studies*, ed. W. J. T. Mitchell and Mark B. N. Hansen (Chicago: University of Chicago Press, 2010), 49.
7. Susan Broadhurst, *Digital Practices: Aesthetic and Neuroesthetic Approaches to Performance and Technology* (Basingstoke: Palgrave Macmillan, 2007), 142.
8. Purse, 'New Spatial Dynamics', 156.
9. John Gaeta, 'New Realities: The Matrix Revolutions Completes a Trilogy of Films that Introduced a New Style of Visual Effects', interview by Barbara Robertson, *Computer Graphics World* 26.12 (2003): 56–7.
10. José Arroyo, 'Mission: Sublime', in *Action/Spectacle Cinema: A Sight and Sound Reader*, ed. José Arroyo (London: British Film Institute, 2000), 22.
11. Scott Bukatman, *Matters of Gravity: Special Effects and Supermen in the 20th Century* (Durham, NC: Duke University Press, 2003), 118, 125.
12. Wells, *The Time Machine*, 77. Subsequent page references are given in parentheses in the text.
13. See Keith Williams, *H.G. Wells, Modernity and the Movies* (Liverpool: Liverpool University Press, 2007).

14. H. G. Wells, *The Definitive Time Machine: A Critical Edition of H.G. Wells's Scientific Romance*, ed. Harry M. Geduld (Bloomington: Indiana University Press, 1987), 158.
15. Williams, *H.G. Wells, Modernity and the Movies*, 3.
16. William James, *The Principles of Psychology* (New York: Henry Holt, 1890), 639.
17. Marx and Engels, *The Communist Manifesto*, 38.
18. Wolfgang Schivelbusch, *The Railway Journey: The Industrialization and Perception of Time and Space* (Berkeley: University of California Press, 1986), 64.
19. Martin Jay, 'Introduction: Genres of Blur', *Common Knowledge* 18.2 (2012): 227.
20. Ibid.
21. Ibid.
22. In 1877 Stanford commissioned Muybridge to figure out if Marey's hypothesis about the floating horse was actually true.
23. In the year 3015, this distinction will belong to the photographer Jonathon Keats, who in 2015 set up a camera in Arizona to capture a one-thousand-year pin-hole exposure. See https://petapixel.com/2015/03/05/this-camera-will-capture-a-1000-year-exposure-that-ends-in-3015-for-historys-slowest-photo/ (last accessed 11 October 2018).
24. Sarah Hermanson Meister, 'Open Shutter', in *Michael Wesely: Open Shutter* (New York: Museum of Modern Art, 2005), 9. All remarks from Wesely come from conversations with Meister, April–June, 2004.
25. Ibid. 13.
26. Ibid.
27. Stefan Klenke, 'The Longest Photographic Exposures in History – The Latest', *Itchy I* (blog), 20 July 2010, http://itchyi.squarespace.com/thelatest/2010/7/20/the-longest-photographic-exposures-in-history.html (last accessed 11 October 2018).
28. John Crowe Ransom, 'Flux and Blur in Contemporary Art', *The Sewanee Review* 37.3 (1929): 355, 362.
29. William Faulkner, *The Sound and the Fury: Norton Critical Edition*, ed. David Minter, 2nd edn (New York: W. W. Norton, 1994), 54. Subsequent page references are to this edition and are given in parentheses in the text.
30. Jean-Paul Sartre, 'On *The Sound and the Fury*: Time in the Work of Faulkner', in *Literary and Philosophical Essays*, trans. Annette Michelson (London: Rider, 1955), 79; J. Hillis Miller, 'Time in Literature', *Daedalus* 132.2 (2003): 92.
31. Sartre, 'On *The Sound and the Fury*', 80.
32. Ibid. 82.
33. Justin Skirry, 'Sartre on William Faulkner's Metaphysics of Time in *The Sound and the Fury*', *Sartre Studies International* 7.2 (2001): 17.
34. Ibid. 22–3. 'Faulkner, on the other hand', says Skirry, 'presupposes that time is chronological in that it is an external force composed of a collection of discrete instances that determine us to be what we are (In-itself) without regard for what we are not (For-itself)' (17).
35. Sartre, 'On *The Sound and the Fury*', 80, 83.
36. Douglas Messerli provides a comprehensive review of 1950s–1960s criticism focused on time in *The Sound and the Fury*, starting with Sartre's essay, which

he sees as establishing transcendence as the only option, and generating the long-standing focus on the ambivalence in Faulkner between subjective duration and transcendent/mythic temporality. Messerli cites and summarises the major readings up to that point in the mid-1970s. Douglas Messerli, 'The Problem of Time in *The Sound and the Fury*: A Critical Reassessment and Reinterpretation', *The Southern Literary Journal* 6.2 (1974): 19–41.

37. Perrin Lowrey, 'Concepts of Time in *The Sound and the Fury*', in *English Institute Essays*, ed. Alan S. Downer (New York: Columbia University Press, 1952), 57–82; reprinted in Michael H. Cowan (ed.), *Twentieth Century Interpretations of The Sound and the Fury* (Englewood Cliffs, NJ: Prentice-Hall, 1968), 53, 60. For Benjy, 'time does not exist [. . .] Because Ben is unaware of the lapse of time, he is always approaching, but never quite reaching, a pure specious present' (54–5); 'What Quentin really wants is to get outside of time, to get into eternity [. . .] [A] state in which change and motion are transcended' (56); and Jason 'attempts to steal and hoard time just as he does money', but is 'always just a little too late' (59).

38. Olga W. Vickery, '*The Sound and the Fury*: A Study in Perspective', *PMLA: Publications of the Modern Language Association of America* 69.5 (1954): 1020.

39. Olga W. Vickery, 'Faulkner and the Contours of Time', *The Georgia Review* 12.2 (1958): 192. Douglas Messerli asks 'Is Faulkner's sense of time represented best by Dilsey?' ('Problem of Time', 34), and makes a case that Dilsey's ethical and religious overcoming of isolation and her future orientation stand in opposition to the nihilism of the Compsons.

40. Vickery, '*The Sound and the Fury*', 1024.

41. Ibid. 1026.

42. Vickery, 'Faulkner and the Contours of Time', 192; Vickery, '*The Sound and the Fury*', 1037.

43. Cleanth Brooks, *William Faulkner: Toward Yoknapatawpha and Beyond* (Baton Rouge: Louisiana State University Press, 1990 [1978]), 255.

44. Ibid. 254; Cleanth Brooks, *William Faulkner: The Yoknapatawpha Country* (New Haven, CT: Yale University Press, 1963), 329.

45. Brooks, *William Faulkner: The Yoknapatawpha Country*, 329, 328.

46. Arthur Geffen likewise argues that 'the black Easter Sunday service' is 'a time out of time', and that its 'antihistorical and timeless quality' stands in stark contrast with profane temporality and the failed attempt at the sacred that is 'Confederate time', 'an order which promises but never delivers fulfillment'; Arthur Geffen, 'Profane Time, Sacred Time, and Confederate Time in *The Sound and the Fury*', *Studies in American Fiction* 2.2 (1974): 180, 181, 191.

47. Brooks, *William Faulkner: The Yoknapatawpha Country*, 329, 330.

48. Ibid. 328, 330, 342.

49. Ibid. 342–3, 345.

50. John Rieder, *Colonialism and the Emergence of Science Fiction* (Middletown, CT: Wesleyan University Press, 2008), 5.

51. Ibid. 32.

52. Galison, *Einstein's Clocks and Poincaré's Maps*, 37.

53. Adrian Mackenzie, 'The Technicity of Time: From 1.00 Oscillations/Sec to 9,192,631,770 Hz', *Time & Society* 10.2–3 (2001): 236.
54. Zemka, *Time and the Moment*, 1.
55. Mackenzie, 'Technicity of Time', 242.
56. Carlene Stephens, '"The Most Reliable Time": William Bond, the New England Railroads, and Time Awareness in 19th-Century America', *Technology and Culture* 30.1 (1989): 8.
57. Ibid. 8.
58. Leonard Waldo, 'The Distribution of Time', *North American Review* 131.289 (December 1880), 528, quoted in O'Malley, *Keeping Watch*, 95.
59. O'Malley, *Keeping Watch*, 88.
60. Galison, *Einstein's Clocks and Poincaré's Maps*, 112.
61. Edward Everett, 'The Uses of Astronomy', quoted in O'Malley, *Keeping Watch*, 63–4.
62. Waldo, 'Distribution of Time', 534.
63. Ibid. 529.
64. Ibid. 534.
65. See Robert Levine, *A Geography of Time: The Temporal Misadventures of a Social Psychologist, or How Every Culture Keeps Time Just a Little Bit Differently* (New York: Basic Books, 1997), 21.
66. *McGuffey's Fifth Eclectic Reader* (New York, 1920 [1881]), 161–3; quoted in O'Malley, *Keeping Watch*, 148.
67. Levine, *Geography of Time*, 70. Levine cites historian John Cawelti on Horatio Alger's stories: 'The new watch marks the hero's attainment of a more elevated position, and is a symbol of punctuality and his respect for time'; John Cawelti, *Apostles of the Self-Made Man* (Chicago: University Chicago Press, 1965), 118.
68. See Stephens, 'Most Reliable Time', 11; Ian R. Bartky, 'The Adoption of Standard Time', *Technology and Culture* 30.1 (1989): 47–8.
69. 'Sketch of William Cranch Bond', *The Popular Science Monthly*, July 1895, 407. For an excellent treatment of the personal equation, see Jimena Canales, *A Tenth of a Second a History* (Chicago: University of Chicago Press, 2009).
70. See Stephens, 'Most Reliable Time', 12–14.
71. Galison, *Einstein's Clocks and Poincaré's Maps*, 103–4.
72. Stephens, 'Most Reliable Time', 11.
73. Ibid. emphasis in original.
74. *Records of New England Association of Railway Superintendents, Organized in Boston, Mass. April 15, 1848, Dissolved, October 1, 1857*, quoted in Stephens, 'Most Reliable Time', 7.
75. Bartky, 'Adoption of Standard Time', 47–8. Bartky argues that the railways' standardisation of time based on Greenwich had less to do with the 'chaos of railroad timetables' (because they could manage the profusion of local times) than with the railways' paranoia about government legislation, the first instance of which was the result of Waldo's influence on Connecticut to pass a statute mandating New York City's local time as the state standard (Ibid. 25). However, it is not difficult to argue that government legislation was itself a response to the confusions and dangers of

temporal 'chaos', in which terminal cities each had two or three time standards, rail lines and their different time standards 'touched or overlapped at three hundred points in the country' (28), and trains had already collided. Standard time did not become a matter of law until the Standard Time Act in 1918.

76. Cynthia Dobbs, '"Ruin or Landmark"? Black Bodies as Lieux de Mémoire in *The Sound and the Fury*', *Faulkner Journal* 20.1/2 (2004): 38.

77. George B. Ellenberg, 'African Americans, Mules, and the Southern Mindscape, 1850–1950', *Agricultural History* 72.2 (1998): 382.

78. Ibid. 396.

79. Cheryl Lester, 'Racial Awareness and Arrested Development: *The Sound and the Fury* and the Great Migration (1915–1928)', in *The Cambridge Companion to William Faulkner*, ed. Philip Weinstein (New York: Cambridge University Press, 1995), 135.

80. Ibid. 130. The first peak was 1915–18; 'Faulkner took the train from Mississippi to New Haven in April 1918 and from Mississippi to Toronto the following July' (Ibid. 130).

81. Ibid. 131.

82. Ibid. 126.

83. See Wayne W. Westbrook, 'Skunked on the New York Cotton Exchange: What Really Happens to Jason Compson in *The Sound and the Fury*', *The Southern Literary Journal* 41.2 (2009): 53–68. According to Westbrook, 'Jason Compson's losses are breathtaking. He had sold short one cotton futures contract (month unknown) at 12.61 on the market's opening. The closing of his account late in the trading session at 20.62 means that the broker paid $10,310 to buy his contract back, or cover his short sale. The result is a stunning loss of 801 points – or $4,005' (57).

84. Michael Hanchard, 'Afro-Modernity: Temporality, Politics and the African Diaspora', in *Alternative Modernities*, ed. Dilip Parameshwar Gaonkar (Durham, NC: Duke University Press, 2001), 281.

85. Ibid. 284.

86. Ibid. 285.

87. Frank M. Kirkland, 'Modernity and Intellectual Life in Black', *Philosophical Forum* 24.1–3 (1992): 159; quoted in Hanchard, 'Afro-Modernity', 277.

88. Kirkland, quoted in Hanchard, 'Afro-Modernity', 278.

89. Karl Marx, *The Poverty of Philosophy* (Moscow: Foreign Languages Publishing House, 1962 [1847]), 51.

90. Eugene D. Genovese, *Roll, Jordan, Roll: The World the Slaves Made* (New York: Pantheon Books, 1974), 286; quoted in Mark M. Smith, *Mastered by the Clock: Time, Slavery, and Freedom in the American South* (Chapel Hill: University of North Carolina Press, 2000), 9.

91. Smith, *Mastered by the Clock*, 130.

92. Mungo Park, *Travels in the Interior Districts of Africa* (London: John Murray, 1815), 478; quoted in Smith, *Mastered by the Clock*, 132.

93. Smith, *Mastered by the Clock*, 163–4.

94. Ibid. 16.

95. Waldo, 'Distribution of Time', 534.
96. Smith, *Mastered by the Clock*, 130.
97. John Streamas, 'Closure and "Colored People's Time"', *The Study of Time* 13 (2010): 220.
98. Ibid. 226.
99. Smith, *Mastered by the Clock*, 165.
100. Hanchard, 'Afro-Modernity', 274.
101. David Lloyd, *Ireland After History* (North Bend, IN: University of Notre Dame Press, 1999), 392.
102. Ibid. 392.
103. Hugues Azérad, 'A New Region of the World: Faulkner, Glissant, and the Caribbean', in *The New Cambridge Companion to William Faulkner*, ed. John T. Matthews (Cambridge: Cambridge University Press, 2015), 168; Ramón Saldívar and Sylvan Goldberg, 'The Faulknerian Anthropocene: Scales of Time and History in *The Wild Palms* and *Go Down, Moses*', in Matthews (ed.), *The New Cambridge Companion to William Faulkner*, 188.
104. Homi K. Bhabha, *The Location of Culture* (London: Routledge, 1994), 177.
105. Ibid. 177, 171.
106. Ibid. 195.
107. Satoshi Mizutani, 'Hybridity and History: A Critical Reflection on Homi K. Bhabha's Post-Historical Thoughts', *Ab Imperio* 4 (2013): 37.
108. Bhabha, *Location of Culture*, 176.
109. Keya Ganguly, 'Temporality and Postcolonial Critique', in *The Cambridge Companion to Postcolonial Literary Studies*, ed. Neil Lazarus (Cambridge: Cambridge University Press, 2004), 170. The quotation in full from Theodor Adorno reads: 'No universal history leads from the savage to the human, but there is one leading from the slingshot to the megaton bomb.' Theodor Adorno, *Negative Dialectics* (London: Routledge, 2003 [1966]), 320.
110. Ganguly, 'Temporality and Postcolonial Critique', 177.
111. See Rifkin, *Beyond Settler Time*. Rifkin's term refers to the integrity and legitimacy of indigenous peoples' refusals in the face of the settler-colonial insistence on historical assimilation, even one that promises to make space for many cultures.
112. Simon Gikandi, 'Globalization and the Claims of Postcoloniality', *The South Atlantic Quarterly* 100.3 (2001): 641.
113. Ibid. 642.
114. Neil Lazarus, 'Modernism and African Literature', in *The Oxford Handbook of Global Modernisms*, ed. Mark Wollaeger and Matt Eatough (Oxford: Oxford University Press, 2012), 233.
115. Ibid. 235.
116. For an excellent reading of the spectacular imprisonment of the Philippines in Hagedorn's novel, see Myra Mendible, 'Desiring Images: Representation and Spectacle in *Dogeaters*', *Critique: Studies in Contemporary Fiction* 43.3 (2002): 289–304. See also Hagedorn's introduction to *Charlie Chan Is Dead: An Anthology of Contemporary Asian American Fiction* (New York: Penguin Books, 1993): 'growing up in the fifties and sixties [. . .] what was really important, what was

inevitably preferred, was the aping of our mythologized Hollywood universe. The colonization of the imagination was relentless and hard to shake off. Everywhere we turned, the images held up did not match our own' (xxiii).

117. Jessica Hagedorn, *Dogeaters* (New York: Penguin Books, 1990), 3.
118. Ibid. 248.
119. For evaluations of the authenticity of the Tasaday at the 1989 symposium organised by the American Anthropological Association, see Thomas N. Headland (ed.), *The Tasaday Controversy: Assessing the Evidence* (Washington, DC: American Anthropological Association, 1992).
120. Jessica Hagedorn, *Dream Jungle* (New York: Viking, 2003), 134. Subsequent page references are to this edition and are given in parentheses in the text.
121. Anderson, 'Modernity and Revolution', 101.
122. See Lazarus, 'Modernism and African Literature', 233. Lazarus is citing Harry Harootunian, *History's Disquiet: Modernity, Cultural Practice, and the Question of Everyday Life* (New York: Columbia University Press, 2000), 62–3.
123. Shyh-jen Fuh, '"At Home in the World": Transnationalism and the Question of Belonging in Jessica Hagedorn's *Dream Jungle*', *Tamkang Review: A Quarterly of Literary and Cultural Studies* 40.2 (2010): 28.
124. See photos 12 and 18 in 'American Development of the Philippines', *National Geographic Magazine* 14.5 (May 1903): 202, 209; Shu-ching Chen, 'Run through the Jungle: Uncanny Domesticity and the Woman of Shame in Jessica Hagedorn's *Dream Jungle*', *Tamkang Review: A Quarterly of Literary and Cultural Studies* 43.1 (2012): 5.
125. Kenneth MacLeish, 'The Tasadays: The Stone Age Cavemen of Mindanao', *National Geographic* 142 (August 1972): 231–2.
126. Ibid. 232.
127. The Moro Rebellion, which began in 1972, was a demand for an independent Muslim state on Rizalina's home island of Mindanao.
128. Chen, 'Run through the Jungle', 7.
129. Anne McClintock, 'The Angel of Progress: Pitfalls of the Term "Postcolonialism"', *Social Text* 31–32 (1992): 30; emphasis in original.
130. Hsiu-chuan Lee, 'The Remains of Empire and the "Purloined" Philippines: Jessica Hagedorn's *Dream Jungle*', *Mosaic: An Interdisciplinary Critical Journal* 45.3 (2012): 54.
131. Vernadette Vicuña Gonzalez, 'Headhunter Itineraries: The Philippines as America's Dream Jungle', *The Global South* 3.2 (2009): 149.
132. Ibid. 149.
133. Ibid. 150.
134. Ibid. 153.
135. Amy E. Kaplan, '"Left Alone with America": The Absence of Empire in the Study of American Culture', in *Cultures of United States Imperialism*, ed. Amy E. Kaplan and Donald E. Pease (Durham, NC: Duke University Press, 1993), 18–19.
136. Ibid. 19.
137. Chen, 'Run through the Jungle', 10.

138. Hagedorn, *Dogeaters*, 233.
139. Warren Liu, 'Queer Excavations: Technology, Temporality, Race', in *Techno-Orientalism: Imagining Asia in Speculative Fiction, History, and Media*, ed. David S. Roh, Betsy Huang and Greta A. Niu (New Brunswick, NJ: Rutgers University Press, 2015), 67.
140. Ibid. 72.
141. McClintock, 'Angel of Progress', 86.

4

TEMPORAL SCALE, THE FAR FUTURE AND INHUMAN TIMES: FORESIGHT IN WELLS AND WOOLF, TIME TRAVEL IN OLAF STAPLEDON AND TERRENCE MALICK

Earth
Solar System
Milky Way Galaxy
Local Group
Virgo Supercluster
Observable Universe

Neil deGrasse Tyson, *Cosmos*

Class of Elements
Clongowes Wood College
Sallins
County Kildare
Ireland
Europe
The World
The Universe

James Joyce, *Portrait of the Artist as a Young Man*

EXPANDED PERSPECTIVES ON TIME

In the first episode of the 2014 reboot of Carl Sagan's *Cosmos*, Neil deGrasse Tyson presented the list above as the sobering 'long address' of the human.[1] Often the long view evokes awe-inspiring totality: think of the earliest pictures of earth from space, such as 'Earthrise' taken from *Apollo 8* in 1968 and the whole-earth photograph 'Blue Marble' taken from *Apollo 17* in 1972. However, as our view grew more and more distant – relayed from 3.7 billion miles away, for instance, by *Voyager 1* in 1990 – our *here we are* pictures seemed to offer only humbling vantages, perspectives from which we could see that the entirety of everything we care about is contained, as Sagan famously put it, 'on a mote of dust suspended in a sunbeam'.[2] As is typical in grand reflections on our inconsequence, Sagan's meditation on the *Voyager 1* image tacks from the 'demonstration of the folly of human conceits' to perhaps the most desperate conceit of second modernity – that we must 'deal more kindly with one another and [. . .] preserve and cherish the pale blue dot, the only home we've ever known'.[3] Our long address, while always partly a litany to our expansive technological abilities, is largely a set of directions to humility: we arrive at our contingency and global responsibility by enfolding a decentred humanity in ever-larger totalising frames. Such shifts in perspective are not only about celebrating technological know-how or recognising that everything we've ever known is *here*. As this chapter will argue, they are sometimes also about rethinking context itself, and not simply in a way that disables shorter *durées*. To modify an idea popularised by the astronomer Jill Tarter, perhaps the most radical lesson of scoping out is not so much the parochialising of 'here' as the presence of other histories 'out there', and further, the constitutive entanglement of our present in a wide array of histories right 'now' (Plate 8).[4]

Often using big views of/from space, recent work in literary studies has aimed to enlarge our understanding of situatedness, scoping out to ever wider arenas of action and interdependence, pushing beyond the national to the planetary. For example, in *Sense of Place and Sense of Planet*, Ursula Heise shows how the 'Big Blue Marble' contributed to the 'holistic understanding of ecological connectedness' that emerged in the 1970s. As environmental concerns increased in urgency, 'cultural imagination [shifted] from a sense of place to a less territorial and more systemic sense of the planet'; this shift finds expression in an updated version of 'collage or montage' – the Google Earth experience of 'the infinite possibility of zooming into and out of local, regional, and global views'.[5] In modernist studies, Susan Stanford Friedman's definitional expansion of modernism entails a 'planetary epistemology' that links an 'infinitely expandable' modernity to a transformed sense of 'the plurality of modernisms and the circulations among them'.[6] This transformation involves not merely additions to the syllabus but also a modification of our readings of familiar sites in relation to larger wholes. Scoping out from narrow definitions changes what the particulars look like in the more familiar horizon.

One of the most important aspects of this critical telescoping is the way spatial scales involve temporal and historical ones. Paralleling the move beyond nation to planet is the expansion of historical context from shallow diachrony to what one might call 'deep historicism'. In *Through Other Continents*, Wai Chee Dimock argues that in nationalist historicisms, to 'contextualize [. . .] is simply to synchronize' with a date, to aggregate only the most proximate phenomena within 'such thin slices of time' of a nation-state's narrow chronology.[7] To counter the use of 'time as a measuring tape, uniform and abstract', she looks to the 'large-scale sciences' whose vantage points and objects alter 'the threshold of differentiation, raising the bar so high that what once looked like huge differences now fall below the line'.[8] Against the chronological synchronisations of the nation and its parochial frames of reference, Dimock stretches 'American literature' across wide 'expanses of slow-moving history' and brings distant and disparate phenomena together in a larger continuum.[9] As critics have pointed out, the results of Dimock's commitment to 'nonstandard space and time' turn out to be enduring, cross-cultural 'categories of experience, such as beauty or death', 'long-lasting genres, such as epic and the novel', and the institution of literature itself.[10]

Deep historicism gives us a view of what lasts, of Braudelian mini-hyperobjects strewn across the ages and places of the world; but scaling up just as often shows us what does not or will not last.[11] Instead of bringing new units of analysis to light, it provokes apocalyptic anxieties about the perishability of all units – including, needless to say, literature, its genres, and the 'universal' categories of experience associated with the humanities. As Mark McGurl points out in his responses to Dimock, to stretch literature across spans larger than Braudelian durations is really to foreground the failure of human institutions.[12] This perilous outcome of scalar operations becomes even clearer in 'big history', the multidisciplinary effort, associated with historians such as David Christian and Fred Spier, to generate a single 'universal history, a history of all time'.[13] Spier recounts that the inspiration for his 'detached overview of history' and his environmental commitments came from the Earthrise photograph, which he saw in *Time Magazine*'s 1969 spread 'The Awesome Views from Apollo 8'.[14] Christian's chronologies and timescales in *Maps of Time: An Introduction to Big History* – from the Big Bang to the emergence of humans and death of the universe – demonstrate the precarious contingency produced by the attempt to think big, which puts into almost hilarious relief the 'Goldilocks' conditions just right for the evolution of complexity. His conception of big history as a 'new creation myth', which answers 'universal questions at many different scales', 'appears to have a nested structure similar to a Russian matryoshka doll', and this doll continually threatens to become a kind of meta-Saturn: the bigger this Saturn gets, the more temporal scales he devours.

Zooming out at the beginning of the twentieth century had very different purposes than the grand history of all time. It included but went beyond the identification of hyperobjects and the dissolution of familiar solidities. The expansion of historicity not only served to critique the myopia of the short term, the close-up immersion in the momentary that we often take as aesthetic modernism's primary focus; the big-historical lens also generated a new and bewildering sense of heterochrony, the clash of multiple timescales. In previous chapters, I have argued that modernism explores not simply the experience of modernity but those aspects of time that estrange modernity's dominant understanding of time itself. The experiments in literature and the visual arts of this period, such as the reconfiguration of narrative as more than just a vehicle for moving around in time, both revealed and produced these unfamiliar features of time. When seen in relation to certain time-travel fantasies, this interrogation appears as part of the century's larger heterochrony machine, a discursive network focused on defamiliarising the very medium in which we move, generating new ways of conceptualising and experiencing it.

The aim of this chapter is to link the period's visions of the far future with modernism's engagement with deep time in order to show how the big historicising that begins in the nineteenth century is not solely about the expansion of historicity but the multiplicity and alternative futurity that follows from it. McGurl gives the name 'posthuman comedy' to examples of horror and science fiction that explore timescales so large that the fit between the object and the representation is laughably bad. Both the form and the content of such texts 'risk artistic ludicrousness in their representation of the inhumanly large and long'.[15] These works are not marked by the longevity of genre but are instead examples of the deterioration of literariness. This issue of aesthetic badness has an established place within modernist studies, but it is not confined to those critical conversations in the way we think it might be. Douglas Mao and Rebecca Walkowitz explored the period's various refusals and repudiations of dominant aesthetic values and social conventions as a commitment to badness, one that allowed us to expand the purview of modernist studies and the definition of modernism itself.[16] In this arena, too, many of the geographical, social and topical transgressions are temporal in a strangely heterochronic way. That is, the temporal expansion in modernist studies is not simply limited to stretching 'the historical period to the late twentieth century' or the early twenty-first.[17] Rather, some of modernism's refractory and risible tactics scope out from conditions specifically known as modernity to their after-effects in the posthuman future, to what Ulrich Beck has theorised as the long-term 'bads' that lie beyond sense and imagination.[18]

The failure of aesthetic scale in the face of 'what can barely be gotten into the representation' reveals the multi-scalar incoherence and uncertainty that haunts posthuman timescales. Thus, while the heterochrony of modernist temporal zoom includes the dissolution characteristic of immense expansions of perspective, it is not centred solely on the absorption of a small frame into some more certain, fundamental backdrop. The bad incongruity between the aesthetic's imperative to scale itself to what we care about and the immensity of things that can only be registered from far away – temporal hyperobjects, speculative outsides, far-futural risks – is valuable not only for the critique of modernity's compressed timescapes that it enables, but also for the way it reveals the plurality of times that cannot be nested within one another. By drawing connections between Virginia Woolf's far futurism, J. B. S. Haldane's essay 'The Last Judgment' (1927), Olaf Stapledon's unprecedented prolepsis of two billion years in *Last and First Men* (1930) and Terrence Malick's more recent end-of-time film *Tree of Life* (2011), this chapter constructs a relationship between genre fiction's scope and modernism's long-range aesthetics – the connection between SF's literal movement away from earthly temporal units (days, years, events, lives, the career of the human as such) and modernist attempts to picture human life from an estranging distance. Modernism's technique of expanding perspective connects to and even culminates in SF's extraterrestrial settings and themes by means of which we can view the fundamentally human and planetary temporal units from a position beyond the earth's rotation and our revolution around the sun. But modernism's exploration of inhuman times – the blowing up of our sense of the human that was also an explosion of the now – was moreover an embrace of the 'fragmentation of the now into multiple irreconcilable futures'.[19]

SECOND MODERNISM, DEFAMILIARISATION AND
THE MOMENT'S FAR FUTURES

We live in a present distended by our concerns about the long-term risks generated by an excessive modernity, the lifespan of our institutions and infrastructure that might contain or remedy those hazards, and the chances that our species will outlive what we have made. This is a period that Beck called second or reflexive modernity, marked by a shift in focus from modernity's short-term distribution of goods to the management of its long-term bads.[20] However, this reflection on the future impact of the modern was already a part of early twentieth-century examinations of the present. As Aaron Jaffe suggests, a 'second modernism [. . .] was implicit from the start', since the 'future effects of the deep time of modernity' had already begun to elongate time-consciousness.[21] Second modernism – in Joyce's Icarian distancing, Eliot's interest in the afterlife of waste, or Woolf's meditations on a world 'when you're not there' – had commenced its stretching of ordinary time over the timescale of modern dangers and their slow unfolding. While the big view and the long address of the human were responses to the dangers within this specific historical moment, they were also responses to the danger *of the moment itself*. That is, for a certain strain of canonical modernism, such a compressed and accelerated form of temporality was itself one of modernity's gravest hazards.

Modernism's aesthetics of transitoriness arose in relation to a modernity characterised by brevity and evanescence, the fractioning of the present and the compressive force of global simultaneity. In this well-known account, new technologies of transport, communication and coordination not only shrank distances with speed, but also eliminated lag and temporal difference through synchronisation.[22] Barbara Adam argues that this 'changed temporal context' or 'timescape' depended crucially upon the domination of clock time, whose rise began with the synchronisation of the globe to Greenwich at the International Meridian Conference in 1884, and the worldwide, wireless transmission of standardised time, first broadcast from the Eiffel Tower in 1913. This 'rationalised time', which was 'severed from local contexts and conditions' except for England's, drew the world and its previously disparate and distant time horizons together 'at near the speed of light, displaced variable local times, and imposed one uniform, hegemonic world time for all'.[23] Stephen Kern has described the way that this new sense of simultaneity revised our sense of the present not simply by including 'multiple distant events' in any local *now*, but by subdividing it into the technological constructions of smaller and smaller instants. This subdivision redefined the present either by rendering it a 'specious' amalgamation of infinitesimal moments or by whittling it down to a slim divider between past and future.[24]

In Jimena Canales's history of *A Tenth of a Second*, modernity is defined by the emergence of this hegemonic micro-time. Science and technology could register tiny moments in a lucid multiplicity, but art often seemed to render micro-time only in a limited way as the experience of blur – as the limits of perceptibility.[25] Nevertheless, it is clear that many paintings and texts of the period tried to engage or even emulate the analytic fractioning of movement or to dilate the small interval's specious dissimulation of rich dynamism. Indeed, the moment was reclaimed from the machinery that produced it (the factory system, the railway, the telegraph), as Sue Zemka has argued.[26] Against the domination of clock time, the acceleration of the pace of life and the imposition of 'one uniform, hegemonic world time for all', moments were reconceived as crucial perceptual vertices 'that emerge from an undifferentiated flow', that 'break routines and habits' and that 'bring insight, a concentration of meaning, ecstasy'.[27]

However, there was a strain in modernism that concerned itself with deeper and longer futures of the moment. In contrast to the familiar fascination with the small and fleeting and its recuperation by intense subjectivity, second modernism attempts to build inhuman speculation into the small-scale window of perception itself. Well before the recent 'speculative turn' in philosophy – itself precipitated by 'looming ecological catastrophe' and oriented in part towards an inhuman, diachronic exteriority – modernism began to inject into the moment and literary form a scaling up and a scoping out to inhuman times. The interest in scale and scope was, among other things, a way of grappling with the long-term impact of the fetish for ephemerality and the limitations of narrative as an anthropocentric down-scaling device.[28] '[I]n order to recognize risks at all', as Beck writes, 'that which is by nature beyond perception, that which is only connected or calculated theoretically' must become an *unproblematic element of personal thought, perception and experience* [. . .] [G]eneral knowledge devoid of personal experience becomes the central determinant of personal experience.'[29] Consider the typical modernist expansions of perspective: a deepening of the historical sense; a tunnelling beyond (inter)personal memories to 'the age of the tusk and mammoth'; or the distribution of feeling across bad forms of incomprehensible scope. These gestures take on new significance when we frame the defamiliarisation of limited human scales alongside the science-fictional examination of time quite literally from a distance, and the period's cultivation of posthuman foresight.[30]

Getting distance on time during this period is typically filed under 'primitivism' and 'palaeomodernism' – the clearly identifiable attempt to critique modernity by retreating, ironically, into the very deep past and singular progressive history that has underwritten modern, imperialist schemes to exploit those marked as permanently anterior. However, the fantasy of going backwards to escape the culture of the instant does not fully prepare us to understand the rise of the inhuman future in response to intellectual and aesthetic short-sightedness. In the latter direction, terms such as 'futurism' and 'neomodernism' do not come close to describing the extent of the exploration forwards, since they designate merely the rush of the immediate future speeding into the present and smashing into tradition, habit and custom. While critics have seen in futurism an 'effort to move beyond the present and create forms for the future', that future is simply the edge of the violently accelerated present, a present reconfigured as a 'forge' that ignites 'the potentialities of the future', to use Renato Poggioli's description of the avant-garde, in the aggressive and 'hygienic' act of destroying the past.[31] Such departures from the past and present do not fare too far forward. To get to the far future, one must usually leave modernist territory for genre fiction – SF or utopian literature.

However, the runway of modernism's techniques of 'artistic ludicrousness' extends quite far into the realm of genre fiction's badness. With respect to modernism's content, little attention has been given to the way in which the distant future is part of the twentieth century's aesthetic exploration of timescales in general, of which palaeomodernism's journey to the deep past is but half the story. Chapter 1 attempted to clarify the heterochronic element in palaeomodernism, despite our tendency to read heterochrony under the sign of primitivism as a fantasy of authentic primordiality – opposed to capitalist modernity and normative plots – in a longer but still singular progressive history justifying racist, imperialist schemes. However, it is not even necessary to expand what we mean by modernism via heterochrony in order to see that one aspect of modernism thematised the long address of the human as a counterpoint to modernity's relentless analytics of the short term, and that this big view implied or explicitly included the future.

For instance, and as a precursor to Neil deGrasse Tyson's lesson on situatedness, we might recall Joyce's Icarian distancing in the second epigraph. While this expansion of scope creates a view of the nightmarish nets in which Joyce's characters are enmeshed – their embedding in increasingly capacious and confining structures oriented towards the past – we might begin to consider the ways in which these outward movements might also be read in relation to Joyce's flight into 'possibilities of the possible as possible' in unevenly modernised landscapes, as well as to the forays in form that marked him as a 'Contemporary of the Future'.[32] Joyce's encyclopaedic and epic scoping, which is held together by the organising device of the body or Greek mythology, also features stylistic melange and internal tensions that imply a more complex understanding of possibility than we are used to pursuing. Similarly, recent criticism has helped us see that Eliot's historical sense goes deeper than we thought by including Magdalenian cave paintings, and Woolf's characters frequently tunnel beyond their personal memories to the deep past.[33] However, the content of Eliot's tradition did not simply evoke agricultural or prelapsarian holdouts but also pointed forwards to the apocalyptic afterlife of waste and the byproducts of modernity.[34] The song of Woolf's battered woman in Regent's Park not only covers 'the age of the tusk and mammoth', but looks ahead to the heat-death of the sun, the earth as a 'cinder of ice' and the closure of 'the pageant of the universe'.[35] Although the modernist fascination with inhuman scales – those aspects of a world 'when you're not there'[36] – are often understood in relation to a backward-looking primitivism, big views of timespace inevitably include the future.

Indeed, in the nineteenth century, there was already a desire 'to commandeer the future [. . .] the conquest of height complementing geology's annexation of the subterranean world', which Robert Stafford correlates with the 'upsurge of enthusiasm for mountaineering during the second half of the century'.[37] In intellectual history, the currents of geology and biology flowed forwards as well as backwards. To consider the age of the earth and the history of bodies gave rise to questions about the different fates that follow from deepdown things, and familiar anxieties about planetary catastrophe, extinction and racial degeneration. As Paul Alkon argues in *Origins of Futuristic Fiction*, 'It was extrapolation to a geological and evolutionary past envisioned as ever more remote from the present that by the nineteenth century had widened temporal perspectives in a way favoring tales of the future no less than historical novels.'[38] Critics have argued that this widening of temporal perspective to the future was responsible not just for SF as such, but also for the first phase of the sub-genre of time-travel fiction.[39] According to David Wittenberg, the rise of time travel at the end of the nineteenth century is the direct result of

Darwinian extrapolation intersecting with the utopian romance, a combination that produced well-recognised aspects of the genre, such as its macrologia – its explanatory long-windedness about the realistic derivation of the far future. The synthesis of the adventure to a better point in history with the idea of slow change over time 'impels a general shift toward specifically temporal models of sociopolitical extrapolation: plausible utopian futures must be directly "evolved" from actual present-day conditions, not merely envisaged or conjectured'.[40] In addition to marking a largely twentieth-century literary genre, the operation of tracking a causal line deep into the far future is for some scholars a defining epistemological feature of the larger terrain of intellectual history. As Marie-Hélène Huet points out, the 'metaphor of the chain [. . .] and more specifically, the conceptualization of time as a chain' rose up 'in the wake of eighteenth century empiricism' and 'became prevalent in nineteenth century thought'. This chain's unprecedented length in both directions underlies SF's dominant mode of anticipation and its generic identity as the 'modern, postindustrial version of prophecy'.[41]

The extension of Stafford's argument about the conquest of height helps us to see the ways in which the long view of the future functions in similar ways to the imperial domination of history and its 'utopian' fantasies of narcissistically deep impact. There is no doubt that views that rise continually higher throughout the twentieth century – such as Kees Boeke's *Cosmic View: The Universe in 40 Jumps* (1957) and Charles and Ray Eames's *Powers of Ten* (1968) – are always to some extent expressions of the imperial will to transcend history and control ever larger territories, and the masculine will to measure one's influence on things to come. But it is also worth pointing out that going up and out not only intensifies uncertainty, as Beck argues, but also destabilises the unifying impulse of the purely scientific form of deep temporalisation in the direction of both past and future.[42] In instances of modernist zoom and SF's literal distancing alike, scoping out and scaling up makes possible and reveals an aesthetics of multiple clocks, differential rates of change, plural timelines and scales. In particular, both participate in a critique of literary forms that render the world familiar and manageable by pushing past narrative's limits. Before turning to Woolf's and Haldane's far futurism, Stapledon's extreme prolepsis and Malick's omega-point fantasy, I want rearticulate modernism's technique of defamiliarisation in relation to SF's 'cognitive estrangement' and its temporal scale. Second modernism and SF work together to expose and repudiate our everyday scope, tempos and historical sense as not only too small but too singular.

Defamiliarisation sometimes functions to critique the moment, and the timeline of which it is a crucial part, in a way that aligns it with SF's attempt to historicise forward. In other words, this technique in both modernist and SF texts produces a similar kind of badness, which connects aesthetic subversion to temporal expansion forward. However, in the modernist domain, defamiliarisation is normally construed as an attempt to access an extraordinary now that has been obscured by habits, whereas in SF, 'cognitive estrangement' is understood as a technique for imagining an alternative future that forces us to historicise the now as 'the determinate past of something yet to come'.[43] The former was theorised by Viktor Shklovsky, who saw a need to 'increase the difficulty and length of perception' to counter an understanding of the world that had become so automatic as to constitute a blindness. In 'Art as Technique', Shklovsky described the endeavour 'to make objects "unfamiliar", to make forms difficult' as a process of stripping away the various layers with which 'habitualisation' has coated reality, of disrupting customary modes of seeing in order to wallow in the difficulties of a more primordial kind of perception.[44] Likewise, in Darko Suvin's influential definition of cognitive estrangement, SF constructs 'an imaginative framework alternative to the author's empirical environment' such that it exposes the contingency of an entire, habitualised social order by presenting a new and shocking future version whose differences from the naturalised present render the latter precariously historical.[45] Second modernism's themes of the far future and telescoping formal violations likewise aspire to reveal temporal alternatives. However, these alternatives are not just possibilities existing virtually in the now, but rather actual timelines and scales cutting across the present.

Although he distinguishes between what he sees as modernism's mere violations of form and SF's diagnostic historicising, Fredric Jameson remains the best theorist for articulating defamiliarisation and estrangement together. In his account of the difference between modernist and SF badness, the former becomes fixated on its own aesthetic operations and compartmentalised moments in the process of subtracting the accretions that block a direct experience of the present; by contrast, the latter's 'cognitive function' generates a historicist deepening and lengthening. That is, as he writes in *Archaeologies of the Future*, cognitive estrangement's 'experimental variation on our own empirical universe' is a historical critique of the moment and a utopian exercise in unearthing the bits and pieces of potentiality within the present as the seeds of a fundamentally different future. Unlike modernism's departures from cultural norms, SF's cognitive function prevents the 'aesthetic and artistic status of the SF or utopian work' from 'neutraliz[ing] its realistic and referential implications'.[46] Whereas modernism defamiliarises the present by violating form alone, thereby giving us access to an extraordinary now obscured by habits, SF attempts 'to defamiliarize and restructure our experience of our own present' by extrapolating the future that follows from the content of our present and exposing how the current now is *constituted* by mindless habits and disciplining structures.[47]

However, Jameson's work on SF can in fact be seen as attempting 'to recover a more radical modernism': indeed, in Phillip Wegner's view, one of Jameson's 'most original contributions' in *Archaeologies of the Future* is that he 'enables us to understand science fiction itself as a *modernist* practice'.[48] That practice turns on a badness that should redefine defamiliarisation as a repudiation of conventional tempos and scope, a critique of the now that Jameson has continually described as dehistoricised, tail-less, ephemeral and yet somehow never-ending under capitalism. Jameson allows SF's badness to be salutary: implausibility, silliness and even silence – what the text is unable to describe – are part of a diagnostic historicising. Indeed, the impossibility of a clear and compelling view of the future, the fact that 'an utterly transformed, radically other, and/or redeemed existence [. . .] is fundamentally unrepresentable', as Wegner writes, is one of the major takeaways of SF.[49] While the failures of imaginative leaps, such as the always poorly represented encounter with alien existence, might make 'the post-human thereby [seem] more distant and impossible than ever', Jameson argues that to think the future, however badly, is to begin to transform the present 'into the determinate past of something yet to come', and to affirm the possibility and necessity of 'the radical break as such'. In our fragmented and atomised present, 'the Utopian form itself is the answer to the universal ideological conviction that no alternative is possible'.[50] This genre in which our present will be the past condition of some future plot is in fact a telescopic '"method" for apprehending the present as history', a technology for redeeming the present's free-floating condition, and thus a way of imagining the multiplicity of 'radical alternatives' that might follow from it.[51]

And so too, in many instances, with modernism. The same significance attaches to modernist badness, which issued from the same conditions and was, in more cases than SF, a deliberate tactic. If SF is a modernist practice, then conversely modernism's scalar zoom and its defamiliarisation of the dominant unilinearity of time can be a science-fictionally historicising estrangement – of the shape and composition of history itself. Second modernism's bad futurising may not be utopian in the way Jameson desires, but it does employ a 'method for apprehending the present as history' and a big-historical technique for critiquing the present's free-floating condition.[52] And what the badness of the long view reveals is not simply multiplicity and possibility buried within a singular modernity awaiting archaeological rescue, but the fiction of a singular present necessary for aligning and collocating different lines of history for specific purposes, and beneath that fiction, an alternativity that striates the future, present and past alike.[53] What we are already used to seeing as the critique of the one, true clock and its timescape of short-term nows crucial to empire, industrialisation and globalisation also enables and makes use of a heterochronic estrangement of the proximity of the future horizon and its absorption of the many non-standard timelines already coursing through the cross-section of any present.

FACULTIES OF FORESIGHT AND LONG-RANGE MODERNISM

In 1927 the Cambridge geneticist and popular science writer J. B. S. Haldane published 'The Last Judgment', an apocalyptic and generically hybrid essay that was deeply influenced by H. G. Wells's thirty-million-year trip to the future in *The Time Machine* and his subsequent calls to 'forecast [. . .] the way things will probably go'.[54] Wells occupies a crucial position in the story of second modernism: he was the first to propose institutionalising foresight and future studies, and he invented a literary device that enables both the voyeuristic tracking and the defamiliarisation of time. It is arguably his later reflection on the time machine that seemed to reveal both the conditions for short-sightedness and the need for the long view. Just a few years after the publication of *The Time Machine*, Wells wrote a series of articles – eventually published as the best-selling *Anticipations of the Reaction of Mechanical and Human Progress Upon Human Life and Thought* (1901) – that offered a 'forecast of the way things will probably go in this new century', and predicted, among other things, the traffic jams and urban sprawl that would follow from new technologies of transport.[55] In 1902 Wells delivered a lecture at the Royal Institution called *The Discovery of the Future*, in which the mere anticipations and speculations of the year before had given way to a diffident proposal: 'the time is drawing near when it will be possible to suggest a systematic exploration of the future'.[56] By 1932 this proposal had become the much more assertive BBC radio broadcast that called for 'whole Faculties and Departments of Foresight' to counter the dangers of 'the abolition of distance' and the threat of global destruction resulting from time-space compression.[57] But already in *Discovery*, in a lecture given at an institution for public engagement with science, Wells was asking if the nineteenth century's great discovery was the existence of big history. Was his period distinguished by the 'great discovery of the *inductive* past' – an 'outer past' that 'no living being has ever met, that no human eye has ever regarded', a 'prehuman past' inferred from 'odd-shaped lumps of stone, streaks and bandings in quarries and cliffs, anatomical and developmental detail' (28–32)? If so, why should the twentieth century not be able to study the 'inductive future', to 'throw a searchlight of inference forward instead of backward' (32)? The question of the future arises for Wells not only as a consequence of his ontology – which his Time Traveller described as 'Four-Dimensioned being', in which any given stability is a mere section or cut of a longer process, striated by other processes and extending in both directions – but also as an issue of methodological symmetry.

Notwithstanding the work accomplished by his time machine, it is more difficult to claim the Wells of this lecture for the heterochronic than the two thinkers he inspired – Haldane and Stapledon. In *Discovery*, Wells does continue the project of *The Time Machine* by problematising the belief that humans are the be-all and end-all, which he says would be 'perfectly comprehensible in a thinker of the first half of the nineteenth century' (49). 'Since the *Origin of Species*', he writes, thinkers must now consider that all of human culture 'is no more than the present phase of a development so great and splendid that beside this vision epics jingle like nursery rhymes, and all the exploits of humanity shrivel to the proportion of castles in the sand [. . .] Man is not final' (50). This 'great unmanageable, disturbing fact' is that we are in a process that ensures our impending unrecognisability and, further, that 'this sun of ours must radiate itself toward extinction' (55). Yet Wells also reaffirms 'the greatness of human destiny', the trajectory of Western progress (as opposed to 'oriental' and submissive pastism), and exclaims triumphantly that 'Worlds may freeze and suns may perish, but there stirs something within us now that can never die again' (56). It is as if, standing without his time machine before an audience of scientists in the Royal Institution, Wells cannot get quite enough distance on time itself. He resorts to the unitary block-universe model of time rather than a model of alternativity to justify the study of deep futures: the future is 'in absolute fact [. . .] just as fixed and determinate [. . .] just as possible a matter of knowledge as the past' (23).[58] The future must be there already in order for it to be an object of knowledge, let alone a destination for travel.[59]

Where Wells's fear of contraction to a destructive global present might lead us to regard his earlier recovery of the future from the realm of non-being as a snapping of the singular present into an enormous, thirty-million-year line, Haldane, the Cambridge geneticist and popular-science writer, used the long view more clearly to emphasise the difficulty of incorporating smaller timescales into larger ones, as well as the challenge of imagining the large-scale, four-dimensioned being of the human. Further, his scope worked to defamiliarise fundamental temporal units of presence such as the day. In 1927 Haldane published 'The Last Judgment', an essay deeply influenced by Wells's worry about the future brought about by the foreshortening and short-sightedness of the present. Framed by an explicitly scientific vision of the apocalypse, the essay's conceit is a lesson delivered by a primary school teacher to our descendants living on Venus forty million years from now (ten million years beyond Wells's time-travel narrative), after all life has been extinguished on earth.[60] The lesson recounts the anthropogenic destruction of earth, but in a twist on Wells's Victorian hope for the essence of the human 'that can never die again', it also separates the fate of our species from the death of the planet. In untethering human evolution from the future of the planet, Haldane stretches our history on to a different time structure and puts all earthly measures of time – 'day', 'month', 'year' – into quotation marks. We thus move from geocentric clocks to a far-futural clock with cosmic periodicity, or at least one scaled to what Haldane conjectures is the lifespan of the galaxy ('80 million million years' [309]) rather than that of our solar system.

On such an enormous stage, the 'human' drama must try to show up and play out; but what kind of aesthetics are involved? Instead of casting the problem in terms of plot structure or scene, Haldane initially frames it in relation to character and its recognisability:

> I shall attempt to describe the most probable end of our planet as it might appear to spectators on another. I have been compelled to place the catastrophe within a period of the future accessible to my imagination. For I can imagine what the human race will be like in forty million years, since forty million years ago our ancestors were certainly mammals, and probably quite definitely recognizable as monkeys. But I cannot throw my imagination forward for ten times that period. Four hundred million years ago our ancestors were fish of a very primitive type. (292)

Wells's posthuman crabs, which Gregory Benford calls 'the first great image of the far future', might have been ambitious thirty years before, but *The Time Machine* was operating on a smaller timescale than Haldane's 'Last Judgement'.[61] Wells's figures of hybridity (the sphinx, the griffin, the human itself) are imaginable; the creature at the end of his novel – 'a round thing, the size of a football perhaps' – comically resembles Wells's sketch of 'the Man of Tomorrow'.[62] However, while Haldane justifies the limit of his narrative scope as the limit of his ability to imagine the shape of the posthuman, the problem at the heart of his story is actually more general and structural – that is, more than a simple matter of casting.

Scaling up, in Haldane as in much of SF, of course means refocusing on populations and collectives rather than individuals. The question *how much longer do we have as a species?* had been an urgent one since Lord Kelvin calculated the expiration date of the sun in 1862 and shrank the future of life on the planet down to mere tens of millions of years – from biologists' and geologists' timescale of hundreds of millions of years.[63] The large body of scholarship on degeneration and the rise of eugenics tracks this urgency as it makes its way into conversations about race, society and the direction of history. As a geneticist, Haldane was a part of these conversations, and in his work and Stapledon's, the motif of bio-engineering our species is, as one might expect, not unproblematic.[64] In 'The Last Judgment', however, Haldane places more emphasis on the refocusing than on the composition of the population: while most earthlings trap themselves in the aesthetic pleasure of sensation or intersubjective drama, a small minority formulate long-term plans for the species' survival in Venus's environment. Becoming 'members of a super-organism', these new humans witness the destruction of the home planet and all earth-dwellers, and plan to continue genetically engineering the species so that it can survive beyond the solar system (304).[65] Because the ultimate question about our career as a 'race' on earth was not just a reflection of modernity but had become simultaneously *reflexively* modernist, that is, a second-modernity query about the hazards of historical myopia, the problem of the future often appears in terms of age but is clearly about temporal scale as such. As in George Bernard Shaw's play *Back to Methuselah* (1921), where humans in the modest year 31,920 evolve into virtually immortal beings, the genetic extension of lifespan is meant to engage long-term problems about which our mortality prevents us from making any headway. But headway comes not only from living longer but from thinking differently.

The issue on which Haldane focuses is the intellectual and aesthetic short-sightedness that has become the primary risk to human history, and whether or not the flare of human existence will last long enough to show up in *any* record. Haldane's Venusian teacher instructs us on the history of this problem. The demise of the earth begins with our depletion of fossil fuels, which leads us to harness the planet's tidal energy. This new source of power exacerbates the slowing of the planet's rotation to the point where, in the year 17,846,151, the fundamental temporal unit of the day is dilated to forty-eight times its original length. As a consequence, the earth undergoes massive climate change and witnesses widespread extinctions of 'practically all the undomesticated' species (300). By the year 25 million, the moon's orbit has tightened and its eventual collision with the earth is only several million years away. While human beings have genetically extended their lifespan to three thousand years, the effect of the addition is not a broadening of their scope but the mere prolongation of their present. As the Venusian lecturer points out, the biggest hazard for humanity was the temporal myopia underlying its inertia:

> it was characteristic of the dwellers on earth that they never looked more than a million years ahead [. . .] The continents were remodelled, but human effort was chiefly devoted to the development of personal relationships and to art and music, that is to say, the production of objects, sounds, and patterns of events gratifying to the individual. (295)

In this humorous hyperbole, human beings had foresight that extended for a million years, which was not far enough to curb their self-destructive extraction of energy from the planet, and they remained committed, like Walter Pater's 'children of this world', to 'art and song' and to 'getting as many pulsations as possible into the given time'.[66]

In tracking the catastrophic impact of the short *durée* and exposing the limitations of *aesthesis* to the sensuous life, Haldane's enormous scope does not simply resolve the problems of short-termism by extending the history of progress into a much longer line. Weird trips through time and proleptic zoom – the operations of time machines and modernist experiments alike – produce scales beyond the scope of literary concern in order to generate badness, bewilderment and instances of faltering imagination. Haldane's story-within-an-essay refuses aesthetic gratification not only by treating the expansively imaginative as an extension of the expository, but also by defamiliarising the fundamental units that undergird narrative structure and provide a clear sense of temporal setting. In 'The Last Judgment', the newly formed earth initially experiences 1,800 days in a year, and each of these days last 'only a fifth of the time taken by a day when men appeared on earth' (293). At this early stage, the moon was closer to earth, and therefore 'the month was only a little longer than the day' (293). As the tides slowly hinder the spin of the earth, 'the effect of tidal friction was to make each century, measured in days, just under a second shorter than the last' (294). That is, because the planet's rotation was slowing and the days grew longer, the number of days it took to fill a century (one hundred revolutions around the sun) diminishes slowly by tiny fractions. After burning through all the fossil fuels on the planet, human beings develop 'tide engines' to harness the earth's rotational energy and its hydropower, and consequently the 'braking action of the tides was increased fiftyfold, and the day began to lengthen appreciably' (294). The unit of the day, therefore, begins to take up a longer portion of the total revolution around the sun. 'By the year eight million', continues the lecturer, 'the length of the day had doubled, the moon's distance had increased by twenty per cent., and the month was a third longer than it had been when it was first measured' (296). Because of our energy needs, what would have taken 'fifty thousand million years [. . .] before the day became as long as month' (295) – presumably the month that is already longer than our 29-day month by a third, and that comprises days that are 48 hours long – has only taken around eighteen million years:

> In the year 17,846,151 the tide machines had done the first half of their destructive work. The day and month were now the same length [. . .] [T]he earth dwellers could only see the moon from one of their hemispheres. It hung permanently in the sky above the remains of the old continent of America. The day now lasted for forty-eight of the old days, so that there were only seven and a half days in the year. (298)

The account above is extremely confusing but instructive: Haldane's big view stands in contrast to short-sightedness, but it also enables one to see a plurality of clocks keeping various times. The duration and periodicity of natural phenomena that determine time are themselves changing in Haldane. While we think of nature as the ground of our understanding of time as a singular medium of uniform measure, the changes in nature's many clocks force us to acknowledge that timespace is mutable and in varying degrees irregular. In Haldane, we are not just watching the running down of a clock on which we live from the perspective of another clock. The alteration of time, not just our understanding of it, by the culture of brevity – the onset of the 48-day day – *is* climate change itself and the destruction of the planet: because the 'long nights were intensely cold', the equator 'contracted, causing earthquakes and mountain-building on a large scale' (298–9). A new ice age begins; the moon's orbit tightens and begins to move in the opposite direction in relation to the earth; finally, in the year 39 million, the disintegrating moon collides with the earth, destroying all life still residing on the planet. While the essay's lesson seems to be the simple one that we should not separate our present distended by a million years from the longer timeline that contains our fate, a fate resulting from that present, the effect of scaling up is also to destroy the assumption that our sense of history is the right timescale and that all timescales are one.

The significance of Haldane's essay, less obvious than what the teacher intends for her Venusian pupils, is that all clocks are radically local, unstable – and ultimately, multiple. As a result of global catastrophe, humanity must not only find other places to live, but *other clocks to live by*. Finding new homes is a matter of plot: after unsuccessful attempts to settle on Venus around the year 10 million, human beings finally move there in the year 25 million, after ten thousand years of 'deliberate evolution' towards a body suited for survival there (302). However, finding new clocks is implicit and forces Haldane out of the fiction into the epilogue, out of the narrative's Venusian lecture and into first-person exposition. In the epilogue, Haldane claims that 'the end of the world which we have just witnessed' – the end of old temporal and historical coordinates –

> was an episode of entirely negligible importance [. . .] [W]e must use the proper time-scale [. . .] As we come to realize the tiny scale, both temporal and spatial, of the older mythologies [of the end of the world], and the unimaginable vastness of the possibilities of time and space, we must attempt to conjecture what purposes may be developed in the universe that we are beginning to apprehend. Our private, national, and even international aims are restricted to a time measured in human life-spans. (309; 310–11)

The very act of getting distance on the medium that narrative is meant to organise (time) means departing from the aesthetic, as well as reconfiguring its object (experience) to include 'general knowledge devoid of personal experience'. For Haldane, to conjecture means to distrust sense and imagination and to think long-range beyond a singular reference frame: as Haldane writes in a different essay, 'On Scales', we are unable to 'imagine the eighteen billion miles which is the unit in modern astronomy when we leave the solar system [. . .] Of course one cannot imagine a parsec. But one can think of it, and think of it clearly.'[67] The models necessary to understand interstellar scales and rates of change would '*show* us very little, for not only the earth, but its orbit around the sun would be invisibly small, and even the orbit of Neptune would be comfortably contained on a pin's head, which would also represent the size of the largest known star'.[68] In a model in which we were to shrink a planet down as much as the earth is resized to fit a 16" globe, the fastest thing in the universe, light, 'would creep much more slowly than a snail'.[69]

HETEROCHRONIC SWEEP IN WOOLF AND STAPLEDON

The search for new clocks and the defamiliarisation of old ones are not just SF scenarios but quintessentially modernist projects. Modernism's interrogations of form often probed the limits of the aesthetic as a technology of the short term – art's default periodicity centred on moments, days, decades, generations, centuries and, of course, most radically, the career of the human itself. One end of this spectrum generates affective power and intensity; the other end generates increasing levels of not only aesthetic badness but also speculative, second-modernist badness. To move across this spectrum towards the end of the human and beyond, as mentioned above, tends to lead one out of modernism and into SF. But the thought experiment of imagining time itself from a distance, that is, estrangement not simply of common-sense measures but of earthly units based on planetary rotation, is modernist too. These probing explorations yield new ways of envisioning the future, ways that encompass SF's alternative futurity as a modernist gesture. Before turning to Stapledon's distension of narrative over an unprecedented two billion years and Malick's more recent exploration of cosmic timescales, let us return to canonical modernism in order to examine its heterochronic scaling up and zooming out, and to see how its expansion of perception joins up with SF's alternative futurity.

In modernism we see for the first time a long-range aesthetics developing in response to the rise of two technologies: the large telescope, which allowed for the perception of faraway things; and the aeroplane, which provided the experience of everyday things from far away. Both technologies are legible within the discourses of empire and its conception of history: the ability to scale new heights, envision ever larger territories and experience realms beyond the unaided senses appear as extensions of the imperial will to sublimity, the sublime control over history. Indeed, the telescope began as the seventeenth-century 'Dutch perspective glass' that gave rise to military field-glasses (binoculars), while the engine-driven, controlled aeroplane, invented in 1902, was immediately conscripted into the First World War as a reconnaissance device.[70] The martial history of these two technologies seems to suggest that expansions of perspective are primarily techniques of expansionism. Because spatial distance is also temporal distance, the period's fictions of geographical movement and range are often and rightly characterised in terms of the colonisation of time, especially the past, since such fictions coincided with and even served to justify the colonisation of those territories and bodies that signified the past.

However, the view from both the telescope and the aeroplane also had effects quite antithetical to the power and mastery generated by empire, war and power. First, as Holly Henry shows in *Virginia Woolf and the Discourse of Science*, big telescopes contributed to Woolf's long-range aesthetics, her 'modernist human decentering and re-scaling'.[71] The 100-inch Hooker telescope at the Mount Wilson Observatory, which was the largest in the world from 1917 to 1948, allowed Edwin Hubble to determine in 1922 that the Milky Way was not the entire universe but only a single galaxy among others, and then, within the decade, to discover that the universe was expanding. Hubble used the telescope to calculate that the Andromeda Nebula was almost a million light years from our own island of stars and therefore extragalactic; and he was able to detect that remote galaxies seemed to be receding at astonishing speeds.[72] While seeing faraway things in an expanding universe may have granted a sense of scoping power, the refusal of the object to remain within the scope of the scope, as it were, more frequently provoked a humiliation of human time frames and our fantasy of an all-comprehending sight. Quoting James Jeans, one of the first British cosmologists who also popularised new views of the universe, Henry points out that distant seeing helped us 'discover that the "inconceivably long vistas of [cosmological] time [. . .] dwarf human history to the twinkling of an eye"', and that this dramatically enlarged universe had become 'terrifying because of its vast and meaningless distances'.[73] Seeing may in many cases be panoptic knowing, but it can also be the beginning of knowing the immensity and multifariousness of what one does not and cannot know.

Henry demonstrates convincingly that the new technologies of distant seeing were at the heart of Woolf's 'narrative scoping strategies' and her 'global aesthetic'.[74] Through Ottoline Morrell, Woolf was patched into a robust scientific intellectual network that discussed these technologies and their expansion of perspective. Henry points out that 'telescopes or telescopic devices [. . .] appear literally or metaphorically in six of Woolf's nine novels, and in multiple essays and short stories'.[75] The famous, inhumanly distant section of *To the Lighthouse*, 'Time Passes', in which a number of moving and tragic events in the lives of the Ramsays occur in almost offhanded brackets, is not just rendered but figured as a telescopic view: Mrs McNab remembers Mrs Ramsay as if she were an image appearing in 'the circle at the end of a telescope'.[76] The optical instrument's reversible visual fields – that is, the magnification, in one end, of far-off, virtually imperceptible objects, and the shrinkage, in the other, of nearby, everyday things as if they were distant and unfamiliar – provided Woolf with a key aesthetic model for registering ordinarily invisible things, whether such phenomena fall within the compass of the ordinary or beyond it.

In the critical literature on Woolf's scope, the palaeomodernist paradigm often eclipses the modernist ambition to encompass the far future, since, as Michael Whitworth points out, 'references to the continuing presence of prehistory are not far to seek'.[77] For example, in *Night and Day*, Katherine Hilbery – a character who desires to 'calculate things, and use a telescope' like an astronomer – imagines witnessing the birth of Christ, and beyond that, the 'ape-like, furry form' of human origins; and in *Between the Acts*, Lucy Swithin – who is reading the progenitor of David Christian's 'big history', Wells's *Outline of History* (1920) – rewinds the present-day image of Picadilly back to a time when it is populated by 'the iguanodon, the mammoth, and the mastodon; from whom presumably, she thought, jerking the window open, we descend'.[78] However, 'tokens of memory' in Woolf can often function in the opposite direction – to explore the 'relation to posterity'.[79] Whitworth's summary of Camille Flammarion's *Lumen* (1872), one of the most influential thought experiments in nineteenth-century popular-science discourse, provides the context for Woolf's interest in thinking about scale forwards as well as backwards:

> if we were to look at earth from a suitably distant planet, we would in theory be able to see the battle of Waterloo happening 'now', in our present moment. An observer moving away from the earth faster than light would be moving deeper and deeper into the earth's past, and would see events reversed.[80]

Because light is not instantaneous but takes time to travel from place to place, what we experience as a present view in the sky is in fact the appearance of a faraway event 'after travelling for millions upon millions of years', as the character Bernard notes in Woolf's *The Waves*.[81]

Like palaeomodernist frameworks, the astrophysical discourse about the finite speed of light recasts starlight falling in the now as an inscription of an immensely long and 'eternally present' cosmic history, and the fantasy of overtaking light does express a desire to go back in time. However, modernism's long view was equally influenced by the corollary question about an elsewhen in some relative future, a distant view which seems to Lily Briscoe, in Woolf's *To the Lighthouse*, 'to outlast by a million years [. . .] the gazer'.[82] In Woolf's *Night and Day*, this 'outlasting' perspective arranges the Victorian social world in relation to a modern present and, moreover, stretches the world of human concerns on to the longer history of our species and the inhuman history of the cosmos:

> the stars did their usual work upon the mind, froze to cinders the whole of our short human history, and reduced the human body to an ape-like furry form [. . .] This stage was soon succeeded by another, in which there was nothing in the universe save stars and the light of stars.[83]

In these moments where Woolf examines starlight – the comparison in *To the Lighthouse* of Mrs Ramsay's own 'little strip of time' with the life and death of stars, or Louis's reminder in *The Waves* of how human beings' 'lighted strip of history' is extinguished in the 'roar' through the 'abysses' of space and time – the question of the future looms, and not simply as a destiny-pathos generator.[84]

Woolf's interest in the far future is as important for rethinking the way time is configured in this period (and in modernist studies) as it is for bringing humility to any technological fantasy of an all-comprehending sight. Associated most often with phenomenological moments of being and intermittent, deep-past insights, Woolf is also a key figure in modernism's more bizarre, heterochronic estrangements which are produced in its connections with time machines. Henry remarks that 'Woolf saw [. . .] that the telescope is a time machine of sorts, in that looking out into space always marks a looking back in cosmological time'.[85] But with respect to bad heterochrony, the most important aspect of this time machine is that its scope, in raising the issue of the finite speed of light across great distances, also raises the issue of the irregularity and unevenness of timespace – its plurality of non-Euclidean frames – which Woolf was so patently good at tracking in the social sphere. In Woolf, the telescopic time machine does not simply trouble our common sense that something seen is something that exists here and now, that the images reaching us from far away must be contemporary with our perception; the big view also negates the intuition that there is a single, unified frame in which we might see it.[86]

In ways similar to the telescope, the aeroplane enabled canonical modernism to think heterochronically. Not much more than a decade after its invention in 1902, the engine-driven aeroplane was enlisted in the war effort, because its perspectives were so comprehensive in reconnaissance and so useful in planning attacks. The photo-mosaics constructed from aeroplane photographs came to be associated – in some cases, causally – with cubism, a cubism that can be construed as complicit in its 'reduction of depth, elimination of unessential detail, composition with simplified forms, and unification of the entire picture surface'.[87] The literal as well as figurative obliteration of 'unessential detail' in First World War reconnaissance photos and cubism could be seen as a kind of training in how to look at the world, as Paul K. Saint-Amour has pointed out.[88] But to look at the world from far away is not simply about erasure by an all-seeing lens, as modernists knew, but about the conditions for things showing up, and more importantly, for the appearance of incongruous and even clashing temporal multiplicity. As Saint-Amour argues, while reconnaissance photography may have contributed to 'a fantasy of all-powerful vision', the aerial perspective could not conceal the fact that its 'integrated, synchronic image [. . .] was in fact a series of images patchworked and blended together'.[89] Thus, '[w]hen the illusion of spatial integration fails, it does so principally because the composite image separates into *tiles of nonsynchronous time* [. . .] A photomosaic is perforce a mosaic of temporalities.'[90]

The view from above and far away, rather than exemplifying pure 'disembodied omniscience', reveals a multiplicity of partial views, which themselves imply a number of rates of change generated by speed and distance from the earth.[91] Saint-Amour emphasises this multiplicity at the level of moments and subjects:

> the photomosaic partook of a tendency shared by many Western modernisms – literary as well as visual ones – to view the total from the vantage of the radically site-specific, subjective, or fragmentary, underscoring in the process how portraits of a given totality can be both generated and apprehended only from viewpoints that are optically and ideologically partial.[92]

However, while urban *flânerie* or the view from the railway carriage certainly contributed to this familiar aspect of cultural ephemerality and perspectival simultaneity, perhaps 'the earth seen from an airplane is something different', as Gertrude Stein put it in *Picasso* (1938).[93] Whatever else Stein may have meant by this difference in her description of the aerial view of 'the earth as no one has ever seen it', marked by 'the mingling lines of Picasso',[94] we can say that the controlled scaling of abstraction and the process of rising in altitude reveal not simply the immersive rush based in moments and subjectivities, but an equally important insight generated by cubism: namely, that the modernist departure from the smooth timespace of static, single-point perspective yields the characteristic crinkling of timespace and the asynchronous collisions of mingling timelines.

In Woolf's essay 'Flying over London' (1928), for instance, the combination of the aeroplane and telescopic zooming abilities does more than simply defamiliarise the realist perspective on the city. By looking through 'Zeiss glasses' during Flight-Lieutenant Hopgood's shifts in altitude, we notice the uneasy nestability of various frames of history as we pass from one level to the next. It may be that 'Habit has fixed the earth immovably in the centre of the imagination' and 'everything is made to the scale of houses and streets'.[95] Flight-Lieutenant Hopgood's name alludes to the comparison of grasshoppers and aeroplanes at the start of the essay, and also, as Henry points out, to the astrophysicist James Hopwood Jeans and the telescopic imagination itself. But it also allows the speaker to leave the 'inveterately anthropocentric' (187) and envision, at one level, the deep past, and at another level, the far future.[96] The speaker sees first 'the River Thames [. . .] as the Romans saw it, as paleolithic man saw it, at dawn from a hill shaggy with wood, with the rhinoceros digging his horn into the roots of rhododendrons' (187); then she sees, at a higher altitude, 'not immortality but extinction' (188). More importantly, the speaker notices the relation between different levels: a small dot 'the size of a bluebottle' whose 'movement [seems] minute' is in fact a galloping horse, 'but all speed and size were so reduced that the speed of the horse seemed very very slow' (190). The speaker thus finds herself converting 'air values into land values. There were blocks in the city of traffic sometimes almost a foot long; these had to be translated into eleven or twelve Rolls Royces in a row' (191). The scale of 'social grades' (191) gives way not only to the fantasy of withdrawing to a tiny private room, but also to the value of altitude and abstraction. While Henry and others have noted how metaphors of flying in other Woolf texts represent the powers of the mind 'to imagine other worlds', we can see that the distant view also affords a sense of the temporal differences between worlds.[97]

Although Woolf is more often associated with moments of being and intermittent deep-past insights, it is not difficult to connect her aesthetic zoom to that of Olaf Stapledon, whose novel *Last and First Men* (1930) covers two billion years of human history. Indeed, we can think of Stapledon's absurd narrative ambitions as an extension of Woolf's high aims, a desire to go beyond the connoisseurship of intimate spaces, small moments and fleeting thoughts. Where the scope of the one makes visible differential temporalities, the distancing moves of the other reveal a mosaic of historicities. As Henry points out, Woolf and Stapledon in fact knew each other's work, emulated each other's scope, and entered into correspondence in the 1930s. Stapledon had read *The Years* 'with delight, and also with despair at the thought of the contrast between your art and my own pedestrian method'.[98] Woolf's novel, which she worried was a 'complete failure' (but a 'deliberate' one), examined a number of years in the life of the Pargiter family, from 1880 to the 1930s, and placed the private moments of individual characters in tension with the point of view of seasonal weather.[99] On the other end of this correspondence, Woolf read *Star Maker*, Stapledon's sequel to *Last and First Men*, which goes beyond human history in the solar system to the entire inhuman history of the cosmos. Woolf wrote to Stapledon:

> I have understood enough to be greatly interested, & excited too, since sometimes it seems to me that you are grasping at ideas that I have tried to express [. . .] But you have gone much further, & I can't help envying you – as one does those who reach what one has aimed at.[100]

Because he went so much further and farther – in his work our descendants with weird pinky fingers and a third 'upward-looking astronomical eye on the crown'[101] make it to Neptune – Stapledon's high-flying emulation of Woolf's inhuman aims deserves a better adjective than 'pedestrian'. His ambitions in similar fashion relocate narrative operations from rich subjective and intersubjective textures to a much more encompassing fabric. Henry sees this fabric as crucial to the global and pacifist aesthetic of both authors, since Woolf and Stapledon alike sought to imagine new worlds and 'alternative narratives for our human future' out of the fears of destruction and extinction that intensified in the space between the nineteenth century and the Second World War.[102] Both were readers of Jeans who, like Sagan, tacked from the nihilistic reading of our fate – 'clinging on to a fragment of a grain of sand until we are frozen off [. . .] strut[ting] our tiny hour on our tiny stage' – to an optimistic reading of 'the message of astronomy'.[103] 'In terms of time', wrote Jeans, that message 'becomes one of almost endless possibility and hope [. . .] [A] day of almost unthinkable length stretches before us with unimaginable opportunities for accomplishment.'[104] Thus it is not hard to see the impact of scale on their understanding of the political context of the interwar period and the appeal of what Masood Ashraf Raja and Swaralipi Nandi call the 'postnational fantasy' – the dream of utopian cosmopolitanism and ever-larger structures of social organisation that has become one of the hallmarks of SF.[105] But for my argument, the temporal implications that lie beyond the humiliation of the human or its heroisation mean that the alternativity generated by zooming is as crucial as the need to resituate the human context within the fantasy of the biggest, absolute and singular reference system. Woolf's desire to 'call in all the cosmic immensities' – as a way of generating alternatives to the narrowness of what is – feeds directly into Stapledon's take on scale.[106] As Stapledon wrote in the 'Note on Magnitude' that ends *Star Maker*, 'Immensity is not itself a good thing [. . .] But immensity has indirect importance through its facilitation of mental richness and diversity.'[107]

The diversity of interest in *Last and First Men* is represented not just by the stuff contained within a mentality or immensity, but by the number of timelines in which such stuff becomes meaningful or even shows up ontologically. Indeed, the most striking features of the novel – its five 'Time Scale' illustrations – do not merely supplement the novel's chronicle of our evolution into seventeen additional human species. Rather, these timelines exemplify the novel's basic formal procedure of zooming out, as well as contributing to the novel's critique of modern historical thinking. From the published timescales, we can see that, as the horizon expands to cover new events, significant details from the previous timeline disappear from view as they compress into the 'Today' of the succeeding timescale. The first scale covers four thousand years, and each one thereafter scopes out by a factor of one hundred. By Time Scale 3, Stapledon has outstripped the scope of Wells's *Time Machine* and has begun to pull away from Haldane's forty-million-year sweep. After hitting four billion years in Time Scale 4, Stapledon zooms out ten thousand times in order to cover fifteen trillion years in Time Scale 5, which presents the bookends of

'Today' – comically, tragically – as 'Planets formed; End of Man.' While psychologists had attempted to measure the phenomenological present as a matter of seconds, Stapledon anticipated the stretching of the day along the lines of the Long Now Foundation.[108] In Stapledon's manuscript timelines, we can see the progenitor of Boeke's *Cosmic View* and the Eames' *Powers of Ten*: eleven timescales in logarithmic order, in which each scale increases by a power of ten and includes the entirety of the preceding scale as a small portion of its centre (Figs 4.1, 4.2 and 4.3).

At first glance, the rhetorical impact of these timescales seems less about temporal diversity and plurality than about unitary nestings, cosmic containment and the diminishment of all sets of coordinates of significance and historical meaning into ever-shrinking subsets of an infinitely expandable context. Indeed, as Daniel Rosenberg and Anthony Grafton show in *Cartographies of Time*, the recent invention of the timeline, just over two centuries old, often effaces what preceding charts and matrices were able to communicate: instead of 'many intersecting trajectories of history', the timeline often 'emphasized overarching patterns and the big story'.[109] Further, the timeline's 'single axis and regular, measured distribution of dates' projects values that have become thoroughly naturalised in historical thinking, namely as the presumption of 'the uniformity, directionality, and irreversibility of historical time'.[110] However, Stapledon's illustrations seem to use this historicising technology against itself. While the text is explicit that the 'vast proportions' are meant to underscore 'the littleness of your here and now' (14) – to denaturalise and bring low 'our most cherished ideals [that] would seem puerile' to other, later and 'more developed minds' (9) – it also seems to go beyond resituating the human context in the biggest, absolute and singular reference system: as Rosenberg and Grafton suggest in their brief gloss, Stapledon's multiple timelines are 'self-consciously estranging forms of temporal mapping' that 'shake up his readers' assumptions about the values implied in the very scale of our historical narratives'.[111] After the first, conventional line that begins with the birth of Christ and goes two thousand years beyond the present, the timelines begin to operate more like medieval annals, which, Rosenberg and Grafton observe, mash up 'categories helter-skelter like the famous Chinese encyclopedia conjured by Jorge Luis Borges' and 'make no distinction between natural occurrences and human acts'.[112]

In *Last and First Men*, all three heterochronic devices – the figure of scoping, the trope of flight and the idea of time travel – are at work to trouble the ultimate historicisation that might integrate and make coherent the entirety of time. Telepathic time travel allows Stapledon's enormous 'future history' to be narrated by a voice that is literally doubled, simultaneous voices whose co-presence is instantaneous and faster-than-light: one belongs to a member of the 'Last Men', someone from the eighteenth human species two billion years hence, who lives

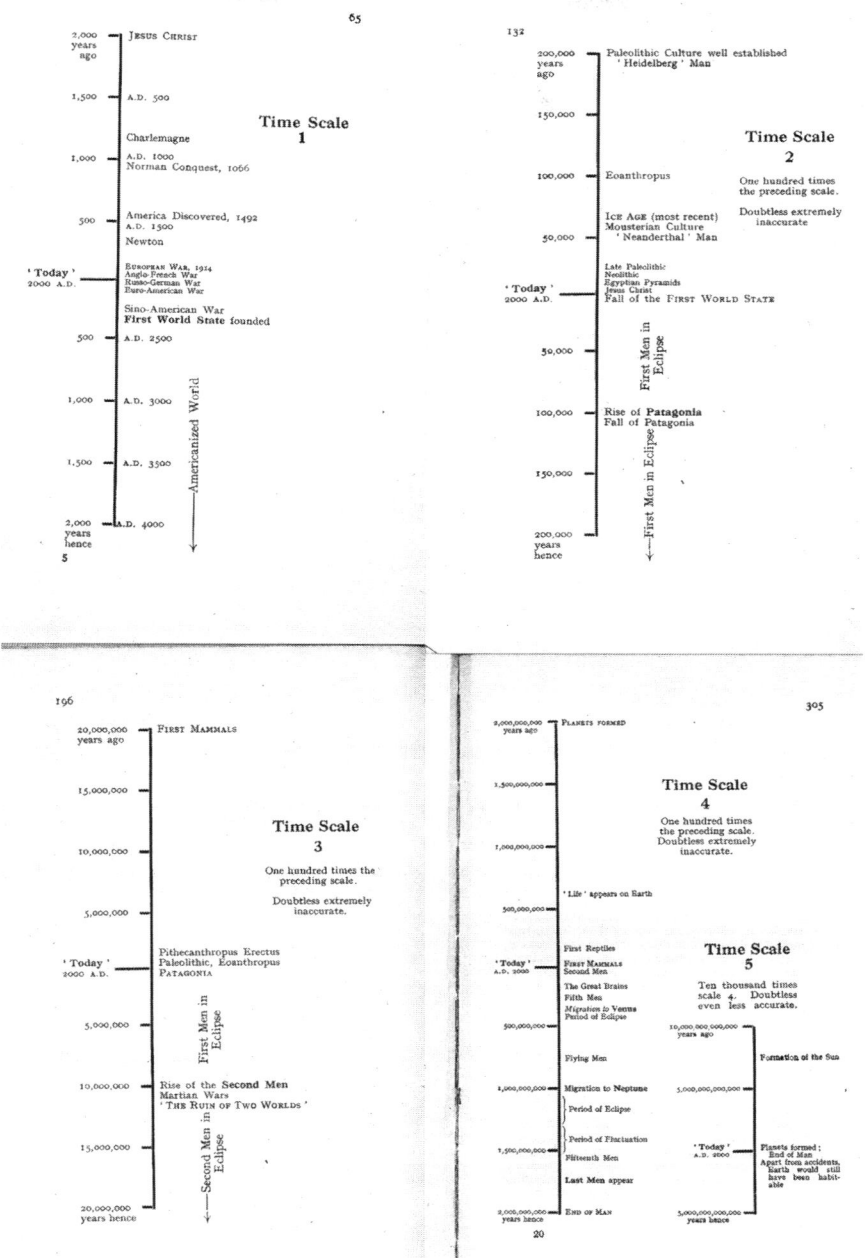

Figure 4.1 Olaf Stapledon's five Time Scales in *Last and First Men* (1930). Courtesy of Jason Shenai

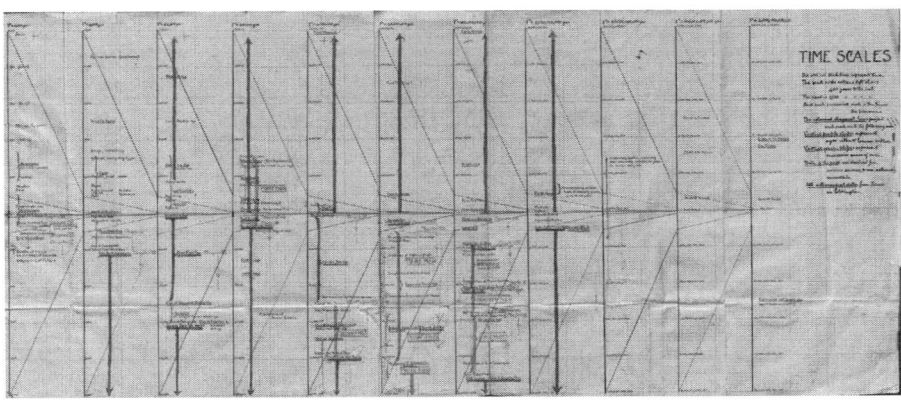

Figure 4.2 Olaf Stapledon's manuscript Time Scales for *Last and First Men*. University of Liverpool Special Collections and Archives. Courtesy of Jason Shenai

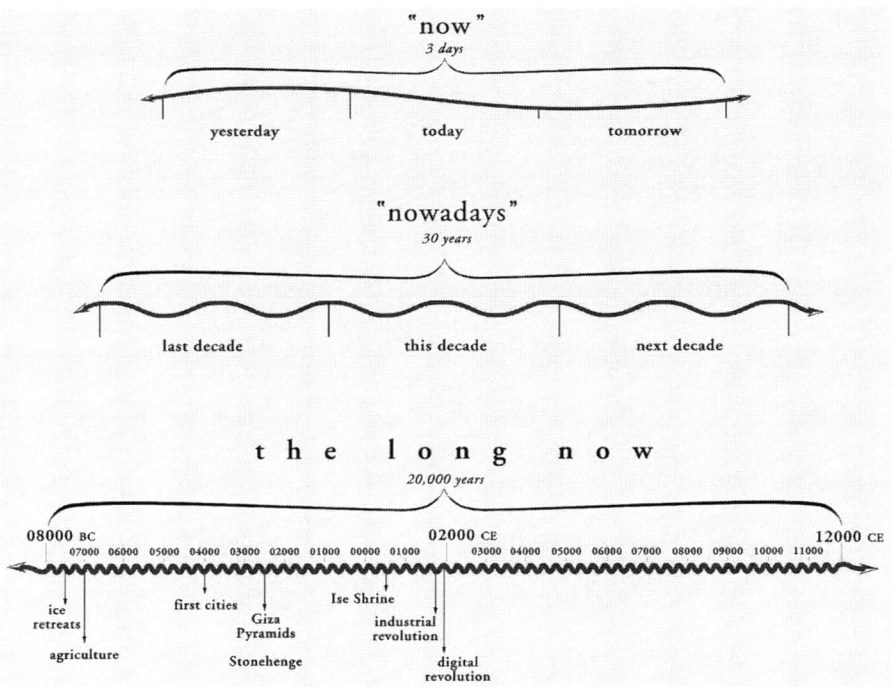

Figure 4.3 The Long Now Foundation's definition of the long now

on Neptune in the final days of a scorching solar system; the other belongs to the person he inhabits, someone from the days of the 'First Men', who 'lives in the time of Einstein' (13). We discover later in the book that the time-travel technique employed to possess the speaker who is the reader's contemporary – a method pioneered by the 12-foot-tall, mentally networked 'Fifth Men' – is akin to the 'inspection of a minute tract of space-time [. . .] as through an optical instrument' (181), an instrument whose frustrating limitations tell us about the nature of timespace itself. Finally, in order to complicate the fact that those who 'romance of the future [. . .] too easily imagine a progress toward some kind of Utopia' that would exist for beings with 'a fixed human nature', the narrator invites us 'to travel in imagination through the aeons' to witness the non-teleological rise and fall of multiple forms of social organisation and 'human nature' (13). This requires the period's other technology of the distant view. The aeroplane appears as the narrative's justification for the extreme breadth, speed and variety of the novel's coverage: 'Clearly we cannot walk at leisure through such a tract [. . .] We must fly. We must travel as you do in your aeroplanes, observing only the broad features of the continent' (15). Although the narrator says in the introduction that this flight must be punctuated by 'many descents [. . .] even alighting at critical points to speak face to face with individuals' (15), Stapledon's novel almost never drops to this high-aesthetic level: the novel has no plot, no characterisation and virtually zero dialogue.

The out-zooming, flying and time travelling produce a predictable aesthetic badness that critics have tried to recuperate by emphasising the ultimate oneness of history from an ahistorical, cosmic point of view. As Louis Tremaine observes, the long-standing view of Stapledon as mythmaker has treated his work as attempting 'to carry us outside of historical time and into a realm of eternally recurring cycles'.[113] Rather than engaging with the moral and practical dilemmas of his day, Stapledon has been seen 'to escape into a world so vast that those dilemmas shrink into insignificance'.[114] For K. V. Bailey, Stapledon's scope is an 'ultimate vision' characterised by correspondences and 'the all-inclusive cosmos/human/atom hierarchical concept'.[115] Such a reading overemphasises another of Stapledon's organising tropes – history as a 'symphony' (109). From this perspective, to go big is to affirm a fundamental unity: while an individual life itself may be 'a universe, rich and poignant', and the large spans of human history that Stapledon flies over are marked by 'great diversity' and 'teeming with variegated life' (143), all these are contained by the largest musical orchestration of the cosmos. The use of music as a figure for the form of history as well as the form of the novel generates, in John Huntington's view, 'artistic coherence': 'music [. . .] supplies a way of seeing that envisions all reality, even those aspects that other modes exclude or condemn, as part of a developing whole meaningful because it contains such parts'.[116]

Certainly Stapledon invites this view. But his other devices work to neutralise the function of the symphonic as a synthetic, all-encompassing whole,
an organising principle without which, Huntington fears, the novel and the
history would disintegrate into 'a hodgepodge, a set of gestures and starts,
of incomplete episodes which are often unconnected'.[117] Notwithstanding his
commitment to the artfulness and larger beauty of Stapledon's text, Huntington is in fact the first to consider that the aesthetic gambit of Stapledon's work,
in its attempt 'to generate real disorientation of the sort we associate with the
future', might be 'for it to fail as a novel [. . .] to render the quotidian disarray
without artistic shape'.[118] In this aspect of his argument, futurity, SF's primary
dimension, is by its very nature estranging, though most fiction usually defuses
this 'potential for the unforeseen' by transforming it into a version of the past,
bringing futurity into the structure of 'retrospective understanding' and intelligibility. However, some future-oriented SF texts such as Stapledon's are similar
to modernism's paradoxical experiments: in both, 'if the pattern makes any
sense, the surprise fails'; if the surprising future succeeds at being utterly alien,
'then by most standards the novel must fail'.[119] Reading the novel in this way
leads Huntington to focus on its enormous gaps and ludicrous compressions,
its absence of a 'rational pattern' and its refusal of a 'teleological principle'
in favour of 'a single imaginative rule that demands that any state of understanding, however secure and satisfactory it may seem in itself, recognize some
contrary state: sometimes an alternative mode of life, sometimes a contrasting
awareness [. . .] Such a mode imitates the future.'[120] For this modernist version
of Huntington, the untotalisability of a discontinuous, choppy and open-ended
time frustrates aesthetic form and is figured by the absence of all the details that
the novel, by flying far and scoping out, cannot provide. If we can call the novel
dialectical, as Huntington does, it is a chronicle not punctuated by antitheses
but advanced by mind-boggling variations in the degrees of contrast and difference resulting from variations in altitude and distance.

Stapledon seems fully aware of the problems in going beyond the art of the
short view, and he says in the preface that his aim is not primarily 'to create
aesthetically admirable fiction' (9).[121] If in this work he appears unwilling to
let go of the aesthetic and its timescales, he is more clear-eyed about the consequences of his ludicrously expansive scope in *Star Maker*. In the preface to
this sequel – where the entirety of the two-billion-year history covered in *Last
and First Men* takes just one paragraph – Stapledon takes some pride in say-
ing that 'Judged by the standards of the Novel', this 'extravagant work [. . .]
is remarkably bad. In fact, it is no novel at all.'[122] But this badness applies
equally to *Last and First Men* and is translatable into the modernist discourse
of novelty and its interrogation of anthropocentric aesthetic scales. As the literary scholar John Dover Wilson wrote in a letter to Stapledon about *Last and
First Men*, 'You have invented a new kind of book, & the world of Einstein

& Jeans is ready for it.'[123] In this new book, the fullest critique of historical thinking requires maximum badness: this critique goes beyond showing how narrow views exclude events to how they ignore multiple frames of reference. Such badness cannot be salvaged by a single, overarching, nesting framework because the absence of the latter is precisely what the aesthetic inadequacy is meant to demonstrate. Stapledon's ludicrous posthuman comedy generates the poor fit not only between the representation and the size of the history to be narrated, but between aesthetic form and history's number.

Stapledon uses the tropes and techniques of time travelling, flying and telescoping to produce irresolvable discrepancy and dissonance. For instance, the telepathic link to the present from two billion years in the future produces a clash within the narratorial voice between the perspective of our contemporary 'First Man' who anticipates, and the 'Last Man' who looks back on a finished history. Both are narrating the novel, and as Huntington points out, the anachronic gestures of prolepsis and analepsis produce a juxtaposition of 'contradictory attitudes', as well as an awareness of what Wells's *Time Machine* calls 'the infirmity of the flesh' – the bodily limitations on perception (our inability to see a flying bullet or bicycle spokes), as well as on interpretation (the illegibility of the transformed earth and its unfamiliar social situation). In Stapledon's novel, 'we feel the discrepancy between his [the Last Man's] understanding and our own' because the last species of human being has undergone two billion years of evolution punctuated by long periods of genetic engineering.[124] But the 'anachrony' is not just biologically epistemological – not merely a result of the fact that, as the narrator says, 'your sense organs, and therefore your perceptions, are too coarse-grained to discriminate' (14) our tiny now in relation to the whole of human history. Rather the discordance is also the relation between different timescales themselves.

Stapledon thematises this scalar discordance directly in his account of the history of telepathic time travel. The 'direct inspection of the past' that our distant descendant uses to narrate this 'future history' – a telepathy pioneered by the 'Fifth Men', a 12-foot-tall, mentally networked species created by the 'Fourth Men', who themselves are giant brains genetically engineered by short, six-fingered members of the third human species – is for a long time unsuccessful in its calibration of large-scale historicism to an individual organism's minor purchase on history. As in Chris Marker's film *La Jetée*, the 'medium' initially suffers 'mental disintegration', paralysis and death. The traveller slips 'so easily into the trance that his days were eaten up by the past' (180), much like Borges's 'Funes the Memorious', whose reconstructions of memories take precisely as long as the original past event.[125] 'Still more distressing', continues the narrator, the medium, like the dreamers in *Inception*, 'might not keep pace with the actual rhythm of those events themselves [. . .] might behold the events of a month, or even a lifetime, fantastically accelerated so as to occupy a trance of no more than a day's duration' (180). The perfection of this technique is likened to lordly reading, and the refined possession of a past mind is described in familiar liberal-humanist terms for literary experience and empathy: individuals can enter the mind of past humans, and '[w]hile experiencing the past individual's perceptions, memories, thoughts, desires, and in fact the whole process and content of the past mind, the explorer continued to be himself' (181). Although the narrator describes this 'supra-temporal experience' as a glimpse into eternity, it is also a zooming-in marked by differential scaling. The telescope must simultaneously be a microscope: both focus their vision through the past mind, on the one hand, and the medium's own re-scaling aperture, on the other. The modernist disjunction between these two historical registers, the unlordly forms of misreading and the temporal dangers of this telepathy, is important for understanding the way the novel undoes its own premise of one time's intervention in another.

Finally, the novel's interesting badness also relies on the elision and compression (rather than containment) produced by the high-flying and out-scoping. In chapter 10, having examined only the first and second species of humanity (forty million years), the narrator says that, to cover the Third and Fourth Men, we must 'accomplish a swift flight at great altitude over a tract of time more than three times as long as that which we have hitherto covered' (143). By chapter 14, and with only forty pages to go (but nine additional human species left to describe), the narrator hilariously braces the reader for the necessarily spotty treatment: 'Now we shall travel at a greater height and with speed of a new order [. . .] [W]e must consider things from the astronomical rather than the human point of view' (205). From this perspective, the 'period between the first mammal and the first man, some twenty-five millions of terrestrial years, seems now inconsiderable' (205), and ascending farther for a 'still wider view, we see that this aeon of four thousand million years [the period from the formation of our solar system's planets to the death of our sun and our species] is itself no more than a moment' (205). While the height and 'the breath-taking acceleration that is central to the novel's form'[126] leaves out everything that we might care about, the compression of major swathes of time allows the narrative to render scalar discordance in the experience of large-scale, geological processes. For example, Stapledon's narrative presents time-lapse shots such as these:

> a new land rose to join Brazil with West Africa. The East Indies and Australia became a continuous continent. The huge mass of Thibet sank deeply into its disturbed foundations, lunged West, and buckled Afghanistan into a range of peaks nearly forty thousand feet above the sea. Europe sank under the Atlantic. Rivers writhed shiftingly higher and thither upon the continents [. . .] New strata were laid upon one another under new oceans. (97)

As in Haldane, the increasing distance of narration that enables us to see this literally forces the reader into frames with different clocks. In the novel, the ninth species of human, having finally settled on Neptune, experiences a year that 'was at this time about one hundred and sixty-five times the length of the old terrestrial year' (207).

By distending the form of *Last and First Men* over a timespace that is Einsteinian and disjunctive, as well as Jeanian and cosmologically vast, Stapledon's work has much in common with modernist subversions. As Patrick McCarthy has noted, not only do the unconventional stylistic departures of *Last and First Men* express the same accelerated lifeworld of incoherence and radical discontinuity of canonical modernist artists, they also seem to imply the same time concepts traditionally attributed to modernism.[127] McCarthy tracks the similarities between modernism's anti-historicist interest in 'the transcendent moment and the mythological cycle', on the one hand, and Stapledon's 'study of the temporal' that treats 'the heightened perspective' as 'a means of gaining entrée to the eternal', on the other.[128] However, both modernism and Stapledon's text can be seen in more radical terms. *Last and First Men* uses the big view of the future and the 'bewildering device' of time-travel telepathy not only, as the narrator says, to 'embody the possibility that there may be more in time's nature than is revealed to us' (10). Like modernism, the novel tries to reconfigure the very understanding of time by which plot would be, according to Frank Kermode, 'an organization that humanizes time by giving it form'.[129] That is, if modernism is, in Jeff Wallace's succinct formulation, *'the moment at which art stops making sense'*, then Stapledon contributes to this refusal by failing to give time the intelligibility generated by narrative.[130] Indeed, Stapledon dehumanises time by stretching the novel – 'objects, sounds, and patterns of events gratifying to the individual' – beyond its breaking point, and by calling attention to the impossibility of unifying discordant and clashing timescales.

SECOND MODERNISM'S INHUMAN TIMES IN TERRENCE MALICK

In his 1972 *New Yorker* piece, 'Onward and Upward with the Arts: S.F.', Gerald Jonas, praising Stapledon's work as the epitome of SF's unification of wonder and reason, remarks that Stapledon 'wrote a number of novels that most S.F. fans regard as masterpieces and almost everyone else finds unreadable'.[131] 'In fact', he continues, 'two of his most famous books, "Last and First Men" (1931) and "Star Maker" (1937) [. . .] contain no plot, no characterization, and no dialogue [. . .] What they offer instead is a scope so vast it defies synopsis.' Stapledon's method, he argues, is 'basically cinematic':

> First, he dazzles us with an awe-inspiring vision, and then he pulls back his zoom lens until what we have been staring at is revealed to

be nothing but a tiny detail in an even more dazzling vista. And then he pulls his lens back again, and again, and once again.[132]

If modernist and science-fictional defamiliarisation goes well beyond the present on which it is typically thought to focus, the scalar zooming that persistently estranges the temporal horizon itself – again, and again, and once again – engenders a second-modernist insight: the early twentieth-century lesson about perspectives, points of view beyond the human that confound the experience of perspective itself, is that there are many times in our period's much vaunted temporal multiplicity that are unreadable, and that cannot be nested into a metaphysically single 'Time'.

The cinematic eye is, as Dziga Vertov memorably put it, 'the microscope and telescope of time', and Terrence Malick's Palme d'Or-winning film *Tree of Life* (2011) shows how second modernism's elastically expansive scope uncovers a range of scales, disparate cinematic-narrative rhythms, and the ultimate unnestability of such heterochronic complexity. None of the approving viewers – those who were not bored or put off by the film's obvious courting of a unified explanatory structure for the appearance of everything in the universe – would be likely to construe the film as a heterochronic alternate history, but this may be the best way to read *Tree of Life*. Only by reading the film outlandishly can one see its contribution to the century-long thematic and formal exploration of the non-subjective plurality of timespaces and concurrent histories. One might thereby discern in the film clear counterpoints to its most obvious features, such as the religious themes generating the structuring tension between nature and grace, violence and compassion; the 'mythopoetic' trope of the tree of life itself suggesting arboreal nesting structures that finally collapse into a single common origin; and the conspicuously bad overemphasis on the human scale, the 1950s family drama in Waco, Texas, intensified by some truly awful voice-over.

The latter list of obvious attributes is at the heart of why half of the film's viewers loved it, while the other half of the audience, as was widely reported, booed, stood up and walked out of the cinema. At first glance, *Tree of Life*'s cosmic vision of the interconnectedness of all things, as Kent Jones points out, seems to express a majestic unity in a 'grand consistency of forms ([. . .] the same spindly tentacles in a ball of primal energy, in a waving undersea plant, in a dinosaur's tale [*sic*], in the branches of trees blowing in the wind, in human hands and fingers)'. Citing the film's 'fluid shifts of scale' and its 'signature action of dilation and contraction', Jones approvingly quotes Emerson on 'the whole of history [. . .] in one man', 'a relation between the hours of our life and the centuries of time'.[133] Similarly, David Sterritt, riffing on Baudelaire, writes that the mercurial scenes and highly mobile camera blend 'the transitory and the enduring, the breathless and the timeless. From the standpoint of eternity, Malick poetically suggests, the feeling of an instant and the meaning of a lifetime are interwoven parts of a seamless whole.' For Sterritt as for so many others, the movie ultimately makes sense because the jarring juxtapositions of scale 'eventually jell into a fairly linear, if highly unconventional, narrative' – one that privileges the human drama of the O'Brien family as the perfect aperture on to the cosmic story of the origins of life, consciousness and conscience.[134]

However, the impatient reactions of the disapproving audience to the film's shifts from cosmic montage to microscopic footage register what I think is the film's equally important failure to make sense. The counterpoint to the emphasis on seamless wholes, gelling and the nested scales of narrative – that is, the film's resistance to ultimate sense-making in the shifts, dilations and contractions of camera and story – is generated by the very content of the film itself: the multiplicity of time frames. Our expectations of both cinema and narrative as conventional time machines are frustrated by this content. The film's grating failure to gel makes us recognise that, as physicist Robert Jaffe points out, 'the times of our lives [. . .] are not the natural rhythms of the world', which include such irreconcilable scales as the electron's orbit ('the beat of the electromagnetic force', 10^{-16} second), the quark's vibration ('the natural rhythm of the strong force', 10^{-22} second), but also 'the unit of cosmological time' of 10 billion years, measured, of course, from our reference frame.[135] Unhappy viewers were most frustrated by the film's incommensurable scales and images, expressed most efficiently by the title of a blog post, 'Daddy didn't love me. Hey look, a dinosaur!'[136] But perhaps the film's greatest contribution is in fact indexed by frustration, since this reaction is produced by the film's demonstration of the impossibility of making the pathos of the narrative mode universal. While the drama of 1950s American life is placed in the blink-of-an-eye flashback of a middle-aged Jack, the whole of history cannot be simply in one man. The theological emphasis on the problem of evil, evoked by the quotation from Job at the beginning of the film and the sermon in the middle, and of course by the death of Jack's brother, is indeed a result of the *incompatibility* of the processes of larger natural scales with the human frame.[137] It is this inability of scales to be reducible to one another in some final cosmic totality that is the real subject of *Tree of Life*, perhaps in spite of itself (Fig. 4.4).

To refer to the cosmos – in those gorgeous manipulations of Hubble images, shots of the formation of the universe, slow views of the flamelike coalescence of gas and dust into galaxies – is already to acknowledge the relativity of reference frames and what modernism troped as the proliferation of clocks. The twenty-minute stretch in the film that time-travels from the earliest moments of the universe, to the birth of microbial life on the planet, to the plesiosaur on the prehistoric beach, to the birth of consciousness in the predatory Troodon, to the birth of Jack, seems to form a single, thin, long line, resulting in 'the dawn

Figure 4.4 Multiple scales in Terrence Malick's *Tree of Life* (2011)

of all human life' and the appearance of grace.[138] But in fact, we have many disparate lines, some of which make their way into the present, some of which have completely independent trajectories and pace, and some of which are long extinct. The visual clash of the various scales, if it is the function of any tree, is better seen as the dense entanglements of Darwin's 'great Tree of Life', the only illustration in his *On the Origin of Species* (1859), which he described as 'fill[ing] with its dead and broken branches the crust of the earth, and cover[ing] the surface with its ever-branching and beautiful ramifications'.[139] While the film appears to use its voice-overs as a way of unifying and arborealising the cosmic lineage of grace, I think the weird way in which the soundtrack and monologue carry over impossibly across a series of shots produces not theophanic transcendence but cineophanic immanence in which frame rate is not in any natural relation to the rate of occurrence within any particular reference frame. Moreover, as Martin Woessner has pointed out, Malick has used voice-over before as the vehicle for cliché (e.g., in *Badlands*), and thus the film invites a *suspicion* of the voice-overs, the visual rhymes and the homological power of the human drama in general.[140]

Like H. G. Wells's *Time Machine*, *Tree of Life* appears to conclude with a vision of the end of human time – after the death of the sun. But Malick gives his ending a distinctly Christian cast: the beach, where the dead have risen and are walking around, is a literalisation of the mother's insight about time dilation ('unless you love, your life will flash by') and the site of her graceful release of her dead son ('I give you my son') in divine sacrifice. However, this closure, like the Traveller's theories in Wells's novel, is clearly facile in contrast to the rest of the film's interest in the relations and interference of timescales that produce all temporal effects, including the dilated instant that Jack is in fact experiencing outside his office building. It is this type of instant, not a point but a portal to just this temporal difference, in which one strain of modernism was clearly invested. As Eliot's J. Alfred Prufrock says, before he too ends up on a beach, 'in a minute there is time'.

In this newly estranged time is the play of relations among locally inflected sequences and disparate lines of occurrence. Our perception of something condensed or capacious, fast or slow, modern or archaic is not a feature of the event alone, measured in some singular abstract medium, but is a function of the pace of these timelines or reference frames in relation to one another. For Wells's Traveller, it might be the difference between 'the spoke of a wheel spinning, or a bullet flying through the air' and the perceptual rates of the human sensorium.[141] For Henri Lefebvre, in his description of 'rhythmanalysis', it might be the contrast between 'an apparently immobile object, the forest' and some smaller scale in which 'the movements of the molecules and atoms that compose it' become visible.[142] It is also the difference between multiple histories running concurrently through the body of the present.

The zooming out of second modernism reconfigures time along these lines. Not only does its scoping teach us how seeing works; its movement across multiple scales contests the 'ultimate vision' that Bailey attributes to Stapledon by emphasising the discordance that cannot be dissolved by any symphonic harmonisation. Thus, the very understanding of time normally generated by plot, which is, according to Frank Kermode, 'an organization that humanizes time by giving it form', is redefined by second-modernist distentions that do not absorb badness but foreground it.[143] Long-range modernism across the long twentieth century not only refused and continues to refuse to give time the intelligibility generated by narrative; it also often dehumanises time by stretching it beyond the orbit of those 'objects, sounds, and patterns of events gratifying to the individual' – beyond its breaking point, where it splinters into a number of discordant and clashing timescales that are impossible to unify. If in second modernity 'literary studies is particularly well-equipped to explore' a present that has been 'derealize[d] [. . .] by stretching it out, suffusing it with the quality of "speculative fiction"', the reason is that contemporary historicist literary criticism, as McGurl puts it so perfectly, 'attempts to travel through time'.[144] From our time machines, we are starting to see that earlier journeys away from time itself yielded some of the best bad views of common-sense measures – earthly units based on planetary rotation in a minor reference frame.

NOTES

1. Ann Druyan, *Cosmos: A Spacetime Odyssey*, season 1, episode 1, hosted by Neil deGrasse Tyson, directed by Ann Druyan, Brannon Braga and Bill Pope, broadcast 9 March 2014 (Twentieth Century Fox).
2. The earliest photographs were taken in 1946 by 35-mm cameras mounted on V-2 missiles. Carl Sagan is reflecting on the 1990 image from *Voyager 1* in Carl Sagan, *Pale Blue Dot: A Vision of the Human Future in Space* (New York: Random House, 1994), 6. Similarly, Tyson makes use of this deflationary containment: 'We humans only evolved in the last hour of the last day of the cosmic year. 11.59, 46 seconds: all of recorded history occupies only the last 14 seconds, and every person you've ever heard of lives somewhere in there. All those kings and battles, migrations and inventions, wars and loves, everything in the history books, happened here – in the last second of the cosmic calendar' (Druyan, *Cosmos*).
3. Sagan, *Pale Blue Dot*, 7.
4. See http://www.ted.com/talks/jill_tarter_s_call_to_join_the_seti_search (last accessed 12 October 2018). Tarter is the scientist on whom Carl Sagan modelled his protagonist Ellie Arroway in his novel *Contact*.
5. Ursula K. Heise, *Sense of Place and Sense of Planet: The Environmental Imagination of the Global* (Oxford: Oxford University Press, 2008), 23, 56, 10–11.
6. Susan Stanford Friedman, 'Planetarity: Musing Modernist Studies', *Modernism/ Modernity* 17.3 (2010): 473, 474.
7. Wai Chee Dimock, *Through Other Continents: American Literature across Deep Time* (Princeton: Princeton University Press, 2006), 124.
8. Ibid. 2, 55.
9. Fernand Braudel, 'History and the Social Sciences: The Longue Durée', in *On History*, trans. Sarah Matthews (Chicago: University of Chicago Press, 1980), 27, quoted in Dimock, *Through Other Continents*, 5.
10. Dimock, *Through Other Continents*, 4, 5. Bruce Robbins thinks the focal points of Dimock's scaled-up view 'look like the old universal "themes" [. . .] Disguised by the fashionable notion of liberating ourselves from the nation-state, what you get here is a rejection of history itself.' Bruce Robbins, 'Many Years Later: Prolepsis in Deep Time', *The Henry James Review* 33.3 (2012): 193. By contrast, Robbins uses 'disaster prolepsis' to show how the apocalyptic leap forward beyond the bounds of narrative is actually a way of raising the question of who is included in political communities of different sizes and who shares sympathetically in the same fate. Literature's value is not to archive everything on an infinitely expanding scale that approximates timelessness, but to engage the problem of 'what is *worth* remembering and why' in an attempt to 'motivate us to build and inhabit collective agents, whether national or [. . .] transnational' (203).
11. Timothy Morton defines hyperobjects as 'things that are massively distributed in time and space relative to humans'. Examples of such large-scale entities that offer no phenomenal access to experience include black holes, the biosphere and climate change. Timothy Morton, *Hyperobjects: Philosophy and Ecology after the End of the World* (Minneapolis: University of Minnesota Press, 2013), 1.

12. Mark McGurl, 'The Posthuman Comedy', *Critical Inquiry* 38.3 (2012): 533–53; Wai Chee Dimock, 'Low Epic', *Critical Inquiry* 39.3 (2013): 614–31; Mark McGurl, '"Neither Indeed Could I Forebear Smiling at My Self": A Reply to Wai Chee Dimock', *Critical Inquiry* 39.3 (2013): 632–8.

13. David Christian, *Maps of Time: An Introduction to Big History* (Berkeley: University of California Press, 2011 [2004]), xxiii.

14. Fred Spier, *Big History and the Future of Humanity* (Oxford: Wiley-Blackwell, 2010), ix–x.

15. McGurl, 'Posthuman Comedy', 539.

16. See Douglas Mao and Rebecca L. Walkowitz, *Bad Modernisms* (Durham, NC: Duke University Press, 2006), and Douglas Mao and Rebecca L. Walkowitz, 'The New Modernist Studies', *PMLA* 123.3 (2008): 737–48. McGurl, '"Neither Indeed Could I Forebear Smiling at My Self"', 633.

17. Mao and Walkowitz, 'New Modernist Studies', 738.

18. See Ulrich Beck, *Risk Society: Towards a New Modernity*, trans. Mark Ritter (London: Sage, 1992). For a succinct description of bads, see Beck's essay, 'The Reinvention of Politics: Towards a Theory of Reflexive Modernization', in Ulrich Beck, Anthony Giddens and Scott Lash, *Reflexive Modernization: Politics, Tradition and Aesthetics in the Modern Social Order* (Stanford: Stanford University Press, 1994), 6: 'With the advent of risk society, the distributional conflicts over "goods" (income, jobs, social security), which constituted the basic conflict of classical industrial society [. . .] are covered over by the distributional conflicts over "bads".'

19. Aravamudan, 'Return of Anachronism', 351. Aravamudan is summarising Chakrabarty to argue for the return of those who have been anachronistically remaindered and 'the multiplicity of historicities': 'The subject of anachronism [. . .] goes beyond historicism by refashioning an explanation of himself or herself in the wake of multiple futures that exist in the now, rather than by yielding to the tyranny of a totalized now that purportedly leads to a singular future' (351).

20. Beck, *Risk Society*.

21. Aaron Jaffe, *The Way Things Go: An Essay on the Matter of Second Modernism* (Minneapolis: University of Minnesota Press, 2014), 18, 19.

22. See Harvey, *Condition of Postmodernity*; Kern, *Culture of Time and Space*.

23. Barbara Adam, *Timescapes of Modernity: The Environment and Invisible Hazards* (London: Routledge, 1998), 107.

24. Kern, *Culture of Time and Space*, 68, 82–3.

25. Canales notes how Louis Olivier, a 'prominent editor of a scientific journal' in the nineteenth century, used crisp, high-speed photography to establish a 'tenth-of-a-second limit' for art – a limit based in the human eye's inability to register clearly more than ten images per second. Whereas science could go beyond this limit by atomising blurry or invisible motion into a lucid multiplicity of tiny fractions, Olivier felt that art should remain committed to the actual experience of encountering such a present. Paintings, said Olivier, 'should represent objects as we see them [. . .] faithfully rendered [. . .] [providing] us with the sensation which we had in seeing'. Louis Olivier, 'Physiologie: La Photographie du mouvement', *Revue scientifique* 30 (1882): 809, quoted in Canales, *A Tenth of a Second*, 120. Canales's

excellent book is actually about small-scale non-simultaneities within media not normally thought to contain lag time, including the human body itself, with its distances between eye and ear, brain and hand.

26. Zemka, *Time and the Moment*, 1.
27. Adam, *Timescapes of Modernity*, 107; Zemka, *Time and the Moment*, 1.
28. Levi Bryant, Nick Srnicek and Graham Harman (eds), *The Speculative Turn: Continental Materialism and Realism* (Melbourne: re.press, 2011), 3.
29. Beck, *Risk Society*, 72.
30. Woolf, *Mrs. Dalloway* (1981), 81.
31. Astradur Eysteinsson, *The Concept of Modernism* (Ithaca: Cornell University Press, 1990), 149; Renato Poggioli, *The Theory of the Avant-Garde*, trans. Gerald Fitzgerald (Cambridge, MA: Harvard University Press, 1968), 73.
32. James Joyce, *Ulysses: The Corrected Text*, ed. Hans Walter Gabler (New York: Random House, 1986 [1922]), 9.349–50; Evelyn Scott, 'Contemporary of the Future', *The Dial* (October 1920), 353–67. For a reading of Stephen's worldly identity in relation to the debates over Martha Nussbaum's argument for cosmopolitanism and the dangers of the global's erasure of the local, see Rick Livingston, 'Global Tropes/Worldly Readings: Narratives of Cosmopolitanism in Joyce, Rich, and Tagore', *Narrative* 5.2 (1997): 121–34.
33. See Patey, 'Whose Tradition?'; Michael Whitworth, 'Virginia Woolf, Modernism, and Modernity', in *The Cambridge Companion to Virginia Woolf*, ed. Susan Sellers, 2nd edn (Cambridge: Cambridge University Press, 2010), 107–23.
34. Aaron Jaffe reads Eliot's palaeofutural 'oceanic trash vortex' briefly but suggestively in his reframing of modernist novelty within a 'second modernism'. Aaron Jaffe, 'Modernist Novelty', *Affirmations: Of the Modern* 1.1 (2013): 120–3. McGurl is also interested in using Ulrich Beck's sociology to re-examine modernism's deep-time engagement with modernity's present: the sociological concept of reflexive modernity 'has a prominent precursor in the reflexive relation to modernity found in literary modernism. Oriented, in Eliot's case, primarily toward the past, it nonetheless allows us to reconfigure both our conception of the future and our relationship to that future, to move away from a position of automatic critique to a position as interested in the conservation and value of institutions as in their limitations.' Mark McGurl, 'Ordinary Doom: Literary Studies in the Waste Land of the Present', *New Literary History* 41.2 (2010): 343.
35. Woolf, *Mrs. Dalloway* (1981), 81.
36. Woolf, *To the Lighthouse*, 23.
37. Robert Stafford, 'Scientific Exploration and Empire', in *The Oxford History of the British Empire*, ed. Andrew Porter, vol. 3 (Oxford: Oxford University Press, 1999), 314.
38. Paul K. Alkon, *Origins of Futuristic Fiction* (Athens: University of Georgia Press, 1987), 46.
39. Veronica Hollinger writes that SF is 'conventionally understood to be a future-oriented genre': Veronica Hollinger, 'A History of the Future: Notes for an Archive', *Science Fiction Studies* 37.1 (2010): 24. Hugo Gernsback defined SF as prophecy and prediction in 'Wanted: A Symbol for Scientifiction', *Amazing Stories* 3 (April 1928), 5. John W. Campbell, Jr, the editor of *Astounding Science-Fiction*, called SF 'an attempt to forecast the future, on the basis of the present

[. . .] a form of extrapolation': John W. Campbell, Jr, 'The Perfect Machine', *Astounding Science-Fiction* 25 (May 1940), 5. Samuel R. Delany identified its speculative quality as 'subjunctivity': Samuel R. Delany, *The Jewel-Hinged Jaw: Notes on the Language of Science Fiction* (Middletown, CT: Wesleyan University Press, 2011), 1–16.

40. Wittenberg, *Time Travel*, 30. Wittenberg argues that the fiction from this early phase, including H. G. Wells's *Time Machine*, is not yet time-travel fiction proper, since its movement through time is 'subsidiary' to the imperatives of the utopian macrologue: 'to furnish a realistic mechanism for the temporal transportation required of an evolutionary narrative, and to insert the viewpoint of an embodied and believable observer into a directly extrapolated future' (85). For Wittenberg, time-travel fiction becomes its own autonomous form in the 1920s under the sign not of Darwin and evolution but of Einstein and relativity, at which point, like the aesthetics of modernist self-reflexivity, its focus becomes the temporality of literary form itself, 'above all [. . .] the forms and mechanisms of storytelling itself' (31).

41. Marie-Hélène Huet, 'Anticipating the Past: The Time Riddle in Science Fiction', in *Storm Warnings: Science Fiction Confronts the Future*, ed. George Edgar Slusser, Colin Greenland and Eric S. Rabkin (Carbondale, IL: Southern Illinois University Press, 1987), 39–40, 35.

42. '[I]n risk society, the unforeseeable side and after-effects of this demand for control [by instrumental rationality], in turn, lead to what had been considered overcome, the realm of the uncertain' (Beck, 'Reinvention of Politics', 10).

43. Jameson, *Archaeologies of the Future*, 211.

44. Viktor Shklovsky, 'Art as Technique', in *Modernism: An Anthology of Sources and Documents*, ed. Vassiliki Kolocotroni, Jane Goldman and Olga Taxidou (Chicago: University of Chicago Press, 1998), 219.

45. Suvin, *Metamorphoses of Science Fiction*, 7–8.

46. Jameson, *Archaeologies of the Future*, 270, 410.

47. Ibid. 286. This persistent idea is quoted in Jameson's early, 1982 piece 'Progress versus Utopia, or, Can We Imagine the Future?' reprinted in *Archeologies of the Future*, 281–95.

48. Wegner, 'Jameson's Modernisms', 11, 7; emphasis in original. SF is 'a form of what we might call *realist* (cognitive) *modernism* (estrangement)' (9).

49. Phillip E. Wegner, 'Utopia', in *A Companion to Science Fiction*, ed. David Seed (Oxford: Blackwell, 2005), 79.

50. Jameson, *Archaeologies of the Future*, 211, 288, 231–2.

51. Ibid. 288, 416.

52. Ibid. 288.

53. For Jameson, multiple and alternative modernities are the fictions, and they belong to neoliberalism and free-market fundamentalism. However, modernism not only 'attempts to look through [. . .] macrostructural modernity to the more complex temporalities it conceals', as McGurl says, but adds literal times and histories to the understanding of modernism as 'complex temporalities' (McGurl, 'Ordinary Doom', 339–40).

54. Wells, *The Time Machine*; H. G. Wells, *Anticipations of the Reaction of Mechanical and Scientific Progress upon Human Life and Thought* (London: Chapman & Hall,

1901). On the influence of Wells, Mark B. Adams writes: 'So pervasive was his influence that most contemporaries assumed there was no need to mention it; as Olaf Stapledon remarked in 1931, "A man does not record his debt to the air he breathes in common with everyone else"'; Mark B. Adams, 'Last Judgment: The Visionary Biology of J. B. S. Haldane', *Journal of the History of Biology* 33.3 (2000): 470; Haldane, Adams notes, felt similarly: 'The very mention of the future suggests him [Wells]'; J. B. S. Haldane, *Daedalus; or, Science and the Future; a Paper Read to the Heretics, Cambridge, on February 4th, 1923* (New York: E.P. Dutton, 1924), 9, quoted in Adams, 'Last Judgment', 470.

55. Wells, *Anticipations*, 1.
56. H. G. Wells, *The Discovery of the Future: A Discourse Delivered to the Royal Institution on January 24, 1902* (London: T. Fisher Unwin, 1902), 33. Subsequent page references are to this edition and are given in parentheses in the text.
57. H. G. Wells, 'Wanted: Professors of Foresight', radio broadcast, BBC, 19 November 1932, http://www.bbc.co.uk/archive/hg_wells/12403.shtml (last accessed 11 October 2018).
58. On the one hand, Wells's interest is not in the 'great man' but 'in the larger forces behind the individual man'. On the other, these larger forces close the openings for intervention in the future: 'if by some juggling with space and time Julius Caesar, Napoleon, Edward IV, William the Conqueror, Lord Rosebery, and Robert Burns had all been changed at birth it would not have produced any serious dislocation of the course of destiny' (*Discovery*, 42–3).
59. Elana Gomel treats the block-universe model as the foundation of the time-travel chronotope, whereas the alternate-history chronotope is based on evolutionary contingency (Gomel, 'Shapes of the Past and the Future'). However, not only are these two chronotopes often conflated in both types of story, but moving in time is not necessarily confined to the limits of the block. Aside from the diagnostic capacity of tracking various open-ended threads, one might also consider how Einsteinian forward time travel is in fact just the confluence of two rates of change: one that runs at a slower pace for the twin moving at a very high speed; one whose earthbound history involves many more revolutions around the sun, to which the younger, speedy twin returns.
60. J. B. S. Haldane, 'The Last Judgment', in *Possible Worlds* (New Brunswick, NJ: Transaction Publishers, 2002 [1927]), 287–312. Subsequent page references are to this edition and are given in parentheses in the text.
61. 'His doomed crab scuttling on a reddened beach was the first great image of the far future': Gregory Benford (ed.), *Far Futures* (New York: Tor, 1995), 11.
62. Wells, *The Time Machine*, 148.
63. See Nicholas Ruddick's introduction in Wells, *The Time Machine*, 32.
64. For an account of Haldane's complicated and shifting career, see Adams, 'Last Judgment', 459–62, 474–7. Haldane's eugenic vision of 'ectogenesis' and his anxieties about 'the greater fertility of the less desirable members of the population in almost all countries' in *Daedalus: Or, Science and the Future* (1924) prompted famous responses: Bertrand Russell's *Icarus, or the Future of Science* (1924) and Aldous Huxley's *Brave New World* (1932). However, Adams argues that *Daedalus* was the first part of a larger vision articulated by 'The Last Judgment'. The

complex context for Haldane's interest in eugenic bioengineering is therefore, he suggests, not only and simply the composition of races against the backdrop of national identity but planetary futures against the backdrop of anthropogenic destruction. 'The futurological account in *Daedalus* is from 150 years into our future, and details how the decline of humanity was forestalled by the universal application of eugenic ectogenesis. The futurological account in "The Last Judgment" is from 40,000,000 years into our future, and details how we have survived the end of our planet and rise to a higher form of consciousness through controlled human evolution' (Adams, 'Last Judgment', 476).

65. By the year 5,000,000, humans have undergone 'artificial evolution' to live 3,000 years. Prior to this, 'the human race on earth was never greatly influenced by an envisaged future [. . .] On the contrary, the earth's inhabitants were often influenced in a curious way by events in the past' (Haldane, 'Last Judgment', 300, 301). But by the time humans have colonised Venus, they have not only engineered their bodies to withstand the heat and lack of oxygen, but they have inserted 'genes such as H 149 and P 783 c' which enable their minds to 'dwell more readily on the future' (Ibid. 301), and they have cultivated dispositions that put the interests of the species before individual desires, becoming eventually members of a super-organism.

66. Pater, *Studies in the History of the Renaissance*, 120.

67. J. B. S. Haldane, 'On Scales', in *Possible Worlds*, 2.

68. Ibid. 3–4.

69. Ibid. 4.

70. See Henry King, *The History of the Telescope* (London: Griffin, 1955); Paul K. Saint-Amour, 'Modernist Reconnaissance', *Modernism/Modernity* 10.2 (2003): 349–80.

71. Holly Henry, *Virginia Woolf and the Discourse of Science: The Aesthetics of Astronomy* (Cambridge: Cambridge University Press, 2003), 3.

72. Ibid. 12–13. As Henry points out, Andromeda is now calculated to be more than twice that distance from us, 2.3 million light years.

73. James Jeans, *The Mysterious Universe* (New York: Macmillan, 1933), 3–4, quoted in Henry, *Virginia Woolf and the Discourse of Science*, 37, 3.

74. Henry, *Virginia Woolf and the Discourse of Science*, 51–70.

75. Ibid. 58.

76. Woolf, *To the Lighthouse*, 136. See Henry, *Virginia Woolf and the Discourse of Science*, 59.

77. Whitworth, 'Virginia Woolf, Modernism, and Modernity', 110.

78. Virginia Woolf, *Night and Day* (New York: Barnes & Noble, 2005 [1919]), 203, 205; Virginia Woolf, *Between the Acts: Annotated* (New York: Houghton Mifflin Harcourt, 2008 [1941]), 7. Wells's *Outline of History* sold over two million copies and begins with a cosmic and geological account of 'The Earth in Space and Time', ending with 'The Great War' and 'The Next Stage in History'. Hilariously, in Olaf Stapledon's *Sirius: A Fantasy of Love and Discord* (London: Secker & Warburg, 1944), the scientifically modified and intelligent dog Sirius is reading *Outline of History*.

79. Whitworth, *Einstein's Wake*, 181.

80. Ibid. 174.

81. Virginia Woolf, *The Waves* (London: Houghton Mifflin Harcourt, 1950 [1931]), 268.
82. Woolf, *To the Lighthouse*, 20.
83. Woolf, *Night and Day*, 172.
84. Woolf, *To the Lighthouse*, 59; Woolf, *The Waves*, 225.
85. Henry, *Virginia Woolf and the Discourse of Science*, 54.
86. Whitworth reports that the inspiration for Mrs Ramsay's stock-taking against the backdrop of the future was Einstein, citing Woolf's letter to Vita Sackville-West, 29 March 1926: 'It seems that Woolf's question about her own posterity was prompted by a dinner the previous evening, at which her companions discussed "how if Einstein is true, we shall be able to foretell our own lives". Though Woolf considered the argument to be "passing my limits", the diary preserves a fragment of a culture in which scientific ideas and unscientific speculations were frequently discussed' (Whitworth, *Einstein's Wake*, 182).
87. Kern, *Culture of Time and Space*, 245.
88. '[M]ilitary reconnaissance was explicitly oriented around equipping, training, and therefore describing human *observers*, which [. . .] is also the case with avant-garde representation during the period' (Saint-Amour, 'Modernist Reconnaissance', 353).
89. Paul K. Saint-Amour, 'Applied Modernism: Military and Civilian Uses of the Aerial Photomosaic', *Theory, Culture & Society* 28.7–8 (2011): 245.
90. Ibid. 246, emphasis added.
91. Ibid.
92. Ibid. 248.
93. Gertrude Stein, *Picasso* (Mineola, NY: Dover Publications, 1984 [1938]), 50; quoted in Saint-Amour, 'Modernist Reconnaissance', 350.
94. Stein, *Picasso*, 50.
95. Virginia Woolf, 'Flying over London', in *The Captain's Death Bed and Other Essays* (London: Hogarth Press, 1950), 186. Subsequent page references are to this edition and are given in parentheses in the text.
96. Henry, *Virginia Woolf and the Discourse of Science*, 66–7.
97. See chapter 2, 'From Hubble's Telescope to "The Searchlight"', and chapter 3, 'Woolf and Stapledon Envision New Worlds', in Henry, *Virginia Woolf and the Discourse of Science*. See also Banfield, *Phantom Table*, 185–6.
98. Stapledon's letter to Woolf, 14 July 1937, quoted in Henry, *Virginia Woolf and the Discourse of Science*, 111.
99. Woolf linked the novel's badness to the 'jerking' changes of scene. Virginia Woolf, *The Diary of Virginia Woolf, Vol. 5: 1936–41*, ed. Anne Olivier Bell (New York: Harvest, 1985), 17. Verita Sriratana argues that Woolf's last-minute insertion of the weather passages were meant to solve these transition problems, but meteorological distance in fact exacerbated the issue of narrative coherence by foregrounding the tension between two very different orders of temporality. Verita Sriratana, '"It Was an Uncertain Spring": Reading the Weather in *The Years*', in *Virginia Woolf and the Natural World*, ed. Kristin Czarnecki and Carrie Rohman (Clemson, SC: Clemson University Digital Press, 2011), 191–5.

100. Woolf's letter to Stapledon, 8 July 1937, quoted in Robert Crossley, 'Olaf Stapledon and the Idea of Science Fiction', *Modern Fiction Studies* 32.1 (1986): 29.
101. Olaf Stapledon, *Last and First Men* (Mineola, NY: Dover Publications, 2008 [1930]), 215. Subsequent page references are to this edition and are given in parentheses in the text.
102. For an excellent reading of Woolf and Stapledon in the context of the 1930s, see Henry's fifth chapter, 'Woolf and Stapledon Envision New Worlds', *Virginia Woolf and the Discourse of Science*, 108–40.
103. Jeans, *Mysterious Universe*, 15, quoted in Henry, *Virginia Woolf and the Discourse of Science*, 63.
104. James Jeans, *The Universe Around Us* (New York: Macmillan, 1929), 331.
105. Raja and Nandi point out that concepts of postnationality as a universalism often scope out from the narrowness of nationalism in a way that obscures 'whose interests are served' by such scaling up. However, postcolonialism helps to reveal that the 'rise of neoliberal capitalism, heralded as a system that defies nationalistic modes of production of advanced capitalism, cannot also erase the nation and the national'. Massod A. Raja and Swaralipi Nandi, 'Introduction', in *The Postnational Fantasy: Essays on Postcolonialism, Cosmopolitics and Science Fiction*, ed. Masood A. Raja, Swaralipi Nandi and Jason Ellis (Jefferson, NC: McFarland, 2011), 8. Moreover, citing Bruce Robbins, they suggest that any 'cosmopolitics' that refuses a 'free-floating view from above' must account for, rather than erase, the 'particular [. . .] unprivileged – indeed, often coerced'. Pheng Cheah and Bruce Robbins (eds), *Cosmopolitics: Thinking and Feeling beyond the Nation* (Minneapolis: University of Minnesota Press, 1998), 1; quoted in Raja and Nandi, 'Introduction', 7.
106. Woolf, *Diary, Vol. 5*, 135.
107. Olaf Stapledon, *Star Maker*, ed. Patrick A. McCarthy (Middletown, CT: Wesleyan University Press, 2004), 265.
108. In the 1880s Wilhelm Wundt determined experimentally that the present is 5 seconds long, and William James argued that the 'specious present' lasts about 12 seconds. See Kern, *Culture of Time and Space*, 82–3.
109. Daniel Rosenberg and Anthony Grafton, *Cartographies of Time: A History of the Timeline* (New York: Princeton Architectural Press, 2010), 20.
110. Ibid. 19.
111. Rosenberg and Grafton, *Cartographies of Time*, 23.
112. Ibid. 11, 12.
113. Louis Tremaine, 'Historical Consciousness in Stapledon and Malraux', *Science Fiction Studies* 11.2 (1984): 130.
114. Ibid.
115. K. V. Bailey, 'Times Scales and Culture Cycles in Olaf Stapledon', *Foundation: The Review of Science Fiction* 46 (autumn 1989): 36.
116. John Huntington, 'Olaf Stapledon and the Novel about the Future', *Contemporary Literature* 22.3 (1981): 359.
117. John Huntington, 'Remembrance of Things to Come: Narrative Technique in *Last and First Men*', *Science Fiction Studies* 9.3 (1982): 263. Huntington is committed

to defending 'Stapledon's narrative art' by making it capacious enough to subsume badness. For him, Stapledon's excellence resides in his ability to play the singular and specific off the iterative, recurrent and patterned. Thus the novel preserves 'the potentiality of the individual and exceptional', while also emphasising 'continuities and orderly, inexorable process' (262).

118. Huntington, 'Olaf Stapledon', 351.

119. Ibid. 350, 351. Huntington's examples are William Burroughs's aleatory juxtaposition/'cut-up' novel *Nova Express* and John Brunner's Dos-Passosian, multiple-strand novel *Stand on Zanzibar*.

120. Ibid. 353–4.

121. He says that his aim is rather to produce myth, which he defines simply as 'the highest admirations possible' in a culture.

122. Stapledon, *Star Maker*, 5.

123. Wilson's letter is quoted in Robert Crossley, *Olaf Stapledon: Speaking for the Future* (Syracuse, NY: Syracuse University Press, 1994), 191. In his notes, Crossley locates the letter in a special file on *Last and First Men* in the Stapledon Archive at the University of Liverpool Library but does not provide the date (n. 26).

124. Huntington, 'Remembrance of Things to Come', 259.

125. Jorge Luis Borges, 'Funes the Memorious', in *Labyrinths: Selected Stories & Other Writings*, ed. Donald A. Yates and James E. Irby (New York: New Directions, 2007), 59–66.

126. Huntington, 'Remembrance of Things to Come', 260.

127. Patrick A. McCarthy, 'Stapledon and Literary Modernism', in *The Legacy of Olaf Stapledon: Critical Essays and an Unpublished Manuscript*, ed. Patrick A. McCarthy, Charles Elkins and Martin Harry Greenberg (New York: Greenwood, 1989), 41.

128. Ibid. 42, 43.

129. Frank Kermode, *Sense of an Ending: Studies in the Theory of Fiction* (Oxford: Oxford University Press, 1966), 45.

130. Jeff Wallace, *Beginning Modernism* (Manchester: Manchester University Press, 2011), 3 (emphasis in original).

131. Gerald Jonas, 'Onward and Upward with the Arts: S.F.', *New Yorker* 48 (29 July 1972): 51.

132. Ibid. 51–2.

133. Kent Jones, 'Light Years', *Film Comment* 47.4 (2011): 26, 28.

134. David Sterritt, 'Days of Heaven and Waco: Terrence Malick's *Tree of Life*', *Film Quarterly* 65.1 (2011): 55, 53.

135. Robert L. Jaffe, 'As Time Goes By', *Natural History* 115.8 (2006): 16, 21.

136. Greg Christie, '"Daddy didn't love me. Hey look, a dinosaur!" Boozie Movies waxes philosophical on *Tree of Life*', *Twitch* (blog), 19 June 2011, https://screena-narchy.com/2011/06/daddy-didnt-love-me-hey-look-a-dinosaur-boozie-movies-waxes-philosophical-on-tree-of-life.html (last accessed 31 October 2018).

137. The film quotes the Book of Job 38: 4, 7–8: 'Where were you when I laid the foundations of the earth? [. . .] When the morning stars sang together, and all the sons of God shouted for joy?' This is the reply to Job's question about why a just God would allow his ten children to die.

138. Jones, 'Light Years', 26.
139. Charles Darwin, *On the Origin of Species by Means of Natural Selection* (London: John Murray, 1859), 105, quoted in S. Brent Plate, 'Visualizing the Cosmos: Terrence Malick's *Tree of Life* and Other Visions of Life in the Universe', *Journal of the American Academy of Religion* 80.2 (2012): 533.
140. According to Woessner, Malick's 'Heideggerian Cinema' always calls attention to the horizons and limits of worlds. See Martin Woessner, 'What Is Heideggerian Cinema? Film, Philosophy, and Cultural Mobility', *New German Critique* 113 (summer 2011): 144–5, 40.
141. Wells, *The Time Machine*, 67.
142. Lefebvre, *Rhythmanalysis*, 20.
143. Kermode, *Sense of an Ending*, 45.
144. McGurl, 'Ordinary Doom', 331, 334.

CONCLUSION

How does one conclude a book about time travel, about the heterochronic function of time machines, at a moment when fascist politics are resurgent in the US and across the globe, and a range of catastrophic arcs, from the social to the planetary, reach into the present from different zones of the future? One imagines Walter Benjamin's angel appearing on these horizons and importuning us to pull the emergency brake on history as it barrels forward. But which track are we on? Ernst Bloch thought that there could be no 'proletarian hegemony' without the ability to master 'the substance of genuine non-sametimeliness and its heterogeneous contradictions'.[1] For some thinkers, this exhortation in 1935 was ineffectual in countering 'fascism's political exploitation of "non-sametimely" social elements and cultural strata' with what Bloch envisioned as a 'Triple Alliance of the proletariat with the impoverished peasants and the impoverished middle classes'.[2] The idea that the left could marshal the forces of non-synchronous and synchronous contradiction – the oppositional power of those who have been left behind in an unfinished past and those whose antagonism comes directly from contemporary relations of production in the dominant socio-economic order – was, as Peter Osborne says, 'already too late'.[3]

We currently see more clearly that our present is simultaneously 'archaic, modern, and futuristic', and that 'every historical era is likewise multitemporal [. . .] with multiple pleats'.[4] Michel Serres's angels fly across and between the pleats in order to understand different kinds of assemblages, which has given rise to accusations that his history is not historicist, that he pilots a time machine. But I imagine that his angel and time machine have learned the lesson of the backward-facing Angelus Novus. These heterochronic devices do not abandon the 'revolutionary chance in the fight for the oppressed past', but rather add to their operations a scaling-up of historiographic replay and, crucially, a forward-facing scan for trajectories already running through what we take as the present. Like the fantasy of moving within the fifth-dimensional bulk, the task of disclosing, tracking and engaging de-synchronised timelines always takes place from another reference frame that is itself shot through with zones of differential pace and timelines of varying length. Giorgio Agamben's answer to the question 'What Is Contemporary?' is that only the thinker 'who perceives the indices and signatures of the archaic in the most modern and recent can be contemporary'; the time machine adds to this 'contemporal' assemblage a set of impending futures.[5]

It has been important to my argument that we see this assemblage not simply *in time* but *of times*. Unitary temporality, linear time, nineteenth-century historicism – these terms and ideas have come to seem like the straw targets of a modernism and postmodernism that have long since been reconfigured. But the desired counter-terms and counterpoints were most often an aesthetic playfulness, freed from the constraints of a singular set of operating procedures and materials; non-linear styles, subversive of oppressive teleology; and subjective and sociological plurality, proliferating in the absence of a unifying cultural clock. I continue to believe that these stances and moves were important and meaningful instances of the dialectical push away from an immediate past, strategies in which time was given a hopeful cast as a virtual repository of 'multiple futures, for open pathways, for indeterminable consequences'.[6]

However, rather than treating the idea of unilinearity as a shibboleth solidifying an aesthetic and historical period dialectically, I have tried in this study to start with unitary time – its putatively isochronic character, its anthropocentric narrativity and its monochronic nature – as a phenomenon that arose in particular technological and cultural conditions, and which provoked or was met with a hotchpotch historicity expressed in certain aesthetic and cultural objects, political orientations and scientific theories (biology and physics). I have no doubt that time has been construed as a stable backdrop in other conjunctures, for other reasons, just as I know that time has been conceived as unstable in other cultural and historical currents in the past. The difference I have tried to underline comes from the insistent attempt to think of timespace and history as literally multiple – with irregular internal consistency and pace, variable scales and distinctive frames of reference. To hold apart timespace and history analytically, and to keep individual experience separate as well, has often resulted in the preservation of unitary time as the fundamental base layer, as that which underlies narrative sense-making at the level of chronology of fabular order, on which we deploy tropes and figures in rendering both individual and collective experience to ourselves. But there are many base layers, many times.

No doubt the distance between experience, figurative elements and structures and some underlying form is often necessary to understand many aspects of modernist cultural production and twentieth-century criticism. But this study has sought to focus on the plurality and relativity of non-subjective times themselves, whose presence immediately complicates the operating principle of a single, absolute time generated by modernity's material processes of coordination, communication and production. The technologies, aesthetic devices and cultural machines that give access to or produce the differential pace, scale and number of times provide different counter-terms to unitary time than the dominant lexica of modernist and postmodernist discourses: instead of playfulness, nonlinearity and subjective and social indeterminacy, modernist time machines make or reveal heterochrony, multilinear zones of occurrence, nonhuman and inhuman scales. The resistance to modernity's regulation of temporal rates, shapes and number has for a long time, and movingly, resulted in the centrality of the vexed experience of and heroic resistance to isochronicity and standardised time. But I hope to have contributed to the critical picture by emphasising another possible focus: one that attends to the exit strategies from downscaled forms, that follows postcolonial historiography and critical geography into sovereign and polychronic timespaces, that thinks through another sort of historicity, and that is haunted by future-oriented, second-modernist calculations about the half-lives of the various 'bads' produced by modernity.

We are surrounded now by many big clocks – the Doomsday Clock, the Clock of the Long Now, registers of the slow violence of environmental disaster – which tell an insensible risk temporality and create a measure for 'a new, nonnarrative future tense'.[7] Facebook and GoogleTimeline are always working to piece together a coherent trajectory for each of us through a monetised dataspace and policeable real time. These clocks seem to enforce a kind of negative universality of planetary fate, 'a countdown to some potential future annihilation', but, as Molly Wallace argues, we are now learning to re-read them as 'measuring different scales of temporality' and a syncopated present 'containing multiple catastrophes, historical and to come, simultaneously'.[8] In our historical situation, possibility and contingency have been reconfigured: they are no longer a matter of finding the right moment for right action in a singular chain of events, but of making different kinds of intra- and multilinear assessments, and of various modes of timing. In the realm of Trumpism, too, Blochian multi-temporality does not confirm (after the fact) the right's claim to outsiderism in relation to the present as a way of arguing for its ownership of it, but rather points to a tactical reality in which the future of 'the future' itself depends upon activating more promising pasts and anticipating the catastrophic processes – social, political and environmental – currently ticking away at different rates and on different scales.

As we think about the modern, and indeed the internal consistency generated by periodisation itself, in relation 'not only to capital but to carbon, not only in modernities and post-modernities but in parts-per-million, not only in dates but in degrees Celsius', we traverse, as Ian Baucom argues, different times and types of time, different domains of agency, causal dynamics and effectiveness. We therefore require 'a new search for a method that will take as its starting point an investigation of the multi-scaled, ontologically plural, simultaneously historical, infra-historical, and supra-historical "situation" in which we find ourselves'.[9] The Anthropocene scenario of extinction, rather than re-imposing the regime of the unitary, calls for an attunement to a present that is 'composed of multiple scales, orders, and classes of time (abstract, hermeneutic, ontic) and multiple corresponding orientations to the possibility of the (just) future fashioning of those times'.[10] Whereas universal apocalyptic forms see a chain of events, the heterochronic angel calculates and speculates on a range of futures that are arriving and not arriving via more than one sequence, at unsynchronised rates and on discrepant units of measure. In the current state of emergency, the brakes must be pulled, but there is more than one track, frame and train. In concurrent domains, the acceleration lever must be pushed. The turbulent dynamics of the wind blowing against the wings of the angel in his time machine tilts them in a number of directions, and the negative universality of apocalypse feels different across discontinuous fields. In each direction, the angel pins his tactically timed and renewed hopes not just on certain streamlined acts but on the persistent engagement with the heterochronic Not-Yet-Become.[11]

NOTES

1. Bloch, *Heritage of Our Times*, 114.
2. Osborne, 'Out of Sync', 43; Bloch, *Heritage of Our Times*, 113.
3. Osborne, 'Out of Sync', 43
4. Serres and Latour, *Conversations on Science*, 60.
5. Giorgio Agamben, 'What Is Contemporary?', in *'What Is an Apparatus?' and Other Essays*, trans. David Kishik and Stefan Pedatella (Stanford: Stanford University Press, 2009), 50.
6. Grosz, *The Nick of Time*, 253.
7. Richard Klein, 'The Future of Nuclear Criticism', *Yale French Studies* 77 (1990): 77. See also Molly Wallace's excellent *Risk Criticism: Reading in an Age of Manufactured Uncertainties* (Ann Arbor: University of Michigan Press, 2016).
8. Wallace, *Risk Criticism*, 17.
9. Ian Baucom, 'History 4°: Postcolonial Method and Anthropocene Time', *Cambridge Journal of Postcolonial Literary Inquiry* 1.1 (2014): 125, 134.

10. Ibid. 142. See also Srinivas Aravamudan's argument that the sense of an ending and the orientation towards apocalypse tend towards the unitary, the 'catachronic' alignment of past and present with a singular 'future proclaimed as determinate but [. . .] of course not yet fully realized'. Srinivas Aravamudan, 'The Catachronism of Climate Change', *Diacritics* 41.3 (2013): 8.

11. Ernst Bloch, 'Introduction', in *Principle of Hope*, vol. 1 (Cambridge, MA: MIT Press, 1986), 3–18. On Bloch's thinking in relation to postcolonial historicity, see Bill Ashcroft, *Utopianism in Postcolonial Literatures* (London: Routledge, 2017).

BIBLIOGRAPHY

Abel, Elizabeth, 'Narrative Structure(s) and Female Development: The Case of *Mrs Dalloway*', in *Virginia Woolf*, ed. Rachel Bowlby (London: Routledge, 2013 [1992]), 77–101.

Achebe, Chinua, 'An Image of Africa', *Massachusetts Review: A Quarterly of Literature, the Arts and Public Affairs* 18.4 (1977): 782–94.

Adam, Barbara, *Timescapes of Modernity: The Environment and Invisible Hazards* (London: Routledge, 1998).

Adams, Mark B., 'Last Judgment: The Visionary Biology of J. B. S. Haldane', *Journal of the History of Biology* 33.3 (2000): 457–91.

Adorno, Theodor, *Negative Dialectics* (London: Routledge, 2003 [1966]).

Agamben, Giorgio, 'What Is Contemporary?', in *'What Is an Apparatus?' and Other Essays*, trans. David Kishik and Stefan Pedatella (Stanford: Stanford University Press, 2009), 39–54.

Alkon, Paul K., *Origins of Futuristic Fiction* (Athens: University of Georgia Press, 1987).

'American Development of the Philippines', *National Geographic Magazine* 14.5 (1903): 197.

Anderson, Perry, 'Modernity and Revolution', *New Left Review* 144 (1984): 96–113.

Antliff, Mark, *Inventing Bergson: Cultural Politics and the Parisian Avant-Garde* (Princeton: Princeton University Press, 1993).

Antliff, Mark, and Patricia Leighten, *Cubism and Culture* (New York: Thames & Hudson, 2001).

Antliff, Mark, and Patricia Leighten (eds), *A Cubism Reader: Documents and Criticism, 1906–1914* (Chicago: University of Chicago Press, 2008).

Aravamudan, Srinivas, 'The Catachronism of Climate Change', *Diacritics* 41.3 (2013): 6–30.

Aravamudan, Srinivas, 'The Return of Anachronism', *MLQ: Modern Language Quarterly* 62.4 (2001): 331–53.

Armstrong, Tim, *Modernism: A Cultural History* (Cambridge: Polity, 2005).

Armstrong, Tim, *Modernism, Technology, and the Body: A Cultural Study* (Cambridge: Cambridge University Press, 1998).

Armstrong, Tim, 'Modernist Temporality: The Science and Philosophy and Aesthetics of Temporality from 1880', in *The Cambridge History of Modernism*, ed. Vincent B. Sherry (Cambridge: Cambridge University Press, 2016), 31–46, https://doi.org/10.1017/9781139540902 (last accessed 11 October 2018).

Arnold, Matthew, *The Poetical Works of Matthew Arnold*, ed. Nathan Haskell Dole (New York: Thomas Crowell, 1897).

Arroyo, José, 'Mission: Sublime', in *Action/Spectacle Cinema: A Sight and Sound Reader*, ed. José Arroyo (London: British Film Institute, 2000), 21–5.

Ashcroft, Bill, 'Archipelago of Dreams: Utopianism in Caribbean Literature', *Textual Practice* 30.1 (2016): 89–112, https://doi.org/10.1080/0950236X.2015.1059587 (last accessed 11 October 2018).

Ashcroft, Bill, *Utopianism in Postcolonial Literatures* (London: Routledge, 2017).

Azérad, Hugues, 'A New Region of the World: Faulkner, Glissant, and the Caribbean', in *The New Cambridge Companion to William Faulkner*, ed. John T. Matthews (Cambridge: Cambridge University Press, 2015), 164–84.

Badsey, Stephen, '"If It Had Happened Otherwise": First World War Exceptionalism in Counterfactual History', in *British Popular Culture and the First World War*, ed. Jessica Meyer (Boston: Brill, 2008), 351–67.

Bailey, K. V., 'Times Scales and Culture Cycles in Olaf Stapledon', *Foundation: The Review of Science Fiction* 46 (autumn 1989): 27–39.

Banfield, Ann, *The Phantom Table: Woolf, Fry, Russell, and Epistemology of Modernism* (Cambridge: Cambridge University Press, 2000).

Barr, Alfred, *Picasso: Forty Years of His Art* (New York: Museum of Modern Art, 1939).

Barrows, Adam, *The Cosmic Time of Empire: Modern Britain and World Literature* (Berkeley: University of California Press, 2011).

Bartky, Ian R., 'The Adoption of Standard Time', *Technology and Culture* 30.1 (1989): 25–56, https://doi.org/10.2307/3105430 (last accessed 11 October 2018).

Bartky, Ian R., *One Time Fits All: The Campaigns for Global Uniformity* (Stanford: Stanford University Press, 2007).

Baucom, Ian, 'History 4°: Postcolonial Method and Anthropocene Time', *Cambridge Journal of Postcolonial Literary Inquiry* 1.1 (2014): 123–42.

Baudelaire, Charles, 'The Painter of Modern Life', in *Selected Writings on Art and Literature*, trans. P. E. Charvet (Harmondsworth: Penguin, 1992), 390–435.

Bauman, Zygmunt, 'Time and Space Reunited', *Time & Society* 9.2–3 (2000): 171–85.

Baxter, Stephen, 'The Technology of Omniscience: Past Viewers in Science Fiction', *Foundation: The International Review of Science Fiction* 29.80 (2000): 97–106.

Beaumont, Matthew, 'Imagining the End Times: Ideology, the Contemporary Disaster Movie, Contagion', in *Žižek and Media Studies*, ed. Matthew Flisfeder and Louis-Paul Willis (Basingstoke: Palgrave Macmillan, 2014), 79–89.

Beaumont, Matthew, 'Introduction', in Walter Pater, *Studies in the History of the Renaissance*, ed. Matthew Beaumont (Oxford: Oxford University Press, 2010), vii–xxix.

Beck, Ulrich, 'The Reinvention of Politics: Towards a Theory of Reflexive Modernization', in Ulrich Beck, Anthony Giddens and Scott Lash, *Reflexive Modernization: Politics, Tradition and Aesthetics in the Modern Social Order* (Stanford: Stanford University Press, 1994), 1–55.

Beck, Ulrich, *Risk Society: Towards a New Modernity*, trans. Mark Ritter (London: Sage, 1992).

Beck, Ulrich, Anthony Giddens and Scott Lash, *Reflexive Modernization: Politics, Tradition and Aesthetics in the Modern Social Order* (Stanford: Stanford University Press, 1994).

Bellour, Raymond, 'To Alternate/To Narrate', in *Early Cinema: Space, Frame, Narrative*, ed. Thomas Elsaesser and Adam Barker (London: British Film Institute, 1990), 360–74.

Benford, Gregory (ed.), *Far Futures* (New York: Tor, 1995).

Benjamin, Walter, 'Theses on the Philosophy of History', in *Illuminations*, trans. Harry Zohn (New York: Harcourt, 1968), 253–64.

Bennett, Jane, and William Connolly, 'The Crumpled Handkerchief', in *Time and History in Deleuze and Serres*, ed. Bernd Herzogenrath (New York: Continuum, 2012), 153–71.

Bergson, Henri, *Creative Evolution*, trans. Arthur Mitchell (New York: Henry Holt, 1911).

Bergson, Henri, *An Introduction to Metaphysics*, trans. T. E. Hulme (London: G. P. Putnam's Sons, 1912).

Bergson, Henri, *Time and Free Will: An Essay on the Immediate Data of Consciousness* (London: G. Allen, 1913 [1889]).

Bernier, Ronald R., *Monument, Moment, and Memory: Monet's Cathedral in Fin de Siècle France* (Lewisburg, PA: Bucknell University Press, 2007).

Bhabha, Homi K., *The Location of Culture* (London: Routledge, 1994).

Bignell, Jonathan, 'Another Time, Another Space: Modernity, Subjectivity, and *The Time Machine*', in *Liquid Metal: The Science Fiction Film Reader*, ed. Sean Redmond (London: Wallflower, 2004), 136–44.

Bloch, Ernst, *Heritage of Our Times*, trans. Neville and Stephen Plaice (Cambridge: Polity, 1991 [1935]).

Bloch, Ernst, 'Introduction', in *Principle of Hope* (Cambridge, MA: MIT Press, 1986), 1: 3–18.

Borges, Jorge Luis, 'Funes the Memorious', in *Labyrinths: Selected Stories & Other Writings*, ed. Donald A. Yates and James E. Irby (New York: New Directions, 2007), 59–66.

Brathwaite, Edward Kamau, 'History of the Voice, 1979/1981', in *Roots* (Ann Arbor: University of Michigan Press, 1993), 259–304.

Braudel, Fernand, 'History and the Social Sciences: The Longue Durée', in *On History*, trans. Sarah Matthews (Chicago: University of Chicago Press, 1980).

Briggs, Julia, *Reading Virginia Woolf* (Edinburgh: Edinburgh University Press, 2006).

Broadhurst, Susan, *Digital Practices: Aesthetic and Neuroesthetic Approaches to Performance and Technology* (Basingstoke: Palgrave Macmillan, 2007).

Brooker, Jewel Spears, and Joseph Bentley, *Reading The Waste Land: Modernism and the Limits of Interpretation* (Amherst, MA: University of Massachusetts Press, 1992).

Brooks, Cleanth, *Modern Poetry and the Tradition* (Chapel Hill: University of North Carolina Press, 1939).

Brooks, Cleanth, *The Well-Wrought Urn* (London: Dennis Dobson, 1968 [1947]).

Brooks, Cleanth, *William Faulkner: The Yoknapatawpha Country* (New Haven, CT: Yale University Press, 1963).

Brooks, Cleanth, *William Faulkner: Toward Yoknapatawpha and Beyond* (Baton Rouge: Louisiana State University Press, 1990 [1978]).

Brown, Bill, 'Materiality', in *Critical Terms for Media Studies*, ed. W. J. T. Mitchell and Mark B. N. Hansen (Chicago: University of Chicago Press, 2010), 49–63.

Brown, Paul Tolliver, 'The Spatiotemporal Topography of Virginia Woolf's *Mrs. Dalloway*: Capturing Britain's Transition to a Relative Modernity', *Journal of Modern Literature* 38.4 (2015): 20–38.

Bryant, Levi, *Onto-Cartography: An Ontology of Machines and Media* (Edinburgh: Edinburgh University Press, 2014).

Bryant, Levi, Nick Srnicek and Graham Harman (eds), *The Speculative Turn: Continental Materialism and Realism* (Melbourne: re.press, 2011).

Bukatman, Scott, *Matters of Gravity: Special Effects and Supermen in the 20th Century* (Durham, NC: Duke University Press, 2003).

Bush, Ronald, 'The Presence of the Past: Ethnographic Thinking/Literary Politics', in *Prehistories of the Future: The Primitivist Project and the Culture of Modernism*, ed. Elazar Barkan and Ronald Bush (Stanford: Stanford University Press, 1995), 23–41.

Calinescu, Matei, *Five Faces of Modernity: Modernism, Avant-Garde, Decadence, Kitsch, Postmodernism* (Durham, NC: Duke University Press, 1987).

Campbell, Jr, John W., 'The Perfect Machine', *Astounding Science-Fiction* 25 (May 1940): 5.

Campbell, Laura E., 'Dickian Time in *The Man in the High Castle*', *Extrapolation: A Journal of Science Fiction and Fantasy* 33.3 (1992): 190–201.

Canales, Jimena, *A Tenth of a Second a History* (Chicago: University of Chicago Press, 2009).

Cantor, Paul A., and Peter Hufnagel, 'The Empire of the Future: Imperialism and Modernism in H. G. Wells', *Studies in the Novel* 38.1 (2006): 36–56.

Cawelti, John, *Apostles of the Self-Made Man* (Chicago: University Chicago Press, 1965).

Chakrabarty, Dipesh, *Provincializing Europe: Postcolonial Thought and Historical Difference* (Princeton: Princeton University Press, 2000).

Charney, Leo, 'In a Moment: Film and the Philosophy of Modernity', in *Cinema and the Invention of Modern Life*, ed. Leo Charney and Vanessa R. Schwartz (Berkeley: University of California Press, 1995).

Cheah, Pheng, and Bruce Robbins (eds), *Cosmopolitics: Thinking and Feeling beyond the Nation* (Minneapolis: University of Minnesota Press, 1998).

Chen, Shu-ching, 'Run through the Jungle: Uncanny Domesticity and the Woman of Shame in Jessica Hagedorn's *Dream Jungle*', *Tamkang Review: A Quarterly of Literary and Cultural Studies* 43.1 (2012): 3–26.

Cheng, John, *Astounding Wonder: Imagining Science and Science Fiction in Interwar America* (Philadelphia: University of Pennsylvania Press, 2012).

Christian, David, *Maps of Time: An Introduction to Big History* (Berkeley: University of California Press, 2011 [2004]).

Christie, Greg, '"Daddy didn't love me. Hey look, a dinosaur!" Boozie Movies waxes philosophical on *Tree of Life*', *Twitch* (blog), 19 June 2011, https://screenanarchy.com/2011/06/daddy-didnt-love-me-hey-look-a-dinosaur-boozie-movies-waxes-philosophical-on-tree-of-life.html (last accessed 31 October 2018).

Cianci, Giovanni, 'Reading T. S. Eliot Visually: Tradition in the Context of Modernist Art', in *T. S. Eliot and the Concept of Tradition*, ed. Giovanni

Cianci and Jason Harding (Cambridge: Cambridge University Press, 2007), 119–30.

Connor, Steven, 'How to do Things with Writing Machines', in *Writing, Medium, Machine: Modern Technographies*, ed. Sean Pryor and David Trotter (London: Open Humanities Press, 2016), 19–34.

Conrad, Joseph, *The Secret Agent* (London: Methuen, 1907).

Cover, Arthur Byron, 'Vertex Interview with Philip K. Dick', *Vertex* 1.6 (1974), http://www.philipkdickfans.com/literary-criticism/frank-views-archive/vertex-interview-with-philip-k-dick/ (last accessed 11 October 2018).

Cowan, Michael H (ed.), *Twentieth Century Interpretations of The Sound and the Fury* (Englewood Cliffs, NJ: Prentice-Hall, 1968).

Cox, Neil, *Cubism* (London: Phaidon, 2000).

Crary, Jonathan, *Techniques of the Observer: On Vision and Modernity in the Nineteenth Century* (Cambridge, MA: MIT Press, 1990).

Crawford, Robert, *The Savage and the City in the Work of T. S. Eliot* (Oxford: Clarendon Press, 1987).

Crossley, Robert, 'Olaf Stapledon and the Idea of Science Fiction', *Modern Fiction Studies* 32.1 (1986): 21–42.

Crossley, Robert, *Olaf Stapledon: Speaking for the Future* (Syracuse, NY: Syracuse University Press, 1994).

Currie, Mark, *About Time: Narrative, Fiction, and the Philosophy of Time* (Edinburgh: Edinburgh University Press, 2007).

Daiches, David, *Virginia Woolf* (Norfolk, CT: New Directions, 1942).

Danius, Sara, *The Senses of Modernism: Technology, Perception, and Aesthetics* (Ithaca: Cornell University Press, 2002).

Dannenberg, Hilary P., *Coincidence and Counterfactuality: Plotting Time and Space in Narrative Fiction* (Lincoln: University of Nebraska Press, 2008).

Danto, Arthur C., review of Linda Dalrymple Henderson, *The Fourth Dimension and Non-Euclidean Geometry in Modern Art*, *The Print Collector's Newsletter* 16 (May–June 1985), 64.

Darwin, Charles, *On the Origin of Species by Means of Natural Selection* (London: John Murray, 1859).

Davies, Paul, *How to Build a Time Machine* (New York: Penguin, 2002).

Davis, Thomas S., 'Late Modernism: British Literature at Midcentury', *Literature Compass* 9.4 (2012): 326–37.

Delany, Samuel R., *The Jewel-Hinged Jaw: Notes on the Language of Science Fiction* (Middletown, CT: Wesleyan University Press, 2011).

Deleuze, Gilles, and Félix Guattari, *Anti-Oedipus: Capitalism and Schizophrenia*, trans. Robert Hurley, Mark Seem and Helen R. Lane (Minneapolis: University of Minnesota Press, 1983).

Deleuze, Gilles, and Félix Guattari, *A Thousand Plateaus: Capitalism and Schizophrenia*, trans. Brian Massumi (Minneapolis: University of Minnesota Press, 1987).

de Man, Paul, 'Literary History and Literary Modernity', in *Blindness and Insight: Essays in the Rhetoric of Contemporary Criticism* (Minneapolis: University of Minnesota Press, 1988), 142–65.

Dick, Philip K., *The Man in the High Castle* (New York: Penguin Books, 2001 [1962]).

DiGiacomo, Mark, 'The Assertion of Coevalness: African Literature and Modernist Studies', *Modernism/Modernity* 24.2 (2017): 245–62.

Dimock, Wai Chee, 'Low Epic', *Critical Inquiry* 39.3 (2013): 614–31.

Dimock, Wai Chee, *Through Other Continents: American Literature across Deep Time* (Princeton: Princeton University Press, 2006).

Doane, Mary Ann, *The Emergence of Cinematic Time: Modernity, Contingency, the Archive* (Cambridge, MA: Harvard University Press, 2002).

Dobbs, Cynthia, '"Ruin or Landmark"? Black Bodies as Lieux de Mémoire in *The Sound and the Fury*', *Faulkner Journal* 20.1/2 (2004): 35–52.

Dohrn-van Rossum, Gerhard, *History of the Hour: Clocks and Modern Temporal Orders* (Chicago: University of Chicago Press, 1996).

Douglass, Paul, *Bergson, Eliot, and American Literature* (Lexington: University Press of Kentucky, 1986).

Dowling, David, *Mrs. Dalloway: Mapping Streams of Consciousness* (Boston, MA: Twayne Publishers, 1991).

Eagleton, Terry, *Criticism and Ideology: A Study in Marxist Literary Theory* (London: Verso, 1976).

Eagleton, Terry, 'Modernism, Myth, and Monopoly Capitalism', in *The Eagleton Reader*, ed. Stephen Regan (Oxford: Blackwell, 1998), 279–84.

Einstein, Albert, and Leopold Infeld, *The Evolution of Physics: The Growth of Ideas from Early Concepts to Relativity and Quanta* (New York: Simon and Schuster, 1938).

'Eliot and Anti-Semitism: The Ongoing Debate', *Modernism/Modernity* 10.1 (2003): 1–70.

Eliot, T. S., *The Annotated Waste Land with Eliot's Contemporary Prose*, ed. Lawrence Rainey (New Haven, CT: Yale University Press, 2005).

Eliot, T. S., 'Books of the Quarter', *The Criterion* 13.52 (1934): 451–2.

Eliot, T. S., *Collected Poems, 1909–1962* (New York: Harcourt Brace, 1963).

Eliot, T. S., 'The Metaphysical Poets', in *The Annotated Waste Land with Eliot's Contemporary Prose*, ed. Lawrence Rainey (New Haven, CT: Yale University Press, 2005), 192–201.

Eliot, T. S., *The Sacred Wood: Essays on Poetry and Criticism* (London: Methuen, 1920), http://bartelby.com/200/ (last accessed 11 October 2018).

Eliot, T. S., 'Tradition and the Individual Talent', in *The Sacred Wood: Essays on Poetry and Criticism* (London: Methuen, 1920), 47–59, http://bartelby.com/200/ (last accessed 11 October 2018).

Eliot, T. S., 'Ulysses, Order, and Myth', in *Selected Prose of T.S. Eliot*, ed. Frank Kermode (New York: Harcourt Brace Jovanovich, 1975), 175–8.

Ellenberg, George B., 'African Americans, Mules, and the Southern Mindscape, 1850–1950', *Agricultural History* 72.2 (1998): 381–98.

Ellison, Ralph, 'Hidden Name and Complex Fate', in *The Collected Essays of Ralph Ellison: Revised and Updated*, ed. John F. Callahan (New York: Modern Library, 2011), 189–209.

Esty, Joshua, *Unseasonable Youth: Modernism, Colonialism, and the Fiction of Development* (Oxford: Oxford University Press, 2012).

Eysteinsson, Astradur, *The Concept of Modernism* (Ithaca: Cornell University Press, 1990).

Fabian, Johannes, *Time and the Other: How Anthropology Makes Its Object* (New York: Columbia University Press, 2014 [1983]).

Falcetta, Jennie-Rebecca, 'Geometries of Space and Time: The Cubist London of *Mrs. Dalloway*', *Woolf Studies Annual* 13 (2007): 111–36.

Farrell, Kirby, 'Wells and Neoteny', in *H.G. Wells's Perennial Time Machine*, ed. George Edgar Slusser, Patrick Parrinder and Danièle Chatelain (Athens: University of Georgia Press), 65–75.

Faulkner, William, *The Sound and the Fury: Norton Critical Edition*, ed. David Minter, 2nd edn (New York: W. W. Norton, 1994).

Foucault, Michel, *The Archaeology of Knowledge*, trans. A. M. Sheridan Smith (New York: Pantheon Books, 1972).

Foucault, Michel, *Les mots et les choses: une archéologie des sciences humaines* (Paris: Gallimard, 1966).

Foucault, Michel, 'Of Other Spaces', *Diacritics* 16.1 (1986): 22–7.

Frank, Adam, *About Time: Cosmology and Culture at the Twilight of the Big Bang* (New York: Simon and Schuster, 2011).

Frank, Joseph, 'Spatial Form: An Answer to Critics', *Critical Inquiry* 4.2 (1977): 231–52.

Frank, Joseph, 'Spatial Form in Modern Literature', in *The Widening Gyre: Crisis and Mastery in Modern Literature* (New Brunswick, NJ: Rutgers University Press, 1963), 3–62.

Franklin, H. Bruce, 'What Are We to Make of J. G. Ballard's Apocalypse?', in *Voices for the Future: Essays on Major Science Fiction Writers*, ed. Thomas D. Clareson (Bowling Green, OH: Popular Press, 1979), 82–105.

Friedman, Susan Stanford, 'Planetarity: Musing Modernist Studies', *Modernism/Modernity* 17.3 (2010): 471–99.

Froula, Christine, 'Mrs. Dalloway's Postwar Elegy: Women, War, and the Art of Mourning', *Modernism/Modernity* 9.1 (2002): 125–63, https://doi.org/10.1353/mod.2002.0007 (last accessed 11 October 2018).

Fuh, Shyh-jen, '"At Home in the World": Transnationalism and the Question of Belonging in Jessica Hagedorn's *Dream Jungle*', *Tamkang Review: A Quarterly of Literary and Cultural Studies* 40.2 (2010): 21–40.

Gaeta, John, 'New Realities: The Matrix Revolutions Completes a Trilogy of Films that Introduced a New Style of Visual Effects', interview by Barbara Robertson, *Computer Graphics World* 26.12 (2003): 56–7.

Galison, Peter, *Einstein's Clocks and Poincaré's Maps: Empires of Time* (New York: W. W. Norton, 2003).

Gallagher, Catherine, 'Undoing', in *Time and the Literary*, ed. Jay Clayton, Marianne Hirsch and Karen Newman (New York: Routledge, 2002), 11–29.

Ganguly, Keya, 'Temporality and Postcolonial Critique', in *The Cambridge Companion to Postcolonial Literary Studies*, ed. Neil Lazarus (Cambridge: Cambridge University Press, 2004), 162–79.

Gaonkar, Dilip Parameshwar, 'Introduction', in *Alternative Modernities*, ed. Dilip Parameshwar Gaonkar (Durham, NC: Duke University Press, 2001), 1–23.

Gaonkar, Dilip Parameshwar (ed.), *Alternative Modernities* (Durham, NC: Duke University Press, 2001).

Geffen, Arthur, 'Profane Time, Sacred Time, and Confederate Time in *The Sound and the Fury*', *Studies in American Fiction* 2.2 (1974): 175–97.

Gennaro, Mara de, 'A Return to *The Waste Land* after Césaire's *Cahier*', *Comparative Literature Studies* 52.3 (2015): 479–509.

Genovese, Eugene D., *Roll, Jordan, Roll: The World the Slaves Made* (New York: Pantheon Books, 1974).

Gernsback, Hugo, 'Wanted: A Symbol for Scientifiction', *Amazing Stories* 3 (April 1928): 5.

Giddens, Anthony, *The Consequences of Modernity* (Stanford: Stanford University Press, 1990).

Gikandi, Simon, 'Globalization and the Claims of Postcoloniality', *The South Atlantic Quarterly* 100.3 (2001): 627–58.

Gilman, Sander L., *Difference and Pathology: Stereotypes of Sexuality, Race, and Madness* (Ithaca: Cornell University Press, 1985).

Golding, John, *Cubism: A History and an Analysis, 1907–1914* (London, 1959).

Gomel, Elana, 'Shapes of the Past and the Future: Darwin and the Narratology of Time Travel', *Narrative* 17.3 (2009): 334–52.

Gonzalez, Vernadette Vicuña, 'Headhunter Itineraries: The Philippines as America's Dream Jungle', *The Global South* 3.2 (2009): 144–72.

Gordon, Lyndall, *Eliot's Early Years* (Oxford: Oxford University Press, 1977).

Gould, Stephen Jay, 'The Uses of Heterochrony', in *Heterochrony in Evolution: A Multidisciplinary Approach*, ed. Michael L. McKinney (New York: Plenum Press, 1988), 1–13.

Green, Christopher, 'An Introduction to *Les Demoiselles d'Avignon*', in *Picasso's Les Demoiselles d'Avignon*, ed. Christopher Green (Cambridge: Cambridge University Press, 2001), 1–14.

Green, Christopher, '"Naked Problems"? "Sub-African Caricatures"? *Les Demoiselles d'Avignon*, Africa, and Cubism', in *Picasso's Les Demoiselles d'Avignon*, ed. Christopher Green (Cambridge: Cambridge University Press, 2001), 128–50.

Grosz, Elizabeth, *The Nick of Time: Politics, Evolution, and the Untimely* (Durham, NC: Duke University Press, 2004).

Gunning, Tom, 'Attractions: How They Came into the World', in *The Cinema of Attractions Reloaded*, ed. Wanda Strauven (Amsterdam: Amsterdam University Press, 2006), 31–40.

Gunning, Tom, '"Now You See It, Now You Don't": The Temporality of the Cinema of Attractions', *Velvet Light Trap: A Critical Journal of Film & Television* 32 (autumn 1993): 3–12.

Gunning, Tom, '"Primitive" Cinema: A Frame-Up? Or, The Trick's on Us', in *Early Cinema: Space, Frame, Narrative*, ed. Thomas Elsaesser and Adam Barker (London: British Film Institute, 1990), 95–103.

Habib, M. A. R., *The Early T.S. Eliot and Western Philosophy* (Cambridge: Cambridge University Press, 2008).

Haeckel, Ernst, *Anthropogenie: oder, Entwickelungsgeschichte des Menschen* (Leipzig: Engelmann, 1874).

Haeckel, Ernst, *The Evolution of Man: A Popular Exposition of the Principal Points of Human Ontogeny and Phylogeny* (New York: D. Appleton, 1879).

Haeckel, Ernst, 'Die Gastrula und die Eifurchung der Thiere', *Jenaische Zeitschrift fur Naturwissenschaft* 9 (1875): 402–508.

Haffey, Kate, 'Exquisite Moments and the Temporality of the Kiss in *Mrs. Dalloway* and *The Hours*', *Narrative* 18.2 (2010): 137–62.

Hagedorn, Jessica, *Dogeaters* (New York: Penguin Books, 1990).

Hagedorn, Jessica, *Dream Jungle* (New York: Viking, 2003).

Hagedorn, Jessica Tarahata (ed.), *Charlie Chan Is Dead: An Anthology of Contemporary Asian American Fiction* (New York: Penguin Books, 1993).

Haldane, J. B. S., *Daedalus; or, Science and the Future; a Paper Read to the Heretics, Cambridge, on February 4th, 1923* (New York: E.P. Dutton, 1924).

Haldane, J. B. S., 'The Last Judgment', in *Possible Worlds* (New Brunswick, NJ: Transaction Publishers, 2002 [1927]), 287–312.

Haldane, J. B. S., 'On Scales', in *Possible Worlds* (New Brunswick, NJ: Transaction Publishers, 2002 [1927]), 1–6.

Hanchard, Michael, 'Afro-Modernity: Temporality, Politics and the African Diaspora', in *Alternative Modernities*, ed. Dilip Parameshwar Gaonkar (Durham, NC: Duke University Press, 2001), 272–98.

Harootunian, Harry, *History's Disquiet: Modernity, Cultural Practice, and the Question of Everyday Life* (New York: Columbia University Press, 2000).

Harvey, David, *The Condition of Postmodernity: An Enquiry into the Origins of Cultural Change* (Cambridge: Blackwell, 1990).

Headland, Thomas N. (ed.), *The Tasaday Controversy: Assessing the Evidence* (Washington, DC: American Anthropological Association, 1992).

Hegeman, Susan, *Patterns for America: Modernism and the Concept of Culture* (Princeton: Princeton University Press, 1999).

Heise, Ursula K., *Sense of Place and Sense of Planet: The Environmental Imagination of the Global* (Oxford: Oxford University Press, 2008).

Hellekson, Karen, *The Alternate History: Refiguring Historical Time* (Kent: Kent State University Press, 2001).

Henderson, Linda Dalrymple, 'Editor's Introduction', *Science in Context* 17.4 (2004): 423–66.

Henderson, Linda Dalrymple, 'Four-Dimensional Space or Space-Time? The Emergence of the Cubism-Relativity Myth in New York in the 1940s', in *The Visual Mind II*, ed. Michele Emmer (Cambridge, MA: MIT Press, 2005), 349–97.

Henderson, Linda Dalrymple, *The Fourth Dimension and Non-Euclidean Geometry in Modern Art* (Princeton: Princeton University Press, 1983).

Henderson, Linda Dalrymple, 'X Rays and the Quest for Invisible Reality in the Art of Kupka, Duchamp and the Cubists', *Art Journal* 47.4 (1988): 323.

Henry, Holly, *Virginia Woolf and the Discourse of Science: The Aesthetics of Astronomy* (Cambridge: Cambridge University Press, 2003).

Herbert, Christopher, 'Frazer, Einstein, and Free Play', in *Prehistories of the Future: The Primitivist Project and the Culture of Modernism*, ed. Elazar Barkan and Ronald Bush (Stanford: Stanford University Press, 1995), 133–58.

Herbert, Christopher, *Victorian Relativity: Radical Thought and Scientific Discovery* (Chicago: University of Chicago Press, 2001).

Hollinger, Veronica, 'A History of the Future: Notes for an Archive', *Science Fiction Studies* 37.1 (2010): 23–33.

Hollington, Michael, 'Some Art-Historical Contexts for "Tradition and the Individual Talent"', in *T. S. Eliot and the Concept of Tradition*, ed. Giovanni Cianci and Jason Harding (Cambridge: Cambridge University Press, 2007), 131–46.

Hopwood, Nick, 'Pictures of Evolution and Charges of Fraud: Ernst Haeckel's Embryological Illustrations', *Isis* 97.2 (2006): 260–301.

Huet, Marie-Hélène, 'Anticipating the Past: The Time Riddle in Science Fiction', in *Storm Warnings: Science Fiction Confronts the Future*, ed. George Edgar Slusser, Colin Greenland and Eric S. Rabkin (Carbondale: Southern Illinois University Press, 1987), 34–42.

Huntington, John, 'Olaf Stapledon and the Novel about the Future', *Contemporary Literature* 22.3 (1981): 349–65.

Huntington, John, 'Remembrance of Things to Come: Narrative Technique in *Last and First Men*', *Science Fiction Studies* 9.3 (1982): 257–64.

Jaffe, Aaron, 'Modernist Novelty', *Affirmations: Of the Modern* 1.1 (2013): 105–38.

Jaffe, Aaron, *The Way Things Go: An Essay on the Matter of Second Modernism* (Minneapolis: University of Minnesota Press, 2014).

Jaffe, Robert L., 'As Time Goes By', *Natural History* 115.8 (2006): 16–22.

James, William, *The Principles of Psychology* (New York: Henry Holt, 1890).

Jameson, Fredric, *Archaeologies of the Future: The Desire Called Utopia and Other Science Fictions* (New York: Verso, 2005).

Jameson, Fredric, 'Future City', *New Left Review* 21 (May/June 2003): 65–79.

Jameson, Fredric, *Postmodernism, Or, The Cultural Logic of Late Capitalism* (Durham, NC: Duke University Press, 1991).

Jameson, Fredric, *The Seeds of Time* (New York: Columbia University Press, 1994).

Jameson, Fredric, *A Singular Modernity: Essay on the Ontology of the Present* (London: Verso, 2002).

Jarvey, Natalie, '"The Man in the High Castle" Is Amazon's Most-Watched Original', *The Hollywood Reporter*, 21 December 2015, http://www.hollywoodreporter.com/live-feed/man-high-castle-is-amazons-850422 (last accessed 11 October 2018).

Jay, Martin, 'Introduction: Genres of Blur', *Common Knowledge* 18.2 (2012): 220–8.

Jeans, James, *The Mysterious Universe* (New York: Macmillan, 1933).

Jeans, James, *The Universe Around Us* (New York: Macmillan, 1929).

'Jeremy Shaw – Degenerative Imaging in the Dark | LambdaLambdaLambda | Artsy', https://www.artsy.net/show/lambdalambdalambda-jeremy-shaw-degenerative-imaging-in-the-dark (last accessed 15 May 2017).

Johnson, Peter, 'Unravelling Foucault's "Different Spaces"', *History of the Human Sciences* 19.4 (2006): 75–90.

Jonas, Gerald, 'Onward and Upward with the Arts: S.F', *New Yorker* 48 (29 July 1972): 33.

Jones, Kent, 'Light Years', *Film Comment* 47.4 (2011): 24–9.

Joyce, James, *Ulysses: The Corrected Text*, ed. Hans Walter Gabler (New York: Random House, 1986 [1922]).

Kahnweiler, Daniel-Henry, *Der Weg zum Kubismus* (Munich: Delphin, 1920).

Kaplan, Amy E., '"Left Alone with America": The Absence of Empire in the Study of American Culture', in *Cultures of United States Imperialism*, ed. Amy E. Kaplan and Donald E. Pease (Durham, NC: Duke University Press, 1993), 3–21.

Katz, Tamar, 'Pausing, Waiting, Repeating: Urban Temporality in *Mrs. Dalloway* and *The Years*', in *Woolf and the City*, ed. Elizabeth F. Evans and Sarah E. Cornish (Clemson, SC: Clemson University Digital Press, 2010), 2–16.

Kermode, Frank, 'The Modern', in *Modern Essays* (London: Collins, 1971), 39–70.

Kermode, Frank, *Sense of an Ending: Studies in the Theory of Fiction* (Oxford: Oxford University Press, 1966).

Kern, Stephen, *The Culture of Time and Space, 1880–1918* (Cambridge, MA: Harvard University Press, 2003).

Kettler, David, and Colin Loader, 'Temporizing with Time Wars: Karl Mannheim and Problems of Historical Time', *Time & Society* 13.2–3 (2004): 155–72.

Keynes, John Maynard, *The Economic Consequences of the Peace* (London: Macmillan, 1920).

Kincaid, Paul, 'Time Travel', in *The Greenwood Encyclopedia of Science Fiction and Fantasy: Themes, Works, and Wonders*, ed. Gary Westfahl and Neil Gaiman (Westport, CT: Greenwood Press, 2005), 2: 819–21.

King, Henry, *The History of the Telescope* (London: Griffin, 1955).

Kirkland, Frank M., 'Modernity and Intellectual Life in Black', *Philosophical Forum* 24.1–3 (1992): 136–65.

Klein, John, 'The Dispersal of the Modernist Series', *Oxford Art Journal* 21.1 (1998): 121.

Klein, Richard, 'The Future of Nuclear Criticism', *Yale French Studies* 77 (1990): 76–100, https://doi.org/10.2307/2903216 (last accessed 11 October 2018).

Klenke, Stefan, 'The Longest Photographic Exposures in History – The Latest', *itchy I* (blog), 20 July 2010, http://itchyi.squarespace.com/thelatest/2010/7/20/the-longest-photographic-exposures-in-history.html (last accessed 11 October 2018).

Korg, Jacob, 'Modern Art Techniques in *The Waste Land*', *Journal of Aesthetics and Art Criticism* 18.4 (1960): 456–63.

Kortenaar, Neil ten, 'Where the Atlantic Meets the Caribbean: Kamau Brathwaite's "The Arrivants" and T. S. Eliot's "The Waste Land"', *Research in African Literatures* 27.4 (1996): 15–27.

Kracauer, Siegfried, *History: The Last Thing before the Last* (Princeton: Markus Wiener Publishers, 1969).

Kramer, Hilton, *The Age of the Avant-Garde, 1956–1972* (New York: Farrar, Straus and Giroux, 1973).

Krulwich, Robert, 'Time Travel On The Cheap', *The Picture Show: Photo Stories on NPR* (blog), https://www.npr.org/sections/pictureshow/2010/01/looking_backwards.html (last accessed 22 December 2017).

Lamont, Elizabeth Clea, 'Moving Tropes: New Modernist Travels with Virginia Woolf', *Alif: Journal of Comparative Poetics* 21 (2001): 161–81.

Larsen, Lars, 'PCP: Pop/Conceptual/Psychedelic: Interview with Jeremy Shaw', *C Magazine* 101 (2009): 16–21.

Lazarus, Neil, 'Modernism and African Literature', in *The Oxford Handbook of Global Modernisms*, ed. Mark Wollaeger and Matt Eatough (Oxford: Oxford University Press, 2012), 228–45.

Le Goff, Jacques, *Time, Work, and Culture in the Middle Ages*, trans. Arthur Goldhammer (Chicago: University of Chicago Press, 1980).

Lee, Hsiu-chuan, 'The Remains of Empire and the "Purloined" Philippines: Jessica Hagedorn's *Dream Jungle*', *Mosaic: An Interdisciplinary Critical Journal* 45.3 (2012): 49–64.

Lefebvre, Henri, *Rhythmanalysis: Space, Time, and Everyday Life* (London: Continuum, 2004).

Leighten, Patricia, 'Colonialism, l'art Negre, and *Les Demoiselles d'Avignon*', in *Picasso's Les Demoiselles d'Avignon*, ed. Christopher Green (Cambridge: Cambridge University Press, 2001), 77–103.

Leinster, Murray, 'Sidewise in Time', *Astounding Stories* 13.4 (1934): 10–47; repr. in *The Time Travelers: A Science Fiction Quartet*, ed. Robert Silverberg and Martin Harry Greenberg (New York: D.I. Fine, 1985), 67–142.

Lester, Cheryl, 'Racial Awareness and Arrested Development: *The Sound and the Fury* and the Great Migration (1915–1928)', in *The Cambridge Companion to William Faulkner*, ed. Philip Weinstein (New York: Cambridge University Press, 1995), 123–45.

Levenson, Michael, 'The Time-Mind of the Twenties', in *The Cambridge History of Twentieth-Century English Literature*, ed. Laura Marcus and Peter Nicholls (Cambridge: Cambridge University Press, 2004), 197–217.

Levine, Robert, *A Geography of Time: The Temporal Misadventures of a Social Psychologist, or How Every Culture Keeps Time Just a Little Bit Differently* (New York: Basic Books, 1997).

Lewis, Wyndham, *Time and Western Man* (Santa Rosa: Black Sparrow Press, 1993 [1927]).

Linnett, Richard, 'The Gondry Effect', *Shoot* 39.19 (1998): 25.

Liu, Warren, 'Queer Excavations: Technology, Temporality, Race', in *Techno-Orientalism: Imagining Asia in Speculative Fiction, History, and Media*, ed. David S. Roh, Betsy Huang and Greta A. Niu (New Brunswick, NJ: Rutgers University Press, 2015), 64–75.

Livingston, Rick, 'Global Tropes/Worldly Readings: Narratives of Cosmopolitanism in Joyce, Rich, and Tagore', *Narrative* 5.2 (1997): 121–34.

Lloyd, David, *Ireland After History* (North Bend: University of Notre Dame Press, 1999).

Lomas, David, 'In Another Frame: *Les Demoiselles d'Avignon* and Physical Anthropology', in *Picasso's Les Demoiselles d'Avignon*, ed. Christopher Green (Cambridge: Cambridge University Press, 2001), 104–27.

Lowrey, Perrin, 'Concepts of Time in *The Sound and the Fury*', in *English Institute Essays*, ed. Alan S. Downer (New York: Columbia University Press, 1952), 57–82.

Löwy, Michael, *Fire Alarm: Reading Walter Benjamin on the Concept of History*, trans. Chris Turner (London: Verso, 2005).

Lumley, Robert (ed.), *The Museum Time-Machine: Putting Cultures on Display* (London: Routledge, 1988).

Lunn, Eugene, *Marxism and Modernism: An Historical Study of Lukács, Brecht, Benjamin, and Adorno* (Berkeley: University of California Press, 1984).

Mackenzie, Adrian, 'The Technicity of Time: From 1.00 Oscillations/Sec to 9,192,631,770 Hz', *Time & Society* 10.2–3 (2001): 235–57.

MacLeish, Kenneth, 'Tasadays, Stone Age Cavemen of Mindanao', *National Geographic* 142 (August 1972): 218.

Manganaro, Marc, '"Beating a Drum in a Jungle": T. S. Eliot on the Artist as "Primitive"', *Modern Language Quarterly* 47.4 (1986): 393–421.

Manganaro, Marc, *Culture, 1922: The Emergence of a Concept* (Princeton: Princeton University Press, 2009).

Manganaro, Marc, 'Mind, Myth, and Culture: Eliot and Anthropology', in *A Companion to T. S. Eliot*, ed. David E. Chinitz (Chichester: Wiley-Blackwell, 2009), 79–90.

Mannheim, Karl, 'The Problem of Generations', in *From Karl Mannheim*, ed. Kurt Wolff (New Brunswick, NJ: Transaction Publishers, 1993), 351–98.

Manovich, Lev, 'The Poetics of Augmented Space', *Visual Communication* 5.2 (2006): 219–40, https://doi.org/10.1177/1470357206065527 (last accessed 11 October 2018).

Mao, Douglas, and Rebecca L. Walkowitz, *Bad Modernisms* (Durham, NC: Duke University Press, 2006).

Mao, Douglas, and Rebecca L. Walkowitz, 'The New Modernist Studies', *PMLA* 123.3 (2008): 737–48.

Marcus, Jane, *Virginia Woolf and the Languages of Patriarchy* (Bloomington: Indiana University Press, 1987).

Marx, Karl, *The Poverty of Philosophy* (Moscow: Foreign Languages Publishing House, 1962 [1847]).

Marx, Karl, and Friedrich Engels, *The Communist Manifesto: A Modern Edition* (London: Verso, 1998).

Massey, Doreen, *For Space* (London: Sage, 2005).

May, Jon, and Nigel Thrift, *TimeSpace: Geographies of Temporality* (London: Routledge, 2001).

McCarthy, Patrick A., 'Stapledon and Literary Modernism', in *The Legacy of Olaf Stapledon: Critical Essays and an Unpublished Manuscript*, ed. Patrick A. McCarthy, Charles Elkins and Martin Harry Greenberg (New York: Greenwood, 1989), 39–51.

McClintock, Anne, 'The Angel of Progress: Pitfalls of the Term "Postcolonialism"', *Social Text* 31–32 (1992): 84–98.

McGurl, Mark, '"Neither Indeed Could I Forebear Smiling at My Self": A Reply to Wai Chee Dimock', *Critical Inquiry* 39.3 (2013): 632–8.

McGurl, Mark, 'Ordinary Doom: Literary Studies in the Waste Land of the Present', *New Literary History* 41.2 (2010): 329–49.

McGurl, Mark, 'The Posthuman Comedy', *Critical Inquiry* 38.3 (2012): 533–53.

McLemee, Scott, 'Jameson and Son', *Lingua Franca* 5.5 (1995): 10–11.

McNamara, Ken, *Shapes of Time: The Evolution of Growth and Development* (Baltimore: Johns Hopkins University Press, 1997).

Meister, Sarah Hermanson, 'Open Shutter', in *Michael Wesely: Open Shutter* (New York: Museum of Modern Art, 2005).

Mendible, Myra, 'Desiring Images: Representation and Spectacle in *Dogeaters*', *Critique: Studies in Contemporary Fiction* 43.3 (2002): 289–304.

Mendilow, A. A., *Time and the Novel* (New York: Humanities Press, 1965).

Messerli, Douglas, 'The Problem of Time in *The Sound and the Fury*: A Critical Reassessment and Reinterpretation', *The Southern Literary Journal* 6.2 (1974): 19–41.

Metzinger, Jean, 'Notes sur la peinture', *Pan* (October–November 1910), repr. in Mark Antliff and Patricia Leighten (eds), *A Cubism Reader: Documents and Criticism, 1906–1914* (Chicago: University of Chicago Press, 2008), 75–7.

Miller, Arthur I., *Albert Einstein's Special Theory of Relativity: Emergence (1905) and Early Interpretation (1905–1911)* (New York: Springer, 1997).

Miller, Arthur I., *Einstein, Picasso: Space, Time, and the Beauty That Causes Havoc* (New York: Basic Books, 2001).

Miller, J. Hillis, 'Repetition as the Raising of the Dead', in *Fiction and Repetition: Seven English Novels* (Cambridge, MA: Harvard University Press, 1982), 176–202.

Miller, J. Hillis, 'Time in Literature', *Daedalus* 132.2 (2003): 86–97.

Minow-Pinkney, Makiko, *Virginia Woolf and the Problem of the Subject* (New Brunswick, NJ: Rutgers University Press, 1987).

Mizutani, Satoshi, 'Hybridity and History: A Critical Reflection on Homi K. Bhabha's Post-Historical Thoughts', *Ab Imperio* 4 (2013): 27–48, https://doi.org/10.1353/imp.2013.0115 (last accessed 11 October 2018).

Morgan, Lewis Henry, *Ancient Society; or, Researches in the Lines of Human Progress from Savagery, through Barbarism to Civilization* (New York: Henry Holt, 1877), http://catalog.hathitrust.org/api/volumes/oclc/5518778.html (last accessed 11 October 2018).

Morton, Timothy, *Hyperobjects: Philosophy and Ecology after the End of the World* (Minneapolis: University of Minnesota Press, 2013).

Mountfort, Paul, 'The *I Ching* and Philip K. Dick's *The Man in the High Castle*', *Science Fiction Studies* 43.2 (2016): 287–309.

Mumford, Lewis, *Technics and Civilization* (New York: Harcourt, Brace, 1934).

Musser, Charles, *Before the Nickelodeon: Edwin S. Porter and the Edison Manufacturing Company* (Berkeley: University of California Press, 1991).

Narita, Tatsushi, 'Eliot and the World's Fair of St. Louis – His "Stockholder's Coupon Ticket"', *Studies in Social Sciences and Humanities* 26 (March 1982): 1–24.

Newton, Isaac, *Mathematical Principles of Natural Philosophy*, trans. Andrew Motte (Berkeley: University of California Press, 1934 [1729]).

Nochlin, Linda, *Impressionism and Post-Impressionism, 1874–1904: Sources and Documents* (Englewood Cliffs, NJ: Prentice-Hall, 1966).

Nolan, Christopher, *Interstellar*, DVD, Warner Home Video, 2014.

O'Malley, Michael, *Keeping Watch: A History of American Time* (New York: Viking, 1990).

Osborne, Peter, *Anywhere or Not at All: Philosophy of Contemporary Art* (London: Verso, 2013).

Osborne, Peter, 'Out of Sync: Tomba's Marx and the Problem of a Multi-Layered Temporal Dialectic', *Historical Materialism* 23.4 (2015): 39–48.

Park, Mungo, *Travels in the Interior Districts of Africa* (London: John Murray, 1815).

Parrinder, Patrick, 'Introduction', in *Learning from Other Worlds: Estrangement, Cognition, and the Politics of Science Fiction and Utopia*, ed. Patrick Parrinder (Durham, NC: Duke University Press, 2001), 1–18.

Pater, Walter, *Studies in the History of the Renaissance*, ed. Matthew Beaumont (Oxford: Oxford University Press, 2010 [1873]).

Patey, Caroline, 'Whose Tradition? T. S. Eliot and the Text of Anthropology', in *T. S. Eliot and the Concept of Tradition*, ed. Giovanni Cianci and Jason Harding (Cambridge: Cambridge University Press, 2007), 161–73.

Patrides, C. A., *Aspects of Time* (Manchester: Manchester University Press, 1976).

Peters, John Durham, *The Marvelous Clouds: Toward a Philosophy of Elemental Media* (Chicago: University of Chicago Press, 2015).

Pinney, Christopher, 'Things Happen: Or, From Which Moment Does That Object Come?', in *Materiality*, ed. Daniel Miller (Durham, NC: Duke University Press, 2005), 256–72.

Plate, S. Brent, 'Visualizing the Cosmos: Terrence Malick's *Tree of Life* and Other Visions of Life in the Universe', *Journal of the American Academy of Religion* 80.2 (2012): 527–36.

Poggioli, Renato, *The Theory of the Avant-Garde*, trans. Gerald Fitzgerald (Cambridge, MA: Harvard University Press, 1968).

Pound, Ezra, 'Dateline', in *Literary Essays of Ezra Pound*, ed. T. S. Eliot (London: Faber, 1954), 74–87.

Pound, Ezra, *The Letters of Ezra Pound, 1907–1941*, ed. D. D. Paige (New York: Harcourt Brace, 1950).

Pound, Ezra, *Literary Essays of Ezra Pound*, ed. T. S. Eliot (London: Faber, 1954).

Powell, Jason E., 'Looking Into the Past', http://jasonepowell.com/albums/looking-into-the-past/ (last accessed 22 December 2017).

Pryor, Sean, and David Trotter, 'Introduction', in *Writing, Medium, Machine: Modern Technographies*, ed. Sean Pryor and David Trotter (London: Open Humanities Press, 2016), 7–17.

Pryor, Sean, and David Trotter (eds), *Writing, Medium, Machine: Modern Technographies* (London: Open Humanities Press, 2016).

Purse, Lisa, 'The New Spatial Dynamics of the Bullet-Time Effect', in *Spectacle of the Real: From Hollywood to Reality TV and Beyond*, ed. Geoff King (Bristol: Intellect, 2005), 151–60.

Rae, Patricia, 'Anthropology', in *A Companion to Modernist Literature and Culture*, ed. David Bradshaw and Kevin J. H. Dettmar (Oxford: Blackwell, 2008), 92–102.

Raja, Masood A., and Swaralipi Nandi, 'Introduction', in *The Postnational Fantasy: Essays on Postcolonialism, Cosmopolitics and Science Fiction*, ed. Masood A. Raja, Swaralipi Nandi and Jason Ellis (Jefferson, NC: McFarland, 2011), 5–14.

Ransom, John Crowe, 'Flux and Blur in Contemporary Art', *The Sewanee Review* 37.3 (1929): 353–66.

Redmond, Sean, 'The Origin of the Species: Time Travel and the Primal Scene', in *Liquid Metal: The Science Fiction Film Reader*, ed. Sean Redmond (New York: Wallflower, 2004), 114–15.

Rehak, Bob, 'The Migration of Forms: Bullet Time as Microgenre', *Film Criticism* 32.1 (2007): 26–48.

Richards, I. A., *Principles of Literary Criticism* (London: K. Paul, Trench, Trubner, 1924).

Rieder, John, *Colonialism and the Emergence of Science Fiction* (Middletown, CT: Wesleyan University Press, 2008).

Rieder, John, 'The Metafictive World of *The Man in the High Castle*: Hermeneutics, Ethics, and Political Ideology', *Science Fiction Studies* 15.2 (1988): 214–25.

Rifkin, Mark, *Beyond Settler Time: Temporal Sovereignty and Indigenous Self-Determination* (Durham, NC: Duke University Press, 2017).

Robbins, Bruce, 'Many Years Later: Prolepsis in Deep Time', *The Henry James Review* 33.3 (2012): 191–204.

Røsaak, Eivind, 'Figures of Sensation: Between Still and Moving Images', in *The Cinema of Attractions Reloaded*, ed. Wanda Strauven (Amsterdam: Amsterdam University Press, 2006), 321–36.

Rosen, Philip, *Change Mummified: Cinema, Historicity, Theory* (Minneapolis: University of Minnesota Press, 2001).

Rosenberg, Daniel, and Anthony Grafton, *Cartographies of Time: A History of the Timeline* (New York: Princeton Architectural Press, 2010).

Rosenberg, Daniel, and Susan Friend Harding (eds), *Histories of the Future* (Durham, NC: Duke University Press, 2005).

Rosner, Victoria, '"Life Struck Straight through the Streets": *Mrs. Dalloway* as City Novel', in *Approaches to Teaching Woolf's Mrs. Dalloway*, ed. Eileen Barrett and Ruth O. Saxton (New York: Modern Language Association of America, 2009), 39–43.

Rubin, William, 'Picasso', in *'Primitivism' in 20th-Century Art: Affinity of the Tribal and the Modern*, ed. William Rubin (New York: Museum of Modern Art, 1984), 1: 241–343.

Russell, W. M. S., 'Time before and after *The Time Machine*', in *H. G. Wells's Perennial Time Machine*, ed. George Edgar Slusser, Patrick Parrinder and Danièle Chatelain (Athens: University of Georgia Press, 2001), 50–61.

Sagan, Carl, *Pale Blue Dot: A Vision of the Human Future in Space* (New York: Random House, 1994).

Saint-Amour, Paul K., 'Air War Prophecy and Interwar Modernism', *Comparative Literature Studies* 42.2 (2005): 130–61.

Saint-Amour, Paul K., 'Applied Modernism: Military and Civilian Uses of the Aerial Photomosaic', *Theory, Culture & Society* 28.7–8 (2011): 241–69.

Saint-Amour, Paul K., 'Counterfactual States of America: On Parallel Worlds and Longing for the Law', *Post-45* (blog), 20 September 2011, http://post45.research.yale.edu/2011/09/counterfactual-states-of-america-on-parallel-worlds-and-longing-for-the-law/ (last accessed 11 October 2018).

Saint-Amour, Paul K., 'Modernist Reconnaissance', *Modernism/Modernity* 10.2 (2003): 349–80.

Saldívar, Ramón, and Sylvan Goldberg, 'The Faulknerian Anthropocene: Scales of Time and History in *The Wild Palms* and *Go Down, Moses*', in *The

New Cambridge Companion to William Faulkner, ed. John T. Matthews (Cambridge: Cambridge University Press, 2015), 185–203.

Sartre, Jean-Paul, 'On *The Sound and the Fury*: Time in the Work of Faulkner', in *Literary and Philosophical Essays*, trans. Annette Michelson (London: Rider, 1955), 79–87.

Schivelbusch, Wolfgang, *The Railway Journey: The Industrialization and Perception of Time and Space* (Berkeley: University of California Press, 1986).

Schneider-Mayerson, Matthew, 'What Almost Was: The Politics of the Contemporary Alternate History Novel', *American Studies* 50.3 (2009): 63–83.

Scholes, Robert, and Eric S. Rabkin, *Science Fiction: History, Science, Vision* (New York: Oxford University Press, 1977).

Schroder, Leena Kore, '"Reflections in a Motor Car": Virginia Woolf's Phenomenological Relations of Time and Space', in *Locating Woolf: The Politics of Space and Place*, ed. Anna Snaith and Michael Whitworth (New York: Palgrave Macmillan, 2007), 131–47.

Schwarz, Bill, '"Already the Past": Memory and Historical Time', in *Regimes of Memory*, ed. Susannah Radstone and Katharine Hodgkin (London: Routledge, 2003), 135–51.

Scott, Evelyn, 'Contemporary of the Future', *The Dial* (October 1920): 353–67.

Seitler, Dana, *Atavistic Tendencies: The Culture of Science in American Modernity* (Minneapolis: University of Minnesota Press, 2008).

Serres, Michel, *Genesis* (Ann Arbor: University of Michigan Press, 1995).

Serres, Michel, and Bruno Latour, *Conversations on Science, Culture, and Time*, trans. Roxanne Lapidus (Ann Arbor: University of Michigan Press, 1998).

Shanks, Michael, and Christopher Tilley, *Re-Constructing Archaeology: Theory and Practice* (Cambridge: Cambridge University Press, 2005).

Shaw, Bernard, *Back to Methuselah: A Metabiological Pentateuch* (London: Penguin Books, 1990).

Shklovsky, Viktor, 'Art as Device' (1919), trans. Alexandra Berlina, *Poetics Today* 36.3 (2015): 151–74, https://doi.org/10.1215/03335372-3160709 (last accessed 11 October 2018).

Shklovsky, Viktor, 'Art as Technique', in *Modernism: An Anthology of Sources and Documents*, ed. Vassiliki Kolocotroni, Jane Goldman and Olga Taxidou (Chicago: University of Chicago Press, 1998), 217–20.

Singles, Kathleen, *Alternate History: Playing with Contingency and Necessity* (Berlin: Walter de Gruyter, 2013).

'Sketch of William Cranch Bond', *The Popular Science Monthly*, July 1895.

Skidelsky, Robert, *John Maynard Keynes: Hopes Betrayed, 1883–1920* (London: Macmillan, 1983).

Skirry, Justin, 'Sartre on William Faulkner's Metaphysics of Time in *The Sound and the Fury*', *Sartre Studies International* 7.2 (2001): 15–43.

Slusser, George, and Danièle Chatelain, 'Spacetime Geometries: Time Travel and the Modern Geometrical Narrative', *Science Fiction Studies* 22.2 (1995): 161–86.

Slusser, George, and Robert Heath, 'Arrows and Riddles of Time: Scientific Models of Time Travel', in *Worlds Enough and Time: Explorations of Time in Science Fiction and Fantasy*, ed. Gary Westfahl, George Edgar Slusser and David Leiby (Westport, CT: Greenwood Press, 2002), 11–24.

Smith, Mark M., *Mastered by the Clock: Time, Slavery, and Freedom in the American South* (Chapel Hill: University of North Carolina Press, 2000).

Smith, Neil, *Uneven Development: Nature, Capital, and the Production of Space*, 3rd edn (Athens: University of Georgia Press, 2008).

Snaith, Anna, and Michael Whitworth (eds), *Locating Woolf: The Politics of Space and Place* (New York: Palgrave Macmillan, 2007).

Sobchack, Vivian, 'Time Passages', *Film Comment* 50.6 (2014): 20–4.

Soja, Edward, *Thirdspace: Journeys to Los Angeles and Other Real-and-Imagined Places* (Cambridge: Blackwell, 1996).

Spier, Fred, *Big History and the Future of Humanity* (Oxford: Wiley-Blackwell, 2010).

Squier, Susan Merrill, 'Embryologies of Modernism', *Modernism/Modernity* 3.3 (1996): 145–53.

Squier, Susan Merrill, *Virginia Woolf and London: The Sexual Politics of the City* (Chapel Hill: University of North Carolina Press, 1985).

Sriratana, Verita, '"It Was an Uncertain Spring": Reading the Weather in *The Years*', in *Virginia Woolf and the Natural World*, ed. Kristin Czarnecki and Carrie Rohman (Clemson, SC: Clemson University Digital Press, 2011), 191–5.

Stableford, Brian M., *Science Fact and Science Fiction: An Encyclopedia* (New York: Routledge, 2006).

Stafford, Robert, 'Scientific Exploration and Empire', in *The Oxford History of the British Empire*, ed. Andrew Porter (Oxford: Oxford University Press, 1999), 3: 294–319.

Stapledon, Olaf, *Last and First Men* (Mineola, NY: Dover Publications, 2008 [1930]).

Stapledon, Olaf, *Sirius: A Fantasy of Love and Discord* (London: Secker & Warburg, 1944).

Stapledon, Olaf, *Star Maker*, ed. Patrick A. McCarthy (Middletown, CT: Wesleyan University Press, 2004).

Stein, Gertrude, *Picasso* (Mineola, NY: Dover Publications, 1984 [1938]).

Steinberg, Leo, 'The Philosophical Brothel', *October* 44 (1988): 7–74.

Steiner, Wendy, *The Colors of Rhetoric: Problems in the Relation Between Modern Literature and Painting* (Chicago: University of Chicago Press, 1982).

Stephens, Carlene, '"The Most Reliable Time": William Bond, the New England Railroads, and Time Awareness in 19th-Century America', *Technology and Culture* 30.1 (1989): 1–24, https://doi.org/10.2307/3105429 (last accessed 11 October 2018).

Stern, Rebecca, 'Time Passes', *Narrative* 17.3 (2009): 235–41.

Sterritt, David, 'Days of Heaven and Waco: Terrence Malick's *Tree of Life*', *Film Quarterly* 65.1 (2011): 52–7.

Stowell, H. Peter, *Literary Impressionism: James and Chekhov* (Athens: University of Georgia Press, 1979).

Streamas, John, 'Closure and "Colored People's Time"', *The Study of Time* 13 (2010): 219–35.

Suddendorf, Thomas, and Michael C. Corballis, 'Mental Time Travel and the Evolution of the Human Mind', *Genetic, Social, and General Psychology Monographs* 123.2 (1997): 133–67.

Sutherland, John, *Can Jane Eyre Be Happy? More Puzzles in Classic Fiction* (London: Icon, 2017 [1997]).

Suvin, Darko, *Metamorphoses of Science Fiction: On the Poetics and History of a Literary Genre* (New Haven, CT: Yale University Press, 1979).

Suvin, Darko, 'P. K. Dick's Opus: Artifice as Refuge and World View (Introductory Reflections)', *Science Fiction Studies* 2.1 (1975): 8–22.

Szalay, Michael, *New Deal Modernism: American Literature and the Invention of the Welfare State* (Durham, NC: Duke University Press, 2000).

Thompson, E. P., 'Time, Work-Discipline, and Industrial Capitalism', *Past and Present* 38 (1967): 56–97.

Thorne, Kip, *The Science of Interstellar* (New York: W. W. Norton, 2014).

Tomba, Massimiliano, *Marx's Temporalities* (Chicago: Haymarket Books, 2013).

Tomlinson, David, 'T. S. Eliot and the Cubists', *Twentieth-Century Literature* 26.1 (1980): 64–81.

Tremaine, Louis, 'Historical Consciousness in Stapledon and Malraux', *Science Fiction Studies* 11.2 (1984): 130–8.

Tulving, Endel, 'Memory and Consciousness', *Canadian Psychology* 26.1 (1985): 1–12.

Turtledove, Harry, 'Introduction', in *The Best Time Travel Stories of the 20th Century*, ed. Harry Turtledove and Martin Harry Greenberg (New York: Del Rey, 2005), ix–xii.

Valéry, Paul, 'Poetry and Abstract Thought' (1939), in *The Art of Poetry*, ed. Jackson Mathews (Princeton: Princeton University Press, 1989), 52–81.

Vickery, Olga W., 'Faulkner and the Contours of Time', *The Georgia Review* 12.2 (1958): 192–201.

Vickery, Olga W., '*The Sound and the Fury*: A Study in Perspective', *PMLA: Publications of the Modern Language Association of America* 69.5 (1954): 1017–37.

Wagmeister, Elizabeth, '"The Man in the High Castle" Becomes Amazon's Most-Streamed Original Series', *Variety* (blog), 21 December 2015, http://variety.com/2015/tv/news/the-man-in-the-high-castle-amazon-ratings-viewership-1201665925/ (last accessed 11 October 2018).

Waldo, Leonard, 'The Distribution of Time', *The North American Review* 131.289 (1880): 528–36.

Walker, Ronald G., 'Leaden Circles Dissolving in Air: Narrative Rhythm and Meaning in *Mrs. Dalloway*', *Essays in Literature* 13.1 (1986): 57–87.

Wallace, Jeff, *Beginning Modernism* (Manchester: Manchester University Press, 2011).

Wallace, Molly, *Risk Criticism: Reading in an Age of Manufactured Uncertainties* (Ann Arbor: University of Michigan Press, 2016).

Warrick, Patricia, 'The Encounter of Taoism and Fascism in Philip K. Dick's "The Man in the High Castle"', *Science Fiction Studies* 7.2 (1980): 174–90.

Watt, Ian P., *Conrad in the Nineteenth Century* (Berkeley: University of California Press, 1979).

Waugh, Arthur, 'The New Poetry', in *T. S. Eliot: The Critical Heritage*, ed. Michael Grant (London: Routledge & Kegan Paul, 1982), 1: 67–9.

Wegner, Phillip E., 'Jameson's Modernisms, or, the Desire Called Utopia', *Diacritics: A Review of Contemporary Criticism* 37.4 (2007): 2–20.

Wegner, Phillip E., 'Learning to Live in History: Alternate Historicities and the 1990s in *The Years of Rice and Salt*', in *Kim Stanley Robinson Maps the Unimaginable: Critical Essays*, ed. William J. Burling (Jefferson, NC: McFarland, 2009), 98–112.

Wegner, Phillip E., *Life between Two Deaths, 1989–2001: U. S. Culture in the Long Nineties* (Durham, NC: Duke University Press, 2009).

Wegner, Phillip E., 'Utopia', in *A Companion to Science Fiction*, ed. David Seed (Oxford: Blackwell, 2005), 79–94.

Wells, H. G., *Anticipations of the Reaction of Mechanical and Scientific Progress upon Human Life and Thought* (London: Chapman & Hall, 1901).

Wells, H. G., *The Definitive Time Machine: A Critical Edition of H.G. Wells's Scientific Romance*, ed. Harry M. Geduld (Bloomington: Indiana University Press, 1987).

Wells, H. G., *The Discovery of the Future: A Discourse Delivered to the Royal Institution on January 24, 1902* (London: T. Fisher Unwin, 1902).

Wells, H. G., *The Outline of History: Being a Plain History of Life and Mankind* (London: George Newnes, 1920).

Wells, H. G., *A Short History of the World* (London: Cassell, 1922).

Wells, H. G., *The Time Machine: An Invention*, ed. Nicholas Ruddick (Peterborough, ON: Broadview Press, 2001).

Wells, H. G., 'Wanted: Professors of Foresight', radio broadcast, BBC, 19 November 1932, http://www.bbc.co.uk/archive/hg_wells/12403.shtml (last accessed 11 October 2018).

Wells, Spencer, *Deep Ancestry: Inside the Genographic Project* (Washington, DC: National Geographic, 2006).

Westbrook, Wayne W., 'Skunked on the New York Cotton Exchange: What Really Happens to Jason Compson in *The Sound and the Fury*', *The Southern Literary Journal* 41.2 (2009): 53–68.

West-Pavlov, Russell, *Temporalities* (London: Routledge, 2013).

Whitworth, Michael H., *Einstein's Wake: Relativity, Metaphor, and Modernist Literature* (Oxford: Oxford University Press, 2001).

Whitworth, Michael, 'Virginia Woolf, Modernism, and Modernity', in *The Cambridge Companion to Virginia Woolf*, ed. Susan Sellers, 2nd edn (Cambridge: Cambridge University Press, 2010), 107–23.

Wildenstein, Daniel, *Claude Monet: Biographie et Catalogue Raisonné*, 5 vols (Paris: La Bibliothèque des arts, 1974), Vol. 3.

Williams, Keith, *H. G. Wells, Modernity and the Movies* (Liverpool: Liverpool University Press, 2007).

Williams, William Carlos, introduction to *The Wedge* (New York: New Directions, 1969 [1944]), 5–11.

Wittenberg, David, *Time Travel: The Popular Philosophy of Narrative* (New York: Fordham University Press, 2013).

Woessner, Martin, 'What Is Heideggerian Cinema? Film, Philosophy, and Cultural Mobility', *New German Critique* 113 (summer 2011): 129–57.

Wood, Andelys, 'Walking the Web in the Lost London of *Mrs. Dalloway*', *Mosaic: An Interdisciplinary Critical Journal* 36.2 (2003): 19–32.

Woolf, Virginia, *Between the Acts: Annotated* (New York: Houghton Mifflin Harcourt, 2008 [1941]).

Woolf, Virginia, *The Diary of Virginia Woolf, Vol. 2: 1920–24*, ed. Anne Olivier Bell (New York: Harcourt Brace Jovanovich, 1978).

Woolf, Virginia, *The Diary of Virginia Woolf, Vol. 5: 1936–41*, ed. Anne Olivier Bell (New York: Harvest, 1985).

Woolf, Virginia, 'Flying over London', in *The Captain's Death Bed and Other Essays* (London: Hogarth Press, 1950), 186–92.

Woolf, Virginia, 'Modern Fiction', in *The Common Reader*, ed. Andrew McNeillie (New York: Harvest, 2002), 146–54.

Woolf, Virginia, *Moments of Being*, ed. Jean Schulkind (New York: Harcourt, 1985).

Woolf, Virginia, *Mrs. Dalloway* (San Diego: Harcourt, 1981).

Woolf, Virginia, *Mrs Dalloway*, ed. Anne E. Fernald (Cambridge: Cambridge University Press, 2014).

Woolf, Virginia, *The Mrs. Dalloway Reader* (Orlando: Harcourt, 2003).

Woolf, Virginia, *Night and Day* (New York: Barnes & Noble, 2005 [1919]).

Woolf, Virginia, *Orlando: A Biography (Annotated)*, ed. Maria DiBattista (Orlando: Harvest, 2006).

Woolf, Virginia, *To the Lighthouse* (New York: Harvest, 1981 [1927]).

Woolf, Virginia, *The Waves* (London: Houghton Mifflin Harcourt, 1950 [1931]).

Woolf, Virginia, *A Writer's Diary: Being Extracts from the Diary of Virginia Woolf* (London: Hogarth Press, 1953).

Yeats, W. B., *The Collected Works of W.B. Yeats: The Poems*, ed. Richard J. Finneran (New York: Macmillan, 1989).

Zemka, Sue, *Time and the Moment in Victorian Literature and Society* (Cambridge: Cambridge University Press, 2011).

Zhu, Jianjiong, 'Reality, Fiction, and Wu in *The Man in the High Castle*', in *State of the Fantastic: Studies in the Theory and Practice of Fantastic Literature and Film*, ed. Nicholas Ruddick (Westport, CT: Greenwood, 1992), 107–13.

Zwerdling, Alex, *Virginia Woolf and the Real World* (Berkeley: University of California Press, 1986).

INDEX

EU Authorised Representative:

Easy Access System Europe Mustamäe tee 50, 10621 Tallinn, Estonia

gpsr.requests@easproject.com

Printed and bound by CPI Group (UK) Ltd, Croydon, CR0 4YY

22/04/2026

02095387-0001